Moveable Margins

Moveable Margins

The Narrative Art of Carme Riera

Edited by
Kathleen M. Glenn,
Mirella Servodidio,
and Mary S. Vásquez

Lewisburg
Bucknell University Press
London: Associated University Presses

Associated University Presses
440 Forsgate Drive
Cranbury, NJ 08512

Associated University Presses
16 Barter Street
London WC1A 2AH, England

Associated University Presses
P.O. Box 338, Port Credit
Mississauga, Ontario
Canada L5G 4L8

The paper used in this publication meets the requirements of the American National Standard for Permanence of Paper for Printed Library Materials Z39.48-1984.

Library of Congress Cataloging-in-Publication Data

Moveable margins : the narrative art of Carme Riera / edited by Kathleen M. Glenn, Mirella Servodidio, and Mary S. Vásquez.
p. cm.
Includes bibliographical references and index.
ISBN 0-8387-5399-X (alk. paper)
1. Riera, Carme—Criticism and interpretation. I. Glenn, Kathleen Mary. II. Servodidio, Mirella D'Ambrosio. III. Vásquez, Mary Seale.
PC3942.28.I37Z75 1999
849′.9354—dc21 98-42630
CIP

PRINTED IN THE UNITED STATES OF AMERICA

Contents

Introduction

MIRELLA SERVODIDIO

THE INTRODUCTION OF THE MAJORCAN WRITER CARME RIERA TO THE reader presents intriguing complexities. Riera forms part of the veritable explosion of literature by women writers in post-Franco Spain and she is specifically linked to the conspicuously talented constellation of women writing in Catalan. Recognized for their originality and style, Riera's complete works have been translated into Spanish (*Epitelis tendríssims* remains the one exception) and selected stories have found their way to Czech, Dutch, English, German, Greek, and Russian translations. However, Riera is still very much a writer in her creative prime and her oeuvre is resistant to the overview and assessment that are the traditional province of introductions, for these betoken the leaden weight of closure, of eternal repose within stable, definable boundaries. Moreover, the "placement" of her work resonates with the overtones of familiar patriarchal strictures: a woman (writer) most certainly should be "put in her place," should "know her place" and so on. Instead, the motility heralded in the title of this volume signals an opposing, more transgressive truth: the "moveable margins" of Riera's fiction are the signifiers of a refusal to be cornered or encrypted by a geography of exclusion. Moreover, hers is very much a work in progress—fluid, experimental, stretching its literary horizons even as it gains in character and depth.

Clearly, there are unshakable truths that have located Carme Riera at the margins of hegemonic discourse: her status as a Majorcan, as a woman writer in a highly patriarchal culture, and as a speaker and writer of a minority language. Yet, Riera has used these very margins as the site of political contention and contestation, as a literary space constructed from conflicting materials of gender and geography, of class and critical consciousness, a space from which to map alternate pathways that cross cultural, linguistic, and specular boundaries. The denial of impregnable barriers that these incursions and border crossings inscribe, subverts—or, at the least, relativizes—the very notion of centrality or marginality. This destabilization moves in tandem with the shifting political and cultural tides expressly or indirectly chronicled in Riera's opus spanning the last two and a half decades and which necessarily reconfigure the contours of a cultural map of Spain. Surely, the awarding of the prestigious Premio Nacional de Narrativa to Riera in 1995 for her novel, *Dins el darrer blau* [In the Furthest Blue], 1994, exemplifies the changing signposts of Riera's world and is the full-throated proclamation that at last a writer of "minority" language and gender can be embraced as a "major" artist.

Riera's biography jolts us with a set of unexpected conjunctions. Born in 1948 to a well-to-do family in Palma de Majorca, she received a traditional primary education with the nuns of El Sagrado Corazón, who emphasized preparing students for their forthcoming roles as wives and mothers. Her parents' substantial library was kept behind locked doors, in the belief that reading could prove inimical to a young girl's mental health. Although Riera's creative imagination was fueled by reading stories in the Argentinian magazines lying about the house, by a pilfered copy of Valle-Inclán's *Sonata de otoño* [Autumn Sonata] found in the attic, and by the tales, real or imagined, told her by her grandmother, she appeared slated for bourgeois conformity and insularity. Indeed, Riera's attachment to Majorca, its language and its people, is unbendable, and the island is the setting of much of her fiction. Yet, we soon discover that her parents' language of choice at home was Castilian Spanish, that her primary education was in Castilian, and that, in fact, her formation was entirely bilingual. It is also true that in 1965, Riera leaves behind the protected world of Majorca to study at the University of Barcelona and is soon caught up in the heady atmosphere of intellectual and artistic discourse, in the ferment of radical political debate and the consciousness-raising of an insurgent feminist movement whose theoretical writings she begins to explore. Riera takes up permanent residence in Barcelona, completing a degree in 1970 in Spanish philology and discovering a special affinity for Golden Age literature. Married in 1971 to Francisco Llinás, a professor of physics, and already the mother of a son by 1972, Riera embarks on the dual career paths—one academic, one creative—that she has followed to the present and which, by her own account, have nourished each other synergistically to remarkable effect. The scholar earlier smitten with classical literature swerves abruptly to the twentieth century, devoting herself to poetry, the genre most distant from her own. As a professor at the Universitat Autònoma de Barcelona, Riera produces books and essays of literary criticism written in Castilian, including her doctoral dissertation, published with the title "La Escuela de Barcelona" [The School of Barcelona], which receives the 1988 Anagrama de Ensayo Prize. Riera's narrative fiction, on the other hand, is written in Catalan, which takes pride of place as the creative wellspring of her art (editions of her books in Castilian Spanish follow in short order, translated and at times profoundly reworked by Riera herself and/or by her friend and exegete, Luisa Cotoner). She has published four volumes of short stories, one novella and three novels, and is currently completing work on a fourth novel. She has also written a one-act play, *Senyora, ha vist els meus fills?* [Madame, Have You Seen My Sons?], 1982, which appears in print for the first time in this volume. Riera's biography fascinates, then, for a polyvalence that evades unitary or reductive categorizations for, in her life as in her work, she has joined multiple worlds and realities. She is a private person and a public persona, the devoted wife and mother of two children, and a celebrity with marked feminist sensibilities and ambitions; she is a scholar, creator, professor, and provocateur, the explicator of canonical texts, on the one hand, and literary "terrorist," on the other, hurling firebombs into the sacred temples of culture. She is both classical and contemporary, both Majorcan and Continental, both "major" and "minor." And the prose styles she commands range from the lyrical to the self-mocking, from the ludic to the learned.

Riera's fiction centers on a governing set of marginalizations and thematic concerns that give shape, coherence, and continuity to her artistic universe. Yet, perversely (predictably?), a salient feature of her writing is that it defines itself in opposition to fixed meaning or tidy compartmentalization. Rather, her aesthetic imagination is stimulated by ambiguity, mystery, connotation, and overtone, all of which facilitate provisionality and speculation. Exploration of the fluidity of human personality and the solubility of the "I," the portrayal of multiply defined sexuality, the use of doubling and mirroring—all provoke a variety of perspectives that defer the reader's arrival at meaning or reliable truth. Elusive and allusive, Riera's prose is driven by the author's faith in the seductive power of ambiguity. That literature is an act of erotic seduction, first arousing and then sustaining the desire of the Other through wily games of hide-

and-seek, of concealment and disclosure, stands as one of Riera's bedrock convictions. It is a thesis to which she returns repeatedly in interviews, lectures, and books. The metafictional inflection of Riera's work is unmistakable, for it is acutely conscious of its signifying practices and offers a running commentary on its condition of intertextuality. Riera's entire opus is mediated through other literature, the Barthian "déjà lu," for it takes its meaning in relationship to other texts that are cited, parodied, deconstructed, refuted, or mirrored in a formidable display of erudition and literary gamesmanship. Her points of reference range far and wide, from Continental literature to the literature of the Americas, from classical and humanistic traditions to the current vogues of high and popular culture alike.

Riera's first two books, *Te deix, amor, la mar com a penyora* [I Leave You, My Love, the Sea as a Token], 1975, and *Jo pos per testimoni les gavines* [I Call on the Seagulls as Witness], 1977, both collections of short stories, are not only close chronologically but evince a genuine consanguinity of themes, diction, and form. Indeed, both are conflated as one volume in two subsequent Castilian editions: *Palabra de mujer* [Woman's Word], 1980, and *Te dejo el mar* [I Leave You the Sea], 1991. The stories lean preferentially to first-person narration and make frequent use of epistolary, confessional, and interlocutionary modes. More important, with few exceptions, the narrating subjects are women of various stations and circumstance, and Riera succeeds in nuancing their different linguistic registers and sociolects with virtuosic accuracy. The author clearly brings a feminist consciousness to bear on the lives of these alienated female characters for whom self-possession, subjective agency, and self-determination are precarious operations. Several stories that thematize lesbian desire focus on the subversion of cultural representations of difference. Others which portray the lives of working-class women highlight material differences of access to economic means and resources. In her subsequent collection, *Epitelis tendríssims* [Most Tender Epithelia], 1981, Riera experiments with the traditionally male subgenre of erotic literature much cultivated in recent years by women writers in Spain—accentuating the ludic, humorous aspects of eroticism while offering yet another spin on her credo that all literature is an act of seduction. Although the ludic remains a dominant strain of the stories of *Contra l'amor en companyia i altres relats* [Against Love with a Partner and Other Tales], 1991, the paramount focus of the collection is metafictional and intertextual. Riera still privileges first-person narration, and many stories adopt an epistolary or mock-confessional mode. However, the gender-bending of the earlier volumes is noticeably absent. Instead, Riera trains her eye on the world of writers of all stripes and stations—journalists, scholars, creative writers—failed, aspiring, or arrived, whose borrowings, mirrorings, and "dialogues" with other authors create a dizzying textual collage. Especially prominent is the playful interaction with contemporary Latin American masters—Borges, Cortázar, García Márquez—and several stories venture into the fantastic mode. The collection portrays a literary culture in which Riera herself is deeply steeped and which she parodies here with merciless wit and commanding assurance.

This self-reflexive scaffolding is also much in evidence in Riera's longer prose fiction. For example, in the epistolary novella *Qüestió d'amor propi* [A Question of Self-Love], 1987, the female protagonist is herself a creative writer and student of literature, and her life is clearly mediated by other texts. Constructed as a single, confessional letter in which she recounts her failed love affair with another writer and cunningly lays the groundwork for a literary-style revenge that relies on the addressee's complicity, the book explores the relationship of life and literature, makes extensive use of mirroring structures, and draws the reader into a complex game in which erotic and narrative seduction are intertwined. The novels *Una primavera per a Domenico Guarini* [A Primavera for Domenico Guarini], 1981, recipient of the Prudenci Bertrana Prize; and *Joc de miralls* [Game of Mirrors], 1989, winner of the Novel-la Ramon Llull Prize, though written eight years apart, are both exemplars of detective fiction that engage in puzzle-solving, the deciphering of codes, secret messages, and clues that are characteristic of the genre. Clara, the protagonist of *Una primavera*, is a journalist for a Barcelona newspaper who travels to Italy to cover the trial of Guarini, the alleged perpetrator of an act of vandalism against Botticelli's masterpiece, *Primavera*. Clara is not content with the surface reportage of the pieces she sends back to her home paper. Digging for answers to the mystery surrounding this affair, she draws on various literary and visual intertexts and constructs a personal narrative interpretation of Guarini's motives. However, beyond Clara the journalist and Clara the private "eye," there is also Clara the private "I," and a central part of the novel involves her parallel search for personal identity at a critical moment in her life. *Joc de miralls* is part detective story, part political thriller. In the novel's first two sections, the sleuthing is given an academic spin, for the novel plots the encounter of the protagonist, Teresa Mascaró, with the famous Latin American writer and former political prisoner, Pablo Corbalán, whose work she is studying for her doctoral dissertation. His mysterious and sudden "suicide" is the causal factor of her trip to Itálica, his homeland, where she engages in some biographical detective work. Teresa turns up puzzling clues and contradictory evidence that lead her to Antonio Gallego, also a writer and political prisoner, whose life and work are suspiciously entangled with Corbalán's. Within a larger political context of perfidy, abuse, imprisonment, and torture—all amply developed in the novel's final section—Riera gives full play to a game of shifting mirrors, fluid identities, and intertextualities. In her most recent novel, *Dins el darrer blau,* recipient of the Josep Pla Prize as well as the 1995 National Prize for Narrative and considered by some to be her most accomplished to date, the author returns to a pivotal event of Majorcan history—the burning of thirty-seven Jews at the stake in the four *autos de fe* of 1691—with the express purpose of exposing the pervasive and entrenched religious intolerance that has characterized her native island and which casts a long shadow over the history of Spain.

We open our volume with a brief introductory section which we call "In Her Own Voice." Consisting of a preface by Carme Riera, followed by two interviews artfully conducted by Kathleen M. Glenn and Christina Dupláa, it is designed to bring the writer into bold relief and to facilitate the reader's unmediated access to her thinking. The essays that follow are written by scholars who have thought profoundly about contemporary literature. Rather than coalescing around a single theoretical line, they gather and apply widely varying critical perspectives and formal concerns to engage Riera's fiction. The result is a full, fluid exchange of readings ranging from feminist, psychoanalytical, formalist, poststructuralist, new historical, and intertextual to postmodern and postcolonial. Even within single essays there are instances of intersecting levels of theoretical discourse.

The volume's first seven essays have been arranged to reflect the chronolgy of Riera's opus so as to capture the organic changes and continuities therein, as well as the abrupt swerves in new directions found in her most recent writing. Mirella Servodidio returns to two early stories of Carme Riera that thematize lesbian love. She marshals current feminist psychoanalytical theories relative to the construction of gender identity, harnessing them to a new purpose—that of demonstrating the clear interplay of language and desire, of psyche and text. Examining their collocation and linguistic registers, their rhetorical shape and discursive strategies, Servodidio unveils sexual, scriptural, and structural convergences that betray a system of metonymic linkages challenging gender-marked codes of separation and differentiation.

Akiko Tsuchiya applies the insights of recent feminist and poststructuralist theories to a consideration of the centrality of seduction in *Una primavera per a Domenico Guarini* (and, briefly, in *Joc de miralls*). Seduction is examined and understood not only in a thematic or narrative sense, but also as an epistemological model. Jean Baudrillard's concept of seduction, in particular, provides the theoretical framework for Tsuchiya's analysis of the novel. Breaking with previous feminist critics who have seen the protagonist's journey as one of self-discovery, Tsuchiya argues in favor of another species of discovery. In her view, the female hero comes to learn that identity and meaning are unstable constructs that undergo constant transformation through discourse.

Brad Epps's essay takes *Qüestió d'amor propi* and risks reading the title literally, sounding out questions of love and the self, its properties and proprieties. Accordingly, the essay pays special attention to the place of the self in and out of love, to pride and narcissism. At the same time, it heeds the place of the Other, both in and out of love. These "places" do not always coincide and may be fraught, as in Riera's novella, with conflict and contradiction. Correspondence is thus a crucial concern here, not merely in the sense of agreement and harmony but also in that of communication through the exchange of letters. Attending to form and content alike, Epps pushes at epistolarity and, specifically, its connection to gender. This inquiry, conducted largely within the parameters of literary history and contemporary feminism, is supplemented by a Lacanian-inflected inquiry into relationality and desire, into the often strange relays and uncanny returns of signs—and questions—of the self and love.

Drawing on the theories of Gide, Lacan, Derrida, Todorov, and Dallenbach as they apply, generally, to the concept of the *mise en abyme,* Janet Pérez provides a comprehensive study of specular structures in *Joc de miralls.* These involve the use of internal duplication, doubling, parallels, repetition, echoes, reflection, and refraction. Moreover, she demonstrates that the novel is not merely a complex exercise in *mise en abyme,* but also is a self-conscious, metaliterary, "narcissistic" narrative incorporating various other subgenres and layers of intertextuality while contrasting appearance with reality.

Mary S. Vásquez returns to a central conceit of Riera's opus, one taken up earlier by Tsuchiya and Epps—that of seduction—implicitly certifying the thematic continuities encountered in Riera's opus. Vásquez's essay builds on the author's previous work on Riera's *Qüestió d'amor propi* and draws on Elizabeth Macarthur's theoretical constructs pertaining to the inherently seductive nature of epistolarty discourse. She explores the process of textual production of both narratee and reader through the workings of the epistolary mode in two Riera stories, "Letra de ángel" and "La seducción del genio," here in their Castilian versions, for reasons explained in the essay. This textual seduction is propelled by desire for the creation and reception of a text, the narratorial self. Vásquez examines Riera's sophisticated play with voicing, de-voicing, and the recasting of narratorial voice around societal concepts, a favorite Riera emphasis. The gendering and engendering of narrative voice characterize Riera's use of epistolarity in the narratives as both process of and metaphor for the creation of the self.

The two essays that follow are devoted to *Dins el darrer blau,* Riera's most recent and least studied novel, and take differently nuanced approaches. Geraldine Cleary Nichols provides a supple analysis of the novel as a work of historiographic metafiction. Her essay pinpoints the ways in which Riera retextualizes the official, monological version of one of the foundational episodes of modern Majorcan identity (the *autos de fe* of 1691), giving voice to those who were silenced and drawing attention to the subjective nature of historiography. Nichols rounds off her essay by studying the novel's connection to contemporary history and current philosophical debates about identity, memory, and speaking for the Other. Neus Carbonell explores the plurality of writing positions in *Dins el darrer blau,* grounding her analysis in postcolonial theory. Citing David Lowenthal, Edward Said, Gayatri Chakravorty Spivak, Robert Young, and Patrick Wright, among others, she considers the question of how a discourse purporting to represent and defend the practices of heterogeneity can be caught up in a web of heterogeneous contradictions. For Carbonell, Riera's novel embodies all the pitfalls of a contemporary discourse which confronts the ethical issues of responsibility for the Other.

The essays by Catherine G. Bellver and Susan Lucas Dobrian have a thematic focus that cuts across much of Riera's fiction. Their placement in the volume benefits from the solid foundation laid in the previous seven essays which familiarize the reader with the works cited by Bellver and Dobrian. Bellver examines the varying manifestations of the double—both as psychological phenomenon and as literary archetype—in and across Riera's fiction, and her essay acts as an interesting complement to Janet Pérez's study of doubling in *Joc de miralls.* She argues compellingly that the evolving functions of duplication, duality, and reflection stand in apposition to Riera's changing view of the world and of her own art. She also explores the special significance that doubleness, duplicity, and fragmentation have for women, who traditionally have been represented as the mirror for the male subject. Bellver further notes that women's experiences have been grounded in a split perspective and their art in a "double-voiced discourse." Dobrian's essay, thematic and intertextual in its approach, offers a close reading of stories that transform and rewrite the Daphne-Apollo theme (Daphne is the virgin nymph who changes into a tree to escape the pursuit of Apollo). She studies Riera's deployment of the strategy of female disappearance (either enforced or as an act of choice), manifestly integrating the issues of female voice, body, and desire. Dobrian charts the progressive series of disappearances in Riera's prose ranging from self-elimination to excision of the male body from the text and demonstrates their effectiveness in thwarting the use of textual elimination as a tool employed by males against females to subdue and immobilize them.

We close our volume with Patricia Hart's essay devoted to Riera's only dramatic work to date, the one-act play, *Senyora, ha vist els meus fills?,* written as a segment of the six-part *Dones i Catalunya* which is followed by the play manuscript itself, published here for the first time both in the original Catalan and in English translation. Constructed around three women characters, the work is set in the immediate aftermath of the Spanish Civil War. Hart builds her analysis on the contributions of feminist theorists, new historians, and a range of drama theorists that include George Lukács, Arthur Miller, and Peter Brook. She demonstrates that the play's linkage of erotic and political attitudes creates an innovative staging of the "intra-history" of women in the wake of the Civil War.

We trust that our introduction of the Majorcan writer, Carme Riera, and the brief roadmap of the volume's contents will prove a useful guide to our readers as they journey forth to explore the "moveable margins" of Riera's prose (credit goes to Mary S. Vásquez for our title). We conclude by expressing our profound thanks to Carme Riera, whose artistic vibrancy has been the creative catalyst for this venture.

December, 1996.

Moveable Margins

Part I
In Her Own Voice

Una ambición sin límites

Carme Riera

Me piden las editoras de este volumen, con quienes he contraído una impagable deuda de gratitud, que escriba unas páginas introductorias a los ensayos que con tanta generosidad me han dedicado diversas/os investigadoras/es, a quienes antes de nada quiero dar también las gracias.

Debo confesar, de entrada, que me resulta muy difícil tratar de mi propia obra, quizás porque estoy mucho más acostumbrada a analizar la de los demás, pues no en vano soy profesora de literatura. Incluso cuando en conferencias o coloquios se me insta a que me refiera a mis textos procuro escurrir el bulto o salirme por la tangente, planteando aspectos que incluyan a otras/os colegas. El mal rato que paso cuando tengo que revisar pruebas de imprenta me resulta suficientemente penoso para no desear tener que seguir hurgando en lo que ya no puedo corregir.

Desde que en marzo de 1975 di por concluido mi primer libro de relatos, *Te deix, amor, la mar com a penyora,* hasta hoy, septiembre de 1996, en que escribo estas líneas, han pasado veintiún años. Veintiún años en los que no he dejado de sentir miedo no ante la página en blanco, como aseguran muchos autores/as, sino ante la página escrita y todavía más ante la página impresa. En la página en blanco todo es aún posible, en la escrita compruebo siempre que aquello que en mi imaginación parecía nuevo y distinto no lo es y que, en definitiva, el deseo y la realidad poco tienen en común.

Ser una profesional de la enseñanza de la literatura, me permite, creo, conocer mejor los fallos y, en consecuencia, me conduce a una perpetua insatisfacción. La mejor de mis obras es aquella que estoy escribiendo en la cabeza, apenas sin trasladar al papel, susceptible, por tanto, de todo tipo de enmiendas y correcciones. De las demás prefiero no acordarme, aunque me gusta—paradójicamente—que se acuerden los otros. Me gusta que me lean. Considero, como asegura Eco, que es el lector/a con su concurso quien verdaderamente acaba la obra literaria. Para que ese montón de palabras que constituye un libro tenga sentido hace falta el sentido que sólo el receptor puede darle.

Un libro cerrado se diferencia muy poco de cualquier otro de los objetos ornamentales que, a menudo, llenan también los estantes de las librerías domésticas: cachivaches, figurillas o bibelots de calaña diversa. Un libro abierto, un libro leído, en cambio, modifica nuestra experiencia al ofrecernos una representación del mundo. Sin embargo mientras estoy configurando esa representación no me acuerdo en absoluto del lector/a, no le hago la más mínima concesión, escribo aquello que considero que debo escribir para que la obra funcione según la intención propuesta, sin dejarme tentar por reclamos externos, sin pensar siquiera en la dificultad que pueda entrañar, sin otra meta, ni otra exigencia que la estética.

Cuando empecé a corregir la versión original catalana de *Dins el darrer blau* me di cuenta de que los tres primeros capítulos resultaban demasiado morosos, quizás demasiado detallistas, lentos en exceso, comparados con la literatura trepidante que suele atraer al público, pero no quise cambiarlos para hacerlos más accesibles, puesto que mi intención era que el lector se fuera sumergiendo lenta, pero profundamente, en el mundo de los judeo-conversos mallorquines, especialmente en el de dos de los protagonistas desencadenantes de la tragedia, el malsín Rafael Cortés, Costura y el loco de Cap de Trons—Cabeza de Trueno—su primo, llamado también, Rafael Cortés.

Para mostrar las estrechas relaciones de parentesco que caracterizaban a la "gente de la calle"-los todavía denominados xuetas—repetí nombres y apellidos en vez de bautizar de diferente mane—ra a cada uno de los personajes, lo que hubiera resultado más fácil y menos complicado para el lector/a pero le hubiera escamoteado un aspecto característico de quienes, como aseguró Don Américo Castro, tuvieron que aceptar una vida al acecho y su vivir fue un vivir amargo. Me pareció necesario contagiar al lector/a, con todos los medios a mi alcance, la sensación de claustrofobia y acorralamiento, recreando incluso, en lo posible, la particular habla del gueto. Pero si así lo hice no fue para imitar a Góngora (cuyo origen converso le llevó, probablemente, a labrarse un estilo tan peculiar, un mundo estético tan singular, como reducto de su marginación), en su desprecio por los lectores, sino por necesidades de cohesión interna del relato, en atención al lector/a y en consideración a que éste o ésta no deben dejar de exigir una obra compacta, bien organizada, bien trabada, capaz de ofrecer una imagen globalizadora de un mundo personal autónomo en el que los personajes vayan evolucionando a medida que avanza la novela y podamos observar cómo se transforman según los acontecimientos, y no al albur de su creador/a. Mi intención era construir una novela bien edificada en la que cada palabra significara precisamente lo que quise decir, del modo más exacto y a la vez más connotativo posible, de manera que el texto tuviera la solidez de la piedra pero también la gracia leve y alada de una mariposa, la sugestiva delicadeza de una flor que vuela. . . .

Sin embargo el hecho de no hacer concesiones a la facilidad, al lector eventual, el no tener en cuenta los índices de audiencia para tratar de escribir con la receta adecuada para construir un *best seller,* no se contradice con el interés por los lectores/as e incluso, por llegar a contar, con eso que se llama el favor del público. Quienes escribimos narrativa lo hacemos con la primordial intención de llegar a la inmensa mayoría, ávidos de comunicar, de establecer contacto con el receptor, como si le rozáramos con las palabras para despertarle o acariciarle.

Quizá no esté lejos el día en que haya más escritores/as que lectores/as. Es posible que pronto el lector, la lectora se conviertan en especies delicadamente protegidas por hallarse en vías de extinción. Considero que sin el interés, sin la colaboración del público no hay texto, sólo papel. Palabras vanas. Letra muerta.

Ya que esta tarde casi otoñal parece propicia a las confidencias, anotaré que a menudo cuando entro en una librería me suele dar un ataque de furioso pánico, en especial si acabo de sacar un libro, que tendrá que competir necesariamente con la montonada de ejemplares que se exhiben en las mesas y anaqueles. Volúmenes de autores importantes que sin duda tendrán tantas cosas o más que decir que yo, tantas dudas que plantear, y que, por descontado, escribirán mejor y cuyos textos, hasta por fuera, parecerán más sugerentes, con portadas más llamativas y precios tal vez más asequibles. No deja de parecerme extraordinario que, en un país de hábito de lectura tan escaso como es España donde quienes leen lo hacen en contadas ocasiones, pues la inmensa mayoría sólo compra uno o dos libros al año, alguien elija un libro mío, pudiendo escoger entre otras tantísimas posibilidades.

Un lector/a es un pequeño milagro en los tiempos que corren y hay que cuidarle. Cuando en Barcelona o en Mallorca, en un metro o en un autobús encuentro a alguien leyendo un libro mío tengo que reprimir el impulso de acercarme a darle un beso.

Si no lo hago es para que la sorpresa no le resulte demasiado desagradable, se lo tome como una agresión y cambie de libro inmediatamente.

A menudo en actos públicos, a veces incluso por la calle, me sorprendo a mí misma buscando un rostro al que veinte años habrán cambiado posiblemente tanto como a mí, pero cuyos rasgos estoy segura que reconocería enseguida. Entonces, hace veinte años, veintiuno para ser exacta, el día del libro de 1975, con Franco en la cabecera de pista para el despegue final y el optimismo de ser joven y de tener el primer libro en la calle, apareció él. Lo recuerdo todo como si fuera ahora, recuerdo mis nervios de aquella mañana detrás de un improvisado mostrador en las Ramblas de Barcelona donde los libreros ofrecen las novedades y a los escritores como reclamos de ventas. La gente pasaba. Unos miraban, otros hasta se acercaban pero a mí ni me veían. Mientras a mi lado firmaban mis colegas, cuyos montones de ejemplares iban decreciendo a ojos vista para mayor afrenta, yo seguía allí, aburridísima, parapetada detrás de los libros azules de la primera edición de *Te deix, amor, la mar com a penyora*. . . . Ya estaba pensando en huir sin que lo notaran cuando de repente llegó él. Debía de tener más o menos mi edad de entonces, era de una guapura compacta y parecía dado al placer solitario de la lectura. Se paró delante de mi montón de libros, que con el paso de las horas aún se me antojaba mayor, y tomó uno. Lo abrió con cuidado, quizás hasta leyera unos párrafos y entonces yo, sospechando que aquélla podría ser mi única oportunidad, le dije, tímidamente: Si te lo quedas te lo dedico . . . Se lo compró, se lo firmé y fue el primer libro que dediqué en mi vida, el único en aquella penosa mañana. . . . Por eso, a pesar del tiempo pasado todavía sigo queriéndoselo agradecer.

Cuando miro mucho más atrás, mucho antes de empezar a publicar, incluso antes de empezar a escribir, y busco en el vasto y lejanísimo territorio de la infancia los motivos que pudieron impulsarme a escribir, se me aparece la imagen de una niña (*d'una nina,* como decimos en el catalán de Mallorca) de breves trenzas y ojos tristes, que mira el mar lejano desde la ventana de una casa grande y vacía del barrio antiguo de *Ciutat* de Mallorca.

La imagen de aquella niña que rechazaba atemorizada los espejos porque no era guapa como su madre, y sí fea como su padre, vuelve a llenar a menudo mi retina: no juega, mira como juegan sus hermanos en el jardín de la casa, desde el balcón del cuarto de la abuela, la *senyora àvia* que le cuenta durante casi todo el día viejas historias de un pasado familiar rancio, tan glorioso como periclitado. Historias de amor con lujos de pasiones incontrolables, de raptos, incluso, que desbocan la fantasía de la niña, y la impulsan a fabular otras similares.

La niña triste que rechaza los espejos porque teme verse reflejada en ellos con el bigote que luce su padre, comienza a escribir a los ocho o nueve años variantes de los relatos que le cuenta la abuela y hasta pretende, para no tener que enfrentarse directamente con el hombre negro que todas las semanas la interroga detrás de las pequeñas rendijas del odioso confesionario, confesarse por escrito.

Sólo de este modo, escamoteando la presencia, se considera capacitada para vencer su timidez infinita e incluso, para diluir entre las líneas de la caligrafía, las posibles culpas. Digamos que el papel en blanco le sirve de espejo, un espejo cómplice en el que se observa favorecida y hasta gratificada.

No negaré que siento bastante ternura, mucha más que cuando éramos la misma, por aquella niña que fui, en cuyas vivencias, quedan explicados, en parte, los motivos que me impulsan a escribir. Ahora sé que empecé a escribir, en primer lugar, por culpa de la abuela, incitada por su capacidad de contar historias, y, en segundo lugar, porque la escritura me servía para ahuyentar los fantasmas y sobre todo para explicarme el mundo, para conocer la realidad que me rodeaba y clarificarla.

Estoy absolutamente convencida de que muchas de mis obsesiones de escritora y bastantes de mis personajes nunca hubieran existido de no ser por mi abuela. El mundo elegíaco de mis primeros cuentos, los reunidos en *Te deix, amor, la mar com a penyora,* por ejemplo, suelen estar protagonizados por mujeres altas, pálidas y tristes, que contemplan el mar, el mundo, desde ventanas y balcones. Estoy segura de que todas ellas fueron creadas como homenaje a mi abuela ya que ella, cuando era joven, fue el prototipo de la heroína finisecular, tal como nos la puede describir Gabriel Miró en *Nuestro Padre San Daniel* o *El obispo leproso.* Sin sus referencias a la sociedad mallorquina cerrada, estamental, intransigente y cobarde, que utilizó como bestia negra a un determinado grupo de compatriotas, simplemente porque tenían apellidos de origen converso, nunca hubiera escrito *Dins el darrer blau,* hasta hoy mi última novela publicada.

No soy ni mucho menos la primera escritora a quien las historias contadas por otros, los cuentos narrados en la infancia le han llevado a la literatura. Clarín recordaba como iniciador de su vocación de escritor nada menos que al conserje del gobierno civil de León, donde su padre fue gobernador, que de niño le contaba cuentos. En los cuentos de Clarín los niños felices son precisamente aquellos a quienes alguien les cuenta cuentos. Las niñas desgraciadas, como Ana Ozores, son huérfanas de cuentos y esa carencia planea luego sobre su vida de un modo negativo. . . .

Algunos psicólogos opinan que es en la infancia recién estrenada, en los dos o tres primeros años, cuando se configuran los rasgos dominantes de nuestro carácter y es posible que tengan razón. Por lo que a mí respecta, creo que un 80% de mi imaginario creador procede de aquella época. Mi vinculación desde la niñez a un determinado paisaje de la costa norte de la isla de Mallorca es para mí tan fundamental que constituye un omnipresente recuerdo. Recuerdo que ha motivado la presencia del mar en casi todos mis libros, algunos escritos en la casa que mi familia tiene en Deià, pueblo literario donde los haya y donde vivieron y escribieron también Anaïs Nin y Robert Graves. Desde las ventanas y terrazas de la casa la vista rebosa de mar. He podido contemplarlo a todas horas, siempre cambiante, según la luz, las nubes, el viento, la tempestad o la calma, el mar ofrece rostros diferentes, alterna y hasta casi simultanea gestos distintos, cosa que nunca ocurre con la tierra. Desmemoriado, nos impide dejar rastro alguno sobre su superficie que, según se le antoje, puede ser sábana tersa, mantel tendido, espejo sin fisuras, lámina intacta o, por el contrario, puede convertirse en aquella bestia fiera, con la que no quería tratos Paul Valery.

Todos los veranos no sólo hundo las manos a la búsqueda del mar perdido en el pozo de la infancia sino que sigo contemplándolo con la misma obsesión que cuando era niña, la obsesión de tocarlo, de llegar hasta él para sumergirme en sus aguas. La casa está construida junto a un acantilado. El mar parece al alcance, se le ve y se le oye muy cerca, y sin embargo permanece inasequible. Desde pequeña tengo un sueño que se repite: encontrar una escalera milagrosa que me permita bajar hasta la playa a la que sólo se puede llegar a nado. El mar pronto se convirtió para mí en el símbolo de la belleza inaprensible y también en una necesidad absolutamente vital que poco o muy poco tiene que ver con la literatura y sí mucho con mis circunstancias infantiles. Mi memoria primera es memoria del mar.

Por mar, naturalmente, pretenden huir en mi novela *Dins el darrer blau* los judíos conversos que el 7 de marzo de 1687 deciden embarcarse rumbo a Livorno ante la inminencia de un apresamiento masivo que les conducirá a la hoguera. La obsesión por pasar el mar y el miedo a emprender un viaje lleno de probables zozobras—con piratas, tempestades y naufragios—debió de llenar muchas de sus horas previas al embarque, pero al final siempre prevalecía la esperanza de la libertad. Por eso preferí aludir en el título de mi novela al color azul antes que al rojo de la hoguera. Pues en la línea del horizonte crece aquella flor de la que habla Novalis. Es para mí azul y no verde el color de la esperanza, del deseo y de la quimera.

Cuando yo era pequeña mi abuela siempre que el viento movía los árboles del jardín me hacía rezar por los navegantes. Debía de considerar que aquel viento que se entretenía en fatigar el escobón de la palmera que crecía frente a su ventana levantaba también olas terribles en todos los mares del mundo. Mi abuela suponía, igual que sus antepasados, que todos los meridianos y todos los paralelos pasaban por el centro de nuestra isla, que Mallorca era el ombligo del mundo. Hoy la sociedad mallorquina ha cambiado mucho, tenemos la renta per cápita más alta de España, el turismo nos ha hecho, al menos, aparentemente cosmopolitas y desde la posguerra hasta ahora hemos evolucionado más que en tres siglos. Creo que a estas alturas ya no encontraría modelos vivos de los que partir si tuviera que escribir muchos de los cuentos que integran mis primeros volúmenes de relatos y que no pretendieron ser otra cosa que un homenaje a una serie de mujeres que conocí, para dejar constancia de unas vidas que, como las de la inmensa mayoría de personas son insignificantes y a las que sólo la literatura puede ofrecer una cierta trascendencia. Ellas, como otros personajes de mis cuentos, tomaban entidad mediante el recurso de la primera persona, eso es mediante la propia palabra.

Diagnosticaba Freud que el escritor/a padece una neurosis de la que sólo podrá curarse si abandona la escritura cosa que no está dispuesto/a a hacer. Posiblemente lo que nos ocurre a los escritores/as es que no podemos dejar de escribir. Al menos yo escribo porque no puedo evitarlo, no puedo sustraerme a la necesidad de fabular, de imaginar alternativas a la realidad, al entorno, a todo cuanto tengo a mi alcance. Umberto Eco ha apuntado que el hombre es un animal fabulador . . . a mi juicio, son las mujeres quienes han desarrollado mejor esa facultad como desquite de la monotonía de sus existencias sin otra perspectiva que el opresivo mundo doméstico, aunque sus fabulaciones a menudo ni siquiera hayan pasado al papel. No me cabe duda de que en esa alternativa a la vida que es la fabulación hay implícito un acto de rebeldía. Es posible que Virginia

Woolf se refiera a esa rebeldía cuando observa que la cólera es inherente a la literatura femenina de sus antepasadas.

Mario Vargas Llosa ha señalado con acierto que escribir es negar el mundo real "si estás reconciliado con la realidad no tiene ningún sentido crear otra realidad distinta a través de la palabra escrita. Escribir es ya un acto de negación simbólico, verbal, desde una realidad que no nos gusta." Por su parte, Esther Tusquets, parafraseando a Hölderlin, ha afirmado que escribe "para escapar de tanta miseria." Y es que, en efecto, estamos rodeados de miseria. Una miseria propia, personal y particular y otra ajena que, no obstante, repercute en nuestras vidas. A veces resulta casi imposible aguantar un índice de miserabilidad tan alta, en especial, cuando desarrolla niveles demasiado nocivos para la salud humana y el equilibrio psíquico. Las barbaridades terroristas, la injusticia, las calamidades de cualquier tipo a las que solemos asistir a través del ojo televisivo representan una realidad francamente obscena, auténticamente repulsiva de la que sólo puede salvarnos la esperanza en una vida futura, si tenemos la suerte de ser creyentes.

Para mí, que soy agnóstica, la conciencia de la derrota que conduce a la claudicación final—al fin y al cabo la vida es una batalla perdida de antemano—ha llegado a ser tan acuciante, a partir de los cuarenta, que sólo por higiene mental hago el esfuerzo de minimizarla. La literatura ayuda a eso pues es uno de los fármacos más eficaces que conozco para transgredir las leyes que nos conducen a la caducidad porque convierte en duraderas las palabras destinadas a ser sólo efímeras y nos permite, como a Scherezade, hacernos la ilusión de que continuamos aplazando la muerte. Además mientras fabulamos vivimos muchas otras vidas e inventamos otros mundos posibles e imposibles que nos ofrecen una enorme cantidad de alternativas y hasta nos permitimos decir mentiras a manos llenas para ir a la búsqueda de la verdad de la literatura que no va a resolvernos la vida, naturalmente, pero que nos ayudará a reinterpretarla. Claro que eso sólo ocurre con las grandes novelas, con el *Quijote,* con *Madame Bovary,* con *Las olas* o con *El bosque de la noche* de Djuna Barnes y algunas más, quizás porque son libros cuya lectura nos hace distintos/as, nos imprime carácter, nos revela algún entresijo misterioso que afecta a la incertidumbre de nuestra condición. . . .

Mi meta no es otra que conseguir escribir una novela de ese tipo y considero que aquel escritor o escritora que no se plantee llegar a ser Cervantes, llegar a escribir de nuevo el *Quijote,* no merece tal nombre aunque haya alumbrado el *best seller* más comercial, haya alcanzado ventas supersónicas y sea famoso/a en el mundo entero. No me importa declararme públicamente como una escritora de una ambición ilimitada, pese a conocer, desgraciadamente, mis muchas limitaciones.

An Ambition Without Limits

CARME RIERA

THE EDITORS OF THIS VOLUME, WHOM I CAN NEVER REPAY, HAVE asked me to write an introduction to the essays that various scholars, whom I also wish to thank, have so generously dedicated to my work.

I must confess, from the outset, that it is very difficult for me to discuss my own work, perhaps because I am much more accustomed to analyzing the work of others. I am, after all, a professor of literature. Even when I am pressed at conferences or colloquia to refer to my texts, I try to dodge the issue or go off at a tangent, bringing up questions that pertain to my colleagues as well. The discomfort I feel when I have to read galley proofs is so intense that I have no desire to continue poking around in what I no longer can correct.

Twenty-one years have passed between March 1975, when I finished my first book of stories, *Te deix, amor, la mar com a penyora,* and now, September 1996, when I write these lines. Twenty-one years in which I have never stopped being afraid—not of the blank page, as many writers declare they are, but of the written page and, even more so, of the printed page. The blank page offers unbounded possibility. The written page, however, confirms that what seemed new and different in my imagination is, in fact, not—in short, that desire and reality have little in common.

Being a teacher of literature by profession enables me, I believe, to recognize shortcomings more clearly, and this leads to my perpetual dissatisfaction. My best work is the one I am writing in my head, not yet set down on paper and, therefore, open to all manner of emendations and corrections. I prefer not to remember my other works, although, paradoxically, I do like to have other people remember them. I like to be read. I believe, as Umberto Eco assures us, that it is the reader who truly completes the literary work with his or her active participation. In order that the heap of words that constitute a book have meaning, it is necessary that the reader confer meaning, something only he or she can do.

A closed book differs very little from any of the other ornamental objects that frequently fill the shelves of our private bookcases: knickknacks, figurines, assorted bibelots. An open book, a book that has been read, on the other hand, modifies our experience by offering us a representation of the world. Nevertheless, while I am giving shape to that representation, I do not think at all about the reader; I make not the slightest concession to him or her. I write what I must in order for the work to function as I intend, without letting myself be tempted by external inducements, without even thinking about the difficulty it may entail, without any goal or exigency other than the aesthetic one.

When I began to correct the original, Catalan version of *Dins el darrer blau,* I realized that the first three chapters were too deliberate, perhaps too detailed, excessively slow-moving, compared with the fast-paced literature that usually appeals to the public; but I refused to change them to make them more accessible, since it was my intention that readers immerse themselves gradually, but deeply, in the world of the Majorcan converted Jews (*conversos*), especially in the world of two of the protagonists who set the tragedy in motion: the informer Rafael Cortés, known as Costura, and the madman Cap de Trons—Cabeza de Trueno—his cousin, also named Rafael Cortés.

In order to show the close relationships of the "people of the street"—who are still called *xuetas* [descendants of Jews]—I repeated names and surnames instead of baptizing each character differently, which would have been easier and less complicated for readers but would have eliminated a characteristic aspect of people who, as Américo Castro affirmed, had to live constantly on guard and whose existence was a bitter one. I thought it necessary to use all the means at my disposal to communicate to the reader the sense of claustrophobia and entrapment, and even to re-create, to the extent possible, the speech peculiar to the ghetto. I did this not to imitate Góngora (whose *converso* origins probably led him to forge such an idiosyncratic style, such a singular aesthetic world, as a redoubt of his marginalization) in his scorn for his readers, but rather because of the need for internal coherence in my narrative. I was also mindful that the reader should not shrink from demanding a compact, well-developed, well-elaborated work capable of offering a totalizing image of an autonomous personal world, one in which the characters evolve and change in response to events, not because of the whim of their creator. My intent was to construct a well-built novel in which each word would mean precisely what I wanted it to mean, as exactly and as connotatively as possible, so that the text would have the solidity of stone but also the light, winged grace of a butterfly, the suggestive delicacy of a flower in flight.

However, my unwillingness to make things easy for potential readers or to follow popular, audience-tested "recipes" for producing bestsellers is not inconsistent with my interest in readers and even my counting on what is known as the public's favor. Those of us who write novels do so with the primordial intent of reaching the immense majority. We long to communicate, to establish contact with our readers, as if we were touching them with words so as to awaken or caress them.

Perhaps the day is not far off when there will be more writers than readers. It is possible that readers soon will become a protected species, because they are on the verge of extinction. I believe that without the interest, without the collaboration of the public, there is no text, only paper. Empty words. Dead letters.

Since this almost autumnal afternoon favors the exchange of confidences, I will note that often when I enter a bookstore I am overcome by panic, especially if I have just published a book that will, necessarily, have to compete with the mountains of volumes displayed on tables and shelves. Books by important authors who assuredly have as much to say as I or more, as many doubts to set forth, and who, it goes without saying, write better than I and whose texts, even from the outside, seem more attractive, with their showier covers and prices that may be more reasonable. Because Spain is a country where reading is not widespread and where those who do read do so only on occasion (the immense majority buy just one or two books each year), I always find it extraordinary that someone would choose a book by me, when there are so many other possibilities.

Nowadays, a reader is a minor miracle and must be cosseted. When in Barcelona or Majorca, in the subway or on a bus, I find someone reading one of my books, I have to repress the impulse to approach and kiss that person. If I refrain from doing so, it is because I don't want the surprise to be too disagreeable, to have it interpreted as an act of aggression which would cause the person to switch, immediately, to another book.

Frequently in public ceremonies, at times even on the street, I catch myself looking for a face that twenty years may have changed as much as they have changed me, but whose features I am sure I would recognize at once. Twenty years ago—twenty-one, to be exact—on Book Day in 1975, when Franco was at death's door and I was filled with the optimism of youth and the elation of having published my first book, he appeared. I remember him as if it were today; I remember my nervousness that morning as I stood behind an improvised counter on the Ramblas in Barcelona, where booksellers offer the latest books and the authors are present as an added inducement. People kept walking by. Some glanced over, others even approached; but they did not see me. While at my side my colleagues autographed books and their stacks of copies visibly diminished, adding insult to injury, I continued there, exceedingly bored, barricaded behind the blue copies of the first edition of *Te deix, amor, la mar com a penyora.* I was already considering fleeing without anyone's noticing when suddenly he appeared. He must have been more or less my age, with compact good looks, and with the manner of one temperamentally suited to the solitary pleasure of reading. He stopped in front of my pile of books, which I felt had grown taller as the hours dragged by, and picked up a copy. He opened it with care, perhaps he even read a few paragraphs, and then, suspecting that that might be my only opportunity, I timidly said to him: "If you take it, I'll dedicate it to you." He bought it, I signed it for him, and it was the first book I had ever dedicated and the only one during that distressing morning. That's why, despite all the time that has passed, I still want to express my gratitude to him.

When I look much further back, long before I began to publish, even before I began to write, and I search the vast and distant realm of childhood for the motives that may have impelled me to write, there appears before me the image of a child (*d'una nina,* as we say in Majorcan Catalan) with short braids and sad eyes, who looks at the distant sea from the window of a large, empty house in the old quarter of Ciutat de Mallorca [Palma].

The image of that child, who out of fear avoided mirrors because she was not pretty like her mother but plain like her father, frequently appears before my eyes. She does not play; instead, she watches her brothers frolic in the garden of the house, observing them from the balcony of the room of her grandmother, *la senyora àvia* who almost all day long tells her old stories about a musty family past, once as glorious as it now is in decline. Love stories with a wealth of uncontrollable passions, even kidnappings, that set free the child's imagination and impel her to invent similar stories.

The sad child who rejects mirrors because she fears she will see her face reflected in them sporting a mustache like her father's begins at the age of eight or nine to write variants of the stories her grandmother tells her and even attempts to confess in writing, so as not to have to face directly the man in black who every week interrogates her from behind the grill of the hated confessional.

Only in this way, avoiding presence, does she consider herself capable of overcoming her infinite timidity and even her possible sins, dissolving them between the lines of her handwriting. Let us say that the blank page serves her as a mirror, a complicitous mirror in which she sees herself favored and even gratified.

I shall not deny that I feel considerable tenderness for the child I once was (greater tenderness than I felt when we were one and the same person), whose experiences explain, in part, the motives that drive me to write. I now know that I first began to write because of my grandmother, spurred on by her ability to tell stories, and secondly, because writing enabled me to drive away phantoms and, above all, to explain the world to myself, to understand the reality around me and to clarify it.

I am absolutely convinced that many of my obsessions as a writer and a number of my characters never would have existed were it not for my grandmother. The elegiac world of my first stories, those collected in *Te deix, amor, la mar com a penyora,* for example, usually have as their protagonists tall, pale, and mournful women who, from windows and balconies, contemplate the sea and the world. I am sure they all were created as a tribute to my grandmother who, in her youth, was the prototype of the fin-de-siècle heroine, much as Gabriel Miró describes her in *Nuestro Padre San Daniel* or *El obispo leproso.* Without her references to Majorcan society—closed, stratified, intransigent, and cowardly, that used as its bête noire a certain group of compatriots simply because the latter had surnames of *converso* origin—I never would have written *Dins el darrer blau,* my most recently published novel.

I am far from being the first writer who has been drawn to literature because of stories told by others, stories narrated during childhood. Clarín reminisced that the abettor of his vocation as a writer was the doorman of the civil government building in

León (where Clarín's father was governor), who used to tell him stories when he was a boy. In Clarín's own stories, happy children are primarily those to whom someone tells stories. Unfortunate children, like Ana Ozores [protagonist of Clarín's best-known novel, *La Regenta*], are ones who have been deprived of stories, who are "storyless," and that lack later hovers over their lives in a negative fashion.

Some psychologists are of the opinion that it is in early infancy, at the age of two or three, when the dominant traits of our character are formed, and they may be right. As far as I am concerned, I believe that 80 percent of my creative imagination stems from that period. My connection since childhood to a particular landscape on the northern coast of the island of Majorca is so fundamental that it constitutes an omnipresent memory. I recall that it has motivated the presence of the sea in almost all my books, some of which have been written in the house my family has in Deià, a literary town, if ever there was one, and where Anaïs Nin and Robert Graves lived and wrote. From the windows and terraces of the house, one's eyes are filled with the sea. I have been able to contemplate it at every hour, ever changing according to the light, clouds, wind, storm, or calm. The sea offers different faces, it alternates and almost simultaneously presents different expressions, something that never happens with the land. Forgetful, it prevents our leaving the slightest trace upon its surface which, according to its whims, can be a smooth sheet, an outspread tablecloth, a mirror without fissures, an intact lamina. Or, on the other hand, it can turn into that wild beast with which Paul Valéry wished to have no dealings.

Every summer I not only plunge my hands into it in search of the sea lost in the well of childhood, but I also keep on looking at the water with the same obsession as when I was a child, the obsession of touching it, of submerging myself in it. The house is built near a cliff. The sea appears to be within reach, one sees and hears it nearby, and yet it remains inaccessible. Since I was a child I have had a recurring dream: that of finding a miraculous stairway that allows me to descend to the beach, which can be reached only by swimming. The sea soon became for me the symbol of unattainable and incomprehensible beauty and also an absolutely vital need that has little to do with literature and much to do with the circumstances of my childhood. My first memory is of the sea.

It is by sea, naturally, that in my novel *Dins el darrer blau* the converted Jews seek to flee on 7 March 1687 when they decide to embark for Livorno, threatened by the imminent, massive seizure that will lead them to the bonfire [of the Inquisition]. The obsession with crossing the sea and the fear of undertaking a voyage likely to be rife with worries—pirates, tempests, shipwrecks—must have filled many of their hours prior to embarking, but in the end, the hope of freedom always prevailed. That is why I preferred to allude in the title of my novel to the color blue rather than to the red of the bonfire. For, on the horizon grows that flower of which Novalis speaks. Blue, and not green, is, for me, the color of hope, of desire, and of chimera.

When I was small, my grandmother had me pray for sailors whenever the wind moved the trees in the garden. She must have thought that the wind which agitated the fronds of the palm tree that grew in front of her window also stirred up terrible waves in all the seas of the world. My grandmother, like her ancestors, assumed that all meridians and all parallels passed through the center of our island, that Majorca was truly the center of the world. Today, Majorcan society has changed considerably. We have the highest per capita income in Spain, and tourism has made us, at least in appearance, cosmopolitan, and since the end of the Civil War we have evolved more than during the previous three centuries. I think that at this point I could no longer find live models to use as my starting point, if I had to write many of the stories that make up my first volumes and which were intended as a homage to a series of women I knew. I wrote them to leave a record of lives that, like those of most people, are insignificant and to which only literature can offer a certain transcendence. The women, like other characters in my stories, took shape through the device of the first person, that is, through their own words.

It was Freud's diagnosis that writers suffer a neurosis which can be cured only if they abandon their writing, which they are not disposed to do. Possibly what happens to us writers is that we cannot stop writing. I, for one, write because I cannot help but do so. I cannot resist the need to fabulate, to imagine alternatives to reality, to my surroundings, to all that is within my reach. Umberto Eco has pointed out that man is a fabulating animal. In my opinion, it is women who have best developed that faculty as compensation for the monotony of their existence, lacking any perspective other than that of the oppressive domestic world, even if their fabulations often may not even have been set down on paper. There is no doubt in my mind that an act of rebellion is implicit in that alternative to life which is fabulation. It is possible that Virginia Woolf is referring to that rebellion when she observes that anger is inherent in the feminine literature of her forebears.

Mario Vargas Llosa has pointed out correctly that to write is to deny the real world: "If you are reconciled to reality it makes no sense to create another, different reality by means of the written word. Writing is already a symbolic, verbal act of negation, originating in a reality that is not to our liking." Esther Tusquets, for her part, paraphrasing Hölderlin, has affirmed that she writes "to escape from so much wretchedness." And we are, in effect, surrounded by wretchedness. Our own personal, individual wretchedness and that of others which, nonetheless, affects our lives. At times, it is almost impossible to endure so much wretchedness, especially when it reaches levels that are harmful to human health and psychic balance. The acts of barbarity perpetrated by terrorists, injustice, and all manner of calamities which we witness on the television screen represent a reality that is frankly obscene, authentically repulsive, from which only hope in a future life, if we are so fortunate as to be believers, can save us.

For me, an agnostic, the consciousness of the defeat that leads to the final surrender—life, after all, is a battle lost in advance—has become so pressing since I turned forty that, for the sake of mental health, I make the effort to minimize it. Literature helps, for it is one of the most effective medications I know for transgressing the laws that lead us to decrepitude, because it makes lasting words that are otherwise destined to be merely ephemeral, and it allows us, like Scheherazade, to cherish the illusion that we continue to ward off death. Besides, while we fabulate, we live many other lives and invent other worlds, both possible and impossible, that offer us an enormous number of alternatives and even permit us to lie liberally in order to search for the truth of literature, which is not, naturally, going to resolve our life but which can help us interpret it. That, of course, only happens with great novels, like *Don Quixote, Madame Bovary, The Waves,* or with Djuna Barnes's *Nightwood* and a few others, perhaps because they are books whose reading makes us different, imparts character, reveals to us some mysterious secret that affects the uncertainty of our condition.

My goal is none other than to write a novel of that type, and I consider that the writer who does not propose to become Cervantes and to write *Don Quixote* anew does not deserve the name of writer, even if he or she has given birth to the most successful bestseller, has attained supersonic sales and is famous throughout the world. I do not mind declaring publicly that I am a writer whose ambition is without limits, despite my rueful recognition of my limitations.

Translated by Kathleen M. Glenn

Conversation with Carme Riera

KATHLEEN M. GLENN

Barcelona
27 June 1996

KMG: YOU'VE COMMENTED THAT YOU BEGAN TO WRITE AFTER YOUR first communion, that confessing was, in a sense, the equivalent of telling stories to your confessor and that you liked to talk without seeing or being seen.

CR: Yes, because I was a very timid child. I have brothers but no sisters, and my mother to a degree abdicated her responsibility toward me and left me with my grandmother in a very large house. My parents and my brothers slept downstairs and I slept upstairs, in my grandmother's quarters. This created a different relationship. I felt that I was in another house, in another environment.

KMG: And in another era.

CR: Indeed, another era. It was more the nineteenth century than the postwar period, because of Grandmother's influence. Also, she was very religious, and that religiosity was quite important in my childhood. I remember my first communion as a transcendental event, very positive in that it signified entering a new and different realm, but also very negative because the man in the cassock frightened me. I would have liked to be able to make my confession in writing and thus avoid that terrible sensation of having to speak. It's been years since I went to confession, and so I don't know what confessors are like now; but when I was a child, they asked appalling questions. My confessor was absolutely obsessed with sexuality, and the questions he asked me were dreadful. They had a great effect upon me. At any rate, I continue to believe that literature begins, at least in part, as self-examination. The act of confessing—and Saint Augustine is the antecedent here—of delving into one's own wretchedness, one's faults, is an antecedent of literature. So maybe I should be grateful to the nuns who educated me and to my grandmother.

KMG: You studied with the nuns of the Sacred Heart, who emphasized the importance of writing letters as a stylistic exercise and an indispensable part of the upbringing of young ladies.

CR: Yes. The nuns of this religious order educated a good many writers, and the order figures in *Les Liaisons dangereuses* [Dangerous Liaisons]. In retrospect, I'm very grateful to the nuns, because they taught me social graces, which it's always nice to know, and certain norms which later you can ignore, transgress, if you choose to do so. They're the ones who taught me to write. My first story, "Te deix, amor, la mar com a penyora" [I Leave You, My Love, the Sea as a Token], is a letter. I owe to the nuns my facility, my command of the epistolary form. We wrote many letters.

KMG: Use of the epistolary form is a repeated feature of your works.

CR: Not in my last novel, but in almost all my others, yes.

KMG: I was thinking, in particular, of your four books of short stories, all of which include letters. Another constant of your work is the theme of seduction. Àngela Caminals of *Qüestió d'amor propi* [A Question of Self-Love] is fond of declaring that all writing is a love letter, and Pablo Corbalán of *Joc de miralls* [Game of Mirrors] confesses that seduction is his first concern as a writer. You've made similar statements to interviewers, and in your interviews of Carmen Balcells, your literary agent, and of José Manuel Blecua, one of your former professors, you emphasized the charm, the seductiveness, of both persons.[1] Would you comment on the importance to you, as a writer, of seduction?

CR: I believe that a writer's first mission is to seduce, because the world is full of books, and if you don't seduce the reader in the first few lines, your book will surely not be read and, in that case, why publish it? Therefore, seduction is an absolute necessity. The problem always is the dialectic between having to seduce the reader and doing so without resorting to cheap tricks. If seduction were the only thing that mattered, we would all write bestsellers, which are what really please people. I'm not opposed to bestsellers per se, but I *am* opposed to those bestsellers that don't attain a minimal level of literary quality.

KMG: There are two aspects to seduction. To seduce is to attract but also to deceive, and deception is important in your work.

CR: No!

KMG: I'm thinking of the story "Te deix, amor, la mar com a penyora" and. . . .

CR: No. I think you should never deceive the reader. When a writer deceives me, it makes me furious. You can't pull a rabbit out of your hat as if you were a prestidigitator. No, definitely not. You must give the reader clues. At times, it may seem that I'm deceiving readers, but it's more a matter of giving clues—not false clues—and not showing all my cards, giving sufficient data so that readers can make certain suppositions, but surprising them. Surprise is one of the most important elements in literature, and I think it's fine to surprise readers. I'm delighted when a writer surprises me.

KMG: Surprise is a better term. There's a delightful story in *Epitelis tendríssims* [Most Tender Epithelia], "Estimat Thomas" [Dear Thomas], which illustrates what you are saying. The ending takes us by surprise. When we discover that Montse's love letters are addressed to her dog, we see things in a new light. The references to Thomas's interest in trees take on a different significance, as does the passage in which Montse remarks how the feel of his red tongue licking her body drives her wild.

CR: Yes. Stories and jokes are a lot alike. A really good joke is one that surprises us.

KMG: With respect to seduction, film director Pilar Miró has commented that it is a means of achieving power, a weapon. Do you think it is a weapon wielded more by women than by men? Is it a particularly feminine strategy?

CR: I don't know. I don't think so. Rather, I believe it is inherent to the artist, to the male as well as the female writer, the male as well as the female painter. The seducer par excellence is Don

Juan, a man, and if we consider that the seducer is the powerful one, it is men, not women, who have had power. In literature, of course, seduction is a means of appropriating power, of making it ours. I believe that it is not with strength, but with weakness, that one seduces. Strength leads to rejection. I believe that the seducer's weakness at times manifests itself in not displaying power but dissimulating it and making the other person think he or she is the central figure, when in reality the seducer is. To seduce is to proceed sinuously, indirectly, to conceal some of your cards. I believe the artist often does this because art is, or should be, ambiguous; what is obvious holds little interest.

KMG: The figure of the double is a recurrent one in your fiction. Is there a particular reason for this interest in doubling?

CR: I believe that all of us, in a given moment, decide our fate. We choose one thing over another, one path rather than another that would have led us to be different or at least to do different things. This as far as life is concerned. In literature, since the Romantic era, the theme of the creation of identity, of the mask, has been a recurrent one. Thus, both life and literature have led to my interest in the double. I often think that writers are privileged beings in that we have the opportunity to invent characters, to split ourselves in two, to live other lives.

KMG: To live vicariously.

CR: Exactly.

KMG: In his study of your story "*Mon semblable, mon frère*" [My Double, My Brother], the German critic Horst Hina quoted your statement, apropos *Joc de miralls,* that questions of identity fascinate writers, who cannot help but wonder if their ideas are really theirs and to what degree their works are their own, in the sense that all works depend on previous ones.

CR: It's true. Everything has already been said. There is nothing new under the sun. Perhaps all we can do is add nuances. The problem of what constitutes originality is extremely interesting. Postmodernism has said that everything is a matter of intertextuality, reflections, references to other works. That's what literature is. It draws on a tradition and constantly reflects that tradition. And in my case, remember that I am a professor of literature and constantly explicate literary texts.

KMG: Yes. You are a professor, a scholar, and a creative writer. Is there a synergy among the three activities? Do they nourish one another?

CR: Absolutely. With regard to "*Mon semblable, mon frère*," a young critic, José Teruel, has noted that my work on the Escuela de Barcelona [Barcelona School] lies behind the story and that it deals with two members of that group. The poet Jaime Gil de Biedma wrote in Castilian and Gabriel Ferrater in Catalan, but if the two had written in the same language, they would have been the same poet, because what they say and how they say it, the tone of their work, the verse forms they use are so similar.[2] "*Mon semblable, mon frère*" is a literary wink at this group of poets, who closely resemble one another.

KMG: As I recall, the very titles of several of Gil de Biedma's poems ("Contra Jaime Gil de Biedma" [Against Jaime Gil de Biedma] and "Después de la muerte de Jaime Gil de Biedma" [After the Death of Jaime Gil de Biedma]) foreground doubling. It's been suggested that the whole question of identity and the theme of the double have been cultivated most extensively by writers who are bilingual or who live in a bilingual society and experience a feeling of being in two worlds at the same time, of being two who are one and one who is two. Here in Barcelona, you, Cristina Fernández Cubas, and Gil de Biedma, for instance, have been drawn to doubles.

CR: That hadn't occurred to me, but it strikes me as accurate. In my case it's not just a matter of being bilingual—and at times I don't know in which language I think—but also that I write and I teach. I have to lead a double, almost schizophrenic existence. As a child I was constantly going up and down a staircase, because I didn't know if I was to eat in my parents' part of the house or sleep in my grandmother's, if I belonged in one place or the other, and I think that sensation of being divided, split in two, has pursued me my entire life.

KMG: And so your use of doubles is logical.

CR: Assuredly. Moreover, I was subjected to a great deal of tension. There was another person near my grandmother, my aunt, who got along very badly with my mother, her sister-in-law. I was caught between the two of them, absolutely silent, without saying a word, watching—very frightened—and observing what was going on. It was an extremely tense situation. I would never allow my children to experience anything similar. I was in the middle between two opposing worlds, a bit like a pawn between the two.

KMG: Were your grandmother and mother cognizant of your situation?

CR: Not so much my grandmother, but my mother and aunt were.

KMG: You've spoken of "the beautiful myth" of the androgyne. Do you associate the artist with the androgyne?

CR: Perhaps so. I believe that the complete person is the androgyne.

KMG: Before being split in two.

CR: Yes, before being split. I don't know if there is a feminine literature, but what *does* exist is a feminine way of seeing the world, as well as a masculine way. Joining these two gazes in a single being would offer a much more complete vision of the world than is possible from a single perspective. When I put myself in a man's shoes and attempt to see the world through his eyes, it's an imposture, because I continue seeing as a woman. When Flaubert says that Madame Bovary is *he,* it's a lie; she is his mistress, Louise Colet. He has to put himself in Louise Colet's place so as to be able subsequently to portray Madame Bovary.

KMG: Gabriel Valls, of *Dins el darrer blau* [In the Furthest Blue], is a magnificent character. Did you model him upon a particular person?

CR: No. Rather than try to picture what I would be like if I were Valls, I tried to imagine what *he* might be like. I had very few facts, only the accounts of the trials and Valls's strength of character in the face of death, which comes through in Francisco Garau's *Fe triunfante* [Triumphant Faith], as does Father

Garau's reluctant admiration for his antagonist. Valls dies like a hero, not so much for the sake of religious ideas but in the name of human dignity. I had a lot of trouble with the character. I spent several years living with Valls, practically sleeping with him, spending all my time at his side, trying to make him and his story come alive for the reader not so much through my words as through Valls's behavior. It was a challenge, particularly so because people had said that I'd never created a major male character.

KMG: Offhand, I can't think of one who stands out.

CR: I tried with Corbalán, but I understand that my female characters turn out better.

KMG: These last few weeks when I was rereading your novels and stories, I was struck by the coherence of your work. The first two collections contain, at least in embryonic form, almost all the elements found in subsequent books, with the possible exception of *Dins el darrer blau,* your most ambitious work. There is a great variety of registers: lyricism, eroticism, and humor. With regard to this last aspect and the collection *Contra l'amor en companyia i altres relats* [Against Love with a Partner And Other Tales], the target of this humor is often the literary world of conferences, lectures, literary contests, prizes, book presentations: a world you know well as an insider.

CR: You're right. Almost everything was already present in my first books. As for *Contra l'amor en companyia,* I thought it would be best to articulate the book around a central theme, that of writing, and that the constant presence of writers and literary referents would unify the collection. As you say, I know the literary world well.

KMG: In *Qüestió d'amor propi,* too, you satirize the posturing and jockeying for power of certain literary figures.

CR: Yes. I know many writers.

KMG: You also make fun of the stupidity of some critics or types of criticism. The critic who figures in "Uns textos inèdits i eròtics de Victoria Rossetta" [Some Unpublished Erotic Texts by Victoria Rossetta], from *Epitelis tendríssims,* is singularly myopic, pedantic, and pompous. He reads Rossetta's poems as if they were autobiographical documents, and a reference to *pàrquings* [parking garages] in a poem leads him to conclude that her lover was a chauffeur.

CR: I never reread what I've written. Some of my colleagues do nothing but reread their work. I'm the direct opposite, but I now remember the story to which you're referring. Yes, I wanted to write a satire. Since I'm a professor of literature, I spend almost all my time with the same people, the living and the dead.

KMG: Year after year.

CR: Yes, year after year. And I'm thoroughly familiar with what goes on in literary circles and behind the scenes, as well as the tricks of the trade. The bigwigs are fond of saying that they read only the classics, because what is being written today is trash. In contrast, I read my contemporaries, not only because they interest me but because when I'm asked my opinion, I can't say that I don't read them. Besides, I teach their work in my classes.

KMG: Is your field of specialization Golden Age or contemporary literature?

CR: I've worked on Golden Age literature and have written on María de Zayas and Golden Age poetry, and I've been asked to prepare an edition of the work of an almost unknown Golden Age poet, but I've done much more on twentieth-century literature, especially poetry.

KMG: The only one of your books of fiction which has not been translated into Castilian is *Epitelis tendríssims*. Is there a particular reason why? Is it because you have combined humor and eroticism, because of your irreverence?

CR: No. I normally do the Castilian translation of my works, and then my literary agent finds a publisher for me, but I haven't had time to translate *Epitelis tendríssims*. Other projects have interested me more. I believe that a translation of one of the stories, "Una mica de fred per a Wanda" [A Cool Breeze for Wanda], which is probably my favorite, appeared in *Ronda*, Iberia's magazine, and a translation of "Estimat Thomas" was published in a collection of erotic fiction. I'll translate the others some day, when I have time. Lack of time is my main problem. But I have to rewrite the stories, because there are possibilities in them that need to be developed.

KMG: You don't translate; you rewrite. There are some stories where the changes made in the Castilian version are major. "Jo pos per testimoni les gavines" [I Call on the Seagulls as Witness] and "Y pongo por testigo a las gaviotas" in the *Palabra de mujer* [Woman's Word] version are very different texts, and yet there is only a three-year time span between the two.

CR: I don't remember. I haven't reread them.

KMG: It's logical that there would be minor changes, changes in names, cultural references, things that "work" in one language but not in the other. The changes made in "Y pongo . . . ," however, go beyond mere details. The atmosphere is more oppressive, more suffocating in the second text; the protagonist is angrier, more rebellious; and she speaks of male doctors who prescribe tranquilizers for her. In "Jo pos . . .," there is no mention of doctors or sedatives.

CR: I don't remember. I don't know. If another person were translating my work, that person would have to be faithful to the original, but when I translate my own work. . . . What *is* fresh in my mind is *En el último azul.* There, too, there are changes, because Castilian, which has a long literary tradition that includes writers like Quevedo and Borges, is a language that presents problems.

KMG: Problems of linguistic register?

CR: Yes, and there are words that have been used so much they are worn out.

KMG: Can you give me an example?

CR: Words relating to feelings. The word *tendresa* [tenderness] works in Catalan but *ternura,* in Castilian, does not. It's been overused.

KMG: You find it affected, in bad taste?

CR: Yes, it sounds rather affected. You have to be careful in Castilian, because you can easily fall into pretentiousness.

KMG: And that would radically alter the tone of a passage.

CR: Precisely. And the melodiousness of Catalan makes certain words sound better; Castilian, on the other hand, is harsher, more metallic, and it has words that grate on my ear or that are unacceptable. The word *entrañable* [dear] is currently in vogue, but I would never use it. It's horrible; it reminds me of butcher shops.

KMG: Because of *entrañas* [entrails]. So it is less a question of your setting out to modify fundamental aspects of a text than that the switch in language necessitates certain changes which lead to other changes, and you also become aware of new possibilities in the text.

CR: And I find flaws. When I was working on *En el último azul,* I realized that there were repetitions in *Dins el darrer blau* and sequences that were badly organized. I've corrected them in the sixth edition of the novel. And in the first edition, I had spoken of the heat in Valls's cell, but I later realized that was absurd, because the cell was very damp. When you go back to a text after a period of time, you catch mistakes.

KMG: You have been awarded a number of prizes.

CR: Well, I live in a small country.

KMG: It's far more than that; you're being modest. You have received the Premio Anagrama de Ensayo for your *La Escuela de Barcelona,* which was the first part of your doctoral dissertation; the Prudenci Bertrana for *Una primavera per a Domenico Guarini* [A Primavera for Domenico Guarini], and I understand you were the first woman writer to receive this prize; the Ramon Llull for *Joc de miralls;* and four prizes for *Dins el darrer blau:* the Josep Pla, the Crexells, the Lletra d'Or 1995, which is awarded to the best literary work of the year, and the Premio Nacional de Narrativa.

CR: The Crexells is a long-established and prestigious award given by the Ateneo [Atheneum] of Barcelona. Mercè Rodoreda received it for her novel *Aloma*. The Lletra d'Or, also prestigious, is awarded by readers and critics. During the Franco era, it was given to writers like Salvador Espriu and J. V. Foix, who were dissidents and couldn't receive "official" prizes. It has a distinguished tradition here. These two awards do not have a monetary component; in other words, they are given on the basis of literary merit rather than commercial prospects. That's why I was so pleased by both of them.

KMG: I suspect that the Premio Nacional de Narrativa had special significance for you, because never before had it been awarded to a novel written in Catalan.

CR: All prizes are gratifying, but yes, the Premio Nacional was special because Spain's four languages—Castilian, Catalan, Galician, and Basque—were in competition, as were a number of well-known authors, including Javier Marías, Almudena Grandes, Manuel Vicent, and Justo Navarro. Chance always plays a role in these competitions.

KMG: But merit, too.

CR: I think that at times it is not so much a question of literary merit as of a series of factors. The novel, of course, with or without the prize, would be the same.

KMG: Some years ago, after the publication of your first two books, you remarked that you were not interested in being read only by women, that you wanted to get out of the literary ghetto. I assume you have done so with your last novel.

CR: Yes, but the majority of readers are women, and that's nothing new. The pastoral novel was written with a feminine public in mind. There are certain types of literature which attract women more than men. I meant by my remark that I wanted everyone to read my work.

KMG: This year, for the first time, you signed books at the annual Feria del Libro [Book Fair] in Madrid.

CR: Yes, but I autographed only a few copies. In Madrid, the authors who sign a lot of books are ones whose names frequently appear in the media or who are extraliterary figures.

KMG: Like Antonio Gala?

CR: Yes, like Gala or Arturo Pérez-Reverte, a former television reporter.[3] Carmen Martín Gaite, who is a fine writer, is also widely known.

KMG: I hoped you had autographed a great many books.

CR: No, very few, but that's normal.

KMG: Is it normal in Barcelona?

CR: No. Here, when I have a new book, people come to have me autograph it on Book Day, April 23.[4] But remember that I live here and I have a good relationship with my Catalan public. The other day I gave a lecture and a man came up to me afterward and said: "Do you realize that you have many friends you don't know?" "Yes," I replied, "I feel privileged." And he continued: "You can even call me if you want me to go grocery shopping for you." "Fine," I said, "give me your phone number." He was a very nice man, who lives here in the Sarrià neighborhood. At times when I enter a store or am on the street people tell me they have read my latest book. This is very pleasant, but it only happens to me here in my city, in Barcelona.

KMG: Did it happen prior to the publication of *Dins el darrer blau?*

CR: Less so. This last book has been the most important one. Just yesterday, a television producer called to inquire if I'd be interested in writing the script for a series.

KMG: Like the soap operas from Latin America?

CR: Yes, but here in Catalonia, they are written by local authors who are popular.

KMG: Like Maria Mercè Roca?

CR: Yes, and Josep Maria Benet i Jornet, the dramatist.[5] It's a sign of popularity. I don't think I'm going to do it, however.

KMG: You have more important projects.

CR: Definitely.

KMG: In the note appended to *Dins el darrer blau,* you say that Majorcans of good will ought to ask forgiveness of the descendants of the Jews who were burned in the *autos de fe*. Was the intolerance of which you've written primarily a Majorcan phenomenon, or was it far more widespread?

CR: I think it was more intense in Majorca, an island, a closed, self-absorbed, endogamic society, and the intolerance was of longer duration here. Elsewhere, as in the case of Saint Teresa's family, the descendants of converted Jews could obtain letters patent of nobility within a period of several generations, but not in Majorca.

KMG: Your interest in the story of the converted Jews and the persecution they suffered is long-standing. You have mentioned that your grandmother talked to you about them. And in one of the stories in *Epitelis tendríssims,* "La senyoreta Àngels Ruscadell investiga la terrible mort de Marianna Servera" [Miss Angels Ruscadell Investigates the Horrible Death of Marianna Servera], you refer to the 1691 *autos de fe.*

CR: The subject of the Jews had been on my mind for years, and it surfaced in *Epitelis tendríssims.* Furthermore, it is a subject that allowed me to combine both facets of my double life, research and fabulation. I thoroughly enjoy archival research.

KMG: Did you work in the Simancas archives?

CR: Yes, and in Italy, in the Archivo Histórico Nacional in Madrid, in various archives in Majorca, and I read biographies about the Jews.

KMG: I understand that you are now working on a novel set in the nineteenth century, dealing with relations between Majorca and Cuba. Is it another historical novel?

CR: Yes, a similar work. My great-great-grandfather, about whom my grandmother spoke at length, took part in the Cuban War of Independence, fighting on the Spanish side. My mental image of this ancestor is very vivid, because when I was a child I spent hours listening to stories about him, about how he captured Maceo, about Maceo's saddle. . . .

KMG: Who was Maceo?

CR: One of the heroes of Cuban independence. José Martí was the theoretician, and Antonio Maceo, a mulatto, was one of the leaders of the Cuban resistance movement. He was killed while trying to break through the Spanish lines. I'm now writing about all this.

KMG: The historical novel has been in vogue for some time now, and in your case, clearly, there are personal reasons for your interest in the past.

CR: And I enjoy having to do research, to collect data, something that I don't have to do when I write about the present.

KMG: It's a matter of intellectual curiosity, I assume.

CR: A desire to know what went on in other periods, how people lived. If I were to write that in the seventeenth century, in Majorca, windows were curtained, it would be a lie. There were neither curtains nor glass. Discovering this and knowing what daily life was like on the island, being surprised by the fact that pigs ran loose on the streets and could even eat children—these are things you would never learn if you didn't do archival research. As I said, research is part of my life as a university professor, and I find it fascinating. I have more fun when I write about the past.

KMG: We've remarked that Valls is a superbly drawn character, but there are also extraordinary female characters in *Dins el darrer blau:* the visionary Sara de les Olors; the prostitute, Beatriu Mas, for whom you developed a special affection; Isabel Tarongí, mother of two children; the widow, Blanca Maria Pires; Caterina Bonnín, who is mentally unbalanced. In *Jo pos per testimoni les gavines,* as well, there are memorable female characters, especially in the section entitled "Bisti de Càrrega" [Beast of Burden], like the washerwoman of "Te banyaré i te trauré defora" [I'll Wash You and Hang You Out to Dry] and the protagonist of "Es nus, es buit" [The Knot, the Void], who feels like undoing the knot in her stomach and filling the emptiness in her life by swallowing a cupful of bleach.[6] In your work you have repeatedly chosen to give a voice to women, to the elderly, to Jews—people who have long been silenced. And there are many madwomen in your work.

CR: Yes. Reflecting upon what I've written and upon the figure of my grandmother, I have realized that I'm drawn to the marginal. In everyday life, as well, I'm attracted to strange people, not to people who are "normal." Perhaps this is another manifestation of my interest in the mysterious. I think that behind every madman there may be a sane individual, and one must search him out. Those who have been marginalized are particularly interesting.

KMG: The Canadian critic Linda Hutcheon has used the word *ex-centric* to highlight what is off center, to make us reexamine the notions of margin and center.

CR: Bear in mind that I am a marginal person, because I am a woman, because in Spain I form part of a minority literature (Catalan rather than Castilian), and furthermore within this minority literature, I'm not from the center (Barcelona) but from an island (Majorca). Thus, I'm the margin of the margin of the margin. And it's strange that a triply marginalized person should receive the Premio Nacional.

KMG: Yes, it makes your winning of the prize even more impressive.

CR: It's a bit like finding a four-leaf clover.

KMG: The stories grouped under the heading "Bisti de Càrrega" reminded me of Mercè Rodoreda. We've spoken of your flesh-and-blood grandmother. What about literary grandmothers? Rodoreda, for instance?

CR: My literary education was strictly Castilian, as was typical when I was growing up. I read Rodoreda after I had written the stories, and I found her fiction absolutely marvelous. She impressed me as a truly extraordinary author. I wrote to her of my fascination and explained that I had just read her work. She apparently took offense and believed I had imitated her, because later when she was asked in an interview about young writers she mentioned Montserrat Roig and me, and said that although I denied it, I imitated her. That really upset me. I sent her a furious letter, which she didn't answer. I told her that I had written my stories before I read her work, but that she was free to believe whatever she wanted to, and that if she didn't respond, I would be convinced she had indeed made the remark attributed to her and that it was not a journalist's mistake. If I had it to do over again, I wouldn't write to her; I acted immaturely.

KMG: You were hurt.

CR: Yes. Her attitude, too, was one that I would not repeat, now that I'm in a position to help people who are younger than I.

KMG: Rodoreda was known for being difficult. She was very unfortunate in her personal life.

CR: Yes. I think she was very unhappy. I can be sarcastic, and I'm sorry for what I later said: that Rodoreda's problem was that she planted flowers and they turned out to be made of plastic. Terrible. I'm sorry I said that. I have the feeling that she was a very harsh and very lonely person.

KMG: Apart from Rodoreda, what about Carmen Laforet? On the fortieth anniversary of the awarding of the Premio Nadal to *Nada* [Nothing], you wrote a tribute to her.

CR: I don't know Laforet and unfortunately I'll never be able to make her acquaintance. She's very ill. I have a curious relation with her too, because my father studied with her at the university and my mother was a friend of hers, although they weren't in the same class. I should write about the real-life characters and incidents on which *Nada* is based. It is an extraordinary novel, one which I greatly admire. I wouldn't consider Laforet a grandmother but perhaps something of a literary mother, although I don't think she influenced me. But I do admire her. One of the themes that interests me is friendship among women, and *Nada* is a novel about feminine friendship.

KMG: In one of your articles you emphasized the importance of that theme in María de Zayas's *Desengaños amorosos* [The Disenchantments of Love]. In addition to Rodoreda and Laforet as literary "foremothers," what about Virginia Woolf?

CR: Definitely. I think that for the women of my generation, Woolf is practically an idol. We read not only her novels but also *A Room of One's Own,* which was a key work for us.

KMG: Attitudes regarding feminism differ somewhat in the United States and in Spain. A few years ago, Fanny Rubio declared that being called a feminist in Spain is like being called a Basque; it is an insult. That may have been an exaggeration, but it is true that most serious women writers in Spain insist that there is no relation between being a feminist and a writer, between feminism and literature. They are completely different matters.

CR: Yes. I'm a feminist and openly declare that I am one, but I'm not a feminist writer. I'm a feminist *citizen,* and this is more important. As a feminist citizen, I have to advocate feminism, because feminism is a moral question for me. I'm opposed to the death sentence and racism and in favor of women. What I would never do is write a pamphlet. If I wrote something in a polemical style, it would be to call attention to an issue that was of particular concern to me.

KMG: In 1981, you published an article in *Poder y Libertad: Revista Teórica del Partido Feminista de España* [Power and Freedom: Theoretical Journal of the Feminist Party of Spain] on sexist language. Would you say that article represents a stage you have now left behind?

CR: I don't know if I've left it behind. I was involved in the founding of the Partido Feminista years ago with Lidia Falcón, but her ideas don't interest me.[7] They don't interest me at all. I think her attitude is totally out of date and absolutely machista. It consists of being just as intransigent as the most intransigent of men and insisting that if you don't believe as she does and act as she acts, you have no right to exist. I believe in Mercè Otero's distinction between authority and power. Lidia Falcón wants power. What I want is authority, which is a different thing, a different form of power. It is, of course, necessary to accept authority, because we could not function without certain canons and values, but authority is granted among equals, whereas power signifies the oppression of one group by another. Lidia Falcón's attitude is one of control, of domination, which doesn't interest me. I believe that what feminists ought to do is implant different social values. That there be women in power—and we now have a number of female cabinet ministers[8]—is less important than that these women act in a different way and that their attitude not be machista. There of course can be, and there have been, men who are feminists.

KMG: We've not discussed your work as a literary critic, particularly of the Escuela de Barcelona.

CR: Not any longer. I'm tired of that subject. Now I'm working on the edition I mentioned earlier. Then I have to prepare an edition of the poetry of José Agustín Goytisolo, a poet who belongs to the Barcelona School and is a very good friend. Next, an edition of Gabriel Miró's *Las cerezas del cementerio* [The Cherries from the Cemetery]. These are my research projects. I should also do something with all the research I did in connection with the competitive exams last year for promotion to full professor. I worked on a fascinating topic: the influence of Golden Age classics on the Silver Age (the 1890–1930 period). I was advised to choose a project that was not feminist because, as Fanny pointed out so well, feminism has very pejorative connotations. The other day when I was working at the Real Academia Española [Spanish Royal Academy], the secretary of the Academy, Víctor García de la Concha, said to me: "Here you go again, with another feminist subject." "No," I replied. "I am working on other things, but I've noticed that in the Academy catalog, 'Feminism' is included under the heading 'Folklore,' and it is followed by 'Gypsies' and 'Jews.'" That strikes me as amusing.

KMG: You are a very respected critic. García de la Concha has described you as the "madrina crítica" [critical godmother] of the Barcelona School. I like the phrase. It is a nice tribute to you.

CR: He is a generous person, and we are friends. It was as a friend that he made that remark, half in jest, half in earnest, about here you go again with feminist topics, and I advise you against it.

Notes

1. Balcells also represents such literary luminaries as Gabriel García Márquez, Mario Vargas Llosa, Augusto Roa Bastos, Juan and Luis Goytisolo, and Juan Marsé. Both interviews appeared in *Quimera:* "Enseñar a dudar: Conver-

sación con José Manuel Blecua, senior" 26 (1982): 20–25; and "Carmen Balcells, alquimista del libro" 27 (1983): 23–29. The second interview is much sought after, since it is the only one Balcells has granted.

2. On the Gil de Biedma–Ferrater relationship, see Riera's *La Escuela de Barcelona* (Barcelona: Anagrama, 1988), 59–63.

3. Books by both writers are currently on the list of bestsellers.

4. On April 23, which is the anniversary of the death of Cervantes and of Shakespeare, as well as the Day of Sant Jordi, patron saint of Catalonia, it is customary to give a book and a rose.

5. Roca's *Secrets de família* [Family Secrets] was a hit series in 1995, and Benet i Jornet's *Nissaga de poder* [Lineage of Power] is currently being broadcast on TV-3.

6. Also memorable is the narrator-protagonist of "Noltros no hem tengut sort amb sos homos . . ." [We've Not Been Lucky with Men] from *Te deix, amor, la mar com a penyora,* which was added to the "Bestia de carga" section of *Palabra de mujer* and *Te dejo el mar* [I Leave You the Sea]).

7. Falcón is perhaps Spain's best-known feminist. She founded the Partido Feminista, published *Vindicación Feminista* (1976–1979), and currently is the editor of *Poder y Libertad.*

8. Women hold the posts of minister of Agriculture, Education and Culture, Environment, and Justice in José María Aznar's Partido Popular government, which came to power in the spring of 1996.

Interview with Carme Riera: "Teaching Literature Is Teaching the World"

CHRISTINA DUPLÁA

CARME RIERA AND I HAD A SHORT CONVERSATION IN BARCELONA ON 22 January 1996, shortly after she was awarded the National Narrative Prize for *Dins el darrer blau*. We discussed the significance of the award and her teaching (Golden Age and twentieth-century Spanish literature) at the Autonomous University of Barcelona. Riera was promoted to full professor last year.

CD: I'd like to congratulate you on the prize and ask you what you think about it within the context of the plurality of languages in Spain.

CR: I'm very pleased by this prize. It's an award for being marginal in every sense: I'm a woman, Catalan, and from Majorca. Regarding the language of the book, let's recall a bit of history. Despite what people may think, Menéndez Pelayo was the first to understand that peripheral literatures (Catalan, Galician, and, to some degree, Basque) belong to Spanish literature. He studied in Catalonia and learned to understand us. In fact, he placed a "y" between his two family names when he saw that Catalans like Rubió i Ors and Rubió i Lluch used an "i," which is the Catalan translation of the "y." This point of view changed with Menéndez Pidal. He gave priority to Castilian literature. Since then, people think that the only Spanish literature is that of Castile.

I really believe that the Spanish government should take into account the fact that a country is richer when it has four languages instead of one. This kind of approach to our multicultural reality is not yet a fact. Last week I was invited to give a lecture at the opening session of the Cervantes Institute in Germany.

Its director confessed to me that the Spanish embassy didn't want to have me there because I write in Catalan and about Jews.

To me, it's incomprehensible that people still don't understand that Catalan is a Spanish language, like Castilian. When, from the center of Spain, are we going to hear that Ramon Llull was the most important Peninsular philosopher in the Middle Ages? In this sense, the prize jury was being conciliatory.

CD: Do you reflect in your teaching the idea or the concept of exclusion?

CR: If you are referring to a project designed to begin changing the historiographical canon, the answer is "no." As an individual, I can introduce authors who are not on the official syllabus. For example, in my Golden Age class, I teach María de Zayas. In her era, she was as widely read and published as Cervantes, but this fact is ignored by Spanish scholars like Francisco Rico, who writes and edits collections on the history of Spanish literature without mentioning her. As always, in these academic projects we can find only two types of women: either those who are mediocre but representative of something, such as Fernán Caballero, or those who are already established, such as Emilia Pardo Bazán. And that's it.

CD: Does this mean that professors of literature, as a group, do not periodically review the canon?

CR: Those who do that kind of work are the scholars of literary theory, not professors of Spanish literature, which is taught in Spain just as it was in the nineteenth century. Traditional and patriarchal textbooks are still used. They ignore all of those writers who are not recognized by the Academia, like Vicente Blasco Ibáñez. He was considered by the orthodox [thinkers] of his time as a "popular" writer, and he still is.

CD: Does being famous and winning prizes as important as the Nacional de Narrativa make a difference in your relationship with your students?

CR: No. They seem happy, and it's fun for them to see me on TV, because at that specific moment I'm no longer a writer: I've become a spectacle. In Spain and probably also in the United States, one is valuable only when one is a spectacle. Regarding the Nacional, two funny things happened to me: the first was that my son (age 23) asked me if the TV stations were going to interview me at home, and the second was that my publisher in Madrid (Alfaguara) called me, very happy, to tell me that someone was interested in the film rights. The fact that both of these had nothing to do with literature left me astonished.

CD: Do you believe in the concept of "generation"?

CR: Not if we're talking about literature. I've changed the title of "The Generation of 1898" course to "The Turn-of-the-Century in Spain." This open title allowed me to introduce the ideologies of the period as well as *modernismo,* which I consider more universal.

CD: Have you taken advantage of that new title in order to teach Catalan *modernisme?*

CR: No, I can't do so in an open way. That area belongs to the Department of Catalan. Nevertheless, I refer to it often, because we can't forget that many aspects of Spanish *modernismo,* like those of romanticism, have their starting point in Catalonia. I always try to take into account this cultural exchange, because it seems to me to generate a kind of common ground, and I feel very motivated by that. As you can see, I love both of these languages. I can write in Catalan and teach Spanish literature written in Castilian at the same time. I consider myself a bilingual person, and I've paid a price for it, because I've never been one hundred percent behind either side. I've never considered myself a Spanish nationalist or a Catalan nationalist.

CD: Have you ever worked with the concepts of memory and testimony to recover part of our literary history?

CR: Yes. In my research on the Barcelona School, I worked with direct testimonies. I talked to Jaime Gil de Biedma, Carlos Barral, José Agustín Goytisolo, Antonio de Senillosa, and Juan García Hortelano. I reconstructed their literary epoque, so to speak, from their books, their testimony, and their memory. This experience was very interesting, because I realized how literary history is reconstructed. There is a selection of facts in our memory that organizes everything, giving it a sense of totality and unity that it never had in reality. Chance plays an important role in this process, and when we recall something, we first organize the reminiscence. That proved to be the case with these writers.

CD: And do you use your memory in your fiction?

CR: Of course. Memory is the writer's eyes. Whoever loses memory loses identity. Words give us rationality, but memory makes us individuals. Without it, we could not live.

CD: Is *Dins el darrer blau* the result of a guilty conscience regarding Jews in Majorca or of a desire to write a historical novel?

CR: Both. I still remember how some classmates whose families had been forced to convert to Catholicism were marginalized. They were mocked by the other students. Since I was a shy child, this attitude toward the Jews was so terrible that it is still etched in my memory of childhood. Memory is crucial for literature. Maybe writing the book was a way of asking forgiveness for the anti-Semitism of our culture.

CD: Do you feel emotionally fulfilled teaching?

CR: I love teaching. It's so easy to teach the authors of the Golden Age. They are so good that I don't have to do much to get an enthusiastic reaction from the students. I've learned a lot teaching, because it helps me to confront the texts and to read certain authors again. In my opinion, teaching literature is teaching the world.

CD: How did you become a professor of Spanish literature?

CR: I was hired by Professor José Manuel Blecua when I finished my B.A. I wanted to become a physician, but my family wouldn't let me. Then, when I told them that I loved writing, they suggested that I study humanities. I never thought that the teaching of literature was going to fascinate me. When I teach an author that I don't like very much, I try not to express my personal opinion until the end of the course. I don't tell them the first day of class that Unamuno was a misogynist or that he never understood Catalan language and culture. But I tell them from the beginning that I am interested in Azorín and in the influence of the classics on turn-of-the-century literature, what we call the "Silver Age." Last year I was working on this project in order to obtain my promotion to full professor. Thanks to my work as a teacher, which I love, I can be a more complete person. Thank you for asking about what occupies such a large part of my day. Teaching has become a passion.

Part II
Critical Essays

Doing Good and Feeling Bad: The Interplay of Desire and Discourse in Two Stories by Carme Riera

Mirella Servodidio

In "Te deix, amor, la mar com a penyora" [I leave you, my love, the Sea as a Token] and "Jo pos per testimoni les gavines" [I Call on the Seagulls as Witness], the imaging of lesbian love is configured in a continuous interplay of desire and form that bespeaks a clear articulation of psyche and text. The social barriers that drive the two lovers apart after eight and a half months are reflected formally through the cleavage of their common story into separate, autonomous units. Yet, their boundaries remain permeable and create a system of metonymic linkages that privilege continuity and symbiosis.

The placement of the stories fluctuates in the several editions in which they appear. They are first introduced under separate cover as the title stories of two volumes written in Catalan: *Te deix, amor, la mar com a penyora* and *Jo pos per testimoni les gavines.*[1] However, the incubation process linking the two has already begun by the time the first volume appears and is explicitly flagged by the last word, "continuarà," of the concluding (untitled) story: barely skimming a page, it not only mirrors various motifs of "Te deix, amor, la mar com a penyora," but also foreshadows "Jo pos per testimoni les gavines," its clear sequel, in important ways, thereby creating an enchainment of signification.

In "Jo pos per testimoni les gavines," which appears in print two years later, the narrator (and implied author) writes to Carme Riera and gives her own version of "Te deix, amor, la mar com a penyora," which, she claims, overlaps with her life in significant ways. An aesthetic of ambiguity is created by the blurring of boundaries between fiction and reality: calling attention to the first story's status as artistic invention and artifact, the narrator purports to "correct" it with biographical truth. Although entire chunks of the subject's life reproduce Riera's story, the concluding episode veers dramatically from the "fictional" version that she hotly contests. Hence, "Jo pos per testimoni les gavines" creates an ambiguous register of sameness and difference, of continuity and separation from its precursor. The narrator's enunciated wish to suspend all further discourse, thereby rendering her account impregnable to destabilizing deconstructions or addenda, will in fact shortly go unheeded.

Indeed, the two stories reappear in a significantly altered state in *Palabra de mujer* [Woman's Word].[2] The book is an anthology of stories drawn from the two earlier collections and now rewritten in Castilian by the author. The original story sequences are not universally upheld. More significantly, "Te entrego, amor, la mar como ofrenda" and "Y pongo por testigo a las gaviotas" are now placed sequentially, creating an unmistakable register of contiguity and connection. Moreover, the second story differs substantially from the Catalan version by upholding a principle of oneness and continuity with its mate and by a refusal to interpose the artificial barriers created by the framing letters of "Jo pos per testimoni les gavines." The immediacy of this connection is fortified by the replacement of the third-person pronoun of the Catalan version with a direct interlocutionary structure; here, an "I" invokes and mentally addresses a "you" (although some slippage into the third person occurs intermittently). My analysis of the two stories is based on this 1980 edition.

In 1991, a composite edition of both volumes is again presented in Castilian under the title *Te dejo el mar* [I Leave You the Sea].[3] The editor and translator Luisa Cotoner returns to the original sequencing of the books and adheres strictly to the Catalan version of the second story.[4] Nonetheless, the cleavage of the two tales is mitigated by their placement under a single cover. Separated by a thin membrane of pages—which is again bridged by the last word of the concluding story (appropriately, now entitled "Final")—their attachment of meaning is clear.

The positional variants found in these several editions reflect Riera's ambiguous, if persistent, engagement with issues of lesbian identity and attachment. Clearly, the meaning of "Te dejo, amor, la mar como ofrenda" and "Y pongo por testigo a las gaviotas" is founded relationally, in both a rhetorical and a psychological sense. Interestingly, metonymy is identified as a ruling trope of Riera's writing by exegete Luisa Cotoner in her introductory essay in *Te dejo el mar*.[5] Both Roman Jakobson, the linguist, and Jacques Lacan,[6] following Jakobson, situate metonymy in the register of contiguity, a register that comports easily with the *jouissance* of female sexuality as described by Jane Gallop in *The Daughter's Seduction* and which is characterized by the "nearness, presence, immediacy, contact" that we find in Riera's stories.[7]

The symbiotic fusion of Riera's tales may also be viewed through the optic of feminist psychoanalytic theory, which highlights the permeability of female ego boundaries as well as the centrality of the mother-daughter relationship in female development. Nancy Chodorow, in particular, has demonstrated that a girl's gender identity arises through her infantile union and later identification with her mother. Although separation and individuation are as crucially important to a girl's development as they are to a boy's, her personality is relational and fluidly defined and her ego boundaries are permeable.[8]

Because the mother is the prototypic erotic image, it is conceded that the homoerotic side has more primitive weight for a girl than for a boy, exacerbating the difficulties of female development and separation. Lesbianism is explained, in part, by the inability to move beyond the pre-Oedipal mother-daughter dyad. In theorizing the mechanisms of primary identification, narcissism, and abjection, Julia Kristeva has pointed to the homosexual facet in the daughter's pre-Oedipal identification with the mother. In her view, it is the particular modality of the semiotic chora, that place of indistinction prior to the various splittings (subject/object, self/other, mother/child) initiated by the mirror stage. In the pre-mirror stage, the child is "face to face with primary narcissism," caught in a primary identification with the mother that, for the girl, along with the mother, positions her on a homosexual continuum.[9] Even Freud came to recognize that a daughter's unconscious homosexual desire for the mother continually impacts her adult life. The insistence on a mother-daughter bond as the foundation for lesbianism has been criticized as homophobic by Teresa de Lauretis, for, in her view, it subsumes the desire *for* another woman to the desire to be (like) a woman.[10] Nonetheless, the definition of lesbianism as an extension of female bonding or mother love is one to which many lesbians have been drawn.

The pre-Oedipal substratum of Riera's stories is unmistakable and has numerous manifestations. The age difference of the lovers (a teacher of math and her fifteen-year-old-student) and the conspicuous absence of the girl's mother establish the baseline of the older lover as surrogate mother. The sea, the supreme signifier of both stories, is feminized (perhaps in concordance with the famous quadripartition of the elements whereby air and fire divide the masculine realm above, while earth and water share the feminine empire below). For countless mythologies, as well as for current writers like Hélène Cixous and Luce Irigaray, water is the feminine element par excellence. Cixous proclaims, "We are ourselves sea, sand, coral, sea-weed, beaches, tides, swimmers, children, waves."[11] For Cixous, the closure of the mythical world contains and reflects the comforting security of the mother's womb. It is within this space that her speaking subject is free to move from one subject position to another, or to merge oceanically with the world. In "La 'Mécanique' des fluides," Irigaray also figures the feminine as fluid, describing the flow of woman's speech as "continuous . . . compressible, dilatable, viscous, conductible, diffusible." More important, "it mixes with bodies in a like state . . . which renders problematic the distinction between one and the other."[12] Clearly, the idyllic, feminized seascape that is the background of the lovers' tryst in Riera's stories connotes a pre-Oedipal realm, one that floats at a safe distance from the reefs and shoals of a symbolic order.[13] It is a pre-verbal, oceanic space that unmakes cultural identities and erases lines of differentiation between subject and object, between same and other.

The moment evoked is one of beginnings and of privileged contact with the maternal (female) body, the constatory present of bliss that locates itself in "un lugar inefable y misterioso, un lugar fuera del tiempo" [some mysterious, ineffable place . . . A place out of time] (17).[14] The younger woman revels in a sense of stasis and wills the continued stoppage of time: "me negaba a dejar pasar el tiempo" [I refused to let time go by] (13). Desire is oculocentric and tactile, situated in inter-reflecting gazes and interfused surfaces that delineate symbiotic bonding and, as in Irigaray's definition of feminine fluidity, render boundary distinctions problematic. Scopic desire, structured in the gaze, has been theorized as phallic activity by Freud. In agreement with Freud, Irigaray posits that "the prevalence of the gaze" has always been "particularly foreign to female eroticism."[15] Although Riera does give us an eye-intense economy of desire, she also creates a reciprocal feminine spectatorial subjectivity, and the boundaries between desiring viewer and the desired object of perception are permeable and undifferentiated.

Yet, this specularity is clouded by the shadows of a surrounding order that introduces the counterclaims of developmental and cultural orthodoxy. From the start, the mature lover is discomfited by the truths acknowledged ten years later by her companion: "Tu influencia era decisiva para que acabara siendo como soy. . . . Mis ojos . . . eran los tuyos, porque yo veía el mundo tal y como tú lo mirabas" [You had a great influence on my getting to be the way I am now. . . . My eyes . . . were your eyes, for I saw the world as you looked at it] (11–12). This teacher/student coupling, with its accompanying imbalance of age, experience, and knowledge, recalls the Greek link between pederasty and pedagogy on which Gallop elaborates in her book, *Thinking Through the Body*: "A greater man penetrates a lesser man with his knowledge. The student is empty, a receptacle for the phallus; the teacher is the phallic fullness of knowledge."[16] In *Speculum,* Luce Irigaray not only returns to pederasty as a paradigm of classic European pedagogy, but also detects a sublimated male homosexuality structuring other social institutions, for example, marriage, commerce.[17] Although Riera enacts a reversal of sorts by assigning authority to a female teacher, a homosexual economy is nonetheless maintained. Power still attaches to knowledge and experience which are "introduced" into the (innocent) student by the teacher, and a symmetry of gender is retained whereby—in Gallop's words—"the student has no otherness, nothing different from the teacher, simply less."

However, having lived longer, the older lover is fully acculturated to the ideologies that label lesbianism as regressive, circular. Is it altruism or cowardice, then, that moves her to reinstate linearity and force separation? The second story will reveal that by "doing good and feeling bad" (in Jean Baker Miller's words)[18] she becomes the agent of a double victimization, her own and that of her lover, with ineradicable consequences for both: the loss of sanity for the one (the teacher is institutionalized) and the loss of life for the other (appearing to yield to cultural indoctrination, the younger woman marries, gives birth and eventually drowns herself at sea, thereby returning to the originating site of their unorthodox idyll).

Riera thus gives us two stories—both different and the same—two versions of a single unhappy tale which each lover reviews and assesses ex post facto. Both are sagas of failure—the failure of love, of nerve—but, most especially, the failure of communication. For the underlying problematic of each is the tyranny of the discursive systems of a sociocultural order in which the lovers are closeted and which places verbal impediments in the way of carnal union; they are both the casualties and the practitioners of a politics of gender, in its double linguistic and cultural sense.

Riera has reflected on the problematic relation of any female subject to language. In her interview with Geraldine C. Nichols,[19] she expounds on this theme: "Para una mujer, escribir literatura es en cierto modo una rebeldía doble. Primero, porque está escribiendo: es mujer y por eso está marginada. Y segundo es el hecho de que está escribiendo en una lengua que la margina, la propia lengua margina a las mujeres" [For a woman, to write literature is, in a sense, a double rebellion. First, because she is writing; she is a woman and because of this she is marginalized. Secondly, there's the fact that she is writing in a language that marginalizes her, language itself marginalizes women] (203; my translation).

Lacan's account of the child's entry into language opposes bodily connection and verbal exchange. To move into a position in language and the social order of the father, the infant must sacrifice its imaginary sense of wholeness and continuity with the mother. Yet, writers like Cixous, Irigaray, and Kristeva have attempted to define the specificity of a mother tongue that is distinctive from patriarchal language and have examined the preverbal character of the pre-Oedipal mother-daughter relation. Diana Fuss has argued that the female subject *as subject* is already situated in the symbolic: "No matter how uncertain the symbolic is for the woman, the mother's face as lost object is fundamentally irrecuperable." Nonetheless, Fuss does allow that the fantasy or promise of "reconnecting (re-fusing?) the homosexual-maternal relation" may persist in varying forms.[20]

Certainly, for Riera's lovers, desire cannot speak its right name. Yet, curiously, both stories represent a coming to language, a cautious and cautionary enunciation of all that has been elided, silenced, or unnamed. Yet, despite their commonalities, the stories evince significant differences in rhetorical shape, authorial voice, and diction.

"Te entrego, amor, la mar como ofrenda" takes the form of a letter written by the younger woman to her lover ten years after their separation and on the eve of giving birth. Twice the length of its companion piece, it is written in a lavish, evocative prose that, consistent with the narrator's impetuous character, is overflowing and excessive and that brims with associative and formal properties rustling beyond mere denotation. The epistolary form and the open question as to whether the addressee will ever receive the message, dramatize the central problematic of communication that both stories share. The letter is at once an act of recapitulation, assessment, and farewell in which the protagonist is forced to think about the meaning of language and the interaction of language and desire.

It is clear that the speaker locates the initiatory phase of her relationship in a realm outside of language. Communication, structured in the gaze and sited in the touch is—in fact—mute: "No solíamos hablar. . . . Tu brazo ceñía mi cintura, a menudo reclinaba mi cabeza sobre tu hombro y tú me besabas como nadie ha vuelto a hacerlo jamas" [We almost never talked. . . . Your arm caressed my back. Sometimes I leaned my head on your shoulder and you kissed me as nobody has ever done it since] (13; 62). Desire is not vocalized, (for example, "el amor del que nunca en aquella época hablábamos" [the love we never at that time talked about]) (14) or is masked by symbolic subterfuge ("Aquel amor que llamábamos amistad" [The love we then called friendship]) (14). The narrator is now able to acknowledge her pervasive yearning to bridge the body/voice divide, to break the silence, to overturn the classifications that locate her in cultural space and to find the verbal equivalent of the face that mirrors her as she truly is. The impulse toward a song of desire, she now understands, was silenced by a lover who viewed their relationship from outside, from social ground and the vantage point of community that proscribed the linguistic inscription of lesbian desire.

Their inevitable fall from a pre-Oedipal realm is, indeed, driven by language—by the words, epithets, and labels hurled at them that are saturated with the valuations of culture. Moreover, the Lacanian social law of the father prohibiting access to the maternal (female) body is directly and literally applied; for it is the girl's father who speaks to her "face to face," issues ultimatums, and banishes her to Barcelona.

On the heels of the abrupt, harsh decloseting of this unorthodox union, the older woman's loss of will is absolute and unadorned, and all bodily contact is withheld or spurned. Fluid boundaries are replaced by solidified barriers, the lines of demarcation created by codes of social propriety which are fortified and sealed by the laws of language that distinguish grammatically between a first and second person. The gap between organic need and linguistic or symbolic demand appears to be unbridgeable. Here, Riera introduces the girl's nascent struggle to arrive at an alternative symbolic order—what Jean Wyatt has called a "maternal symbolic"—that joins bodily communion with the abstraction of verbal exchange.[21] The opposition between body and spirit, matter and language has also been analyzed by Shoshana Felman in *The Literary Speech Act*, where she theorizes that the act of "the speaking body" destroys the metaphysical dichotomy between the mental and the physical.[22] Riera's narrator enlists her "speaking body" in the transgression of the codes of silence she and her lover have upheld. But her bold speech act ("Te dije que te quería" [I told you that I loved you]) (15) falls on unreceptive ears ("me hiciste callar" [you told me not to say anything]) (16). At best, her interlocutor can only summon the hollow platitudes that mirror gendered codes of sexual propriety and that exile visual and somatic images from the symbolic register, quarantining them within the limbo of the imaginary: "Las palabras salían mecánicamente de tu boca como si alguien las dictara. Esto no puede continuar. Nuestras relaciones no tienen ningún sentido" [As if you were an automaton, words came out of your mouth. This cannot go on. We have to bring this senseless relationship to an end] (16).[23] Having internalized a dominant ideology that defines love without reproduction as perverse, she engages in a calculus in which 1 plus 1 must necessarily lead to 3. It is no wonder that she is portrayed as a mathematician: uneasy with language, she favors arithmetic certainty over rhetorical ambiguity. Her responses are formulaic and pat, and she slips into a discursive dishonesty that precipitates a crisis of communication, in which the receiver again refuses the message: "Ya no te escuchaba" [I was no longer listening] (16; my translation).

The girl's need to articulate an alternative discourse of female desire remains strong but is continuously circumscribed by normative language codes. During the first of various separations, her lover blocks all circuits of communication, and the girl's unposted letters are kept in a "cajón cerrado a cal y canto" [a locked drawer] (18), the figurative equivalent of their closeted affair. On her return, she again intuits the possibility of a maternal symbolic in which sight and touch are joined by language as a necessary third term. The enunciation of her lover's name alone creates a verbal *jouissance* in which the word and the flesh become one: "Pronuncié tu nombre . . . deslizando consonantes, vocales, casi tangibles, casi de caricia, entre mis labios" [I pronounced your name . . . gliding over consonants, vowels, almost tangible, almost like caresses, between my lips] (24; my translation). This oral gratification is reminiscent of a Barthian aesthetic of writing aloud: "What is searched for (in a perspective of bliss) are the pulsional incidents, the language lined with flesh, a text where we can hear the grain of the throat, the patina of consonants, the voluptuosness of vowels, a whole carnal stereophony, the articulation of the body, of the tongue, not of meaning, of language."[24]

Yet, the girl's solipsistic, verbal self-pleasuring delivers negligible dividends, at best. Speech is the demand for recognition from the other, the insistence on foregrounding the desire that ravenously demands the desire of the other. When her teacher forecloses all contact with her outside the public sphere of the classroom, she makes this the site of her campaign against the spiritual and physical mutilation that censorship causes. Her strident, aggressive questioning is not only a demand for recognition but also destabilizes the definiteness, the "proofs," the order associated with mathematical discourse: "Me dirigía a ti constantemente, y te pedía que volvieras a repetir la explicación. . . . Te planteaba cuestiones, interrumpía tu lección para hacerte observaciones insolentes. . . . Y utilizaba un tono agresivo que te desconcertaba. Quería, a toda costa, que notaras mi presencia" [I addressed you constantly, I asked you to repeat your explanations. . . . I gave you a hard time, interrupting your lectures to make haughty remarks . . . and I always used an aggressive tone of voice that bothered you. I wanted you to recognize my presence] (22–23). Her behavior comports with the (post)structuralist representation of desire as an autonomous, if language-embedded, entity that inexorably disrupts sociality, the domain of collective codes and conventions.

However, the cultural interdictions that disallow an explicit syntax of lesbian desire first curb and eventually erode her discursive freedom. During a subsequent separation, the letters the women exchange are entirely desexualized and bear no resemblance to conventional models of love letter writing. In "La Lettre d'amour" [The Love Letter] Annie Leclerc—cited by Cotoner as a writer whom Riera has read—asserts that love letters have always been written from the body, in connection with love.[25] Leclerc wants love to enter into general circulation, inscribed knowledge, rather than remain private and secret. In "La Venue à l'écriture," Cixous affirms a model of letter writing as oral love: "To write: to love, inseparable. Writing is a gesture of love . . . Read-me, lick-me, write-me love."[26] Instead, in Riera's story, the girl's *jouissance* is camouflaged, mediated, suppressed. Words of passion are strategically hidden under the envelopes' stamps, smuggled like contraband cargo into the harbor of the public sphere. Or, the execution of writing itself—the gentle stroking of the pen on the page, with its building, climactic rhythm—acts as a compensatory displacement of desire, again signalling the sway of social priorities and constraints on language.

"Te entrego, amor, la mar," then, is the story of the insistence of a desire that may not speak its name and whose lack of satisfaction gives death as the only alternative. Indeed, it is only on the threshold of suicide that the subject fully gains a sense of agency authorizing both the ending of the life and the beginning of textual self-representation. Nonetheless, the governing sign of the story is ultimately one of ambiguity, for it simultaneously suppresses and reveals, as if in response to a kind of partitioning of the mind that puts conflicting impulses into play. Despite its diachronicity, the space of the story is crammed with the past, the locus of a maternal system of relations based on presence and connection. Nonetheless, the articulation of a maternal symbolic is restricted and restrained. The discourse of the story adheres to a principle of substitution that is itself the signifier of the subject's painful acculturation. Taking authorship in the present, the narrator still watches carefully over language, aware of the threats it poses. Learned habits of self-censorship are invasive, affecting narrative strategy and diction. Avoiding overt markers of her lover's gender identity, her story appears to locate itself within the dominant heterosexual economy of desire. Personal pronouns and proper names are elided, corporeality is aestheticized and telltale anatomical features deleted. Moreover, the story's central erotic episode is bathed in a rhapsodic language that is more metaphoric than mimetic.

Riera has commented on the greater latitude and play that the Catalan language affords where gender differentiations are concerned. In her interview with Nichols, she elaborates on how she bends the ambiguities of Catalan to narrative purpose in the story in question:

> En catalán existe la posibilidad de utilizar el término "nosaltres" en un sentido mucho más ambiguo que en castellano. "Nosaltres" puede referirse a dos hombres, dos mujeres, o un hombre y una mujer, mientras que en castellano "nosotras" es muy claro que son dos mujeres. . . . Entonces, al escribir "Te deix," me di cuenta que podía jugar con la ambigüedad de "nosaltres" y me divertía explotar esta posibilidad del lenguaje.
>
> [In Catalan it is possible to use the term "nosaltres" in a much more ambiguous sense than in Castilian. "Nosaltres" may refer to two men, two women, a man and a woman, while in Castilian "noso-

tras" clearly designates two women. . . . So, when I wrote "Te deix," I realized I could play with the ambiguity of "nosaltres" and I enjoyed exploiting this possibility of the language.] (209–10)

The longed-for freedom to be neutral or complex is difficult to achieve in Castilian, for ambiguity is curbed by rules of grammar that decree a compulsory choice between masculine and feminine. Similarly, for Barthes, linguisitic utopia would entail access to the neuter: "Pleasure is a neuter (The most perverse form of the demonic)." In analyzing the "body" of the text in *The Pleasure of the Text*, he differentiates between the body of anatomists and physiologists (the one science sees or discusses, the text of grammarians, critics and philologists) and a body of bliss consisting solely of erotic relations. For Barthes, "the text . . . grants a glimpse of the scandalous truth about bliss: that it may well be neuter."[27]

Despite the sentient charge and clarifying beauty of "Te dejo, amor, la mar como ofrenda," linguistic and cultural confines drive the narrator to the strategic maneuvers that manipulate language, reader, and text. In the story's final paragraph, however, the speaker's silence is broken. The lover's name, María, is revealed and recaptured in a recapitulated moment starting from the end of the story and the end of the life. The repressed signifier floats to the surface, at last, privileging a female gender that refuses to be effaced. Moreover, as Brad Epps has noted, "the sea implicitly infuses its name into others: la mar, amare, mare, María. Given such verbal flow, rigid lines of property and propriety do not seem to hold: mother, daughter, lover are provocatively con-fused."[28] By pledging to name her unborn child "María," the narrator also establishes a sense of feminine filiation and continuity. The coming to language that this story describes, with its various acts of public naming—for example, the naming of the desire, the naming of the desired and of the child that is their spiritual offspring, and the refusal of the very notion of the unspeakable that these acts of naming imply, reinstigate the reading process, obliging the reader to consider the gendered dimension of writing and to engage in retrospective dialogue with the text. While "Te entrego, amor, la mar" is a story that falls short of a full arrival at a maternal symbolic order, it summons sufficient narrative courage to unplug the circuits of communication that carry a message of female desire. The letter may reach its intended reader, after all.

In "Y pongo por testigo a las gaviotas," writing is presented as an act of self-scrutiny, remorse, and negation. The story carries the stench of live burial and decay, for its locus is the constricted space of the speaker's mind which is mirrored by the closet-like room she has occupied in a mental asylum for fifteen years, since breaking with her lover. Within this stale and airless chamber, sealed off from the outside world and its distractions, she surrenders voluptuosly to the past. Heeding the voice of conscience, she endeavors to place her life under her own truth and to submit her emotions to intellectual consideration. But in her obsessive ritual she explicitly circumvents therapeutic remedies or cures, for she courts guilt *not* expiation. In Freud's key essay, "Remembering, Repeating and Working Through," he describes the unconscious repetition that occurs when recollection is blocked through repression and resistance.[29] Turning Freudian doctrine on its head, the speaker wills herself to "remember" *and* "repeat," and most certainly *never* to "work through." Writing is an act informed by a conscious, if irrational, desire for regression, a quasi-Orphic descent intended to bring back a lost love.

The speaker's self-analysis turns explicitly on her troubled relationship to language. Unable to pry herself loose from dominant language practices and the ideological premises that undergird them, she submits to a vocabulary and syntax in which Sapphic love is the *synonym* of perversion, deviance, inutility (for example, "generaba desorden . . . revolución" [it engendered disorder . . . revolution]) (37) and the *antonym* of functionality, orthodoxy and stability (for example, "los preceptos establecidos" [established precepts]) (37). Its predicate is the inevitable conclusion that hers was "un tipo de amor inútil, que no conducía a ningún fin y del que no se podía sacar ningún provecho" [a useless type of love leading nowhere and carrying no benefit] (37). Submitting wholesale to the "fear of pronouncing prohibited words" (35), she has lived out the unspeakable by refusing to invest desire in any form of telling or hearing. When forced to break the silence, her language is caught in the net of its own inauthenticity. Her loss of nerve is primarily verbal, as much a matter of words as of actions. Moreover, she is forced to confront her discursive incompatibility with her lover and the discomfort that the girl's passionate utterances cause her. Her own coagulated language is overrun by words like "códigos" [codes] "leyes" [laws] "normas" [norms] "preceptos" [precepts], and "contratos" [contracts].

"Y pongo por testigo a las gaviotas" veers from its Catalan counterpart in its explicit problematizing of lesbianism within a dominant culture whose ideology is a fertile, reproductive sexuality. Even from a distance of fifteen years, the narrator smarts from the hurt of an incident that emblematized her marginalization: hovering on the periphery of a wedding party gathered outside a church, she remembers her envy of the groom, of his assured manner, and she recalls her own confused yearnings:

> Deseé haber nacido hombre. Pensaba que en mi sexo residía la causa de todos mis males. . . . Luego me he dado cuenta que no tenía razón y que de nuevo ellos, los demás . . . habían hecho lo posible para que llegara a sentirme culpable. Culpable de no poder ofrecerte un contrato que, bajo la vigilancia de intermediarios, laicos o sagrados, legalizara nuestras relaciones.
>
> [I wished I had been born a man. I believed that the cause of all my troubles resided in my sex. . . . Later I realized that I wasn't right and that once again they, the others . . . had done everything possible to make me feel guilty. Guilty of not being able to offer you a contract, under the supervision of secular or religious intermediaries, that would legalize our relations.] (38)

Yet, as she now realizes, these sparks of rebellion were quickly extinguished, for she had already internalized the social censure codified in the normative language of cultural orthodoxy. Bending to "the angry voices," she places verbal roadblocks in the way of carnal desire, the "frases de moral al uso, en las que no creía" [the customary moral phrases, in which I did not believe] (39).

The story we get is the subject's attempt to seize the word, at last, and become master of her own experience, and it brings the act of its own making into the work itself. Yet, it is her lover's death that powers her cautious coming to language. For the irrevocability of absence raises desire to the second power, obliging her to put a signifier where her lover's body used to be. Even in the absence of a listener, desire is kept alive in the very project of telling. Oscillating between the past and the present, she creates a composite "now" in which the lover is powerfully represented.

The unplugging of self-expression first takes the form of nocturnal cries and whimpers, the pre-verbal utterances that rise—inchoate—from the subconscious. The distance they travel may be measured by the self-reflexive manipulations of language that parse intentions, action, and beliefs. Words like "culpa" [fault] and "rebeldía" [rebellion] are revisited and assigned new valuations that challenge the prevailing sociolect and its misprisions. Former obsessions with silence fluctuate toward a need for verbal exposure, a need to leave the closet and bring mourning from the margin to the center which comports closely with Diana Fuss's definition of "coming out" as a movement into a metaphysics of presence, speech and cultural visibility and into a space in which she can attend to what otherwise might never be made manifest: "no me resigno a encerrar para siempre este manuscrito en un cajón . . . deseo, con todas mis fuerzas, que alguien más que el médico conozca este escrito" [I cannot resign myself to shutting this manuscript in a drawer forever. . . . I wish, with all my might, that someone besides the doctor get to know this piece of writing] (33).[30] The pull to "publish" her story, to leave a trace, recalls Stéphane Mallarmé's words of advice to a comrade who confided to him his need to act: "To act . . . signified . . . *to produce on many a movement that gives you in return the feeling that you were its cause, thus that you exist. . . . Your act always applies itself to paper,* for to meditate without traces becomes evanescent."[31]

Although Riera's narrator is now convinced that there can be no act without linguistic inscription, the governing sign of the story—like that of its mate—is one of verbal ambiguity. The speaker's relation to language is marked by habits of distrust that oblige her to return again and again to her manuscript to "erase," "rewrite," "polish," and to "control verbal violence" and "aggression." Even then, she is persuaded that verbal translations of feelings serve only to traduce them and, despite her remorse at past failures of utterance, she cannot authorize herself to inscribe desire in explicit terms. Instead, she falls back on her habitual circumlocutions and indirections, for example, read "to love" for "el ejemplo más bello de todos los verbos transitivos" [the most beautiful example of all transitive verbs] (41). As in the first story, personal pronouns and proper names are eradicated or deferred (some gender markings appear midway and a final naming does occur). Most significantly, the central act of erotic consummation, described with shimmering lyricism in "Te dejo, amor, la mar," is left open to question here. In the Catalan version of the story, the lesbian love act is categorically denied as if, in Epps's words, "Riera had to amend the sexual act, the lesbian fact of the earlier text: correct it, unwrite and undo it, volatilize and virtualize it."[32] Here, the treatment of the same episode is ambiguous and figurative: the sea is restored as the reigning trope of desire wherein body of water and body of lover are erotically con-fused:

> Persigo el tacto anacarado de las caracolas. La suavidad de las algas entre blondas y encajes de espuma que me envuelven. Me dejo llevar por el ritmo de las olas y el fluir. El oleaje me arrastra hacia las profundidades. Bordeo las paredes de una gruta rezumante . . . y me pierdo en el torbellino de las aguas de fondo.
>
> [I pursue the mother-of-pearl touch of the shells. The smoothness of the algae amidst the silken lace of foam that envelops me. I let myself be carried along by the rhythm of the waves and their flow. The surge carries me towards the deep. I border the walls of an oozing grotto . . . and lose myself in the whirlwind of the deepest waters.] (41)

Yet, even these veiled allusions unnerve the narrator, as the disclaimers of the next paragraph show, and she makes haste to arrest the uncensored verbalization that is crucial to the finding and making of meaning. The virtuality or actuality of this act is thus left open to the reader's interpretation.

While the narrator hovers on the threshold of a genuine representation of the past, hers is ultimately a failed telling which stands as the analogue of the psychosis that obstructs a therapeutic "working through." Her final enunciations are, indeed, final, for they trace her movement away from language and the symbolic, and back to the imaginary, where primary narcissism is restored: "Rechazaría . . . la voz y las palabras. . . . Que nada me estorbara para mirar fascinada aquel cuerpo desnudo" [I would reject . . . voice and words. . . . That nothing impede me from looking upon that nude body in fascination] (39). Holding her goose-down pillow to her breast, she suckles—acting as mother to herself ("succiono una punta a modo de chupete . . . crecida, adulta ya" [Already grown up, adult . . . I suck on the tip as if it were a pacifier]) (42)—and engages in delusional imaginings that return her to an originary intimacy with her lover.

It is only in the last paragraph that the narrator reveals the cause of her lover's death and finally gives her name—"Marina"—a name that not only relocates her in a feminized seascape, but echoes euphoniously with her own and which—but for the discordant consonant—is the perfect mirror image of her own. Indeed, the echoing and mirroring effects of Riera's stories are unmistakable. In part, because in "Te pongo por testigo a las gaviotas," the act of writing is, in fact, an act of incessant rereading of two tales already told: one aborted, the other reaching full term; the first beckoning with the promise of fulfillment, the second tragic, sterile, closed. Unwilling—perhaps unable—to authorize an alternative story, the narrator comes to discover her primary identity as that of reader, and she pledges the remainder of her life to the circular rereading of these two discordant tales. Central to this act of memory is the naming (albeit retarded) of the deceased, for to elide the name would be tantamount to granting death the final word. The survivor's memento mori, through the specificity of its naming, is thus able to create the illusion of eternal witness and presence.

With this, we come full circle. The demarcation and differentiation of Riera's two stories are clear, the apparent signifiers of normative codes of Oedipal and post-Oedipal development. Each is whole with a beginning, middle, and end. And yet both stories "touch," for they create a conceptual and physical space that is communal and shared, and they are melded by continuous cross-references, citations and migrations that create an unmistakable register of contiguity. Lying defiantly side by side, they complement and complete each other, and their fluid, permeable boundaries establish a discourse of bodily connection that overturns gender-marked codes of silence and separation.

Notes

1. Carme Riera, *Te deix, amor, la mar com a penyora* (Barcelona: Editorial Laia, 1975), and *Jo pos per testimoni les gavines* (Barcelona: Editorial Laia, 1977).

2. Carme Riera, *Palabra de mujer* (Barcelona: Editorial Laia, 1980). I will base my analysis of the two stories on this edition. Subsequent references to this volume appear in the text. All citations in English, but two, come from Alberto Moreiras' translation, "I Leave You, My Love, the Sea as a Token," which appears in *On Our Own Behalf: Women's Tales from Catalonia* (Lincoln: University of Nebraska Press, 1989). I provide two translated passages in English, which Moreiras omits in his version. To date, there is no published English translation of "Y dejo por testigo a las gaviotas"; all the citations in English are my translation.

As noted, the translation from Catalan to Castilian in *Palabra de mujer* is that of Carme Riera. In her interview with Geraldine C. Nichols, Riera discusses her linguistic background. She grew up hearing both Catalan and Castilian in her home. Interestingly, her parents' preferred language of communication with each other was Castilian. Her primary school education was also conducted in Castilian. She concludes by saying, "De modo que mi situación de bilingüismo es total" [So that my situation is one of total bilingualism] (195). All the citations in English are my translations.

3. Carme Riera, *Te dejo el mar* (Madrid: Espasa Calpe, 1991).

4. Cotoner enumerates the following departures from the original sequencing: four stories from *Te deix* are omitted, and a fifth has been placed with those of *Jo pos* for reasons of internal coherence. In turn, three stories have been omitted from *Jo pos*. Although the balance hold to the original order, two base themselves on the Castilian version found in *Palabra de mujer*. The precise titles of the stories concerned may be found in footnotes 35 and 36 on page 41 of Cotoner's edition.

5. Cotoner speaks of an aesthetic of "indefinición" produced by a confusion of boundaries between the imaginary and the real and by an admixture of sensorial perception: "Esta aportación que . . . se expresa en complejas asociaciones sinestésicas y metonímicas, es el ingrediente que configura . . . la mayoría de los relatos" [This contribution which . . . expresses itself in complex synesthesic and metonymic associations, is the ingredient that configures . . . the majority of the stories] (21).

6. Jakobson, "Linguistics and Poetics," in *The Structuralists: From Marx to Lèvi-Strauss*, ed. Richard and Fernande De George (New York: Anchor Books, 1972), 85–123; Lacan, *Écrits* (Paris: Éditions du Seuil, 1966).

7. Gallop, *The Daughter's Seduction* (Ithaca: Cornell University Press, 1982), 30.

8. Chodorow argues these points in "Family Structure and Feminine Personality," in *Woman, Culture and Society*, ed. Michelle Z. Rosaldo (Stanford: Stanford University Press, 1974), 43–66; and in *The Reproduction of Mothering: Psychoanalysis and the Sociology of Gender* (Berkeley: University of California Press, 1979).

9. Kristeva, *Desire in Language: A Semiotic Approach to Literature and Art*, trans. Thomas Gora, Alice Jardine, and Leon S. Roudiez, ed. Leon Roudiez (New York: Columbia University Press, 1980), 265.

10. de Lauretis, "The Female Body and Heterosexual Assumptions," in *Semiótica* 67 (1987): 3–4.

11. Cixous, "The Laugh of the Medusa," trans. Keith and Paula Cohen, ed. Elaine Marks and Isabelle de Courtrivon, in *New French Feminism* (Brighton: Harvester, 1980), 260.

12. Irigaray, "La 'Mécanique' des Fluides," *L'Arc* 58 (1974), 52.

13. The narrator is separated from her lover by both time and space. In Barcelona, she evokes the sea that now separates, as it once joined, two bodies of land and the bodies of the two lovers. Yet, with all that, a powerful maternal imagery is retained in the personification of the sea, for example, "Ya no canta nanas; de entre sus dedos se escurrieron hace tiempo todas las caricias" [She no longer sings lullabies; all the caresses slipped from her fingers a long time ago] (9; my translation). With the fall from the pre-Oedipal, the sea is "(un) espejo que no reproduce nada" [(a) mirror that reflects nothing] (9; my translation).

14. Cotoner characterizes the type of love most frequently found in Riera's stories: "Amor casi siempre fijado por la autora en lo que Francisco Alberoni ha llamada 'el estado naciente,' en el momento que el enamoramiento transfigura el mundo y todo resulta nuevo y estremecedor" [Love always fixed in what Francisco Alberoni has called "an incipient state," the moment in which

the infatuation transfigures the world and everything seems new and overwhelming] (24; my translation).

15. Luce Irigaray, *Ce sexe qui n'en est pas un,* trans. Claudia Reeder, in *New French Feminisms,* ed. Elaine Marks and Isabelle de Courtivron (Brighton: Harvester, 1980), 101.

16. Gallop, *Thinking Through the Body* (New York: Columbia University Press), 43. Also on page 43 is the subsequent quotation from Gallop found at the end of the paragraph.

17. Irigaray, *Spéculum de l'autre femme* (Paris: Minuit, 1974). In Spanish literature, lesbian desire between teachers and students has also been thematized in *Julia* by Ana María Moix and *El mismo mar de todos los veranos* by Esther Tusquets. See Mirella Servodidio, "A Case of Pre-Oedipal and Narrative Fixation: Tusquets' *El mismo mar de todos los veranos,*" *Anales de la literatura española contemporánea* 12 (1987): 157–73.

18. Miller, *Towards a New Psychology of Women* (Boston: Beacon Press, 1976), 48–59.

19. Nichols, *Escribir, espacio propio: Laforet, Matute, Moix, Tusquets, Riera y Roig por sí mismas* (Minneapolis: Institute for the Study of Ideology and Literature, 1989), 203 and my translation.

20. Fuss, "Fashion and the Homospectatorial Look," *Critical Inquiry* 18:4 (1992): 736.

21. Wyatt, "Giving Body to the Word: The Maternal Symbolic in Toni Morrison's *Beloved,*" *PMLA* 108:3 (1993): 475.

22. Felman, *Literary Speech Act* (Ithaca: Cornell University Press, 1983), 94.

23. In *Philosophy and the Mirror of Nature* (Princeton, N.J.: Princeton University Press, 1979), Richard Rorty asserts: "We must get the visual, and in particular the mirroring out of our speech altogether," 79.

24. Rolande Barthes, *The Pleasure of the Text,* trans. Richard Miller (New York: Hill & Wang, 1975), 66.

25. Leclerc, "La Lettre d'amour," *La Venue à l'écriture,* ed. H. Cixous, M. Gagnon, and A. Leclerc (Paris: Union Générale d'Editions, 1977).

26. Cixous, "La Venue à l'écriture," *La Venue à l'écriture,* ed. H. Cixous, M. Gagnon, and A. Leclerc (Paris: Union Génèrale d'Editions, 1977), 48.

27. Barthes, 65, 16.

28. Epps, "Virtual Sexuality: Lesbianism, Loss and Deliverance in Carme Riera's 'Te deix, amor, la mar com a penyora,'" *¿Entiendes ?: Gay and Lesbian Writing and Performance in Spain and Spanish America,* ed. Emilie L. Bergmann and Paul Julian Smith (Durham: Duke University Press, 1995), 325.

29. Sigmund Freud, "Remembering, Repeating and Working Through." *The Standard Edition of the Complete Psychological Works of Sigmund Freud.* James Strachey, Ed. and Trans. (London: Hogarth Press: 1953–74), vol. 12, 145–156.

30. Fuss, *Inside/Out: Lesbian Theories, Gay Theories,* ed. Diana Fuss (New York: Routledge, 1991), 4.

31. Mallarmé, "L'Action restreinte," *Oeuvres complètes* (Paris: Gallimard, 1945), 369.

32. Epps, 331.

Seduction and Simulation in Carme Riera's *Una primavera per a Domenico Guarini*

AKIKO TSUCHIYA

IN HIS INFLUENTIAL THEORETICAL WORK, JEAN BAUDRILLARD presents a critique of interpretive discourse in favor of a model of seduction that privileges the play of appearances over the search for a hidden meaning. He exposes as an illusion, as an impossible task, the fundamental desire of interpretive discourse to get beyond the "circulation of signs on the surface": "All appearances conspire to combat meaning . . . and to convert it into a game, according to some other rules of the game, arbitrary ones this time, to some other elusive ritual, more adventurous and more seductive than the mastery of meaning."[1] Furthermore, he associates seduction with the "feminine," with that which transgresses phallic economy and blurs the distinction between authenticity and artifice. In his words, seduction is "an ironic, alternative form, one that breaks the referentiality of sex."[2] My reference here to Baudrillard is not meant to imply a wholesale adoption of his anti-representational rhetoric, which tends to deny culture and the structures of power operative within it. From a feminist perspective, the postulation of the "feminine" as a disembodied sign, as an abstract concept without relation to real cultural and social structures that produce gendered identities, is clearly problematic.[3] At the same time, his postmodernist suspicion of essential truths, master narratives, and unified identities can provide a useful framework of analysis for works by contemporary Spanish writers who are immersed in a literary and theoretical milieu that has challenged traditional notions of literary discourse, representation, and identity.

Carme Riera, who came of age as a writer in this literary and theoretical milieu, repeatedly calls attention to the centrality of seduction, not only as a theme or as a narrative strategy, but also as an epistemological model. In her essay, "Grandeza y miseria de la epístola" [Greatness and Misery of the Epistle], she suggests that the seductive intention of the letter, with its "búsqueda de un destinatario . . . con el objeto de captar su atención y, si es posible, atraerle y aún persuadirle" [search for an addressee . . . with the object of capturing his/her attention and, if possible, attracting and even persuading him/her], represents a model for all literature.[4] Similarly, the female narrator of Riera's epistolary novel, *Qüestió d'amor propi* [A Question of Self-Love, 1987] identifies narrative and erotic seduction with the words, "Qualsevol escriptura és una carta d'amor" [All writing is a love letter] (24), as does the novelist figure, Pablo Corbalán, in *Joc de miralls* [Game of Mirrors, 1989], in the following statement about his own work:

> M'interessa d'entrada seduir el lector perquè segueixi llegint. Mitjançant l'aparença de la meva escriptura, mitjançant els signes, les ambigüitats i connotacions que li ofereix el meu discurs, envoltar-lo, conduir-lo i atracar-lo cap a mi, fer-lo meu, això vol dir seduir.

> I'm interested in seducing the reader from the start so that he will continue reading. Through the appearance of my writing, through the signs, ambiguities and connotations that my discourse offers, I try to ensnare him, lead him and bring him toward me, to make him mine, that is called seduction.[5]

Riera's first novel, *Una primavera per a Domenico Guarini* [*A Primavera for Domenico Guarini,* 1981], like many of her other works, is a highly self-conscious text that dramatizes the seductive nature of literary discourse through a narrative game of simulation and deceptive appearances.[6] Both of the novel's epigraphs call attention to the notion of the mask, thus introducing the dichotomy between surfaces and concealed meanings, between signs and their referents, a dichotomy which becomes a structuring device for the entire work. The first epigraph is a fragment of a poem by Dante Gabriel Rossetti: "Quin misteri es llegeix aqui d'homenatge o esperança? Però, com fer respondre Primaveres Mortes? I com demanar a aquestes màscares pel desolat Any Nou?" [What mystery here is read of homage or of hope? But how command Dead Springs to answer? And how question here these mummers of that wind withered New Year?], which captures the impossibility of reaching a transcendent reality beyond the signs on the surface.[7] Given the context of the novel, the "Primaveres Mortes" clearly evoke Botticelli's famous painting, an arcane work of art which defies the search for a hidden interpretation. The second quote, from Luis Racionero, describes the circular journey of the self, through its various masks, in its quest for identity, a journey that inevitably leads the self back to its point of origin. Both textual fragments reveal the absence of a transcendent essence behind the seductive appeal of the mask.

In *Una primavera per a Domenico Guarini*, "seduction takes the form of an enigma to be resolved," to borrow Baudrillard's words.[8] The novel contains two fundamental plot lines, both of which dramatize the search for truths and veiled meanings. On one level, it is a detective story, directed toward the resolution of the mystery that surrounds Domenico Guarini's vandalism of Botticelli's *Primavera*. This mystery story, at the same time, parallels the narrative account of the female protagonist Clara's quest for identity at a moment of personal crisis. The hermeneutic code that structures both narratives leads us through myriad (inter)texts that mediate her search for the true motive behind the destruction of Botticelli's famous painting, on the one hand, and her journey to self-discovery, on the other.

Critics have examined the diversity of voices and perspectives that Riera weaves together in *Una primavera* to construct these two levels of narration.[9] Part 1, which focuses on Clara's personal reflections during her train journey from Barcelona to Florence, is narrated by the protagonist to herself in the second person. Part 2 alternates between her second-person narration, centering on events in her own life, and a third-person journalistic account of the Guarini case, also written by her. The third part takes the form of an autobiographical narration that captures fragments of Clara's past from her perspective; this personal narration is set against the backdrop of a professor's academic exegesis of Botticelli's *Primavera*. Finally, the epilogue brings us back once again to the protagonist's reflections, addressed to herself in second person, as she heads back for Barcelona on a train.

Within these principal narrative threads are embedded many other texts that call attention, not only to the literary nature of these narratives but also to the acts of interpretation and creation in which the characters are constantly engaged. During her train journey to Florence in the first part of the novel, Clara imagines herself to be a character in the novels of Pardo Bazán, Galdós, and Tolstoy, as she evokes memories of her past. Her words—"El que no et doni la vida ho trobaràs als llibres" [What life doesn't give you, you'll find in books]—capture her propensity to interpret her entire life through literary texts (27). Even her newspaper reports on the Guarini case which, in one critic's opinion, are "written in the highly objective, impersonal journalistic style," are, in reality, highly subjective, stylized, even fictionalized narratives structured according to the conventions of what Roland Barthes has called the "hermeneutic narrative."[10] Like a mystery or serial novel, Clara's narrative is propelled by an enigma and the expectation of its resolution, an ultimate desire for truth and closure. In an attempt to uncover the motive for his mysterious crime, Clara, her former lover Alberto, Guarini's lawyer, the press, and the entire Florentine society participate in deciphering ambiguous, even contradictory signs. At the same time, the reconstruction of the actual "truth" behind Guarini's crime appears to become secondary to the creation of narratives that conform to the literary imagination of a society (108). Guarini's lawyer, Franchi, appeals to the conventions of the serial novel to compose a sensationalistic account of the defendant's life, "una història grata als fulletonistes" [a story to the liking of serial writers], which will evoke the public's sympathy for his client (56). Life imitates art, as the twists and turns of his trial, with the appearance of Guarini's supposed lover, Laura, and her possible connection to a terrorist group, transform his case into a "melodrama" that "alguns dels mitjans de comunicació tracten de 'novelesc'" [some media outlets call "novelistic"] (107).

Not only does Clara (re)construct the Guarini case in her journalistic reports by structuring her account as a hermeneutic narrative, but in the middle of Part 2, she essentially rewrites the story of his life by imaginatively adopting his point of view, alternately in first- and third-person forms. She makes sense of an apparently unintelligible chain of events by organizing them into a coherent narrative with a logical beginning, middle, and end. Her fictional re-creation of Guarini's obsession with Laura, which ultimately leads to the latter's murder, constitutes an idealization of his actions based on implicitly patriarchal literary paradigms. In Clara's account, Guarini's obsession transforms Laura into the object of the male gaze, an act that is explicitly equated with her subjection to phallic desire: "Solia mirar les dones provocativament. No es limitava a despullar-les: els seus ulls ejaculaven gairebé amb precisió exactíssima dins l'untuós amagatall del sexe" [He used to look at women provocatively. He didn't merely undress them: his eyes ejaculated with exact precision into the oily recess of their sex] (82). If, as Teresa de Lauretis suggests, the Oedipal plot is the paradigm of all narratives (of desire), which identify the male as the subject/hero of the quest and the female as the object/obstacle/boundary, Laura, by luring Guarini's gaze yet evading submission to it, becomes an obstacle to his desire "to fulfill his destiny—and his story."[11] It is notably Laura's "esguard violeta" [violet gaze] (87) which initially kindles his desire to know her, both as a sexual object and as an object of his discourse. In Clara's imagination, the frustration of Guarini's desire in real life leads him to seek its fulfilment in art—more specifically, in Botticelli's *Primavera,* whose central figure, Flora, appears to bear a resemblance to Laura. Indeed, art mediates his search for the object of his desire, as he literally copies her image onto a canvas with colored pencils, thus consecrating her as the ultimate symbol of love (88). In Clara's version of Guarini's story, his obsession is not with a real woman but with an archetype that he has invented through his artistic imagination. Even the scene of their first encounter has already been written as a script to be followed by its author. Although Guarini finally achieves sexual union with Laura, he comes no closer to fulfilling his desire to know her and thus to removing her as an obstacle to his quest for the ideal. His inability to reconcile, through his artistic reproductions of Botticelli's painting, what he perceives to be the real Laura with the artistic ideal embodied in Flora, reveals his total loss of control over Laura as a text, as an objet d'art:

> Havia perdut la facultat de fer un traç lleuger que li permetés recobrar la delicadesa que trobà al moment de dibuixar Laura copiant una reproducció de Flora, potser perquè Laura, la veritable Laura, era cruel, mentidera, plena de falsedat.
>
> [He had lost the ability to draw a light line that would allow him to recapture the refinement that he found at the moment when he sketched Laura by copying a reproduction of Flora, perhaps because Laura, the true Laura, was cruel, deceitful, full of treachery.] (96)

According to Clara's vision of Guarini, then, the only way in which he is able to regain control over his objet d'art, "perquè l'harmonia perduda sigui recuperada" [so that the lost harmony would be recovered]—that is, the harmony of the autonomous work of art—is to kill the real woman (98). His resolution to "executar la seva obra" [execute his work] suggests that he views the murderous act not as such, but as an act of artistic creation (99). In his mind, as envisioned by Clara, he can become the subject of his own destiny and his story only by recuperating "la imatge de la veritable Laura" [the image of the true Laura] (99).

The clichéd nature of the plot into which Clara has inserted her male protagonist attests to her incapacity to resist the primordial phallic logic that is implicated in the construction of narrative. As Elizabeth Ordóñez has suggested, Clara, as a writer, apparently identifies with the phallocentric ideology that underlies the Western literary tradition—from Greek mythology to Dante to Petrarch—a tradition on which she bases her version of Guarini.[12] In the chapter that follows Clara's textual rendition of Guarini's life, she presents the reaction of her former lover, Alberto, to the text that she has written. Despite his masculine gender, Alberto plays an important role as a reader in the text who challenges the phallocentric vision implicit in Clara's discourse.[13] Adopting a critical attitude toward Clara's idealization of Guarini's discourse of masculine desire that objectifies woman, Alberto points out to his former lover the obvious fact that Laura is no more than a Galatea figure to her male creator, "un objecte fabricat per ell, una nina de conte de fades, una santeta de guix" [an object fabricated by him, a girl in a fairy tale, a plaster image of a saint] (102). Clara has effectively created a discourse in which the woman has no story of her own, but rather acts as the impulse (the desire) that generates the narrative of the male quest.[14] Through the figure of Alberto, who calls attention to the phallocentric nature of Clara's narrative, the implied author exposes the patriarchal nature of the entire Western literary tradition, from the troubadors to Dante to Petrarch, which is predicated on the female's submission to the male-authored text.

Two works of art, which exemplify the Western tradition, play a central role in the development of the detective story in which Guarini figures as the protagonist. Botticelli's *Primavera* and Petrarch's *Canzoniere* lead Clara to the mysterious figure of Laura, whose relationship to Guarini and to the painting he has destroyed purportedly holds the key to his act of vandalism. Laura remains an enigma for her readers (these readers include Clara, Alberto, and the Florentines who avidly follow the case as presented in the media, and, by extension, the implied reader of the novel itself), precisely because she is denied material existence or a voice of her own. There is constant doubt as to whether the Laura, who is detained for questioning, is the same as Guarini's lover in real life—if she does indeed exist as such—or as the beloved he has fabricated in his imagination. Although she is perceived as a key figure in the case, ultimately she exists only as a function of others' narratives. During the trial, the police find a copy of Petrarch's *Canzoniere* under a laurel tree where Guarini claims to have buried Laura's remains. Other sentimental objects—including his diary, love letters, sketches of Laura's face, and a lock of her hair—accompany the book. In her journalist's report, yet another rewriting of Guarini's text, Clara attributes the latter's actions to his desire to enter into an autonomous, artistic universe of his own creation. According to her view, Guarini's imagination, which leads him to live his entire life in imitation of artistic models, alienates him from the truth of life: "Tanmateix l'art no podrà ser mai superior a la vida, molt més quan la imitació d'aquell . . . és un grotesc i anacrònic simulacre" [Obviously art can never be superior to life, even less so when its imitation . . . is a grotesque and anachronistic simulacrum] (115). Yet the seductive nature of all the narratives that circumscribe Guarini's life and actions constantly diverts the reader from any notion of absolute truth. Guarini's self-textualization through the imitation of artistic models is no more or no less "a grotesque and anachronistic simulacrum" than are the interpretive discourses of all those who seek meaning beyond the seductive signs on the surface. Even in her reporter's role, Clara admits that her vision of Guarini "no és sinó una interpretació" [is no more than an interpretation] (115), thus undercutting the journalistic ideals of detachment and objectivity.

The artistic universe Guarini has created for himself mirrors the phallocentric ideology of the "inner" texts (Greek myths, Petrarch's *Canzoniere,* Botticelli's *Primavera*) that serve as his models, as well as the "outer" texts (written by Clara and others) that frame his Neoplatonic quest. The Italian Renaissance tradition established the Petarchan and Neoplatonic doctrines of love as archetypes to be followed in the composition of verse. Petrarch's followers in the sixteenth century imitated his representation of woman as idealized physical and moral beauty, a chaste and angelic figure who "has a miraculous power over men and nature."[15] Needless to say, the archetypical Petrarchan woman, symbolized in the figure of Laura, exists solely as a function of masculine desire (or anxiety): she is denied the autonomy and the discursive authority to define her own subjectivity. As Sandra M. Gilbert and Susan Gubar have shown in their critique of Norman O. Brown's views, Petrarch's Laura "can never herself be a poet because she is poetry."[16] Laura's function as textual object in Petrarch's work—and, by extension, as an archetypal feminine aesthetic ideal in the patriarchal Western literary tradition—parallels her role as Neoplatonic ideal in Guarini's "text." As Clara notes in her journalistic account, Guarini himself appears consciously to identify his world with that of the foundational texts of the Western tradition by burying a copy of the *Canzoniere* under the laurel tree. The laurel tree not only acts as a metonymic link to the figure of the beloved in Petrarch's verse, but also evokes the mythological figure of Daphne, who turns into a laurel tree in order to resist Apollo's sexual advances. The story of Daphne and Apollo, which implicitly glorifies the rape of a female divinity by a member of their pantheon of gods, exemplifies yet another archetypal narrative of masculine invasion and conquest.[17]

The narrative represented by Daphne and Apollo, designated by Annis Pratt as the "rape-trauma archetype," provides yet another link between Guarini's text and the *Primavera,* which plays a key role in his artistic self-creation.[18] A central presence in Botticelli's painting is the mythological goddess Flora, who is identified with the nymph Chloris, the figure to her immediate right. According to Ovid's tale, the wind god Zephyr abducts and rapes Chloris, after which he "makes amends" by marrying her and by transforming her into the goddess of flowers.[19] A common interpretation of the painting sees the abduction scene as an allegory of the downfall caused by female pride or hubris: Chloris/Flora has brought punishment upon herself by straying from her paternal home and by giving in to the urges of lust and concupiscence. According to this narrative, Venus, who stands to Flora's immediate left and at the center of the painting, looks down on the rape scene (and, in particular, on Flora) with a gesture of condemnation, while implicitly celebrating the Platonic love of the figures on her right.[20] In fact, this explanation not only justifies but also glorifies Zephyr's pursuit of Chloris, seeing in his breath (directed toward the startled nymph) not "a malevolent intent" but an expression of divine strength to be absorbed by the mortal.[21] The painting thus embodies the central elements of Neoplatonic philosophy, symbolizing the Platonic cycle through which Zephyr, "personifying human love and the life-giving power of nature," elevates Chloris to a higher plane of spirituality and intellectual contemplation.[22] The exaltation and deification of the male perpetrator of violence, together with the assumption that the female victim willfully seeks her own sexual violation and even enjoys its consequences, once again reveal the misogynistic underpinnings of Renaissance humanism.

Furthermore, an unquestioning acceptance of such a phallocentric vision of this classical scene is not surprising, given that our knowledge of the historical circumstances of the *Primavera*'s origin has, in itself, influenced the ways in which the painting has been interpreted through the ages. It is now accepted that the Medici family commissioned the painting for the moral edification of the young Lorenzo di Pierfrancesco de' Medici. The Florentine philosopher and Neoplatonist, Marsilio Ficino, who was Lorenzo's teacher at the time, was given the task of creating a program for the *Primavera* in which the surface representation of a pagan myth was to conceal an arcane and didactic meaning to be available only to the initiate by means of religious contemplation. The artistic program, which, for Ficino, constituted an expression of the spiritual bond (that is, Platonic love) between two men (Lorenzo and himself), was then presented to Botticelli, who completed the painting around 1480.[23] In this context, it is evident that the higher ideals sought by the Neoplatonists were implicitly understood to be attainable only *by* men, to the exclusion of women, or *through* men, at the expense of women, as in the case of Chloris who undergoes "a process of objectification and silencing by an active male subject."[24]

In Riera's novel, a similar Neoplatonic vision informs the exegesis of the art professor, for whom the rape scene represents the transformation of Chloris, through Zephyr's "love," into a higher plane of being (136). According to the professor, this transfiguration occurs under Venus's gaze. Venus's dominant position at the center of the painting as a symbolic mediator between the figures on either side of her assigns her a pivotal role as a medium through which Flora/Chloris (figures on her right) must pass in order to free themselves from the mundane and attain a higher sphere of transcendence. Elizabeth Ordóñez has shown convincingly how the professor's exegesis of Venus affirms the spiritual nonmateriality of the goddess of divine love (represented by Venus Caelestis) through the denial of the female flesh and of the maternal economy (represented by Venus Generatrix).[25] Despite the prominence of Venus's "ventre voluminós" [voluminous belly] in Botticelli's painting (137), the professor regards her not as Venus Generatrix, but as the more ethereal Venus Humanitas who "engendra l'amor humà que viu dins l'ànima, l'amor que capacita la nostra imaginació i els nostres sentits per a percebre la bellesa" [engenders the human love that lives in the soul, the love that enables our imagination and our senses to perceive beauty] (139). In the same exposition, he insists on the even greater superiority of Venus Caelestis, who "engendra l'amor diví perquè procedeix només d'Urani" [engenders divine love because she is born only of Uranus] (140). This privileging of the celestial Venus echoes Pausanias' words in Plato's *Symposium,* in which the goddess is celebrated as the symbol of Platonic love precisely because her "attributes have nothing of the female, but are altogether male."[26] The professor's unquestioning acceptance of the phallocentric and homosocial premises of Renaissance Neoplatonism in his interpretation of the *Primavera* shows how little progress has been made to date in shaking off the patriarchal foundations of the Western tradition.

The third part of the novel juxtaposes the professor's academic discourse with Clara's personal reflections on her life, from her childhood to her recent past, chronicling her struggle to come to terms with her sexual role and identity in a patriarchal society. This narrative strategy serves to highlight the analogy between Clara's role as woman in the "text" that she has written of her life in post-Civil War Spain, on the one hand, and the social and discursive position accorded women in the foundational texts of Western culture, on the other. The professor's commentary on Zephyr's pursuit of Chloris in the *Primavera,* for example, frames in a parallel fashion Clara's childhood memory of being sexually harassed by a child molester in a movie theater. The biblical myths of original sin and of female culpability torment Clara throughout her adolescence as she begins to discover her sexuality.[27] In one flashback, Clara recalls a sleepless night in which she imagines a demon-like figure with a horrible grimace and toothless laugh entering from the garden into her room to punish her for her "culpa obscura" [dark sin], her act of masturbation (131–32). Once again, we see in the adolescent's unconscious the powerful effects of the biblical myth of woman's expulsion from the garden as a punishment for her "sins," a cultural myth continuously recirculated by Spanish post-Civil War society. Clara's own mother, who, except on one isolated occasion, has lived resigned to the role that patriarchal society has assigned to women (in accordance with Eve's fate in Genesis), preaches the biblical imperative to her daughter in a literal-minded way:

> Noltros hem vengut al món per a sofrir i agontar. Déu nostro senyor ho volgué així: pariràs amb dolor, obeiràs el teu homo. . . . Ningú no

> pot esmenar la plana de Déu, llevat d'Eva, la que es deixà temptar. Pecà i per això ho pagam noltros ara.
>
> [We've come into the world in order to suffer and to endure. God, our Father, has willed it this way: you will give birth in pain, you will obey your husband. . . . No one can find fault with God, except for Eve, who let herself be tempted. She sinned, so we're paying for it now.] (134).

Alienated from the discourses of patriarchal culture and from her own mother, who has internalized these discourses, Clara seeks a substitute maternal figure in her schoolteacher, who rejects her by telling her to confide in the Virgin. Significantly, the adolescent protagonist's address to her teacher echoes parts of an earlier work by Riera, "Te deix, amor, la mar como a penyora" ["I Leave You, My Love, the Sea as a Token"], in which a lesbian narrator, moments before giving birth to a child, recreates her past love affair with her female teacher/lover. Although Clara's search for intimacy with her teacher in *Una primavera* is not explicitly subversive of compulsory heterosexuality, as it is in "Te deix," it reveals her desire to recuperate an utopian paradise identified with the Mother. In both works, however, society denies woman the fulfilment of her desire and reinscribes her into the dominant discourses of patriarchy. Just as the narrator's marriage to a man and her imminent death in childbirth in "Te deix" symbolize punishments that society metes out to the lesbian woman for her sexual transgression, the adolescent Clara's rejection by her schoolteacher and her reinsertion into religious discourse in *Una primavera* serve to reinforce patriarchal inscriptions of woman's place within the dominant social order. Finally, the professor's negation of the "pregnant" Venus Generatrix, in favor of the disembodied Venus Caelestis (a Virgin figure), in his interpretation of Botticelli's painting, is yet another manifestation of the same repressive Catholic ideology that denies Clara—both adolescent student and adult woman—her body and sexuality.

Faced with the dilemma of being an unmarried woman who finds herself pregnant and without a strong sense of identity, Clara re-creates the events of her past in search of self-understanding. In her process of self-textualization in the third part of the novel, she discovers the extent to which her life has been shaped according to phallocentric discursive models that are completely alienating to women. In her journey to self-discovery, she must come to terms with the inadequacy not only of the traditional discourses of religion, mythology, and art, but also of the alternative discourses of revolutionary politics, hippie culture, and the like, with which she has come into contact in her life. Clara's relationship with the Communist party leader, Enrique, who, despite his revolutionary rhetoric, relegates woman to the secondary role of supportive companion, teaches her to recognize the emptiness behind the seductive lure of words. Similarly, the apparently nonconformist discourse of youth counterculture, represented by the hitchhiker Marta, does no more than advocate self-destructive behavior, without offering a positive alternative to the discourses of the dominant social order. Even feminist discourse, in the mouth of Clara's activist friend, María, is parodied as a dogma with little relevance to the everyday struggles of the average woman. Surrounded by these alienating discourses, Clara redoubles her search for identity, which continually eludes her. As if mirroring the fragmentation of her identity, Clara's discourse becomes increasingly disjointed in this section of the novel.

At the conclusion of Part 3, Clara's personal journey leads her back, once again, to the central text of the *Primavera*. The painting, which has mediated her interpretive quest throughout the novel, becomes a locus where various other texts—Clara's autobiographical narration, the journalistic report on the Guarini case, and the professor's artistic exegesis—converge in the end. Yet, as she struggles for self-discovery through these texts, Clara becomes aware that uncovering the truth behind the seductive signs of language and art is an impossible task. Although she believes that the *Primavera* holds the key to her true identity, as well as a conclusive explanation for Guarini's mysterious act of vandalism, the professor's words in the background remind her that, in the end, both art and life elude any definitive interpretation. The figure of Mercury, in particular, becomes emblematic of the secret at the center of the *Primavera,* which can never be completely dispelled: although he appears to symbolize reason and light/enlightenment on one level, his caduceus "no esvaeix els níguls, només hi passa a través" [doesn't make the mist disappear, but merely passes through it] (169). In his dual role as the human soul's guide to hell and its means of access to Platonic love and transcendence, he is the essence of ambiguity and contradiction. Recognizing the diverse and conflicting interpretations Botticelli's enigmatic figures have elicited, the professor acknowledges the final inscrutability of the artist's work and vision:

> Botticelli tracta només d'insinuar l'evocació quasi sempre malenconiosa d'un món bell i perdut, perseguit a través d'un gest, un fragment, una al·lusió. Botticelli rebutja narrar episodis i es decanta per a presentar-los a través de línies que s'apropen i se separen, conflueixen i s'enllacen amb ritmes lentíssims i quasi trèmuls a vegades, fins i tot angoixosos a causa de la seva reiteració.
>
> [Botticelli only tries to suggest the almost always melancholic evocation of a beautiful and lost world, pursued by means of a gesture, a fragment, an allusion. Botticelli refuses to narrate episodes and prefers to present them through lines that join and separate, converge and intertwine, with a rhythm that's extremely slow and almost tremulous at times, and even agonizing in its repetition.] (175).

The artistic text thus defies the imposition of narrative logic and coherence, seducing us with a symbolic world of appearances, only to deny us its mastery. Notwithstanding his fundamental identification with a (Neo)platonic vision of the *Primavera,* the professor ultimately admits to the impossibility of a single allegorical meaning behind the work and affirms the existence of multiple possibilities of reading.

After the university professor finishes his lecture on the *Primavera,* Clara scrutinizes the painting once again, hoping to discover in its "missatge hermètic" [hermetic message] an answer to the mystery of Guarini's destructive act (178). The solution she believes to have found, in a moment of revelation, however, is not altogether different from the narratives others have constructed previously around Guarini and the *Primavera.* Clara's conviction that Guarini's crime is, in reality, an act of love through which he seeks his self-transformation is founded on the same phallocentric logic that informs traditional Neoplatonic interpretations of the painting. If, in fact, he sees his crime against the painting and, in particular, against the silent and idealized image of Flora, as a noble act of self-sacrifice, as a renunciation of "la capaçitat de ser feliç" [the capacity to be happy], it is to say that man's spiritual rebirth can be achieved only through the symbolic murder of woman (179). In this scheme, furthermore, woman is limited to her function as a mediator between man (and his material world) and a higher sphere of transcendence attainable only through suffering and self-sacrifice.

The new perspective on Guarini's motives that Clara has gained through her scrutiny of the *Primavera* leads her to believe that the solution to her personal crisis is also to be found in the painting. In the final paragraph of Part 3, she imagines the *Primavera* to be a metaphorical mirror, which permits her to recapture the lost unity of her own fragmented subjectivity:

> Tremola la teva pròpia imatge—totes les versions de tu mateixa, totes les possibilitats del teu ésser, totes les màscares—, desapareix, es recompon, calidoscòpica, al fons d'aquest mirall anomenat *La Primavera.*
>
> [Your own image trembles—all versions of yourself, all possibilities of your being, all of the masks—disappears, is reconstructed, as in a kaleidoscope, in the depths of this mirror called the *Primavera.*] (180)

Yet, in reality, the truths she believes she has found at the end of her interpretive journey are no more than fictions which ultimately defy hermeneutic desire. In the epilogue, as she reflects on the events of her recent past on her return journey from Florence, Clara realizes that she has left many loose ends untied: a final closure to the narrative of her life continues to escape her, as does the definitive meaning of Botticelli's painting: "Potser *La Primavera,* com els misteris d'Eleusis, encara guarda quelcom per a mostrar-te" [Perhaps the *Primavera,* like the mysteries of Eleusis, still holds something back from you] (183). Even the last news report that she reads on the train about the outcome of the Guarini case, with its truly novelistic plot of terrorist intrigue, leaves her with a sense that there are still many "punts obscurs" [uncertainties] that remain unresolved (187). Her humble admission at the end of her journey, "Has après que el més important és mirar per a veure" [You've learned that the most important thing is to look in order to see] (183), exemplifies Baudrillard's claim that what is apparent to the eye—the play of signs on the surface of the text—is bound to subvert the quest for concealed meanings, for interior essences.[28] Similarly, Clara's newly discovered identity, which is bound up with a particular interpretation of Botticelli's *Primavera,* is, in the end, exposed as a provisional and eternally unstable construct, subject to constant transformations through discourse.

The final sections of the epilogue highlight the circularity of Clara's quest for identity: on her train journey back to Barcelona, which recalls a parallel scene at the beginning of the novel when she heads for Florence, she is struck by the sensation of having arrived from "un llarg viatge i tot just l'acabes de començar" [a long journey and you've only just begun it] (183). Through evocation of grotesque and monstrous images in a neo-Baroque style, the penultimate section of the epilogue (which constitutes a literal repetition of the first paragraphs of the novel) plunges the reader back into a labyrinth of the protagonist's unconscious desires and fears surrounding her own sexuality and maternity. Feminist critics have tended to focus their readings on Clara's positive trajectory toward self-discovery, seeing in her acceptance of pregnancy a defiance of societal codes and an affirmation of her new identity as an independent woman.[29] Yet the future Clara projects for herself at the conclusion of the novel focuses as much on the birth of her child as a source of pain and suffering, on her bodily subjection, as on the possibility of self-renewal. The scene ends with her screams of agony resounding on the walls of her hospital room, where she is left alone once again to struggle with the definition of her identity as a woman and a mother. Her symbolic rebirth, to which she looks forward, is incomplete as long as the arrival of the child is deferred. The protagonist's train may have emerged from the tunnel this time, yet there will be other tunnels through which she must travel in order to rewrite and continually re-envision the narrative of her life. Finally, the abruptness of the novel's conclusion calls attention to the fact that all endings are arbitrary, serving only to seduce the reader with the illusory pleasure of resolution and closure.[30]

A brief discussion of Riera's later novel, *Joc de miralls,* is useful here, since it reflects on the relationship between seduction and narrative in an explicitly theoretical way. The first section of the novel can be read almost as a literary manifesto, in which the writer figure (and perhaps a spokesperson for Riera), Pablo Corbalán, explains his views on narrative seduction to his interviewer, Teresa Mascaró, a young student and admirer who is writing a thesis on his work. For Corbalán, as for Baudrillard, seduction is predicated on a game of masks and appearances, which subverts the search for a hidden truth or meaning:

> Allò que sedueix és sobretot la coberta, l'embocall, el signe, més que no el sentit al qual condueix. Fins i tot li diria que allò que ens contorba de la bellesa és l'artifici, no la naturalitat.

> [That which seduces is, above all, the cover, the wrapping, the sign, much more than the meaning to which it leads. I would even tell you that what bewilders us about beauty is its artifice, not its naturalness.] (24)

Like Baudrillard's position, Corbalán's could be interpreted as a conservative one, particularly with regard to the latter's commentary on the relationship between art and politics. Disclaiming his political commitment in an earlier work, Corbalán now asserts a transparently aestheticist posture, insisting on the separation between the man and the writer, between politics and literature: "la missió de l'escriptor està per damunt de les qüestions polítiques. I consisteix a crear una obra, una obra ben feta" [the mission of the writer is above political questions. It consists of creating a work of art, an accomplished work] (29). At the same time, he maintains that his suspicion of absolute truths and his predilection for the domain of mirages and appearances constitute not a denial of history, but a rejection of political dogma and of ideologically monolithic discourses. Accordingly, Teresa notes a significant change in Corbalán's literary aesthetic between his first work, *Días sin sentido* [*Meaningless Days*], a novel of political denunciation, and his most recent, *El relevo* [*The Shift Change*], characterized by "un marcat interès pel joc, per l'ambigüitat" [a definite interest in games, in ambiguities] and by the theme of "la búsqueda de la identidad" [the search for identity] (27, 40).

The beginning of the novel's first section, which juxtaposes two parallel narratives, self-consciously mirrors Corbalán's theory of narrative seduction. Teresa's first-person narration in diary form is interspersed with segments of a third-person narration, which recounts Bettina Brentano's encounter with Goethe in a remote past. An account of Goethe's relationship with his young admirer mediates Teresa's own encounter with Corbalán, who holds the power to seduce her, both as a man and as a writer. Not only does Teresa model her relationship to Corbalán on her romantic idealization of Goethe's admirer, but she also looks to the latter to give significance to experiences in her own life. By juxtaposing the narratives of these two women, the novel identifies erotic and narrative seduction: just as Brentano's letters to Goethe held a clearly seductive intent, Teresa considers her textual commentary on Corbalán's *El relevo* to be a metaphorical love letter, "carta d'amor que no pot esperar a ser tirada en una bústia i tramesa per correu normal" [love letter that can't wait to be thrown into a letterbox and sent by normal mail] (36). Teresa's words echo Riera's own vision of all writing as a love letter intended to seduce its reader.

The rest of the novel exemplifies the theory of narrative seduction that Corbalán professes in his interview with Teresa. When the writer is found mysteriously dead in his hotel room after his interview with Teresa, the latter takes on the role of a detective who sets out to find the key to his life, identity, and death. Driven by hermeneutic desire, Teresa, like the protagonist of *Una primavera,* embarks on a quest for truth and meaning the minute she arrives at Corbalán's homeland, Itálica, entrusted by the latter's publisher, Celia, with the promotion of his most recent book. Significantly, an account of her investigations and discoveries takes the form of epistolary installments (addressed to Celia in Part 2 of the novel), which seduce the reader with a promise for a resolution to the enigmas surrounding Corbalán's life and death. Rather than finding a solution to these enigmas, however, Teresa, like Clara, soon finds herself entangled in a complex game of signs and masks where nothing is what it seems and where getting beyond appearances becomes an increasingly impossible goal. Her investigations in Itálica not only reveal that Corbalán has given her false clues to his life, but that these clues refer to the life of a former university comrade named Antonio Gallego. In her penultimate letter to Celia, Teresa discloses her discovery that Corbalán is not who he claimed he was, after which she abruptly terminates her communication with a final letter informing her correspondent that she will be sending home a manuscript that Gallego's relative has given her. By deferring the expectation of narrative closure once again, displacing the promise for truth onto another text, Teresa's letters illustrate the fundamentally seductive nature of her discourse.

Part 3 of the novel presents us with yet another text—presumably the manuscript to which Teresa refers in her final letter, containing an account of Antonio Gallego's life and, in particular, of his relationship to Pablo Corbalán. This narrative, like that of Clara in *Una primavera,* dramatizes the protagonist's search for identity in a world of simulacra, where any attempt to achieve a coherent or stable subjectivity becomes an impossible goal. The absence of a unified narrative perspective, exemplified in the use of free indirect style, reflects the instability of the subject constructed by the text. As we follow the narration of Gallego's life, it becomes increasingly clear that his identity is intricately intertwined with that of his rival and alter ego, Corbalán, with whom he enters into a game of disguises. The two characters, who resemble each other physically, are aspiring writers in a fictional Latin-American country under the rule of a dictator. When Gallego is arrested for his opposition to the government, Corbalán takes on the former's identity by substituting him in his job and by entering into relations with Gallego's lover. Five years later, when Gallego is a free man once again, he discovers that, in his absence, Corbalán has stolen and plagiarized his half-written novel, *Días sin sentido,* publishing it under his own (Corbalán's) name. Faced with the imminent dissolution of his personal and literary identity, Gallego determines to take revenge on his imposter by embarking on his own game of the imagination. When Corbalán dies a political prisoner, Gallego, also imprisoned, sees no choice but to adopt his rival's identity and to finish *El relevo* under the latter's name. Significantly, the plot of *El relevo*—with its "joc de les disfresses, les màscares" [game of disguises, of masks], and its "utilització dels miralls" [use of mirrors] (27, 32)—self-consciously reflects the narrative of Gallego's own quest for identity in a world of illusory signs.

Gallego's struggle to transform himself through his rival's persona signals the absence of a true identity behind the mask. The truth is infinitely deferred, as his fictions begin to take on a life of their own. As in the case of Clara, a multiplicity of literary texts mediate the narratives Gallego has authored in an attempt to regain control of his destiny. He imitates Goethe's obsession with disguises, masks, and doubles by publishing translations of the poet's works under the pseudonym of an exiled writer whom he has invented. When he seeks to revindicate his name as the winner of a literary prize, he discovers that Corbalán has already jumped one step ahead of the game, having convinced the jury of the actual existence of the fictional writer Gallego has created. Gallego's subsequent resolve to rewrite his destiny by donning the mask of a double finds echoes in the stories of Borges and Kafka, as does his faith in writing as a means of postponing death. If it is a fact, as Gallego (in the guise of Corbalán) has stated in his interview with Teresa, that "les grans històries de seducció acaben en la mort, condueixen inevitablement a la mort" [the great stories of seduction end in death, they lead inevitably to death], the only way to defer the moment of death is by combatting meaning, by remaining in the domain of appearances (24).[31] Only the veil of language, which allows him the possibility of composing an alternative ending to his life, offers him the hope of self-transformation. By rewriting Corbalán's novel, he seeks to empty language of meaning, to reinvent words, which, for him, represent the key to freedom:

> ell podria posar-los ales, fer-les volar si era capaç de desencantar-les, de deslliurar-les, i trencant argolles, cadenes manilles, treure-les de totes les presons.
>
> [He could put wings on them, make them fly if he's capable of disenchanting them, of liberating them, and take them out of prison by breaking chains and handcuffs.] (177)

Yet, even in his role as the supreme manipulator of language and director of his fictional representation, Gallego fails to transform the world and his identity. Rather than return to life when Corbalán disappears, as is his wish, he ends up trapped in his own game as a perpetual shadow of the other, ultimately meeting his destiny not only in his physical death, but in his death as a subject.

Having completed Part 3 of the novel, the reader can still only speculate about the true circumstances of Gallego/Corbalán's death in Part 1. The epilogue, written by Teresa's correspondent, Celia, explains the former's disappearance in Itálica shortly after she wrote her final letter. The manuscript that presumably holds the key to the enigma of the writer's identity seduces the reader into yet another game of mirrors, thus infinitely deferring any definitive closure to the hermeneutic gaps in the novel. In *Joc de miralls,* as in *Una primavera per a Domenico Guarini,* seduction serves as an epistemological model which challenges truth, privileging, instead, the symbolic world of appearances. Just as the personal quests of Riera's characters inevitably divert them from the "truth of signs," the self-consciously literary nature of Riera's novelistic discourse involves the reader in a game of seduction, leading him or her from sign to sign, from text to text, awakening the desire for meaning, only to subvert its possibility.[32]

Notes

1. Baudrillard, *Selected Writings*, ed. Mark Poster (Stanford: Stanford University Press, 1988), 150.

2. Baudrillard, *Seduction*, trans. Brian Singer (New York: St. Martin's Press, 1990), 21.

3. In fact, Baudrillard openly dismisses feminism on a number of occasions, denying the entire history of patriarchal domination and reducing the goals of the feminist movement to the recuperation of Freud's notion of anatomical destiny (*Seduction*, 8–11, 15–17). Andrew Ross views Baudrillard's rejection of feminism as a symptom of the latter's general refusal to acknowledge history, an attitude that reveals "an active or willful complicity with the given, and, consequently, a reluctance to interpret the latent, or ideological features of the culture at large" ("Baudrillard's Bad Attitude," in *Seduction and Theory: Readings of Gender, Representation, and Rhetoric*, ed. Dianne Hunter [Chicago: University of Illinois Press, 1989], 215).

4. In *El oficio de narrar*, ed. Marina Mayoral (Madrid: Cátedra, 1989), 148.

5. Pages 23–24. All quotations from Carme Riera's novels, *Qüestió d'amor propi* (Barcelona: Laia, 1987) and *Joc de miralls* (Barcelona: Planeta, 1989), are cited parenthetically in the text. All translations of these novels are my own. Elsewhere, I have explored the mechanisms of narrative seduction in Riera's *Qüestió d'amor propi* (Akiko Tsuchiya, "The Paradox of Narrative Seduction in Carmen Riera's *Cuestión de amor propio*," *Hispania* 75 [1992]: 281–86). Kathleen Glenn also discusses, from a feminist perspective, the relationship between epistolarity and the theme of seduction in Riera's texts ("Las cartas de amor de Carme Riera: El arte de seducir," in *Discurso femenino actual*, ed. Adelaida López de Martínez [San Juan: Editorial de la Universidad de Puerto Rico, 1995], 53–67).

6. See, for example, Mary Vásquez's study of *Qüestió d'amor propi* as a "self-conscious, self-reflective text" that examines the themes of gender, power, and control through the use of dialogic discourse ("Dialogic Discourse, Gender and Power in Carme Riera's *Cuestión de amor propio*," in *Misogyny in Literature*, ed. Katherine Anne Ackley [New York: Garland, 1992], 350–52).

7. *Una primavera per a Domenico Guarini* (Barcelona: Edicions 62, 1981), 7. Subsequent quotations from this work are cited parenthetically in the text. All translations of this novel are my own.

8. *Selected Writings*, 159.

9. See Luisa Cotoner, "*Una primavera para Domenico Guarini*," *Cuadernos Hispanoamericanos* 390 (1982): 712–14; Roberta Johnson, "Voice and Intersubjectivity in Carme Riera's Narratives," in *Critical Essays on the Literature of Spain and Spanish America*, ed. Luis González-del-Valle and Julio Baena (Boulder: Society of Spanish and Spanish-American Studies, 1991), 153–59; and Carmen Martínez Romero, "Relaciones textuales en la novela femenina de la subjetividad: Gaite, Rodoreda y Riera," in *Ensayos de literatura europea e hispanoamericana*, ed. Félix Menchacatorre (San Sebastián: Universidad del País Vasco, 1990), 293–97.

10. Johnson, "Voice and Intersubjectivity," 158. In a hermeneutic narrative, "truth predicates an incomplete subject, based on expectation and desire for its imminent closure" (*S/Z*, trans. Richard Miller [New York: Hill & Wang, 1974], 76). In this type of narrative, "truth . . . is what is *at the end* of expectation" (76).

11. de Lauretis, "Desire in Narrative," in *Alice Doesn't: Feminism, Semiotics, Cinema* (Bloomington: Indiana University Press, 1984), 112–24, 110.

12. Ordóñez, *Voices of Their Own: Contemporary Spanish Narrative by Women* (Lewisburg: Bucknell University Press, 1991), 130.

13. Ordóñez examines in greater detail Alberto's role as critical reader of Clara's text; see *Voices of Their Own,* 130–31.

14. See de Lauretis for an analysis of the mythical paradigms that have defined the woman's place vis-à-vis the narrative of masculine desire (*Alice Doesn't,* 107–12).

15. Alex Preminger, ed., *Princeton Encyclopedia of Poetry and Poetics* (Princeton: Princeton University Press, 1974), 612–13.

16. Gilbert and Gubar, *The Madwoman in the Attic: The Woman Writer and the Nineteenth-Century Literary Imagination* (New Haven: Yale University Press, 1979), 68.

17. Annis Pratt focuses her attention on some of the phallocentric archetypes that recur as plot structures in women's fiction, and calls on feminist critics to resist the recirculation of these myths (*Archetypal Patterns in Women's Fiction* [Bloomington: Indiana University Press, 1981], 3–12).

18. Ibid., 5.

19. Joanne Snow-Smith, *The Primavera of Sandro Botticelli: A Neoplatonic Interpretation* (New York: Peter Lang, 1993), 61–62.

20. Ibid., 72–80.

21. Ibid., 79.

22. Umberto Baldini, *Primavera: The Restoration of Botticelli's Masterpiece* (New York: Abrams, 1986), 90.

23. Snow-Smith, *Primavera of Sandro Botticelli,* 69–70.

24. Ordóñez, *Voices of Their Own,* 132.

25. Ibid., 133.

26. Snow-Smith, *Primavera of Sandro Botticelli,* 71.

27. Geraldine Nichols conducts an illuminating study of contemporary Spanish women writers' appropriation and subversion of biblical myths, which have long relegated women to a position of subalternity "'Mitja poma, mitja taronja': génesis y destino literarios de la catalana contemporánea," *Anthropos* 60–61 [1986]: 118–25).

28. Baudrillard, *Selected Writings,* 149–50.

29. Cotoner, "*Una primavera para Domenico Guarini,*" 714; Johnson, "Voice and Intersubjectivity," 158; Nichols, "'Mitja poma, mitja taronja'," 125; Ordóñez, *Voices of Their Own,* 135.

30. See J. Hillis Miller for a theoretical exposition on the problematics of narrative endings "The Problematic Ending in Narrative," *Nineteenth-Century Fiction* 33 [1978]: 3–7).

31. Compare Baudrillard, *Selected Writings,* 149–50.

32. Ibid., 160.

A Writing of One's Own: Carme Riera's *Qüestió d'amor propi*

Brad Epps

> Qui pourrait ne pas frémir en songeant aux malheurs que peut causer une seule liaison dangereuse!
>
> [Who wouldn't shudder to think about the misfortunes that one dangerous liaison can cause!]
>
> Choderlos de Laclos, *Les Liaisons dangereuses*

Introductory Remarks: *Strange Ladies and Familiar Stories*

If carme riera has any say in the matter, *qüestió d'amor propi* [A Question of Self-Love] (1987) appears to be something of an anomaly in her more recent literary endeavors, a throwback to concerns gone by.[1] Pondering the moves, if not the "progression" or "development," of her work in general, Riera states that "[p]erhaps the protagonists of my later works are more normal, although now that I think about it I realize you cannot say that about Àngela, of *Qüestió d'amor propi*."[2] The remark, interestingly enough, is made with reference to a question, not of self-love, but of madness. Questioned as to why there are so many madwomen in her work, Riera responds, not by disputing the question but by situating madness in the past and by grounding it, at first, in her religious education. "There were," Riera contends, "more strange women in my first stories, perhaps because of the Sacred Heart nuns. When I was studying with them, Spanish society was already beginning to change, but they did not."[3] Resistant to change, denizens of "another world, that was out of tune with the second half of the twentieth century," Riera's nuns are the anchors of something mad and maddening, a drag on, or dissonance in, modernity itself.[4] But if Riera here implies that the "madwomen" in her work are the work, however indirectly, of women who are "out of tune" with a modern, developmental society, and if she seems to imply, moreover, that this is unfortunate, she nuances it all by referring to her grandmother. "Without her," Riera says, "I would not have been a writer. She belonged not to the nineteenth century but to the eighteenth. She was very intelligent but somewhat peculiar."[5] So peculiar, it seems, that "as a result when I began to write my characters too were rather strange."[6] Strangeness—along with madness, peculiarity, abnormality, and so on—appears, then, to be a legacy from one "century" to another, marking Riera's writing in ways that are not easily left behind and that return, again and again.

These turns and returns implicate the author—and by extension, the reader—in interesting ways. Faced with the question of madness and strangeness, Riera faces herself and her past, producing in the process a sketch of the artist as a young woman. Partial as this sketch may be, I want to draw attention to some of its more suggestive traits and thread them back into the story at hand. One is the significance of *older women* (nuns, teachers, Riera's grandmother) putatively at odds with the flow of history, harking back to times (not quite) gone by. A second, bound to the first, is the profoundly personal fate of knowledge and writing. In the autobiographical, even semi-confessional, context of the authorial interview, Riera indicates that what she knows about writing is shaped, at least in part, by older women: peculiar, strange, not quite normal, and tinged with something mad. In recalling these women, Riera recalls that her own "education was not the customary one for girls of [her] age or class," as if she too were, even as a child, "out of tune" with the times.[7] Whatever the case, Riera claims to have learned one thing, not just from her grandmother, but from the nuns as well: how to write and, more specifically, how to write letters. In another interview, Riera refers to the Sacred Heart nuns: "[c]omo educaban señoritas para casarse, la carta, en su modalidad demodé, era muy importante" [since they trained young women to get married, letters, at their most *demodé,* were very important].[8] So framed, the letter is a "practical" instrument in the quest for matrimony, a means, however beautiful, to a socially sanctioned end. It almost goes without saying that the letter here envisioned is one of proper, modest expression, a graphic manifestation of the *pudor* to which we will return later. Such a concept of the letter may indeed seem "demodé," out of tune with contemporary society; but something else is at play. For Riera, in her personal reflections on knowledge and writing, also notes that the nuns of the Sacred Heart were "responsible for the education of the female characters of Laclos's *Les Liaisons dangereuses.*"[9]

The reference to Laclos's work is not gratuitous. Not only is *Les Liaisons dangereuses* one of the masterpieces of eighteenth-century epistolary fiction (the same century, remember, to which Riera links her grandmother), it is also a libertine jewel, rich with manipulative schemers, duplicitous plans, and perverse pleasures. In Laclos's hands, letters are the instruments, not so much of matrimony, modest expression, and proper conduct, but of seduction, deceit, betrayal, and revenge, all of which, by no small coincidence, are engaged in *Qüestió d'amor propi.* By presenting the Sacred Heart nuns as figures bearing on both reality and fiction, and by associating them with something both "proper" and "improper," Riera evokes not only the tried and true interplay of life and literature but also the variety of often contradictory lessons taught and learned. Bearers of something strange, *demodé,* and "out of tune," the older women of Riera's youth are also, however unintentionally, the bearers of something dark, tempting, and deviously imaginative. Their "strangeness," that is, seems to be not simply the effect of prudishness and conservatism, but of an inventiveness that, while prone to formalization, defies neat evaluation. Perhaps, in fact, their "strangeness" is tied to their ability to stimulate, though by no means control, writing: not just of letters, but of fiction—including, of course, fictional letters, epistolary fiction. This last "strangeness" might just be the effect of sexual—or, rather, sexist—history. After all, women writers, and even those who in one way or another induced women to write, have long had to contend with the charge of strangeness. It is with this in mind that Riera's "strange" women might be read somewhat ironically. Less ironic seems to be the indication that these women have somehow left their mark on the writer and her writing. For, if Riera indicates that her writing has moved away from strange, mad women, she also recognizes—now that she thinks about it—some curious insistences and returns. In the movement from one text to another, in the so-called narrative of authorial development, *Qüestió d'amor propi,* for some strange reason, does not quite fit.

And yet, why is this so? What is it that keeps Riera from pronouncing *Qüestió,* or at least its protagonist, normal? What is it that gives her pause? After all, in many respects, *Qüestió* does not seem the least bit strange. Simply put, it consists of one long letter, from Àngela to her Scandinavian friend, Íngrid, in which

Àngela asks Íngrid to forgive her for not writing sooner and then proceeds to tell the story of her brief love affair and long, painful disillusionment with Miquel (the "reason" she has not written sooner). All three characters are writers, which is important because what Àngela also asks Íngrid to do is to "seduce" Miquel and tell him "stories"—tall tales if not outright lies—about Scandinavia which he will presumably incorporate in his own writing as if they were true. The result of this blend of seduction, lying, and writing will be, Àngela imagines, the public ridicule of the man who has betrayed and ridiculed her; it will also be Àngela's own satisfaction. It is no small satisfaction, because, as Kathleen Glenn remarks, "Àngela considers taking her own life, [but] ultimately she chooses another option—that of getting even."[10] Àngela's plan of revenge, formulated in writing, aims at both writing and the writer, and plays, here too, across life and literature. Intricate as this plan may be, it does not exactly warrant being called strange. Nor does Àngela's initial depression and subsequent desire for revenge seem particularly strange either. In fact, the story and the characters actually seem, as I have already intimated, quite familiar. But perhaps that is just the point. For within this fairly conventional story of seduction, betrayal, and revenge, something seems to occur that leads Riera to think twice before stamping Àngela, and by extension the text, with the seal of normality.[11]

What occurs, obstinately and obsessively, what is so strange, may just be normality itself. Or to spin it a bit differently, the normal and normative, all that is familiar and established and conventional, may harbor something strange. This, too, is perhaps so familiar, so "normal," a psychoanalytic insight that it may hardly seem strange at all; yet, it bears repeating. What may be strange about Riera's text may be the impression that the story it tells, as well as the way it tells it, is so "normal," so familiar. After all, it is the story, like so many stories, of the difficulty of human relationships, particularly when love is involved.[12] As Mary Vásquez remarks, certain aspects of Miquel's courtship of Àngela evince "the stereotypical triteness of *a very old story*." Of course, more than content is implicated here, for, like so many old stories, it is one whose form is quite conventional. It does not break syntactical and semantic codes, or demand the willing suspension of disbelief, or waver on the verge of the (in)credible, or push explicitly at the limits of sense. Nor, for that matter, is Àngela—the woman seduced and abandoned, the woman obsessed with revenge—an unfamiliar character. We might here note, amid so much familiarity and conventionality, that Àngela's obsessiveness is not so far removed from the apparent obstinacy of the "strange" (yet familiar, conventional, old) women Riera describes in her interviews. No longer young, Àngela too is resistant to change; she finds it hard to give up certain ideas and ideals about love, sex, men, and women; and she is out of tune with contemporary feminism. All of this might suffice to make sense of Riera's apparently offhanded remark about *Qüestió d'amor propi,* but there may be something more. What if it were just this refusal or inability to let go of norms and conventions—regarding, for example, heterosexual love—that were the gauge of strangeness? What if strangeness were the turn to, or return of, the familiar? What if strangeness were not only, or even mainly, a property of the "new" but of the "old"? More specifically, what if one cannot say that Àngela and her story are normal because they are, if you will, all too normal?

In Freudian terms, *Qüestió d'amor propi* may thus harbor something uncanny: something once familiar (an old story, the knowledge of older women, established norms and conventions) returns in such a way that one *cannot* say that it is normal.[13] So says, or implies, the author. Then again, we, as readers, do not need the author's say to recognize that norms and conventions (of stories, letters, love, and so on) may be quite strange, even maddening. Be that as it may, it is intriguing, though admittedly somewhat predictable, that a question of madness, posed in an interview, should lead to questions of strangeness. What is less predictable, stranger, is that these questions should return in connection with *Qüestió d'amor propi;* that the question of madness should return in and as a question of self-love, of a love of one's own, of pride and of narcissism (all of which are suggested in the story's title); and, finally, that these questions should take the form of a letter. Going—by now, perhaps, predictably—with what is less predictable, I want to consider how these questions are written and read, addressed and received, transmitted and returned. I want to consider, as well, what is at stake in *wanting* to consider these questions, what desires inform a narrative that takes the form of an extended letter, ostensibly of love, and places "question" in its very title. Accordingly, I will turn first to the matter of letter writing: the epistolary form, its history, its connections to gender, and its relation to such issues as correspondence, reciprocity, and open or closed communication. I will then turn to, among other things, the question of "amor propi," giving special attention to the properties and possessions, both real and desired, of love and the self (self-love, the self in love, pride, narcissism). Through it all, we might recall from time to time the specter of something strangely familiar, abnormally normal, newly old.

> l'émetteur, vous disons-nous, reçoit du récepteur son propre message sous une forme inversée.
>
> [the sender, we tell you, receives from the receiver his or her own message in an inverted form].
>
> Jacques Lacan, "Le séminaire sur 'La Lettre volée'"

The Return of the Letter

As promised, I turn now to the turns and returns of letter writing. The return of the letter is more complex than it may appear at first blush, and is here triple, at least. First, on the most embedded level, Àngela, the protagonist, returns to letter writing after a year's silence. Second, on a broader level, Riera herself, as author, returns to the letter writing found in many of her texts, but especially prominent in "Te deix, amor, la mar com a penyora" [I Leave you, My Love, the Sea as a Token] (1975) and "Jo pos per testimoni les gavines" [I Call on the Seagulls as Witness] (1977).[14] And third, on an even broader level, the letter-writing or epistolary form itself returns, turns up, as a form that, supposedly more proper to the past, is "out of tune" with the present.[15] Although the first two levels are intriguing, for the moment I want to stay with the third, with the epistolary form per se. The idea that the epistolary form is out of tune with modern times is not simply the effect of information technology in which cursors and screens replace pens and paper, the mail goes electronic, and literature cedes ground to video. Nor is it simply the effect of a loss of intimacy in a supposedly ever-shrinking communicational world. It is also, and perhaps no less forcefully, the effect of a developmental understanding of literature itself, a "history" of narrative fiction in which some forms are left behind as being behind the times. The epistolary form is one such form, waxing, waning, and, as it were, just waiting to return.

According to Janet Altman, until recently, "it was commonly assumed that the [epistolary] form was a historically limited, archaic one, describable in terms of its 'rise and fall'."[16] An example of such a "common assumption" is evident in the very subtitle of an early work on the subject, *The Epistolary Novel: Its Origin, Development, Decline, and Residuary Influence.*[17] Dating back at least to Ovid's *Heroides* and attaining a certain preeminence in the seventeenth and eighteenth centuries, literary epistolarity is obviously not free from larger developmental, even teleological, configurations. And yet, more than a merely descriptive rise and fall are in question here. In an engaging review of epistolarity and narration, Elizabeth MacArthur shows how a number of influential critics, from Jean-Paul Sartre to Elaine Showalter to Peter Brooks, view the epistolary form not just as old-fashioned or archaic but as "faulty or limited," as "either an obstacle or a development [duly left behind] in a mighty progress towards its more perfect descendant of the nineteenth century."[18] Taking the nineteenth-century novel as a normative model, these and other critics narrate, according to MacArthur, a history of narrative in which epistolarity flourishes in the eighteenth century, wanes with the passing of time, and gives way in the late nineteenth century to a "modernity" marked by control, synthesis, and closure.

In many respects, these critics are not mistaken. Still, MacArthur is right to question the ways in which their critiques, wittingly or unwittingly, replicate, naturalize, and extend into the late twentieth century certain perhaps inevitably ideological assumptions about narrative closure. As MacArthur points out, "[p]erhaps the fascination with closure, which characterized the nineteenth-century novel to a greater extent than its eighteenth-century predecessor, can be linked to a fear of deviance and a desire for stability."[19] Citing both Brooks's and Sartre's notion of narration as a deviance, disturbance, or disorder that impels a drive toward closure *cum* cure, MacArthur suggests that one of the reasons the epistolary form is perceived as being "extravagant" or "out of tune" is that, however much it may drive toward closure, it tends to defer it by addressing an other who may write, or not, in turn. The epistolary form, prone to an openness that is foreclosed in many "model" narratives, is thus prone to deviance, disturbance, and disorder, to a potentially non-normative or uncontrollable performativity. Which may be a way of saying that the epistolary form, for all its conventions, is inclined to "abnormality," to something strange.

MacArthur, for her part, is uneasy about validating such an inclination, preferring to speak of the epistolary form in terms of "extravagance" rather than "deviance."[20] I will not rehearse her reasons for doing so, but merely note that—for all the caveats—deviance, extravagance, strangeness, and even abnormality haunt a certain critical discourse on epistolarity. This may seem at odds with the conventional, "all-too-normal" tenor of epistolarity, but only if we close ourselves off to the openness of the form, an openness that can at times be quite unsettling. Inasmuch as it implies a circuit of exchange that may outstrip normative control, letter writing does indeed tend to be open-ended, even when, as in the case of *Qüestió d'amor propi,* it seeks specific, self-interested ends. In its very address, this and many other "letters," fictional or not, *expect* a response, a reply, a readdressing (or redressing) in turn. Expectation, along with expectancy, hope, and waiting, may likewise invoke an end; but it is, virtually by definition, an end that has yet to come, that is not re-presented in the text of the letter itself. Non-epistolary narratives also engage expectations, but they do not necessarily infold, within their very structure, the ghost of a readerly-writerly reply that, far from fulfilling expectations, may actually dash and undo them. Letter writing is thus never entirely, or neatly, teleological, for its end is almost always a response to come. Its end, in short, is, in some wise, unending. The same goes for the *history* of epistolary literature: as the existence of Riera's text clearly indicates, we are not done with epistolarity as a literary genre or mode.[21] Nor are we done with *not knowing* what its oft-proclaimed ends may be.

Akiko Tsuchiya is therefore on solid—or solidly shifting—ground when she says, "the real reader of Riera's novel will never know whether Ingrid [the letter's most explicit destinataire] will consent to her friend's request once she has finished reading the letter."[22] I will have more to say about the request, or demand, of the letter and the letter writer; but, for the moment, I want to stress that it is just this *impossibility of knowing,* once and for all, that gives a measure of something like desire, particularly if desire is figured, as it often is, as the (im)possibility of knowing. The impossibility of knowing is not just epistemological, but also sexual in scope, and may be placed alongside the impossibility of full closure and, as we shall see, *complete* correspondence. MacArthur, following feminist revisions of Lacan, reads all this impossibility as the insistence of metonymy, itself read, almost metaphorically, as a figure of desire: mobile, unstable, open-ended, fraught with lack, and given to contiguity rather than fusion. Or as a figure of love, for epistolarity, throughout its history, is thick with the slippery dealings of love.[23] Figured thus, figured as the insistent, expectant, ever so imbricated slippage of figures, letter writing, that eighteenth-century staple presumably out of tune with modernity, seems to bear an uncanny affinity with postmodernity.[24]

Part of what enables one to call the epistolary form "extravagant," if not "deviant" or "abnormal," and to have it return in postmodern guise, is the fact that the conventions, norms, and technical limits of letter writing fuel, even as they may resist, the deferral of limits, their potentially endless replication and repositioning in the interplay of readers and writers, receivers and senders.[25] Riera herself, in the aforementioned interview with Kathleen Glenn, describes letter writing as "a deferred dialogue."[26] A deferred dialogue may, however, be a sustained monologue, as Riera indicates by describing *Qüestió d'amor propi* as *other* than a dialogue: "If the story had been written as a dialogue, her friend would have asked her questions, Àngela would have lost narrative control, and it would have been more evident that her version of events is just that, one version."[27] Tellingly, the best way to conceal that her version is just one version is to present only one version. Àngela, though not as forthcoming as "her" author, also undercuts the dialogic force of her letter by referring to it as "el meu monòleg, per desgràcia obsessiu" [my unfortunately obsessive monologue] (10). So, if letter writing is "a deferred dialogue," it is because letter writing is *not* a dialogue, at least not in the sense of a spontaneous, interactive process susceptible to interruption, redirection, and contestation.[28] Riera again makes this clear by saying that "a letter was the appropriate form for allowing the protagonist, Àngela, to tell her point of view without being interrupted or challenged."[29] In a related vein, Mary Vásquez notes not only the lack of interruption in Riera's text, or Àngela's letter, but also the "narratorial appropriation of presumed narratee reaction."[30] Control is indeed tight with possessive, appropriative maneuvers bearing on the other as well as on the self, and is one of the crucial *questions* of Riera's text: one which I will defer addressing in detail.

Instead, in deferral, we find something else: an interruption and challenge that come—or not—not just from the outside but from the inside, "always already." For if a deferred dialogue may be a sustained, obsessive, uninterrupted monologue, it may also be a dialogue doubled and redoubled, a dialogue in which more than two subjects are in play and more than one deferred. Tsuchiya, in one of the few sustained readings of Riera's text, argues that "the epistolary form allows for a constant and explicit presence of the narratee, the recipient of the narrative within the text. In *Questión de amor propio,* the narratee is Ingrid, Angela's confidante, whom the latter sets out to seduce—metaphorically speaking—with her version of the story, and whose complicity she seeks in planning revenge against Miguel."[31] I will return to the question of seduction, complicity, and revenge; but now I want to suggest not only that the narratee is a constant and explicit *absence,* or absent presence, but also that it is by no means certain that the narratee, or destinataire, is Íngrid and Íngrid alone.[32] Inasmuch as Àngela writes Íngrid in order to "get at" Miquel, or better yet at Miquel's writing, the deferred dialogue can be quite errant, shooting off in directions that exceed a dual, let alone dyadic, circuit and implicating any and all readers of the letter/text.[33] By readers of the letter/text, I also mean the readers of any letter/text that issues, however indirectly, from it.[34] Staying with deferral, I will return to the complexity of the communicative scene in Riera's text (all the more complex, in that it involves the previously deferred question of possession, appropriation, and control); but I will insist, here and now, that dialogue may be deferred by being bedeviled with a welter of "voices" that bespeak something less monologic than heteroglossic.

In *Qüestió d'amor propi,* dialogue is deferred, not merely through the agency of a single, uninterrupted voice, but also, and perhaps more importantly, through an insistent citational act that interrupts, as from the inside, the singularity of the letter writer. Àngela's voice, her writing, is shot through with other voices and other writings. From Maragall, Ausiàs March, Pere Serafí, Jordi de Sant Jordi, Salinas, and Lorca to Unamuno, Proust, Delibes, and Isak Dinesen, from Mozart, Brahms, and Piaf to *Celestina, Faust, Doña Perfecta, Misericordia,* and, most significantly, *La Regenta,* both Àngela's letter and *Qüestió d'amor propi* are prime intertextual and intersubjective artifices. The "love" that is therein figured, and questioned, is itself, as Tsuchiya so aptly puts it, "a collage of texts."[35] Along with heteroglossia, the figure of the palimpsest—the figure of figures over figures—comes to the fore: so much so, that one of Àngela's own novels, *Interior amb figures* [Interior with Figures], mentioned in passing and inaccessible to our reading, may be "read" as an abyssal figure of the letter itself. For, inside Àngela's letter and Riera's text, there are figures, rhetorical and otherwise, that gesture to the alterity of the self and that put any discrete property and possession (including, of course, any "amor propi") in question.

The alterity of the self is adumbrated not just in the references to, and quotations of, others, but in self-reference and self-citation as well. Roberta Johnson, in an enlightening overview of Riera's fiction, has noted how "the woman who speaks defines herself in terms of the other" and how she can become "her own interlocutor—her own other."[36] Johnson makes the last remark specifically in relation to *Una primavera per a Domenico Guarini* [A Primavera for Domenico Guarini] (1981), but it holds, I believe, for *Qüestió d'amor propi* as well. There too, among so many narrative figures and narratees—along with Íngrid, Miquel, and ourselves as readers—is the writer of the letter, the author of the text, implicated in its address, in its destination, perhaps indeed in its destiny. The destination of Àngela's letter, let alone Riera's text, is, as I have indicated, less certain that it may seem. Barbara Johnson, glossing Lacan's claim that "a letter always arrives at its destination," states that "the letter's destination is not its literal addressee, nor even whoever possesses it, but whoever is possessed by it;" in this sense, "the letter's destination is thus *wherever it is read*."[37] This is an important observation, pointing to a general epistolary economy in which the reader, any reader, plays a significant role. Be that as it may, it does not erase the fact that letters may, in fact usually do, contain literal addressees and that certain destinations are privileged: named, though not, of course, controlled.

With respect to privileged destinations and explicitly named, though never fully controllable, destinataires and narratees, *Qüestió d'amor propi* is no exception:

> Molt estimada Íngrid: Tens massa raó. Accept el teu rabiós ultimàtum: No voldràs sebre res pus mai de mi si aquesta vegada tampoc no et contest i t'explic, fil per randa, tots els motius que em dugueren a no donar-te noves durant tant de temps. Ja veus que t'escric de seguida—tot just vaig rebre abans d'ahir la teva carta—i començ per demanar-te que em perdonis. Un any—ho sé—és un interval massa llarg per emparar-se en el dret d'asil del silenci quan tu no has fet res per motivar-ho, tot al contrari. No obstant això—creu-me per favor—he rellegit sovint les teves cartes i t'he contestat moltes vegades des dels llocs més impensats, amb l'esperança que tu, que tan bé em coneixes, hauries de notar, per força, que el meu monòleg, per desgràcia, obsessiu, s'adreçava a tu en exclusiva per donar-te fe de vida i, molt més encara, fe d'amor.[38]

> [My Dear Íngrid: You are all too right. I accept your furious ultimatum: Perhaps you will not want to have anything more to do with

> me if this time, once again, I don't answer you and explain to you, in detail, all the reasons for not giving you any news for so long. You can see that I'm writing you immediately—I just received you letter the day before yesterday—and I'll begin by asking you to forgive me. A year—I know—is too long a time to take shelter in silence when you haven't done anything to provoke it, quite the contrary. Despite that—please believe me—I have often reread your letters and I've answered you many times from the least likely places with the hope that you, who knows me so well, will have to see, by necessity, that my unfortunately obsessive monologue was addressed exclusively to you in order to give you a testimony of life, and even more, of love.] (9–10)

Explicitly addressed to "Íngrid," the text, as letter, begins in a tone of anxious submission, submitting itself, and its writer-sender, to its designated destinataire for approval. The writer concedes her right, her "reason," in virtually the first pulse; adopts almost a servile position (a servitude prefigured, as we shall see, in the text's epigraph); and promptly asks for forgiveness. Already, we might note how concession and submission entail a request, even a mild demand, for something in return: for forgiveness, or more precisely for a reply or response that is the token of forgiveness.[39] The request or demand does not stop at forgiveness, however; it moves, as I have indicated, in more retributive, even vengeful, directions. But, if Miquel, Àngela's ex-lover, is subsequently revealed as the designated target of Àngela's epistolary, or perhaps extra-epistolary, demand, here, at the beginning, in what Mary Vásquez calls "the framing story,"[40] the demand, couched in terms of submission and contrition, is for forgiveness. In a sense, it is as if forgiveness were the necessary condition for revenge.[41]

Then again, revenge is suggested from the outset. After all, Àngela has received what she calls a "wrathful ultimatum" from Íngrid, the woman to whom she writes. Íngrid, the privileged implied reader, is thus written as a writer herself, albeit one to whose words we do not have direct access. In the same sweep, Íngrid is written as a writer who makes a demand and who backs it up with the threat of revenge. Simply put, what Íngrid demands is that Àngela write, *that she write to her*. Failure to do so, to break the year-long silence that Àngela has maintained, will result, in turn, in Íngrid's definitive silence, a silence without return. As a demand for a reply, Íngrid's ultimatum is intimately bound to Àngela's reply as a demand, at first, for forgiveness. There is something circular here: a silence for a silence, a letter for a letter. It is a circularity, a communicative circuit and circulation, an epistolary play of mimetic desire. And yet, even as a communicative circuit of reciprocal correspondence (of one for another, B for A) is shadowed forth, it is actually far more involute. In fact, the more we follow this circuit, the more we are entangled in a vertiginous relay: the writer sends a letter in order to receive, or continue receiving, letters; the writer writes in response to reading so that the reader will respond, or continue responding, in writing; the reader who responds in writing is, among others, the critic; the letter that is the text is both the effect and the cause of other letters, other texts; the letter has neither a beginning nor an end. The propositions could well proliferate, turning on one other, and slipping through even the most iron-clad conceptual grills.

Among the conceptual grills most explicitly evoked in *Qüestió d'amor propi* is that of the confession. Fairly early on in her letter, Àngela, the writer, describes herself as "agenollada enfront de la reixa—aquell immens colador vertical que filtrava les culpes i les penitències" [kneeling before the grill—that immense vertical colander that filtered guilt and penance] (22). Àngela confesses, before a confessional grill that is more porous than iron-clad, to a wrongdoing of a decidedly "letteral" sort. What the writer has done wrong is fail to write; or alternately, what the writer is guilty of is nothing less, or more, than silence. Silence is only one of a number of guilty acts in Riera's text, but, inasmuch as it bears on the very existence of the "letter" we read, it is, no doubt, one of the more significant. Silence is so acute that it is not only Àngela's ability to write letters that is affected, but her ability to write anything at all. Inasmuch as she is a writer by profession, this is serious indeed. Furthermore, it is not a willful silence, but rather an apparently uncontrollable effect of her abandonment by Miquel: "mentre va durar la meva malaltia vaig esser incapaç d'escriure un sol mot—una altra dada per justificar el meu silenci" [while my sickness lasted I was incapable of writing a single word—another bit of information to justify my silence] (18). The malady here in question is love, and as in some medieval treatise on love sickness, silence is one of its most eloquent symptoms.

On another level, Àngela's silence toward Íngrid is an ironic extension, if not a replication, of Miquel's silence toward Àngela. Still, one silence does not fully correspond to another (the lack of full correspondence is, as we shall see, crucial), for, while Miquel withdraws from Àngela to throw himself more vigorously, and cynically, into the world and writing, Àngela appears to withdraw from the world and writing almost altogether. Àngela's withdrawal takes the form of narcissism, of self-love. This may seem to signal yet another point of correspondence between Àngela and Miquel, because Miquel is, at least as Àngela presents him, terribly narcissistic, fixated on himself and himself alone.[42] Àngela, fixated on Miquel, is also, and more deeply, fixated on herself. So much so that Àngela's narcissism assumes some quite classical characteristics that do not seem to hold for Miquel. One such characteristic is the response to pain, suffering, or disease. As Sigmund Freud notes in his essay on narcissism, "a person suffering organic pain and discomfort relinquishes his interest in the things of the outside world, in so far as they do not concern his suffering."[43] Àngela's "malaltia" is not strictly organic, but it is certainly not negligible; after all, she invokes it in order to "justify" her silence. Àngela's "malaltia," affecting both the body and the letter, is the consequence, as Freud might put it, of two interrelated acts: first, an "over-estimation" or "idealization" of an other (Miquel) by which the ego is "impoverished"[44] and, second, the collapse of the idealized other—or as Freud puts it, the ego-ideal—that brings the impoverishment of the ego painfully back home.[45] *Giving* herself to Miquel, displacing her ego into his (or is it her?) idealized ego, Àngela confronts, once the ideal of Miquel collapses, an almost unbearable emptiness or poverty that is manifested in an inability to communicate with others and in thoughts of suicide.

So narcissism is thus not simply a given, but instead the effect of a giving, an excess of giving. More precisely, it is the effect of a giving that expects to get something, equally excessive, in return. This excessive, expectant "gift"—in its dual modalities of giving and getting—is nothing other than love. As Freud says, "love in itself, in the form of longing and deprivation, lowers the self-regard; whereas to be loved, to have love returned, and to possess the beloved object, exalts it again."[46] Or alternately, "he who loves has, so to speak, forfeited a part of his narcissism, which can only be replaced by his being loved."[47] The "part" of narcissism forfeited (it is never forfeited in its entirety) is replaced, ideally, with a corresponding forfeiture on the part of the other, that is to say, with a reciprocal act of love. In any case, it is important to note that what is given or given up is not done so unconditionally: a giving or giving up is, I repeat, *expected in return.* Àngela's "malaltia" does not arise because she has given, but because she has given without getting, sent without receiving. And what she has not gotten is love, a love to correspond to *hers*. The desired trajectory—the trajectory of desire—is classically narcissistic. As Freud so succinctly puts it, "to be loved is the aim and the satisfaction in a narcissistic object-choice."[48] The rule of narcissism becomes even tighter, where Àngela is concerned, if we accept Freud's claim that the ego-ideal, the other so highly esteemed, "is merely [the] substitute for the lost narcissism of . . . childhood."[49] The reluctance, if not inability, to give up *on* love is the inability to give up a childhood gratification, the inability, that is, to keep something from the past from marking us, from returning.

We shall see, especially in the play of adult recollections of childhood in Clarín's *La Regenta,* how many of Freud's observations resonate in Àngela's tale. And yet, even as I evoke Freud, I want to offer a note of caution. Freud's formulation of narcissism, compelling as it is, weighs especially heavily on women (and, by Freud's own indication, homosexual men). For Freud, women are simply less inclined to loving than to being loved, and this in spite, if not indeed because, of the idea that they are expected to nurture, to love so much.[50] We should be wary of these psychoanalytic conventions, norms, and prejudices, along with the (ab)normality that they uphold, but we might also do well to see how the same, or similar, conventions, norms, and prejudices are played out in Riera's story, not just between Àngela and Miquel but between Àngela and Íngrid as well. For, when it comes to silence, writing, love, expectations, giving, and getting—all three characters are implicated. In fact, they are enmeshed in a (non)communicative circuit in which gender—Íngrid's, Miquel's, Àngela's, the writer's, and the reader's—is a far from neutral matter. For what Àngela also confesses, along with her guilty silence, is the splintering of her feminist convictions, her inability to live up to, *to respond in kind* to, Íngrid's example as a strong, forthright, "liberated" woman. Àngela writes, asking to be forgiven for her silence, but also for her inability to correspond.

Correspondence or reciprocation, in love as in letters, is as critical as it is complex. For Àngela, it bears not just on Miquel but also on Íngrid. There are, to be sure, some significant differences: whereas Àngela is not corresponded (in love) by Miquel, it is Íngrid who is not corresponded (in letters and in feminist convictions) by Àngela. As a result, Àngela is both the object and the subject of noncorrespondence, both the receiver and sender of silence. This is not to say that silence is equivalent to non-correspondence, for, after all, as Íngrid's ultimatum makes clear, a silence can correspond to a silence; however, it is to say that Àngela's position is far from being simply that of a victim and that, as Riera herself indicates in her interview with Glenn, Àngela maintains a certain narrative control. This control is not limited to the fact that Àngela writes to Íngrid instead of speaking to her, either by telephone or in person; indeed, Àngela's "monologue" is, as we have seen, dialogic or even heteroglossic in its own right, rife with the words of others. Rather, Àngela maintains a certain control by confessing to a certain *loss* of control.[51] Admitting that she, unlike Íngrid, has not maintained her feminist principles and has not remained strong, Àngela invokes failure and weakness in order to justify herself and, better yet, to direct, if not control, Íngrid into forgiving her. In so doing, Àngela also appeals to Íngrid's pride, her "amor propi," by setting Íngrid up as an example of feminist fortitude. For the reader, denied direct access to Íngrid's words, Íngrid's exemplarity is an effect of Àngela's writing and may be yet another tactic of seduction in a text suffused with seduction.[52] It is the seduction of the strong by the weak, a seduction, deep in confession, in which the roles of strong and weak are not self-evident and preestablished but constituted in the discursive act itself. Whatever the outcome of Àngela's letter may be, Àngela does not seem oblivious to a powerful play of confession: in confessing herself to be weak, *she* confers strength on the person to whom she confesses. She gives, in other words, that which she supposedly does not have.

At any rate, the confessional tone of the letter almost necessitates that the other, placed in the position of the confessor-priest, be perceived and represented as superior in one form or another. That the priest is here a priestess, and that her example is not one of purity and chastity but rather of sensual play, does not wreck the confessional apparatus; at most, it ironizes and displaces it. There is, however, another touch of irony, one that slips something unflattering into the seemingly flattering portrayal of Íngrid as feminist example. Àngela "confesses" that she, unlike Íngrid, is sentimental and romantic and that she finds it difficult, if not downright impossible, to be one of "those" women who pride themselves on being, or appearing to be, "fortes, fredes i autosuficients" (22). Íngrid, at least as Àngela styles her, is implicitly among these "strong, cold, self-sufficient" women. Thus, even as Àngela sets up Íngrid as an example, even as she flatters her as a model of freedom, she marks her distance from her—not as an "inferior" might do with respect to a "superior," but as one who holds the truth might do to one who does not.[53] For, what Àngela suggests is that women are, in some true and essential way, prone to tenderness:

> moltes dones de la meva generació i, de manera especial, les que pasàrem per més intel.ligents, vam arribar a avergonyir-nos d'aquesta propensió vers la tendresa perquè ens pareixia una prova de debilitat, de feblesa femenina, i vam estimar-nos més mostrar-nos, especialment davant dels homes, fortes, fredes i autosuficients.
>
> [many women of my generation, and especially those of us who were considered to be more intelligent, came to be ashamed of that tendency towards tenderness because it seemed to us to be proof of weakness, of feminine frailty, and we preferred to show ourselves, especially in front of men, as being strong, cold, and self-sufficient.] (21–22)

The particular context of the "strong, cold, self-sufficient" women, along with the use of the plural and the preterit, is crucial. Implicating both Íngrid and herself in a common past, Àngela nonetheless implies that she, unlike Íngrid, has "moved on," and that she has done so by "moving back" to the eternal, tender truth of femininity.

Subtly, suggestively, Àngela criticizes her past and, by implication and extension, Íngrid's present, which she elsewhere appears to extol. No longer content merely to "pass" herself off as intelligent or to don a mask before men, Àngela is no longer willing to be one of the women who, in their pursuit of a feminism without shame, are supposedly ashamed of femininity, its truth. Àngela's portrayal of feminism and femininity is tendentious and self-serving, and cannot be understood apart from the question of "amor propi," here, hers. The reason behind Àngela's year-long silence and her decision to break it vis-à-vis Íngrid hangs on her highly sentimental and sentimentalized relationship with Miquel. Àngela would seem to agree with Roland Barthes that, among the reversals of history ("renversement historique") is the sense that "ce n'est plus le sexuel qui est indécent, c'est le *sentimental*—censuré au nom de ce qui n'est, au fond, qu'une *autre morale*" [it is no longer the sexual that is indecent; it is the sentimental—censured in the name of what is—at bottom—*another morality*].[54] But, if sentimentality, like epistolarity, is censured as being "out of tune" with the times, Àngela ironically presents herself as strong enough to resist the rush of modernity by being sentimental, weak, and soft, even if it makes her miserable. This last point is important, because if it is indeed true that Àngela opens with an apology and, as Tsuchiya puts it, "a justification of her communicational medium—the letter" ("Paradox" 282), she also strives to justify the sentimentality, the love, that is one of the primary messages of the epistolary medium. Confessing to sentimentality, weakness, and a certain ambivalent loss of feminist control, seeking forgiveness and continued communication, Àngela nonetheless writes a defense of herself that is also, in the same complicated sweep, a critique of Íngrid and a testimony of love.

If, however, *Qüestió d'amor propi* is a testimony of love, the question remains: Who, or what, is the object, or subject, of love? The question is not as simple as it seems; yet seem so, it does. Unlike "Te deix" and "Jo pos," *Qüestió d'amor propi* opens with a clear address. No name is blurred; no name is withheld. On the contrary, a name is given from the outset, as it "should" be, duly marked as dear ("estimada Íngrid"). Furthermore, Íngrid is designated the recipient not only of the text before us but also of the myriad mental messages Àngela claims to have "sent" to her "en exclusiva" in testimony of life and, even more, of love (10). The exclusiveness of address may well be impossible (the letter comes to us, but also, if all goes "well," to Miquel as well), but that does not mean it does not exist.[55] Those of us familiar with "Te deix" and "Jo pos," both recounting stories of love between women, might be inclined to linger on the "dear," the "estimada," and to read it a bit less conventionally. Similarly, we might be inclined to take the faithful declaration of life and love as indeed addressed *exclusively* to Íngrid, as if one lover were trying to make amends to another. These inclinations are soon (but not too soon) dispelled: for if we learn on the second page that it is a woman who is writing to Íngrid; and on the eleventh that the woman writing has failed, beautifully, in marriage ("el meu matrimoni, tan bellament fracassat," [my marriage, so beautiful a failure], 19); and on the fourteenth that, after her breakup with her husband, she had not gone to bed with anyone for seven years; we do not learn until the seventeenth that the writer has had an all too brief and all too memorable affair, the very affair that brings an end to her abstinence and that interrupts her correspondence with Íngrid. Miquel's name appears a few pages later, long after Íngrid's and long after a welter of reflections on writing, loving, time, and memory. As a testimony of love, *Qüestió d'amor propi* may deploy many of the conventions of sentimentality, but it does not exactly address itself straightforwardly to heterosexuality.

Deferral, delay, and suspense, so important in a text like "Te deix," are here also the measure of something seductive. Akiko Tsuchiya places seduction at the center of her reading of *Qüestió d'amor propi* and asserts that "Àngela's account of her seduction by Miquel can be seen as a subtext that reflects the seductive intention of her own epistle. Erotic and narrative seduction are thus inseparable" ("Paradox" 281). Tsuchiya draws on Riera's repeated acknowledgments of the seductive power of narrative, particularly of epistolary fiction, to make her case. In an interview with Neus Aguado, Riera states that "el escritor debe ser un buen seductor y la escritora una buena seductora" [the writer must be a good seducer].[56] To this end, the writer must hit on "un tono confidente, cómplice, envolvente, y ese tono suele darse precisamente en la carta" [a confidential, complicit, caressing tone, and this tone is usually found precisely in letters].[57] Tsuchiya follows the twists of confidentiality and complicity, how the writer "manipulates literary language in order to involve her reader in a complex narrative game."[58] The game is, or at least appears to be, seduction and is prone to ruses of all sorts: coyness, flattery, exaggeration, and digression, to name but a few. Inasmuch as the game of seduction involves Íngrid, it flirts with a non-normative specter. Tsuchiya, however, in spite of all the attention she gives to the dynamics of seduction, at no point mentions the possibility of lesbianism, of what is at stake in the seduction of a woman by a woman.[59] Àngela's seduction of Íngrid is, as Tuschiya remarks, "metaphorical,"[60] a seduction in and of the figure, not in and of the flesh: the literal flesh. Tsuchiya is right, of course, but she is perhaps a little too quick to rely on the division between metaphor and its more material Other. For, while Àngela's seduction of Miquel (or is it Miquel's seduction of Àngela?) does involve the flesh, it is a flesh figured in and out of letters, in and out of literature. If Àngela "sets out to seduce [Íngrid]—metaphorically speaking," earlier she had set out to do the same with Miquel. That is to say, she seduces him in language, through the somewhat sublime agency of the letter.

Before moving on to Miquel, I want to linger a bit longer with Íngrid, with the materiality and metaphoricity of the letter addressed, most explicitly, to her. Àngela does the same, appealing to Íngrid, eschewing direct discourse, reflecting on the time and place of the letter's composition, its specific tools and general mechanics, its relation to the body and the voice. The first pages are devoted to something like the fragility of expression, the inability of the written word to capture and hold the tremor of the tongue. Àngela, writing with a pen given to her by Íngrid, confronts, among so many other losses, the loss of nuance. Letter writing, for her, is "molt menys còmplice que no la veu, car escamotejarà tots els matisos que voldria conjugar amb les meves paraules" [much less complicit than the voice because it eludes all of the nuances that I would like to convey with my words] (10). She also refers to the time and place of writing as contributing to the loss of nuanced communication:

> A tots aquests entrebancs pots afegir-hi, Íngrid, que el paisatge que contempl, tan diferent del teu . . . no em resulta massa favorable per trobar el to just mitjançant el qual pugui explicar-te tantes coses sense que badallis d'avorriment
>
> [To all of these obstacles you can add, Íngrid, that the landscape that I gaze at, so different from yours, does not seem to me very conducive to finding the right tone with which I could explain so many things without boring you to death.] (12)

And, lest Àngela's inability to find the "right tone" in the context in which she writes seem too personal, she proceeds to claim that it is national in scope. She agrees with Unamuno, "tan misogin" [so misogynist] (14), who associated Spaniards' relative lack of interest in memoirs and letters with the aggressive light of the Mediterranean (14). With such a reference, Àngela not only displays her intellectual baggage, she also shifts the burden from herself to her culture and her climate: it is not so much that she cannot get the "right tone," but that her circumstances do not allow her to do so.

Still, Àngela's personality, her intimate self, seems to be wrapped up in her writing, its metaphors and its materiality. One of the most compelling passages underscores the opacity, and not just the fragility and insufficiency, of written language:

> Et promet que m'esforçaré a fer la lletra clara. Acostumada com estic a escriure únicament per a mi o per a la meva mecanògrafa, que la coneix prou, no creguis que em resulta fàcil. A més, el pudor, inevitable—tens proves de la meva timidesa infinita—, tal vegada m'obligui a emprar inconscientment qualque gargotejosa estratagema per organitzar una línia imaginària de protecció. Tenc tendència a enmascarar-me darrera la meva pèssima lletra i així oblig les persones amb les quals mantenc correspondència de tard en tard,

les poques que de veritat m'interessen, que em dediquen una mica més de temps, intentant desxifrar els meus missatges. Però amb tu sempre m'ha passat al revés: He procurat, en tot moment, esser directa i explícita, fins i tot amb la cal.ligrafia. Per això, si alguns trets de la meva lletra se't fan difícils de llegir, no ho atribueixis a aquesta debilitat confessada que mai no t'he demostrat, sinó a les precaucions inconscients que el meu caràcter tancat pren, ja que s'obstina a perllongar, a força d'esborralls, les confidències que tanmateix necessit fer-te. . . .

[I promise you that I will try to write clearly. Since I'm used to writing only for myself and for my typist, who knows my handwriting well, don't imagine that it comes easily. Furthermore, modesty, inevitably—you have more than enough proof of my shyness—may perhaps unconsciously oblige me to use some scribbling stratagem in order to organize an imaginary line of protection. I tend to mask myself behind my terrible handwriting and thus force the people with whom from time to time I maintain correspondence, the few people who truly interest me, to dedicate a little more time to me by trying to decipher my messages. But with you, it's always been just the opposite: I have tried, always, to be direct and explicit, even with my handwriting. Thus, if it's hard for you to read some traits of my writing, do not attribute it to this confessed weakness that I have never revealed to you, but rather to the unconscious precautions that a character as closed as mine takes, inasmuch as it doggedly strives to prolong, by dint of smudges, the secrets that I still need to tell you.] (11)

What Àngela here reveals is the capacity to conceal oneself in writing, to fashion masks out of script and to make handwritten demands. One of the demands, along with forgiveness and revenge, is for attention, dedication, and an investment of time: only someone truly interested in a person will devote time to deciphering that person's handwriting. In a certain sense, the difficulty and density of the script, its intimate manipulations and idiosyncratic traces, are part and parcel of a demand for love. "Read me," this writing seems to say, "stay with me, and read me again, for I do not give myself easily; I do not come without care."

I have written elsewhere about Riera's concern with the graphic nature of writing, the play between the hand and the pen, the often obscure and hidden sites of the script.[61] This concern continues here, where it bears on a far from simple intercommunicative relationship. Àngela confesses to a weakness—another "debilitat confessada"—that is at odds with Íngrid's strength. As noted, this weakness is almost stereotypically "feminine," bound to tenderness, sentimentality, and sexual reserve. It is also tied to a type of modesty, or *pudor,* that leads Àngela to resort, perhaps unwittingly, to "some scribbling stratagem" in order to hide and protect herself. What is nonetheless revealing is that, while modesty and weakness presumably lead Àngela to conceal and protect herself behind an almost indecipherable script, this very script supposedly leads Àngela's reader(s) to desire to decipher it, to decipher her: modesty, "pudor," is a stimulus, not merely an impediment, to desire. Indeed, so bound up in her script does Àngela appear to be that deciphering her script becomes an activity by which the reader proves his or her interest and fidelity, perhaps even his or her love. The nuance of the voice may be lost, but it is sustained, however weakly, in the nuance of the script; something uniquely personal persists. As a result, the strategy of scribbling becomes a strategy of seduction, and an ostensibly modest opacity the tempting lure for an immodest clarity, a penetrating insight on the part of another. At first glance, this may seem to run counter to Àngela's criticism of clarity and sharp definition and her almost symbolist celebration of grayness and imprecision. Yet, if we take the time to "decipher" it, we may begin to see how opacity and obscurity, dissimulation and occultation, modesty and weakness, may turn, in desire, on themselves.

Longing for—and in—the shadows, Àngela seems to understand that desire is never stronger than when it is veiled. After all, the classic distinction between eroticism and pornography depends precisely on the play of light and shadow: against pornography's aggressively direct exhibition, illuminating all nooks and crevices, lies eroticism's indirect suggestion, heightening mystery, and desire, in the promise and deferral of illumination. This does not mean that Àngela aligns Íngrid with something pornographic, but rather that she aligns herself with something more "truly," more "powerfully," erotic. For Àngela, it is an eroticism that does not prosper well under the sun of Spain or under the gaze of feminism. Íngrid's desire for the sharp luminosity of the South, coupled as it is to her "liberated" view of sexuality, stands in contrast with Àngela's desire for the diffuse luminosity of the North and her defense of a supposedly softer, more gentle view of sexuality.[62] To the degree that the text flirts self-consciously with national stereotype, it is as if neither the liberated northerner nor the conservative southerner were entirely "at home" with her desire, as if the subject, in desire, always desired to be elsewhere and otherwise. And as one desiring subject moves across and into another, the way Àngela addresses herself to Íngrid becomes, upon reflection, even more "revealing." For, even as Àngela claims that she is used to writing only for herself and her secretary (her re-writer, if you will); even as she claims that her "modesty" (*pudor*) leads her not merely to conceal and protect herself but also to test the interest, dedication, patience, and love of her reader by obliging her or him to linger on her script in an effort to make sense of it; even as she claims all this, she claims that she will do something different for Íngrid, that she herself will make the effort to write as clearly as possible, to avoid misunderstanding, to save Íngrid the trouble of having to decipher the materiality of her letter. Exceptionally and perhaps "en exclusiva," Àngela will write with the clarity that the Other, not she, supposedly desires.

That Àngela's and Íngrid's desire is at cross-purposes is important in and of itself, but there is more. Àngela's concern with making an effort to write clearly is, for us, almost beside the point. Brought into print, Àngela's letter does not bear any of the idiosyncrasies of the script; published as a book, it evinces not the slightest trace of the writer's effort to control the tremor of her hand. It is thus not just the nuance of the spoken word that has been lost, but the nuance of the handwritten word as well. In the well-consolidated age of mechanical reproduction, it is decidedly more difficult to maintain scribbling than it is to eliminate it. The letter we read is one in which the concern for clarity and opacity can exist only metaphorically, because the trace of the hand has disappeared, as it were, from Àngela's writing, or at least from our reading of it. Our reading is not like Íngrid's reading because it is public and plural, not just private and singular: which is not to say that something private and singular does not endure for us, but rather that it withdraws, inevitably, from the manuscript to the printed script, from the material to something like the spirit of the letter. This withdrawal is such that the intimate, personal, private traces of Àngela—the very traces to which she refers so insistently—must be imaginatively "rewritten" by ourselves. The upshot of all of this is some curiously (im)modest play between the private and the public, the visible and the invisible, the latter open to imagination and fantasy. It should come as no surprise that amid all this play there is also that of sexuality and sexual difference. A bit more surprising, perhaps, may be the way sexual difference runs not just between women and men, Àngela and Miquel, but between Àngela and Íngrid, between women themselves.[63]

According to Pedro Salinas, whom Àngela cites in her letter, women excel in epistolarity in part because letter writing is looser and less regulated than other literary forms, and in part because publication is not, at least in theory, its primary objective.[64] Together, the relative lack of rules and the avoidance of full publication allow for a flowering of spontaneity, sincerity, and freedom without imperiling the conventions of discretion, demureness, and modesty. For Salinas, if women excel in epistolarity, it is because they must reconcile the desire for full expression and communication with the dictates of modesty, or *pudor*. And to Salinas's eyes, *pudor* is virtually femininity itself: "eso del pudor, si no el monopolio, por lo menos la mayor parte, corresponde a las mujeres. Pudor es virtud capitalmente femenina" [if not all, at least the largest share, of modesty corresponds to women. Modesty is a capital feminine virtue].[65] What also corresponds to women is letter-writing, inasmuch as it, more than most other forms of written communication, presumably respects the so-called feminine virtue that is *pudor*. In contrast, all those forms of writing that aim to enter a wider public sphere, that seek publication, must contend with a mark of immodesty.[66] As Salinas puts it, referring to published material, "¿cómo se va a ocultar que representa cierta dosis de impudor, una proporción de inverecundia, que en algunos libros de memorias y confesiones llega al cinismo?" [how can one hide the fact that it reveals a certain dose of immodesty, a portion of shamelessness, that in some memoirs and confessions borders on cynicism?].[67] Immodesty, it appears, is the privilege of men, able to enter and occupy the public sphere without necessarily compromising their "honor." Indeed, they may actually benefit from their "immodesty," garnering a reputation not so much for cynicism as for audacity and verve. Àngela, however, does not appear to aspire to so much, leaving audacity and adventure to women "like" Íngrid, steadfast in their appreciation of clarity and directness. And yet, Àngela, despite her profession of *pudor* and her rather self-protective admiration for opacity and suggestion, is not a writer whose work has never seen the light of day or who writes letters for one person and one alone.

Àngela herself is a novelist. She may have come upon hard times, but she has already entered, and in many respects established herself in, a public literary space. True, Àngela expresses numerous reservations about writing: "el que escric o dic és reflex pàl.lid del que voldria dir" [what I write or say is a pale reflection of what I would like to say] (17); "tenc por que les paraules s'ajustin malament a les sensacions, sentiments i idees que vull descobrir-te" [I am afraid that my words correspond badly to the sensations, feelings, and ideas that I would like to reveal to you] (18). These reservations, however, do not alter the fact that Àngela is, like Riera herself, a published writer, "[a]costumada al tracte íntim amb les paraules" [used to intimate contact with words] (17) but also used to the loss of intimacy in the passage from handwriting to print. She might also be used to the persistence of conventions, codes, and stereotypes of gender and sexual difference that do not allow her to be simply a writer *tout court,* but rather a woman writer, whether or not she upholds certain feminist principles. For, if feminists insist on the significance of gender in cultural production, Àngela's falling away from feminism into a supposedly tenderhearted femininity does not mean she can lay claim to a "neutral" authority; quite the contrary. In fact, Àngela at times comes close to laying claim to a femininity from which Íngrid, depicted as a more direct and steadfast feminist (in some respects almost masculinized), has reportedly fallen away in turn. The relation between the two women—in which Àngela subtly positions herself as "closer" to femininity than Íngrid—is not one of easy feminine solidarity, although it is also not one of feminine rupture.

Whatever the relation between femininity and feminism, Àngela and Íngrid, whatever its materials and its metaphors, a man is lurking in the shadows. It is Miquel, the initially unobtrusive cause of yet another confession, one that does not end with Íngrid but that runs through her, a confession bearing not on forgiveness but on revenge:

> Et prec que dissimulis el teu disgust, Íngrid, que t'empassis els comentaris encara una bona estona. Estic decidida a complir la penitència que vulguis imposar-me, especialment si em concedeixes el favor que necessit que em facis i que, mitjançant aquesta llarguísima carta—tal vegada la seva extensió et pugui compensar d'un *hiatus* tan notable—intent també demanar-te.

> [I beg you to conceal your displeasure, Íngrid, and to keep your comments to yourself a while longer. I am willing to do whatever penance you may impose on me, especially if you grant me the favor that I need you to do and that, by means of this very long letter—

> perhaps its length can compensate for so long a hiatus—I am trying to ask of you.] (42)

This plea is revealing. For, if the letter is a site of confession and an act of penance, if it is a demand for forgiveness and a pledge to continued communication, it is also an immodest proposal. It comes, in other words, at a rather unpleasant price:

> Savoir qu'on n'écrit pas pour l'autre, savoir que ces choses que je vais écrire ne me feront jamais aimer de qui j'aime, savoir que l'écriture ne compense rien, ne sublime rien, qu'elle est précisément là où tu n'es pas—c'est le commencement de l'écriture.
>
> [To know that one doesn't write for the other; to know that what I'm going to write will never make me loved by the one I love; to know that writing doesn't compensate anything, doesn't sublimate anything, that it is precisely there where you are not—that is the beginning of writing.]
>
> Barthes, *Fragments d'un discours amoureux*

Letters Without Return

If I have delayed recounting the heterosexual romance that ostensibly is at the core of Àngela's letter, if I have deferred arriving at questions of complicity and revenge, it is because delay and deferral are, as we have seen, among the letter's hallmarks. Qualified as obsessive from the outset, Àngela's letter is self-consciously fixated on its own difficulty, or rather its writer's difficulty. Along with "la dificultat d'escriure't" [the difficulty of writing to you] (15), Àngela writes of "la història que amb tantes cauteles, amb excessius preàmbuls" [the story that so cautiously, with so many preambles] (16) she finds so difficult to write. "Sé molt bé, Íngrid, que hauria d'evitar les dilacions, les volteres i contar-te les coses sense tant d'embuts" [I know very well, Íngrid, that I should avoid delays, twists and turns, and tell you things without so much beating around the bush] (16); and yet, the delays and digressions are the very stuff of the letter, not only with respect to its content but with respect to the way it is sent and, presumably, arrives. It is, after all, a belated letter, sent only upon receipt of a furious ultimatum.[68] It is a letter of seduction, as Tsuchiya notes, but it is also a letter of love, of a love that comes late and does not stay.

Love comes to Àngela years after her marriage has ended. By this time, she is forty-eight years old and is far from secure about love's coming, let alone its staying. Desiring love, Àngela nonetheless fears it, in part because she is no longer quite familiar with it and in part—in large part—because, as she sees it, love is not something that comes easily to those who are no longer "young," particularly to women who are no longer "young." We might recall the weight of older women—the Sacred Heart nuns and grandmother—on Riera's youthful formation as a writer, but here it is more a question of the rifts between older women and women in love. According to Àngela, the rifts are quite extreme. In fact, she claims that, in literature and in life, for a nearly fifty-year-old woman to love and desire is considered almost obscene (56–57). She is not exactly off base; for, as she tells Miquel, old characters do not exactly abound in fiction, especially when it comes to women (34). She tells this to him shortly after their first meeting, and he attempts to refute it by referring to *Doña Perfecta* and *Misericordia*. For her part, Àngela refutes this refutation, and in the process fascinates Miquel. More pointedly, an "older" woman fascinates a man, seduces him, by arguing that older women are virtually absent from literature as sexually seductive beings. The irony of this situation is as self-evident as it is significant. That the age-old theme of love provokes a passionate response in Miquel points, that is, not only to something "real," albeit late, but to something literary.

Literature permeates Àngela's belated letter and her belated love alike. She is a writer; Íngrid is a writer, and Miquel is a writer—and not only of letters. They do not write the same way, however, nor do they have the same readers or the same number of readers. Both Íngrid and Àngela appear to be "successful" (Àngela refers to the favorable reception of her second book), but it is Miquel who stands out. Not only is he apparently one of the most stylish and critically acclaimed writers around (29), he is also director of the Foundation for Cultural Progress (38). Miquel is both fashionable and official: significantly, the title of his position as director is in Castilian, not Catalan. He is, accordingly, a writer to be reckoned with. Àngela reckons with him with an intensity that merely grows stronger when she realizes that Miquel's passion is, if not feigned, at least very well-rehearsed. But before that moment, long before it, Àngela says that she felt a deep interest in writers:

> durant l'adolescència els vaig retre un culte devot: No sols recollia autògrafs en un quadern impecable sinó que . . . el que és pitjor,

> aspirava en secret a casar-me amb alguna jove promesa encara incompresa, a qui jo ajudaria a triomfar. I ben aviat la glòria i la fortuna el portarien en un baiard i sota pal.li entraria a l'Acadèmia.
>
> [during my adolescence I rendered them devotion: not only did I gather autographs in a spotless notebook but also, and what is worse, I secretly aspired to marry some misunderstood, promising young [writer] and to help him succeed. And soon fortune and glory would carry him on their shoulders and, covered with honor, he would enter the Academy.] (27)

The childhood memory, or adolescent fantasy, is significant, particularly in the light of Àngela's valorization of the recollection and representation of things past. "Des de nina la memòria ho ha estat tot per a mi," writes Àngela, "i crec que el meu poder de convocar-la a cada instant, en moment claus, per capbussarme en els més foscos amagatalls, m'ha abocat, en part, a escriure" [Ever since I was a little girl, memory has been everything for me and I believe that my ability to conjure it up at any time, in crucial moments, in order to dive into its darkest recesses, has led me, in part, to write] (17). The power of memory to provoke writing is evident, of course, in the existence of the very letter we read; it, too, is the effect of recollected emotion.

Àngela's feelings for Miquel are thus partly the return of feelings and fantasies of the past. This return, like so many other returns in the text, is intensely literary. Late as it is, the return of past feelings, of youthfulness in the midst of maturity, fires Àngela's desire, her desire for love. It is a desire, a love, thick with fear, as Àngela's reference to Pedro Salinas makes clear: "Miedo de ti / quererte es el más alto riesgo" [Afraid of you / loving you is the greatest risk].[69] The quote is from *La voz a ti debida* [The Voice Owed to You], a text whose title is itself a quote from Garcilaso de la Vega's *Egloga III* [Eclogue III]. Salinas's title, rich in literary echoes, is echoed in turn in the opening of Riera's text, and in Àngela's letter, where a voice, in writing, is owed to another. Besides expressing the entanglement of fear, desire, and love, Salinas's words are part of an exchange of verses (and an apostrophic relay, a "turning away" to address an absent person that is as apt for poetry as it is for epistolarity) that provides the measure of the lovers' relationship. Àngela quotes Salinas not only because his poetry speaks to her, but because it speaks (back) to Miquel, or more precisely because it replies to Miquel's own use of poetry. In what soon becomes an intimate poetic correspondence, Miquel quotes from a poem of Ausiàs March. As Àngela says, "fins i tot ambdós vam començar una narració en la qual anàvem intercalant paràgrafs com si ens projectéssim en un joc de miralls" [we even started a story in which we kept introducing paragraphs as if we were projecting ourselves in a game of mirrors] (36). Quoting March in Catalan, Miquel "appropriates" Àngela's language, telling her that these borrowed lines will serve him better than his own words (37). The borrowed words are Miquel's words of love; Àngela, far from taking this borrowing as a lack of sincerity and originality, attempts to respond in kind by using a *different* language, "his" language, Castilian.[70] "Amb la intenció de tornarli la seva gentilesa en emprar la meva llengua, vaig servir-me de Salinas" [In order to return the kind gesture of his using my language, I quoted from Salinas] (39). Àngela thus returns a borrowing with a borrowing, a quote with a quote. To quote her, "era un préstec, una citació que em permetia continuar en la mateixa tessitura litèraria establerta per ell" [it was a borrowing, a quote that enabled me to continue in the same literary vein that he had established] (39). In *Qüestió d'amor propi,* poetic correspondence—not unrelated to something like poetic justice—is all but inseparable from epistolary and amorous correspondence, perhaps even from the correspondence of past and present.

I want to get back to the question of correspondence, but not without first sounding out the fear that is expressed, via Salinas, in and around love and desire. Àngela does not mince words when it comes to fear:

> tenia por, Íngrid, de tot o de quasi tot. De l'edat, del meu cos, no precisament en plenitud, que en qualsevol indret exhibia, fins i tot en els plecs més íntims, en els amagatalls més secrets, la lenta, maldestra carícia dels dies, els impetuosos excessos dels anys.
>
> [I was afraid, Íngrid, of everything or almost everything. Of my age, my body, not exactly in all of its splendor, that exhibited, in every part, even in its most intimate folds and most secret recesses, the slow, clumsy caress of time, the impetuous excesses of the passing years.] (39–40)

One of the main reasons Àngela fears love is that she believes, as a sexist society tells us, that past a certain age women cannot be serious protagonists. She fears that "l'oferiment del meu cos en decadència" [the offer of my body in decline] (40) cannot be the occasion for anything but pathos or, even worse, ridicule and rejection. The fear of being "washed up" sexually is realized, tellingly enough, when she finds out that Miquel has been saying that she is "washed up" literarily.[71]

It seems, however, that I am getting ahead of myself. Àngela's fears are realized, but her desires are not. Shifting the emphasis from fear to desire and love, we find that what Àngela seeks is nothing short of the return of the past, be it in the guise of childlike tranquillity or of an almost primal unity. The return of something childlike is expressed as follows: "tal volta el que en realitat m'interessa és la tendresa, una mena de sensació que em retorna al paradís sempre blau de la infantesa, on qualsevol malson era de seguida espantat per la dolça . . . veu de ma mare" [perhaps what really interests me is tenderness, a kind of sensation that takes me back to the ever-blue paradise of childhood, where my mother's sweet voice promptly dispelled every bad dream] (21); and also: "tota la meva vida he desitjat que algú em digués petita mentre m'abraçava, encara que els meus principis feministes se n'anessin en orris per haver acceptat allò que em semblava una degradació: esser disminuïda, infantilitzada, quasi cosificada" [all my life I have desired to be called "little girl" while being embraced, even if my feminist principles were negated by my having accepted what seemed to me degrading: being reduced, infantilized, practically turned into an object] (22). The return of something almost primal is articulated in equally forceful terms. Referring to the *coup de foudre* she experiences in Miquel's presence, Àngela declares: "la meva meitat perduda, després de la catàstrofe que ens condemnà a una llarguíssima escissió, se soldava amb el meu esser" [my lost half, after the catastrophe that condemned us to an excruciatingly long division, bonded with my being] (24). Somewhere between nostalgia, melancholy, and utopianism, Àngela expresses a dyadic desire, be it for the mother or for the other or for both. Better yet, she expresses a desire to make two one, *to secure a full correspondence,* without fissure or rift, that will stand the test of time. With desire so configured, little wonder that its realization should be so feared.[72]

Still, the desire for fusion and unity does seem to be realized, if only for a moment. With respect to the beginning of her relationship with Miquel, Àngela writes:

> El món—sé que és un tòpic assugar-ho, però fou així—va recobrar tot el seu sentit, un sentit primigeni, desacostumat, harmònic, i les frases més o menys oportunes, més o menys brillants, que jo solia

> divulgar en entrevistes i taules rodones—"Qualsevol escriptura és una carta d'amor", "Escric perquè m'estimin", "L'anhel de pervivència que ens empeny a estimar ens empeny també a crear", "El text no és més que un pretext amorós"—havien trobat finalment l'unic destinatari que m'interessava, un tu que justificaria des d'aleshores la meva existència i per al qual, sense saber-ho, havia guardat tantes absències en una virginitat sinó física almenys espiritual.
>
> [The world—I know that it is a commonplace, but that is how it was—regained all of its meaning, a primeval, strange, harmonious meaning, and the more or less felicitous, more or less brilliant, statements that I used to proffer in interviews and round table discussions—"All writing is a love letter," "I write in order to be loved," "The desire for continuity that leads us to love leads us also to create," "The text is nothing more than a pretext for love"—had finally found the only destinataire that interested me, a 'you' that would henceforth justify my existence and for whom, without knowing it, I had kept so many absences in a virginity that, while not physical, was at least spiritual.] (24–25)

It is interesting to note that, among the play of quotations, Àngela quotes herself and, more intricately, her author, Carme Riera; or perhaps it is the author who quotes herself, spectrally, through her character. For Riera's interviews are teeming with similar, if less personalized, observations. Be that as it may, the highly poeticized desire for unity, fusion, and full correspondence is here revealed to be epistolary as well as amorous in nature. Miquel is not just the only man for Àngela, he is also, and no less powerfully, her only true "destinataire." He, and no one else—not even Íngrid, her dear friend who knows her so well—is the designated, almost predestined, subject of Àngela's interest (25). This is evident, presumably, in the striking coincidence of personal interests: they like the same writers, painters, and musicians, the same books, paintings, and symphonies, the same passages, brush strokes, and movements. They like the same foods, fashions, and decorations, and they are both fascinated by northern Europe. So alike are they, that Àngela is certain that Miquel will like Íngrid as much as Àngela (likes her).

If all of this sounds too good to be true, it is. If it sounds precious, hackneyed, and even somewhat silly, it may be so as well. Both Àngela's letter and, by necessary implication, Riera's text toy self-consciously with affectation, with all that is considered "cursi."[73] Regarding her "poetic correspondence" with Miquel and the variations to which it gives rise, Àngela declares:

"[e]ren frases trivials, Íngrid, fins i tot cursis" [they were trivial, even affected, phrases, Íngrid] (38). At the same time, Àngela's letter by no means avoids the lyricism that characterized her intercourse with Miquel; if anything, it replicates, records, and extends it. Riera herself, in an extended interview with Geraldine Nichols, refers to her own lyrical bent, going so far as to say that she finds the lyricism of her first books rather embarrassing: "en estos libros no sólo había tratado de emocionar al lector, sino que me había emocionado yo, y esto era algo impúdico, ¿no?" [in these books not only had I tried to move the reader, but I had also moved myself, and this was somewhat indecent, was it not?][74] What is interesting is not only the connection, in lyricism, between (young) author and character, but also the idea that lyricism can be terribly self-compromising, that its very delicacy, when exaggerated, can be indelicate. Riera goes on to say that lyricism, "uncontrolled" lyricism, is a defect of a literature of adolescence, which is when she wrote her first books.[75] We will remember that one of Àngela's desires is to remember desire, or love, as it was before, in her youth—if not, indeed, in some primeval imaginary—and that this act of remembrance, this return, is thick with lyricism. *Qüestió d'amor propi* is itself, as I have indicated from the outset, something of a "throwback" or "anomaly" in what might otherwise be described—mistakenly, I believe—as the author's developmental trajectory. It recalls, that is, the lyrical, "letteral" qualities of Riera's early texts, but with a kind of veneer, generated over time, that makes a once familiar lyricism seem strange, almost embarrassingly, indecently strange.

Àngela compares her relationship with Miquel to a saccharine postcard Miquel had undoubtedly "written" many times. She also characterizes her own behavior as that of an adolescent girl, as if she were fifteen years old and as if it were not 1985, but the nineteenth century, at the height of romanticism (42). Here, too, something is out of tune and old-fashioned, more suited to Àngela's grandmother (and Riera's nuns) than to her contemporaries, more in keeping with the conventions of femininity than with the principles of feminism. Indeed, for Àngela, it does not matter that "tot això no siguin més que músiques celestials, randes de passamaneria variada amb les quals les persones tan convencionals com jo intenten disfressar l'animalitat humana" [all that is merely heavenly music, delicate, variegated embroideries, with which conventional people like me try to disguise the more animal aspects of humanity]. It does not matter, because Àngela is adamant about one thing:

> mai no m'hagués *entregat* sense la seguretat que d'altres aspectes menys biològics, més anímics o espirituals—sé que odies ambdues paraules [Íngrid]—havien entrat també en estat de fusió, de confusió íntima.
>
> [I would have never *given* myself without being sure that other aspects, less biological and more emotional and spiritual—I know that you hate these last words Íngrid—had entered into a state of fusion, of intimate confusion.] (23–24, emphasis in original)

Once again, (con)fusion is the measure of desire realized, the necessary condition for any giving, any delivery, any "entrega." This word, *entrega,* emphasized here and elsewhere, as we shall see directly, is most telling. What it tells, in this context, is that the giving or gift (of one's body, love, or letter) is contingent on the receiving or receipt of the gift, or rather, that delivery is not delivered until a complete (con)fusion, a full correspondence, appears assured. This is the case, I might add, not only for Àngela's relationship with Miquel, but with Íngrid as well.

The question of correspondence, in writing and in love, is, as I have indicated, crucial. It arises not just in the story told but in the storytelling, not just in the embedded tale of unrequited love, but in the way the tale is conveyed, the form it takes. The possibility that the addressee will not answer—that the interlocutor will not reply, that the beloved will not sustain love by returning it in kind—is inscribed in Àngela's letter as yet another one of the perils of communication: literary, carnal, and otherwise:

> Suposava que la meva *entrega* no seria corresposta i em veia ridícula, sense més horitzó que uns altres ulls que, ben segur, ni tan sols em mirarien de front. Aquesta covardia, o el que vulguis dir-li, em servia d'excusa per escapolir-me de possibles aventures i també de possibles sofriments futurs.
>
> [I imagined that the *giving* of myself would not be corresponded and that I would seem ridiculous, with no other horizon than that provided by other eyes that, quite surely, would not even look at me directly. That cowardice, or whatever you want to call it, provided me with an excuse to avoid possible affairs as well as possible sufferings in the future.] (19, emphasis in original)

The fear of appearing ridiculous is the fear of not being corresponded.[76] To be sure, the delivery (*entrega*) that Àngela fears will not be corresponded is, most literally, that of love; but it is also, more figuratively, that of a letter. This last point may seem odd, because if Àngela is to be believed, it is Íngrid who has been waiting for correspondence, for a response to her previous delivery. Or more precisely, it is Íngrid who, weary of waiting for something that does not come, has decided to *demand* a correspondence. Again, the communicative circuit threatens to become hopelessly entangled, for Àngela's letter is "about," among other things, delivery and the demand for correspondence, communication and its withholding, love and its writing, unwriting, and rewriting. "About" these things, Àngela's letter *is* these things, in the sense, once more, that delivery, the demand for correspondence, communication, and so on, shoot through its form as well as its content, its structure and style as well as its elusive substance.

The fear that delivery will not be corresponded, that a gift will not give way to a giving *in return,* that "you" will not keep intercourse with "me," the fear of appearing ridiculous before another, is here bound up in another fear: the fear of having one's demands fall flat. I have already referred to demand: the demand for forgiveness, for communication, for correspondence, for revenge, for something in return. Yet another demand may be added to this ever-growing list. Jacques Lacan speaks of the demand for love, which is not the same, however, as the demand for satisfaction. "Demand in itself bears on something other than the satisfactions which it calls for."[77] This distinction between the demand for love and the call for satisfaction (or the need, or appetite, for satisfaction) is worth bearing in mind because it bears in turn on desire. According to Lacan, "desire is neither the appetite for satisfaction, nor the demand for love, but the difference resulting from the subtraction of the first from the second, the very phenomenon of their splitting (*Spaltung*)."[78] Barbara Johnson provides a brilliantly concise gloss: "desire is what is left of the 'demande' [for love] when all satisfaction of 'real' needs has been subtracted from it."[79] In other words, desire is something of a remainder, a leftover; or rather, as Lacan elsewhere puts it, in desire something remains, "est reste."[80] This "reste" is restless, an unsettled and unsettling remnant, because it outstrips all material, or even articulable, satisfaction and cannot be "made good." In a sense, it is what hangs impossibly on, not only beyond the appetite for satisfaction but also beyond demand, or better yet, beyond every *reasonable* demand.[81] But love, the demand for love, at least if it is understood radically, is just that: unreasonable, beyond reason. However much it may seem to be satisfied, however close it may come, it is never enough; there is always more.[82] Which may perhaps be a way of saying that, in desire, love too remains.

Struggling with the relationship between love and desire, I do not mean to say that one is the same as the other or that there is some easy correspondence between them. At most, I might say that in desire, as desire, something impossibly remains; something remains impossible: the correspondence, at least in any complete and final way, of the demand for love and the demand, or need, for satisfaction. This too, I recognize, is rather involved. At the risk of oversimplification, the satisfaction of love—the satisfaction of the demand for love—is what is impossible, at least in any full and final sense. Indeed, complete satisfaction would spell the death of desire, its end *without* remainder. Lacan refers to a desire that overflows (*"déborde"*) demand and asserts that this demand cannot be satisfied without desire extinguishing itself. Even more, he asserts that it is precisely to keep this desire from extinguishing itself that a hungry subject will not nourish itself in order to nourish desire, that it will refuse nourishment because it will refuse to let desire, as hunger, disappear.[83] This is only one of many paradoxes bearing on love and desire. Another, deliciously complex, is Lacan's claim that love, demanded of an Other, is "the gift of something which it [the Other] does not have."[84] Another paradox, admittedly more prone to banality, is the claim that "true love opens (*"débouche"*) onto hate."[85] Yet another paradox, following Freud, is the claim that love, ostensibly addressed to and demanded of another, "is in its essence narcissistic."[86] Together, these paradoxes, some more acute than others, fold into Àngela's letter and Riera's story.

The refusal to give up (on) desire, however desperate it may become; the opening of love onto hate; the narcissism of love; even the gift and giving of what one does not have: all are here at work. Refusing to give up (on) desire, Àngela redirects its terms, moving from love to hate; addressing herself to others, she never quite stops looking after herself; demanding love, demanding the correspondence of love, demanding to have love as she would give it, she does not see love as a giving without having or holding, as an untenable gift. Nor does she see love as a gift without return, as a delivery without recompense or reciprocation. Or to put it bluntly, even brutally, Àngela, in love and desire, is tenacious, vengeful, self-centered, and profoundly ungenerous. Of course, the woman who, in love, would give what she does not have (call it, for example, phallic power) bears an uncomfortably close affinity to the self-abnegating woman of conventional male fantasy: the woman who is nothing without a man and who, paradoxically, is nothing with him. Nothing with or without, for identified as lack and lacking to begin with, she has supposedly given what she does not have to him; she has supposedly made him everything at the cost of making, or continuing to be, herself nothing.

Here, we arrive at the core of Àngela's dilemma: her desire to be nothing if not with and through a man (remember her "adolescent" fantasies of marrying a man and assuring his greatness, of being objectified and possessed) and her desire to be something, that is to say, someone, in and of herself. It is no accident that these two contradictory desires, and the demands they entail, are formulated through literature and letters, literary letters. Nor is it an accident that love is not the only question here, but rather that it is also, even primarily, a question of self-love. More precisely, it is a question of self-love in literature, all of which brings me back to the moment when Àngela and Miquel first meet. I have delayed rehearsing this moment, not only because I wanted to accentuate the proleptic, retrospective, belated quality of Àngela's letter, but also because I wanted to consider fear, desire, and love as if they could be "resolved" and as if resolution, in the form of full correspondence, were not in fact gainsaid from the beginning. I mean, quite simply, that whatever Àngela may fear or desire or love, whatever she may fear or desire *as* love, her relationship with Miquel is conflictive from the start.

Put somewhat generally, in Riera's text, the sexual relation is constituted in a contentious, contestatory, *critical* way. Put more specifically, Àngela questions, and refutes, Miquel in a literary colloquium. As noted, both she and he are writers, and while each has heard about and even "read" the other, they first come together in a discussion about someone else's writing. The other writer is Leopoldo Alas, or Clarín, and the writing which is the ostensible site of their encounter is *La Regenta.* That one of the longest, most "developed" masterworks of Spanish realism should be at the center of Riera's short epistolary work is striking, in part because it signals an uncanny return to and of epistolarity through the very form of narrative that supposedly spelled the "end" of epistolarity. It is also striking because what brings Àngela and Miquel together in *La Regenta* is precisely what keeps them apart. Both of Riera's characters focus, that is, on the problem of love and desire in Clarín's main character. For Miquel, it is a problem of sexual appetite, of Ana Ozores's "unsatisfied libido" (30). For Àngela, in contrast, it is a problem of childhood memory, of Ana Ozores's frustrations over the lack of early affection (30). Àngela's belief that Ana's problem is a function of the persistence of a lack (marked by a fleeting moment of tenderness and care) is significant because it dovetails Àngela's own problem, her own story, her own sense of love.

Recounting Ana's "adventure" with Germán, Àngela tells a story that might well be read as her own:

> El que passà aquella nit entre els nins és un dels pocs records agradables d'Ana: Germán li explica per primera vegada un conte i, per primera vegada també, l'acotxa abans de dormir-se. . . . Fins llavors Ana no ha tengut altre remei, per tal de convocar la son, que contarse contes ella mateixa, ni gaudir de més companyia que la que li proporcionava la seva pròpia imaginació. Tota la vida sentimental de *La Regenta* [sic]—vaig insistir—està dominada per la il.lusió de recobrar aquests sentiments, molt més que per la recerca de la seva realització sexual. El seu lliurament a Mesia [sic] obeeix a la seguretat que cada nit, desprès d'estimar-la, li contarà una història diferent.
>
> [What happened that night between the children is one of the few nice memories that Ana has: Germán tells her a story for the first time and, also for the first time, wraps her up before sleep. Up until then, in order to fall asleep, Ana had no other choice but to tell stories to herself, nor did she enjoy any other company than that of her own imagination. The entire emotional life of La Regenta—I insisted—is dominated by the dream of recovering those feelings, much more than the search for her sexuality. The fact that she "gives" herself to Mesía has to do with the certainty that every night, after making love to her, he will tell her a different story.] (30–31)

To see the ties between one character and another, we need only recall Àngela's expressed desire for tenderness; her longing to be cradled and called "petita" [little one]; her fascination with memory; her dream of recapturing the past and filling a persistent lack; and, most important, her love of (love) stories.[87] Returning to Clarín's text, we find that the children's adventure calls forth a more adult story: Germán declares himself and Ana to be husband and wife, and Ana declares herself to be a mother.[88] In addition, we find that "La Regenta . . . creía que, en rigor, de lo que se acordaba no era de las palabras mismas, sino de posterior recuerdo en que la niña había animado y puesto en forma de novela los sucesos de aquella noche" [La Regenta believed that, in fact, what she remembered was not the words themselves, but a later memory when the little girl had animated and given narrative form to the events of that night).[89] Àngela is similarly engaged in narrative activity, weaving pieces of novels into letters and, even more, pieces of life into fiction. As she tells Íngrid, only those stories whose beauty, transfigured by memory, can offer us the chance of deferring death, are worth living (16–17). The very story Àngela relates to Íngrid has been transfigured by memory, though here its beauty, lyrical and precious, leads to revenge.

And yet, even before the thought of revenge there is a contrariness that is far from incidental. Àngela meets Miquel in a writers' symposium in Valencia. She has heard of him, read him, before arriving there, but does not expect much from him—until he talks. And suddenly, in talking, in the nuances of the voice, Miquel is transformed into a consummate showman, a magician of words and, moreover, of Àngela's adolescence (28). He becomes, as Àngela hears and watches him, a man capable of pulling doves out of his vest and of sawing a woman in half and putting her back together again (the latter image is, of course, rich in sexual significance). What is more, Miquel performs his verbal magic in the "Golden Room" of the Llotja in Valencia, and Àngela marvels at his dexterity and prowess. Emotions she believed dead and buried come surging to the surface, amid the applause and approval of the public. The fact that so much magic is played out in public is important because it impels Àngela, already fascinated by Miquel, to make herself stand out as different. She thus decides that "la millor manera de cridar la seva atenció era portar-li la contrària" [the best way to get his attention is to contradict him) (30). What Àngela indicates is that the best way to get Miquel's attention and to enter into contact with him, to relate to him, is to contradict him, to mark (off) her difference and bear him the contrary. I want to maintain the inelegant, overly literal, rendering of "portar-li la contrària" so as to underscore that Àngela's "intervenció," public and verbal itself, is an act, or, better yet, a delivery, of someone who is, or rather wants to be, *equal and different at the same time.* This clashes with Àngela's repeated anti-feminist longings to be objectified, infantilized, and called "petita." It also clashes with her desire for full fusion, for a return of and to the past, whether personal or primal. For what Àngela seeks in "bearing Miquel the contrary" is the recognition of difference as equal. The formulation is paradoxical, but may be restyled as follows: Àngela wants Miquel to recognize her as a woman and, at the same time, as a writer: a writer as he is, equal to him.

At first, it seems to work: "de seguida em féu saber que jo era la persona més interessant que havia trobat al congrés, la primera dona que en un debat li havia posat els punts sobre les is i, sobretot, que era un entusiasta admirador de la meva obra" [he immediately let me know that I was the most interesting person that he had met at the symposium, the first woman who in a (public) debate had made him nuance his position and, most of all, that he was an enthusiastic admirer of my work] (32). Here, Miquel does not just recognize that Àngela is a writer as he is, but also reveals himself to be a reader of Àngela's work, as Àngela is of his. In this "joc de miralls" [game of mirrors] (36), love can flourish because it sees itself infinitely reflected: delivered and returned for delivery anew. The writer reads the writer who is read by the writer in turn; the lover loves the beloved who loves the lover as beloved in turn: and so on, and so on. If this self-reflective circuit seems to augur the loss of the self in the other, it also harbors its tenacious, obsessive insistence. Love, that giving and gift of what one does not have, exposes itself as self-love, that giving and gift, again, of what one does not have. And what "one" does not have, along with love, is the self, forever a function of the other and of otherness, forever striving to have and hold the other in order to have and hold "itself."

Lacan has said that desire is the desire of the Other, and that observation, however it is read, surely holds here. But another Lacanian observation is equally apposite. Referring to the narcissistic "essence" of love, Lacan states that love is powerless, even if it is reciprocal, because it ignores that it is the desire to be *One,* which entails the impossibility of establishing a relation between *two.*[90] More laconically, and more provocatively, Lacan declares: "il n'y a pas de rapport sexuel": there is no sexual relation, if by relation we understand the possibility of making two into one, of attaining fusion and achieving complete correspondence.[91] Interestingly, Lacan's observation dovetails with Neus Aguado's more focused assertion: "the dominant theme in Carme Riera's short stories and novels is the lack of coincidental occurrence, the ways meetings seem destined not to happen and the difficulty in establishing relationships."[92] True as this is, it is not just because, as Aguado says, Riera's characters "do not accept the established order."[93] In fact, it is also precisely because some of them *do accept* the established order that relations are difficult, if not impossible. Part of the problem with the relationship between Àngela and Miquel is that she acts "just like a woman" and he, "just like a man." In this light, Àngela's romantic illusions, in which femininity is at odds with feminism, are just that: illusions.[94] Which is not to say that there exists a reality free from illusions and unmarked by fictions, only that some are more powerfully fixated on fusion, synthesis, and sameness than others.

Of fiction, there is, as always, more. For, if there is no sexual relation in any absolute sense—if fusion is an impossibility, if full and final correspondence is a fiction played out, again and again, in life—that by no means means that the play is happy and sweet, tender and soft. Play, quite the contrary, may be borne as revenge. Àngela may not be able to send Miquel the letter she writes him (64), but she certainly sends it, or some deflected version of it, to Íngrid. It is a letter requesting, "demanding," forgiveness, continued correspondence, and revenge. Or, to put it more precisely, it is a letter "demanding" revenge in place of what now appears to be a "ridiculous" demand for love. Different as they are, the demand for revenge, motivated by something bordering on hate, is not *that* different from the demand for love, in large measure because desire remains at play in both. René Girard would point out that it is mimetic desire, turning and returning on itself, on the self in its inability to be fully corresponded by the other. For Àngela, it entails a return to letters and to Íngrid, her feminist friend from the North whom she on the one hand courts and, on the other, albeit more quietly, criticizes. However sincere this return to letters and Íngrid may be, it is but part of a project for a more vengeful return to Miquel. What Àngela desires now, after the failure and frustration of love, is that Íngrid intercede on her behalf and exercise, as if by proxy, Àngela's revenge: "no debades t'has divertit amb les venjadores de llurs honres del teatre castellà. Mira per on, i per persona interposada, tens una oportunitat magnífica de representar aquest paper" [you have not enjoyed in vain the Spanish theater's avengers of honor] (83). Resorting once again to literary antecedents, writing in terms of roles to be represented, Àngela offers Íngrid a "magnificent opportunity": to replay a Spanish honor play and to be Àngela's avenging angel.

Miquel is scheduled to take a trip to Scandinavia, and Àngela is sure that he will look Íngrid up: "buscarà en tu un altre espill on poder posar en joc tots els reflexos de la seva persona i et complaurà mostrant-te una allau de similituds" [he will seek in you another mirror in which to put into play all of his reflexes and reflections and he will take pleasure in showing you all sorts of similarities] (81). He will look Íngrid up, then, in order to look at himself. Àngela sees Miquel as seeking a mirror, as narcissistically obsessed with finding reflections and replications of himself, as a man, in women. But Àngela, different as she is, is similarly reflected in this game of mirrors. She, too, in seeking out Íngrid to wreak her revenge, is projecting herself onto Íngrid, seeing herself, and perhaps only herself, in her friend. She assumes that Íngrid will be eager to toss off her Northern feminist garb to don that of some Spanish avenger of honor; but, even more, she assumes that Íngrid's pleasure will be the pleasure of knowing that Àngela is pleasingly avenged. Bluntly put, she assumes that Íngrid's pleasure will be Àngela's, that there will be no significant difference between her pleasure, and desire, and the other's. Pleasure and desire are, once more, narcissistic, and they are also, once more, of a decidedly literary sort. If literature is a mirror, here it is not so much of society as of the self.

Àngela does not ask Íngrid simply to seduce and abandon Miquel as he had done with Àngela, in part because that would be "too easy," and in part because, given Miquel's wiles, it would be "too difficult." At the same time, it is almost as if Àngela were afraid that just such a seduction, more fleshly than figurative, could really happen. In this play of mirrors, there is, then, a desired difference: where Àngela used words to get at Miquel's body, Íngrid is to use words to get at his words. Íngrid, as Àngela scripts her, is to stay with the letter, indeed, to insist on it. Of course, when it comes to Miquel, Àngela herself has not exactly let the letter go, and returns to it, as we have seen, again and again. For Àngela asks Íngrid to fill Miquel's head with pretty lies about Scandinavia, to fire his desire to write about it, and to make him appear *ridiculous,* to his future readers, as a writer. One of these readers will be the writer Àngela Caminals, who writes that she is already laughing her head off thinking about how Miquel's articles will be full of nonsense (85). She imagines, in a rush of hyperbole, that the ridicule will be such that Miquel will never receive a Nobel Prize (85). If she once dreamed of making a man a success, she now dreams of making him a failure. It is thus not so much that she has abandoned her dream, that she has extricated herself from a powerful communicative circuit of love, hate, fear, and desire; but, instead, that she holds onto its malfunctioning: with a vengeance.

It remains to be seen, to be written and read, how Íngrid will respond. What is certain is that while Àngela tells Íngrid that the game is now Íngrid's (82), it is also still Àngela's. And it is still Àngela's game because, however Íngrid plays it, she will in a sense be following Àngela's lead, her script. Even if Íngrid follows a different lead, even if she rewrites or unwrites Àngela's script, she is already marked by it. Indeed, even if Íngrid refuses to play along, she is marked in her very refusal. Marked, but not completely, of course, for there is always something that does not quite coincide or correspond. In this sense, Íngrid is *not* marked by Àngela's script. Inasmuch as this noncoincidental marking, this incomplete correspondence, bears on friendship and, more deeply, on love, it might be a matter of some sorrow. Yet, love is—please forgive me—never having to say you're sorry; or rather, it is almost *always* having to say you're sorry about everything *but* your *self* in love. Love, here and perhaps all too often elsewhere, asks for forgiveness and demands satisfaction—usually in the form of complete correspondence—without truly questioning the self's role in love. But such a question or questioning seems to be one of the more insistent messages of the work at hand, where a love of one's own ultimately is as questionable as a writing of one's own.

Insistent as it may be, it is nonetheless far from an easy message, one that, even as I close my reading, opens in various directions. Now admittedly, we could, with relatively few questions, read Àngela's letter, and Riera's text, as yet another story about the hell that hath no fury, the wrath of a woman scorned. To do so, however, would be to read precisely what Àngela imagines that Miquel will read: "l'única lliçó que treurà de tot això és que mai hom ha de confiar, perquè no en tenen, en el criteri de les dones" [the only lesson that he will get out of all of this is that one (a man) should never trust a woman] (85). We could also, or alternately, read it as yet another story about the dubious and duplicitous "criteria" of a man, about how one (a woman) should never trust a man. Steering away from such "age-old," "normal," "familiar" readings, we might do better—though perhaps still not so terribly well—to read the letter and the text as a *mise en question* of the properties, proprieties, and possessions of love, as a questioning of a love of one's own, of one's own love, of self-love and, of course, of the love of another. We might read it, moreover, as a questioning of the kinds of correspondence that the self, in and out of love, may or may not seek, in and out of writing. We might, in this self-questioning, take a clue from the text's epigraph, the verse from Jaime Gil de Biedma's "Contra Jaime Gil de Biedma": "Oh innoble servidumbre de amar seres humanos, / y la más innoble / que es amarse a sí mismo!" [Oh ignoble servitude to love human beings, / and the most ignoble / that is to love oneself].[95] We might take a clue, I repeat, from Gil de Biedma's verse, pushing us from narcissism to masochism, from idealization to degradation; but we might also run the risk of being a bit too sure about finding the truth of one text in another, of *her* text in *his*. There is, after all, something still strange in this seemingly neutral turn, or return, from one text to another, one author to another: something that on second thought might not be as "normal" as it may first appear, that might indeed be all too "normal." But that, too, as I read it, remains open to reading.

Notes

1. Carme Riera, *Qüestió d'amor propi* (Barcelona: Laia, 1987). Mary Vásquez aptly translates the title as "A Matter of Pride." See her "Dialogic Discourse, Gender and Power in Carme Riera's *Cuestión de amor propio,*" in *Misogyny in Literature: An Essay Collection,* ed. Katherine Anne Ackley (New York: Garland, 1992), 349. I have opted, however, for a more literal translation in order to underscore the question of love and the self. In addition, I will be focusing on the Catalan (or Mallorcan) original and not the Castilian translation, apparently by Riera herself, which, however, I have consulted. The Castilian makes explicit some of the terms that I will be stressing in my reading of the text. Where Angela imagines, in the Catalan text, a way of being "reconfortada" [comforted] (10), in the Castilian, it is "egoístamente reconfortada" [egotistically comforted] (12); where she refers, in Catalan, to her letter as "aquest intermediari" [this medium] (10), in Castilian, she refers to it as "este intermediario convencional" [this conventional medium] (12). The translation seems to qualify and make explicit some of the concepts and concerns (egoism, conventionality) that are important, but more subtly suggested, in the original text.

2. Kathleen Glenn, "Conversation with Carme Riera," *Catalan Review* 8:1–2 (1994), 209.

3. Ibid., 208.

4. Ibid., 209.

5. Ibid.

6. Ibid.

7. Ibid.

8. Luis Racionero, "Cada vez tenemos menos imaginación: Entrevista con Carmen Riera," *Quimera* 9–10 (1981), 14.

9. Glenn, "Conversation," 203.

10. Glenn, "Authority and Marginality in Three Contemporary Spanish Narratives," *Romance Languages Annual* 2 (1990), 429.

11. Geraldine Nichols, in "Stranger than Fiction: Fantasy in Short Stories by Matute, Rodoreda, Riera," *Monographic Review/Revista Monográfica* 4 (1988), refers to Riera's work, specifically, "Te deix" and *Epitelis tendríssims,* as being "beyond the pale of normalcy," 40.

12. Vásquez, 353 (emphasis mine).

13. Sigmund Freud, "The 'Uncanny'," in *Collected Papers,* vol. 4, trans. Joan Riviere (New York: Basic Books, 1959).

14. Letters are also employed in *Joc de miralls* [Game of Mirrors] from 1989. The phrase (and concept) *joc de miralls* also occurs at significant points in *Qüestió.*

15. The epistolary form also appears to be, in the opinion of some critics, "out of place" in Spain. Mary Vásquez describes it as "a mode long popular in women's literature in France and the United States but infrequent in Spain," 349–50.

16. Altman, *Epistolarity: Approaches to a Form* (Columbus: Ohio State University Press, 1982), 3.

17. Godfrey Frank Singer, *The Epistolary Novel: Its Origin, Development, Decline, and Residuary Influence* (New York: Russell & Russell, 1963). This work was first published in the 1930s.

18. Elizabeth J. MacArthur, *Extravagant Narratives: Closure and Dynamics in the Epistolary Form* (Princeton, N.J.: Princeton University Press, 1990), 11.

19. Ibid., 15–16. For more on closure in epistolarity see Altman, for whom "the circuit of communication is never closed. Epistolary texts engender prefaces, preprefaces, and postfaces, which dialogue with each other and with the text proper, and which are a continuation of the text's dialogical model," 163.

20. In MacArthur's words, "like deviance, extravagance exceeds conventional limits, but unlike deviance, extravagance is not an abnormality that can be cured," 29. MacArthur indicates that deviance and abnormality imply a cure that is not implied in extravagance. I find the distinction arbitrary and unconvincing, especially inasmuch as one term blurs, even in clinical discourse, into another. Although there are doubtless shades of difference, an extravagant, "wayward," person is also susceptible to discipline and punishment, to insertion into an apparatus of "cure."

21. Riera, of course, is hardly alone. Although epistolarity may have waned or even "fallen," it continues to turn up in the writing of some of the most celebrated artists and intellectuals of the twentieth century. Linda S. Kauffman, in *Special Delivery: Epistolary Modes in Modern Fiction* (Chicago: University of Chicago Press, 1992), examines the epistolary mode in works by Doris Lessing, Alice Walker, Roland Barthes, and Jacques Derrida, among others. Kauffman also distinguishes—following Alastair Fowler—between genre and mode: "mode, unlike genre, seldom implies a complete external form," xiii. The epistolary mode, accordingly, is more ample than the epistolary genre and may inform works not explicitly constructed in the form of letters. Kauffman's earlier study, *Discourses of Desire: Gender, Genre, and Epistolary*

Fictions (Ithaca: Cornell University Press, 1986), focuses, as its title indicates, on the interrelated questions of gender and genre, specifically women and letters. Both studies shed light on *Qüestió d'amor propi.*

22. Tsuchiya, "The Paradox of Narrative Seduction in Carmen Riera's *Cuestión de amor propio,*" *Hispania* 75:2 (1992), 285.

23. For more on the importance of love (and women's writing) to the history of epistolary literature, see Katharine Ann Jensen's *Writing Love: Letters, Women, and the Novel in France, 1605–1776* (Carbondale: Southern Illinois University Press, 1995).

24. Janet Altman refers to "two types of figures so frequently fostered by letter writing as *metaphoric* (a metaphor of the lover is generated by the epistolary situation, which conjures up interiorized images and comparisons) and *metonymic* (the letter itself, by virtue of physical contact, stands for the lover);" *Epistolarity,* 19. The fact that Àngela writes not to her lover but to her friend—or, rather, writes to her lover *through* her friend—only complicates the metaphoric and metonymic dimensions of her endeavor.

25. I am admittedly a bit apprehensive about qualifying *Qüestió* as postmodern. That much-beleagured term is perhaps better suited to works such as Derrida's *La carte postale* and Barthes's *Fragments d'un discours amoureux,* both studied by Linda Kauffman. At the same time, I am also apprehensive about avoiding the term *postmodern* in connection with Riera's work. I let stand, then, my ambivalence.

26. Glenn, "Conversation," 203. Riera makes the same observation to Neus Aguado, "Epístolas de mar y de sol: Entrevista con Carme Riera," *Quimera* 105 (1991), 35–36.

27. Ibid.

28. Terry Castle, in *Clarissa's Ciphers: Meaning and Disruption in Richardson's* Clarissa (Ithaca: Cornell University Press, 1982), underscores the importance of discontinuity and states that "the interruption, rather than the fulfillment of meaning and form may in fact be what fiction is all *about,*" 40 (emphasis in original).

29. Glenn, "Conversation," 203.

30. Vásquez, "Dialogic Discourse," 350.

31. Tsuchiya, 282.

32. Terry Castle examines the ties between letters and absence. Working through Derrida, Castle says, "the letter . . . is a paradigmatic text in that it is motivated by a dramatized human absence, the physical remove of the letter writer. It comes into existence as a substitute for the body of the writer;" *Clarissa's Ciphers,* 44.

33. The destinataire may also well be "Francesc" (the name of Riera's husband), to whom the book is dedicated; but, beyond that, it is the reader in general. In her interview with Aguado, Riera refers specifically to *Qüestió* and says that the destinataire is always the reader, 36.

34. Examples of these other letters and texts might include Íngrid's written response to Àngela, Íngrid's verbal "response" to Miquel (the "stories" Àngela asks her to tell Miquel), Miquel's written "response" to Íngrid's stories (the ridiculous article Àngela imagines he will write after listening to Íngrid), and so on. The fact that these other "letters/texts" are virtual does not diminish their imaginary power: we, the readers, may project them, write them, as possible responses to the letter/text we actually read.

35. Tsuchiya, 283.

36. Roberta Johnson, "Voice and Intersubjectivity in Carme Riera's Narratives," in *Critical Essays on the Literatures of Spain and Spanish America,* ed. Luis T. González-del-Valle and Julio Baena (Boulder: Society of Spanish and Spanish-American Studies, 1991), 153, 157.

37. Barbara Johnson, "The Frame of Reference: Poe, Lacan, Derrida," in *The Critical Difference: Essays in the Contemporary Rhetoric of Reading* (Baltimore: Johns Hopkins University Press, 1980), 144.

38. The Castilian translation substitutes "fe de cariño" [affection] for "fe d'amor" [love]. The substitution is not entirely innocent.

39. Mary Vásquez rightly stresses the manipulative qualities of Àngela's epistle and the self-portrait it contains. According to her, Àngela's letter is "probably designed to create an image of helplessness, to be countered by a surge of sympathy and helpful action" on Íngrid's part, 358.

40. Ibid., 350.

41. As Vásquez puts it, Àngela couches "her letter in one mode—confession—in order to attain a second—retribution," 350.

42. Mary Vásquez notes yet another, very important, point of resemblance (a mirroring?) between Àngela and Miquel. In Vásquez's opinion, "Angela resorts in her approach to her friend Ingrid to a project as tacky, trite, and reprehensible as Miguel's treatment of her or his conduct of their affair," 356.

43. Freud, "On Narcissism: An Introduction," in *General Psychological Theory,* trans. Cecil M. Baines (New York: Macmillan, 1963), 64.

44. Ibid., 69.

45. Ibid., 74.

46. Ibid., 79.

47. Ibid., 78.

48. Ibid.

49. Ibid., 74.

50. Ibid., 70.

51. Vásquez gives a somewhat different twist to the idea of a controlling loss of control by referring to the "stereotypically feminine . . . deprecation of the self in hope of a reassuring protest by one's interlocutor," 357.

52. Akiko Tsuchiya follows Riera's lead, focusing on the dynamics of seduction in the text. Tsuchiya writes of Àngela's epistolary "seduction" of Íngrid but ignores one of the fundamental strategies of seduction the text employs: flattery or the appeal to the other's pride or "amor propi." Kathleen Glenn, in "Authority and Marginality," also examines the intricate play of seductions, 430.

53. Once again, Vásquez is quite persuasive: "Angela has, of course, placed herself in a position of moral superiority over Ingrid. . . . Angela is now quite willing to use and abuse a friend in the name of female solidarity. She suggests that her own body is somehow more sacred, more worthy of dignity, since she insists upon sex with love, than that of Ingrid, to whom one sexual liaison more or less could not possibly matter. The centuries-old division between women lurks again in the dichotomy between the virtuous and the licentious, the Madonna and the harlot"; "Dialogic Discourse," 359.

54. Barthes, *Fragments d'un discours amoureux* (Paris: Seuil, 1977), 209.

55. An absolutely exclusive address may be impossible and yet exist. The formulation is from Philippe Lejeune, who writes: "l'autobiographie a beau être impossible, ça ne l'empêche nullement d'exister" [autobiography might well be impossible, that hardly prevents it from existing]; *Moi aussi,* 31.

56. Aguado, "Epístolas," 35.
57. Ibid.
58. Tsuchiya, "Paradox of Narrative Seduction," 281.
59. Àngela says that she could never dedicate a book, as Íngrid did, "als homes i dones de la meva vida" [to the men and women of my life] (20). The fact that the forthrightly sexual Íngrid dedicates her books to the men and *women* of her life is hardly a "guarantee" of exclusive heterosexuality. Accordingly, Mary Vásquez writes, here, of a "hint of bisexuality"; "Dialogic Discourse," 359.
60. Ibid., "Paradox of Narrative Seduction," 282.
61. See my "Virtual Sexuality: Lesbianism, Loss, and Deliverance in Carme Riera's 'Te deix amor la mar com a penyora,'" in *¿Entiendes?: Queer Readings, Hispanic Writings,* ed. Paul Julian Smith and Emilie Bergmann (Durham: Duke University Press, 1995).
62. The desire for the tonalities of northern Europe is nothing new in Catalan fiction. In Narcís Oller's *La febre d'or,* we find the following: "—Es latino, esto es latino: un cuadro de Roig y Soler. Prefiero le grisâtre del Norte. ¡Siempre este sol, la prosa del paisaje!—exclamà l'Emilia apropiant-se una frase collida al pintor Urgell" ["It's Latin, this is Latin: a painting by Roig y Soler. I prefer the grisâtre [greyness] of the North. Always this sun, this prosaic landscape!"—exclaimed Emilia, taking up a comment by the painter Urgell], 170. Here, but perhaps in Riera's text as well, the desire for Northern greyness is not bereft of affectation and posturing, of something "cursi" (note Emilia's use of Castilian).
63. There is a difference between men as well, but here it is not as strongly at play, though it is suggested in Àngela's initial perception of Miquel as "different" from other men.
64. Rather than Salinas, I will follow Roberta Johnson, who rightly describes "feminine" epistolarity as a "classic form of written self-expression for women who have traditionally been barred from more public forms of writing"; "Voice and Intersubjectivity," 155.
65. Pedro Salinas, *El defensor* (Madrid: Alianza, 1984), 72.
66. Diaries are, of course, another mode of writing associated with femininity; but here the communication is assumed to be more self-contained.
67. Ibid.
68. The belatedness of the letter is evoked in the name, in Catalan, of the very season of its (ideal) writing, "la tardor." What is late in autumn, "tard" in "tardor," is something like a quickness unto death, a fleetingness Àngela describes in detail (15–16). Autumn is also the season of Àngela's affair and, even more, of Àngela herself: she calls herself "una dona autumnal" [an autumnal woman] (57).
69. The poem's punctuation is actually a bit different: "Miedo. De ti. Quererte / es el más alto riesgo." See Pedro Salinas, *La voz a ti debida / Razón de amor* (Madrid: Castalia, 1984), 54.
70. Riera herself wonders if so-called feminine literature is a borrowed language. See Carme Riera, "Literatura femenina: ¿Un lenguaje prestado?, *Quimera* 18 (1982).
71. "Àngela Caminals és una escriptora acabada" [Àngela Caminals is finished as a writer] (69). Miquel tells Àngela that someone else has been saying that she is "washed up," and that he, ever the (hypocritical) gentleman, came to her defense. As Àngela suspects and subsequently confirms, it is actually Miquel himself who has been "writing her off."

72. My sentence is deliberately ambivalent. Clearly, what Àngela fears is that her desire for fusion cannot be realized; but the opposite may be no less fearful.

73. The very word *cursi*—designating affectation, pretentiousness, feigned elegance, and so on—is, according to the *Diccionari de la llengua catalana* (Barcelona: Enciclopèdia Catalana, 1994), a Castilianism.

74. Geraldine C. Nichols, "Carme Riera," *Escribir, espacio propio: Laforet, Matute, Moix, Tusquets, Riera y Roig por sí mismas* (Minneapolis: Institute for the Study of Ideologies and Literature, 1989), 197.

75. Ibid., 198.

76. Àngela says that one of the reasons she did not write Íngrid was that she was afraid of appearing weak, fragile, full of prejudices and, above all, ridiculous (12).

77. Lacan, "The Meaning of the Phallus," in *Feminine Sexuality,* trans. Jacqueline Rose (New York: W. W. Norton/Pantheon, 1982), 80. Lacan tends to reserve the term *demand* for use in relation to love. He distinguishes between need, demand, and desire.

78. Ibid., 81.

79. B. Johnson, "Frame of Reference," 140.

80. Lacan, *Le Séminaire XX: Encore* (Paris: Seuil, 1975), 12. Jacqueline Rose, in the second introduction to Lacan's *Feminine Sexuality,* also defines desire "as the 'remainder' of the subject, something which is always left over, but which has no content as such. Desire functions much as the zero unit in the numerical chain—its place is both constitutive *and* empty," 32.

81. "Reasonable" demand may perhaps be nothing other than need, related, as it is, to so-called real objects rather than fantasies.

82. Desire is this "never enough" and this "always more" that remains beyond every demand for satisfaction. For Lacan, desire holds its place in the margin of demand as such. See his *Le Séminaire VIII: Le transfert* (Paris: Seuil, 1991), 249.

83. Ibid., 238–39.

84. Lacan, "Meaning of the Phallus," 80.

85. Lacan, *Le Séminaire XX,* 133.

86. Ibid., 12.

87. Glenn, in "Authority and Marginality," rightly observes that "Miguel will play Mesía to [Àngela's] Ana," 429.

88. Leopoldo Alas, *La Regenta* (Madrid: Cátedra, 1984) 1:207.

89. Ibid., 209.

90. Lacan's penchant for linguistic play is in full flower here, making it virtually impossible to capture anything but the spirit of his letter: "L'amour est impuissant, quoiqu'il soit réciproque, parce qu'il ignore qu'il n'est que le désir d'être Un, ce qui nous conduit à l'impossible d'établir la relation d'eux. La relation *d'eux* qui?—*deux* sexes," 12. The play, relying on phonetic homology, is between *"d'eux"* and *"deux," "theirs"* and *"two."* That relation of theirs is impossible, inasmuch as it involves two who, at best or perhaps at worst, want to be One: and a relation of One is, of course, unthinkable. What is more, Lacan's use of phonetic homology is itself revealing: it *sounds* as if the two words are one and the same—*"d'eux"–"deux"*—but, *looked* at more closely, they are not.

91. Lacan, *Le Séminaire XX,* 17.

92. Aguado, "Carme Riera or the Suggestive Power of Words," *Catalan Writing* 6. (Barcelona: Institució de les Lletres Catalanes, 1991), 53.

93. Ibid., 53.

94. Àngela's illusions may be less cynical than Miquel's delusions of grandeur, but they are no less fictional. Àngela's complaint that Miquel sacrifices life to fiction turns back on herself as well.

95. Here, too, as with the Salinas quote, the quote that appears in Riera's text—"¡Oh innoble servidumbre de amar seres / humanos, y la más innoble / que es amarse a sí mismo!"—does *not quite correspond* with the "original." The differences may be minor—a mark of punctuaction, a word on one line rather than another—but, then again, narcissism is often a thing of minor differences. For the "narcissism of minor differences," see Sigmund Freud, *Civilization and Its Discontents,* trans. James Strachey (New York: W. W. Norton, 1961), 72; and *Group Psychology and the Analysis of the Ego,* trans. James Strachey (New York: W. W. Norton, 1959), 42.

A Game of Mirrors: Specularity, Appearance, Doubling and Trompe L'Oeil in Carme Riera's *Joc de miralls*

JANET PÉREZ

CRITICS TEND TO SPECIALIZE, NOT ONLY IN PERIODS OR GENRES, BUT also in writers, and still more narrowly, in selected aspects of an author's work. Even with canonical writers, scholarly criticism privileges favorite works, leaving the remainder (usually the bulk) of an author's output in comparative oblivion. Some egregious examples from modern Peninsular narrative are Camilo José Cela, Emilia Pardo Bazán, Gonzalo Torrente Ballester, and Carmen Martín Gaite. Cela, by his count, has authored "more than 100 books," yet seventy-five to eighty percent of extant criticism treats *La familia de Pascual Duarte* and *La colmena*. Pardo Bazán published nineteen long novels, several short ones, and close to 800 short stories, yet nearly three-fourths of relevant critical studies concentrate on *Los Pazos de Ulloa* and/or its sequel, *La Madre Naturaleza*. Of the more than four decades of production by Torrente Ballester, most critics have chosen to focus on either *La Saga/fuga* or *Fragmentos de apocalipsis,* while more investigators of Carmen Martín Gaite's fiction have examined *El cuarto de atrás* than have studied the rest of her work combined.

Critical preferences affect the secondary literature on more recent writers as well, with numerous titles remaining unexamined and others clearly en route to becoming critical favorites. Carme Riera's *Qüestió de amor propi* (1987) [A Question of Self-Love], for example, has attracted far more attention than the rest of this writer's fiction, with little or no notice accorded *Joc de miralls* (1989) [Game of Mirrors], winner of the Ramon Llull Novel Prize, or its Castilian version, *Por persona interpuesta.*[1] This essay will likewise "specialize," therefore, examining only *Joc de miralls.* After briefly situating the novel in the context of Riera's work as a whole and the broader framework of contemporary Spanish fiction and late twentieth-century aesthetics, my examination will focus on the novelist's use of specular structures (internal duplication, doubling, parallels, reflections, echoes and similar mirroring devices).

Perhaps one reason for critical neglect of much of Riera's work concerns genre, inasmuch as short stories generally receive less critical attention than novels (and brevity characterizes Riera's novels as well). Excepting *Una primavera per a Domenico Guarini* (1981) [A Primavera for Domenico Guarini] and *Qüestió de amor propi,* the writer's output prior to *Joc de miralls* (like *Qüestió,* a short novel) consists of essays, a biography, and short stories. Her first two enormously successful collections, *Te deix, amor, la mar com a penyora* (1975) [I Leave You, My Love, the Sea as a Token] with seventeen stories and the thirteen tales of *Jo pos per testimoni les gavines* (1977) [I Call on the Seagulls as Witness] contain the essentials of Riera's artistry.[2] These essentials are intelligence, lyricism mixed with irony, and certain repetitive themes and devices which, over time, emerge as constants—unabashed feminine sexuality; the quest for identity, self-realization, and liberty; mystery; cosmopolitan settings and characters; and interest in or proclivity for the detective genre. Cultural motifs (represented by music, painting and other art forms, literature and literary events: lectures, conferences, readings, etc.) also appear early, along with a penchant for portraying reporters, writers, critics, agents, publishers, teachers, and others involved in the business of publication. Riera frequently depicts the vanity, subterfuge, and self-deception of writers and other people involved in publishing, as evident in her more recent collection of tales, *Contra L'amor en companyía y otros relatos* (1991) [Against Love with a Partner And Other Tales.] Many of the nineteen stories in this volume feature writers as protagonists, portraying a literary world of editors, judges, prizes, theory, poetics, press conferences, and the like. Several story titles from *Contra* suggest this focus: "Esto no es un cuento" [This Isn't a Story]," "Informe" [Report] and "La novela experimental," as well as prior appearances of the motif (for example, "Quasi a la manera de fulletons" [Almost Like a Serial Romance] from *Je pos per testimoni*). All attest to the metaliterary and self-reflective nature of the texts. Riera's experimental and theoretical interest in narrative form appears via variations on fictional modalities, including repeated adaptations of the detective genre and a special fondness for epistolary form (or variants thereof, such as the diary or journal). Similarly, erotic themes, feminist attitudes, seduction, detectivesque or investigative motifs, ludic pursuits, and snatches of myth, along with the reality/appearance dichotomy, emerge as standard ingredients of Riera's fiction.

Roberta Johnson points to the significance for Riera's work of feminine identity and intersubjectivity and the importance of relatedness and dependence on the presence of the other (157–158), while the 1991 interview by Neus Aguado touches on homoerotic themes, which Riera recognizes as persistent in her fiction.[3] Referring to the myth of Zeus's punishment of putative original (unitary, bisexual/androgynous) humans, Riera affirms that "desde entonces buscamos nuestra mitad perdida" [from that time hence, we've been seeking our missing half] (34–35). This concept reappears in *Joc,* whose protagonist recalls the myth, wondering whether he and his antagonist or more successful rival are not, in fact, two halves of a single being (a portentous indicator of the essential identity of Corbalán and Gallego which readers are unlikely to recognize at first reading). Another character jokingly suggests that these rivals are secret lovers. The notion of the "lost half" is briefly suggested in *Qüestió de amor propi.* Varying this search-for-self theme, Elizabeth Ordóñez notes the reiterated presence in Riera's fiction of the quest for identity and textual self-definition (135).[4] And Akiko Tsuchiya foregrounds the concept of narrative seduction, discussed by the writer-protagonist of *Joc* in an early interview with the narrator.[5] The intrusion of criminality and violence into the ivory tower of literature or the world of high culture (as in *Una primavera per a Domenico Guarini*), a specific variant of the reality-appearance duality, receives further elaboration in *Joc de miralls,* which features, in varying degree, those constant characteristics of Riera's fiction already noted.

My critical or theoretical point of departure is Lucien Dallenbach's presentation in *Le reçit speculaire,* subtitled *Essai sur le mise en abyme.*[6] The *mise en abyme* is first termed "une modalité de la reflexion" (16), in other words, a mirror image or reflection whose function it is to underscore the relationship between meaning and form: "faire saillir l'intelligibilité et la structure formelle de l'oeuvre" [bring out the intelligibility and formal structure of the work] (ibid.). Above all a structuring device, it is not limited to literature but often appears in visual arts, taking its name from a heraldic device which Dallenbach affirms Gide discovered about 1891 in the image of a shield bearing in its center a miniature replica of itself. Examples from other genres include Velázquez's painting, "Las Meninas" and the play-within-a-play in *Hamlet.* Broadly defined, *mise en abyme* is "toute enclave entretenant une relation de similtude avec l'oeuvre que la contient" [every portion having a relation of similitude with the work containing it] (18). Dallenbach notes similarities between the concept of "mise en abyme a celui de miroir" [*mise en abyme* and that of the mirror] (19). The *mise en abyme* involves internal duplication, usually in miniature, a possibly infinite regression wherein a structure is repeated on a smaller scale: "toutes ses significations posibles forment une ensemble infini" [all probable meanings combine in an infinite ensemble] (33).

The Quaker Oats box provides one classic example from popular culture of the *mise en abyme:* the Quaker holds a box of oats on which his own image appears holding a smaller box with yet another, smaller Quaker holding a still smaller box, and so on, ad infinitum. Another oft-cited example evokes a marine landscape with a sailor standing with his back to a ship, holding in his hand a picture showing a sailor standing with his back to a ship, holding a picture showing a sailor standing with his back to a ship, and so on. Related literary devices or structures include parallels, repetition, reflection, and echoing, and results may recall the shadow box or magic lantern. Dreams, paintings, and literary representations (for example, the play-within-a-play or within a novel) which, with minor variations, repeat or echo the plot, characters or situations may also function as specular devices or *mise en abyme,* exemplifying Lacan's dictum:[7] "l'emetteur reçoit du récepteur son propre message sous une forme inversée" [the sender gets back from the receiver his own message in inverted form] (298).

Derrida, similarly, uses the concept of *mise en abyme:* ". . . quand on peut lire un livre dans le livre, un origine dans l'origine, un centre dans le centre, c'est l'abîme, le sans-fond de redoublement infini" [. . . when one can read another book within the book, another origin within the beginning, a center within the center, that's the bottomless abyss of infinite repetition] (434; cf. 435).[8] Todorov mentions the image "en abyme" (48)[9] and presents a similar theory of infinite duplication.[10] What Dallenbach terms *Le reçit speculaire* thus involves a more specific, restricted type of writing than what Linda Hutcheon calls "narcissistic narrative," her designation for metafiction and self-reflective literature (though the *mise en abyme,* a frequent device of self-reflective literature, is often narcissistic, as Dallenbach notes, alluding to Gide's writing before his mirror). But the *mise en abyme,* common in much self-reflective writing by European modernists, is not limited thereto, and self-reflective literature possesses numerous characteristics that do not necessarily accompany the *mise en abyme.*

Joc de miralls, being metaliterary and self-reflective, exhibits some "narcissistic" characteristics: As a self-conscious narrative, it is largely self-directed. Combining letters and diary by the participatory narrator (Teresa, the character who functions as detective) with the notebooks or journals of Gallego/Corbalán, the novel offers more than one viewpoint and might be said to have more than one narrative consciousness. None of these narrative voices represent omniscient vision, however; their perspectives are limited and their interpretations sometimes flawed by closeness to events or their emotional involvement therein. A kind of "limited omniscience," thanks to passing time—or hindsight—is provided by the addition of an epilogue, explaining aspects of the mystery, and written by the recipient of the earlier narrative(s). Blurring the boundaries between literature (fiction) and life (reality), the narrator of *Joc* employs fictitious documents—Gallego's notebooks—as supposedly trustworthy sources or objective "proof" within the context of the larger fiction, creating a mirage effect. The novel offers no "message" or moral, although, unlike many self-reflective works, *Joc de miralls* is not an open-ended narrative, due to the demise of its protagonist(s) and the narrator-investigator.

Joc is metaliterary, having literature as a major theme (writing, criticism, translation, the business of publication and editing are activities of focal characters or narrative voices). Though emphasizing the context of production (home or exile, freedom or prison, censored or unfettered) rather than *writing as process, Joc* nevertheless constitutes literature about literature. Unlike much postmodern metafiction, however, this novel neither flaunts its fictive condition, nor does language per se constitute a major theme. The novel falls short of being fully postmodern insofar as readers do not experience ontological plurality, instability or fluctuations, which McHale deems the essential, distinguishing characteristic of the postmodern.[11] Nor are the characters simply abstract constructs, "un conjunto de palabras" [a combination of words] as in *Fragmentos de apocalipsis* or Camilo José Cela's *Cristo versus Arizona* and *La cruz de San Andrés.* The narrator continues to be more of an observer, chronicler, and investigator than a creator of self, characters and text, and the resulting fictional characters do not lack body and/or soul (as in Cela's works, mentioned above, or his *Oficio de tinieblas*).

Also, unlike typical postmodern narratives, *Joc de miralls* employs a relatively conventional, straightforward sequence of events, following a chronological development within each of the three parts (even though Part I constitutes an "ending" for one character and Part II involves a kind of literary detective investigation into his earlier life, while Part III reconstructs that earlier life). Nor does this novel exhibit the extreme lack of plot or story line, the absence of sequentiality or connected action, the constant rewriting of events or "erasure," or the protean, shifting settings of much postmodern narrative. Whereas the unity of postmodern narrative inheres largely in the narrative perspective or viewpoint, in *Joc,* unity results from the essential connectedness of the narrative, its specular structures and "mirroring" of characters, situations, and incidents. Because the plot involves literary detective work and the unraveling of a mystery, its logic is essentially that of the detective story, which McHale terms the "epistemological genre par excellence"—the "dominant of Modernist fiction" (8–14) being epistemological. Further modernist strategies employed by Riera in *Joc* (which include traits mentioned by McHale) include multiplication—that is, mirroring, doubling, internal replication—focalization of evidence through a single consciousness, strategies of "impeded form" or dislocated chronology, and withheld or indirectly presented information. The epistemological quandaries of characters thereby transferred to readers constitute an essential of the successful mystery. McHale's repetition of elements essential to modernism includes "epistemological doubt and metalingual self-reflection" (8ff) and indefiniteness, heightened by successive interpretations by biased, underinformed, or otherwise unreliable informants, perfectly describing the situation in *Joc* and summarizing the perplexities faced by readers.

Given some readers' probable unfamiliarity with this short novel, a brief synopsis of *Joc de miralls* should facilitate understanding the critical discussion that follows. On the level of form, *Joc* proves more complex than the single extended confessional letter constituting *Qüestió de amor propi,* even though in some sense the dominant mode in both is first person and epistolary (abusing critical license, diaries may be considered letters without a known interlocutor). *Joc* comprises three unequal parts, plus a two-page epilogue, with the first part taking the form of the journal or diary of Teresa Mascaró. Entries run from 13 September 1978 to 20 November of the same year, with several gaps. Interspersed with the initial first-person journal entries (from 13 to 15–16 September) are italicized excerpts from an unidentified third-person account of Bettina Brentano's infatuation with the aged Goethe and their encounter (later, Bettina speaks in the first person, a changing perspective "mirrored" by the larger novelistic structure). Part II comprises letters written by Teresa between 12 December 1978 and 12 January 1979. Part III, mostly by another hand (or hands), represents not only a change of narrator and of narratorial gender, but of narrative genre, from the intimate, confessional feminine letter to the anguished, distanced prison diary in what becomes an unexpected—and, for Riera, unprecedented—political thriller.

In Part I, Teresa records her emotional reactions to the long-postponed encounter in Barcelona with Pablo Corbalán, a celebrated Latin American novelist and former political prisoner on whose work she has for many years been preparing a thesis. Certain exchanges in their interviews contradict data she had gathered years earlier on the writer's life and work (an easily missed clue that Corbalán may not be what [or who] he seems). Their flirtatious relationship ends abruptly with Corbalán's sudden and suspicious "suicide" on the eve of departing for an international peace conference in Madrid. Teresa agrees to become editor of his works, undertaking a trip to the late writer's homeland, the fictitious Central American republic of Itálica, to do biographical research.

Part II comprises Teresa's letters to Celia Bestard (erstwhile literary agent of Corbalán and now Teresa's, in the latter's capacity as Corbalán's editor). Initial missives describe the Caribbean capital of Calipso, its geography and culture, and especially the political climate. This section, totaling six epistles, details Teresa's frustrating quest for information on the early life, family, and pre-penal activities of her subject (she does not initially question the implications of such obscurity surrounding the background of an allegedly prominent figure). After several political impediments, bureaucratic obstacles and blind alleys, she follows up on comments recalled from her interviews with Corbalán, incongruous or contradictory references which lead her not to information on him but to the family and past history of Antonio Gallego, who coincides with Corbalán in being both a writer and a former political prisoner. With her last letter to

Celia, Teresa dispatches, via Spanish embassy diplomatic pouch, a package of papers entrusted to her by Gallego's sister, Constanza.

Part III, whose primary author or narrative consciousness appears to be Gallego (though Gallego is frequently treated in the third person), comprises Gallego's papers recounting a tangled history of clandestine activism, literary rivalry, treachery, imprisonment, torture, usurpation—of writings, mistress, and identity—betrayal and death within a larger framework of political intrigue, power struggles and manipulation of information, the media and public opinion. This section expands the "game of mirrors" begun in Part I, a mirroring that initially seemed simply a ludic literary exercise. Things are frequently not what they seem, however, and readers should not forget that in English, a "game of mirrors" connotes deception (as does "mirage"). Reflections only resemble reality, and—significantly for the narrative—essential dimensions of reality not captured within the fragment framed by the mirror are obscured or excluded from view. In the broadest sense, *Joc de miralls* continues Spanish writers' obsessive exploration of the interface between appearance and reality, while more narrowly, the novel constitutes a complex exercise in specularity, intertextual mirroring and "mirage" effects or false images, paralleling and possibly indicting the false images or disinformation purveyed by censorship, controlled media and manipulation of public opinion. The "game of mirrors" turns deadly, for not only does Corbalán die in prison while Gallego allegedly becomes a victim of poisoning (by or in spite of his "bodyguard"), but Teresa's investigations are terminated by her demise immediately after dispatching Gallego's manuscript to Celia. The latter's epilogue, dated eight years later, informs readers that Teresa perished, together with Gallego's sister Constanza and lover-cousin Gabriela, in a suspicious fire which destroyed Gallego's ancestral home.

The first instance of specularity or intertextual mirroring appears with Riera's prefatory epigraph, part of a letter from Emilia Pardo Bazán to Benito Pérez Galdós, clearly dating from a time when their love affair had begun to cool. Pardo Bazán affirms her everlasting love, obviously responding to her interlocutor's new involvement with a much younger paramour. Not surprisingly, their correspondence treats the affair somewhat metafictitiously, alluding to literary precedents or parallels in the relationship between the aged Goethe and his adolescent admirer, Bettina Brentano. The Goethe-Brentano duality provides a microcosm of the novel (or at least of the relationship[s] in Part I), constituting what Dallenbach terms "reduplication a l'infini" [infinite redoubling] (50), whereby a fragment—similar to the work containing it—links to another, also reflecting it. The concept of the admiring young fan who proffers a nubile body to the aging writer provides the key to the first specular structures or *mise en abyme.* Riera employs specularity in several ways, as the title suggests (the English translation, *Mirror Images,* omits the significant connotations of a "game" of mirrors, perhaps because the political "game" is so ruthless and deadly; the Castilian title, *Por persona interpuesta*—via an intermediary—despite being Riera's own rendering, alters the focus and thereby loses the specular connotation, thus reducing the ironic impact of the original).

As the figure of the mirror suggests, specular fiction involves narcissistic and self-reflective or self-contemplative activity. Dallenbach cites the image of Gide writing before his mirror, and Teresa's diary originates partially as a form of self-observation and analysis. Corbalán, definitely narcissistic in the pejorative sense, will ironically be supplanted by a posthumous "reflection" whose life depends on impersonating his deceased rival. The first, most highly visible set of mirror images involves the adoring young fan and famed older writer, with Bettina/Goethe being reflected by Teresa Mascaró/Pablo Corbalán (as well as the duplication in miniature constituted by Galdós and his unnamed young admirer).[12] Teresa's initial diary entry cites several coincidences and differences (13–20), reflecting on various points of similarity between herself and Bettina, such as the long wait before gaining access to the idol, obstacles encountered, the need for lying and other stratagems in order to see him. She reflects that "la meva relació amb Corbalán sembla marcada ja de bon començament per la seva amb Goethe" [my relationship with Corbalán seems marked from the outset by his with Goethe] (14), thereby providing a logical basis for later conversations between them on that topic. Five italicized passages recapitulate key aspects of the Bettina–Goethe encounter, including her difficulties in getting past the famed writer's watchdog-like secretary (mirrored in distorted form in Teresa's problems with the bodyguard). Teresa even wears a blue dress for the initial interview, conscious that Bettina had done the same; like Bettina, she suffers misgivings about her daring but later flirts shamelessly with her idol, leaving little doubt as to her erotic availability.

In both cases, the young admirer represents herself as an aspiring scholarly investigator. However, while the putative biography of Goethe, which constituted Bettina's pretext, seems to have been only a ruse, Teresa's M.A. thesis project was bona fide, having actually begun several years before, when she corresponded with Corbalán during his exile in Europe. Implicitly, Teresa equates the object of her infatuation with Goethe, and Riera establishes parallels between the two, including age, mane of white hair, weakness for intelligent young women, and a purported lack of scruples. In a sense, this duplication of relationships becomes another mirror image—one mirror reflecting another—which is repeated from the other side of the Atlantic when Teresa's quest leads her to discover Antonio Gallego and she feels herself similarly attracted to his writing and literary persona.

Teresa—recalling Corbalán's long-ago interest in Goethe—mentions the Goethe–Bettina antecedent at their second meeting, thus indicating that she considers their relationship a parallel or reflection (35). "Corbalán" (or Gallego masquerading as Corbalán) notes that Goethe never mentioned Bettina by name and affirms that Beethoven—also much taken with the young lady—wrote her letters that were more beautiful than Goethe's (ibid.). By thus attempting to undermine Goethe in the eyes of "Corbalán's" young admirer, Gallego enjoys a surrogate subversion of his rival. His introduction of Beethoven may seem needlessly pedantic, but the attentive reader already suspects that "Corbalán" was not what, or who, he seemed, that the man interviewed by Teresa must be an impersonator. Attentive readers, therefore, will correctly interpret this conversation as an attempt by the "reflection" (Gallego) to resist reduction to nothing but a mirage—that is, to affirm his own identity and defy total absorption by the persona of Corbalán. The interviewee's resistance constitutes a visible exteriorization of the plurality of identity, a constant in the writing of Riera, for whom personality is seldom if ever simple and unitary.

Another "mirror" is that of literature, reflecting life, and the relationship between life and autobiography in which the latter reflects the former (the putative novels within the text are autobiographical, meta-autobiography). Reacting to that concept in good self-reflective fashion, Teresa writes to Celia:

> tot I que moltes vegades els personatges dels llibres em captiven més que els de la vida, mai no cometria la follia de creure'm que no sóc qui sóc.

> [Despite literary characters often attracting me more than those of real life, I won't commit the folly of imagining myself to be someone I'm not.] (62)

Parts of the subsequent discussion provide a reprise of her earlier identification with Bettina Brentano and the latter's infatuation with the famed writer, an echo, reiteration, or "mirror" of previous diary entries. The "mirroring" mosaic of intertexts in *Joc* evokes literary echoes via a series of regressions comparable to the *mise en abyme,* especially in the conversations between Teresa and "Corbalán" involving readings, poetics, theory, and criticism. Dallenbach notes that the *mise en abyme* occurs as part of composition (in the form of repetition, parallels, echoes, and so on) or of the metatextual code—as poetics, aesthetic considerations, manifesto, or credo—all relatively visible and intended to provoke reflection (130). Whereas Corbalán's interest in Goethe is less firmly established (than Gallego's), Teresa's awareness of that interest antedates the substitution of Goethe's translator, Gallego, in Corbalán's identity and position. Gallego's heteronyms or additional identities constitute another example of *mise en abyme* or multiple regression. After release from prison, Gallego had spent some five years translating Goethe, producing an annotated rendering of *Poetry and Truth,* Goethe's memoirs (112–17), published under the pseudonym "Justino Ramírez." Enthusiastic reception of the translation resulted in a contract for "Ramírez" to translate Goethe's *Conversations with Eckermann,* which received a national translation prize. Gallego "arribà a Calipso per tal de recollir l'estatueta de plata I un xec per valor de cent mil pesos en nom del seu amic Justiniano Ramírez" [went to Calipso representing Ramírez, to pick up a silver statue and a check for one hundred thousand pesos] (116), receiving a draft that could be cashed only by Ramírez. Following this frustrated masquerade, and suffering self-loathing at his own fearfulness (which prevented his collecting the reward for his efforts), Gallego attempted to terminate his alter ego, Ramírez. He identified himself as the pseudonymous translator, only to find that this "mirror image" had acquired more substantial literary identity than Gallego's own: he failed to demonstrate to official satisfaction his claim to the prize and honor.

Given Gallego's apparent ineptness and supplantation by his own pseudonym, readers may wonder whether Corbalán was truly the scoundrel Gallego considers him to be and whether

Gallego is indeed the more talented. Objective opportunities to judge are lacking (not only is there no omniscient narrator, but no informed character survives to comment on the somewhat self-serving notebook comprising Part III). Teresa's interviews, however, clearly reveal a better-informed Goethe scholar than the writer with whom she previously corresponded; indeed, Gallego's depth of knowledge surprises her—the retouched photograph is superior to the original (that is, the mirage, copy or reflection surpasses "reality"). These details suggest that Gallego, alleged involuntary "ghost writer" of Corbalán's major successes, is indeed the more gifted creator and that Corbalán did plagiarize or usurp the former's work. Ironically, Corbalán thereby proves to be the "mirage," with his public persona illusory or without substance, lacking a basis in reality.

A major instance of specularity involves Corbalán and Gallego, an instance where the "game of mirrors" involves an elaborate hoax and deception. Especially relevant for applying the notion of *mise en abyme* to *Joc de miralls* is Gide's discussion of that concept, attributing to another character the same activity as that of the narrator.[13] In the lives of Corbalán and Gallego, duplication (or assumption of the same activities) becomes a "two-way mirror," with each completing a novel by the other, loving the same woman, suffering imprisonment and torture for political reasons, and finally dying at the hands of repressive, rightist regimes. Gallego—of approximately the same age, body type, education, and tastes as Corbalán—had crossed paths with him at the university where the two were vaguely acquainted and had a few common associates. Both aspiring writers, they were involved in liberal political opposition activities as members of the Radical Party during their university days. Gallego, a successful emerging journalist, was incarcerated for interrogation after an attempted coup. Despite being tortured, he refused to reveal the conspirators' names. Nevertheless, some were captured and the party expelled him, not believing that he had withstood the interrogators.

While Gallego was in jail, Corbalán took over his newspaper column (an initial usurpation of identity); he then removed Gallego's books and personal effects from the other's boarding house, presumably for safekeeping. Included among Gallego's papers was an unfinished novel which Corbalán adapted and published as his own after supplying an ending (supplantation of ownership), fortuitously achieving enormous political success when publication of the plagiarized work more or less coincided with the downfall of the dictatorship that had jailed Gallego. Not only did Corbalán steal the largely autobiographical novel (and thus usurp Gallego's success along with his personal experience), but, as a result, he began to attribute Gallego's autobiography to himself—making his biography mirror that of his rival—as implied by the biographical data that Teresa repeats in the interviews and reviews in her letters. This usurpation is double-reflected, in reverse, when—after having discovered Gallego—Teresa realizes Corbalán was referring to Antonio Gallego's life as his own during their interviews: "Em deman per què Corbalán tingué el capritx de donar-me dades de la vida de Gallego fent-les passar par seves" [I wonder why Corbalán kept giving me false clues about Gallego's life, claiming them as his own] (67). Corbalán also replaced Gallego in the affections of the latter's mistress, Blanca, a government minister's wife whose affectionately dedicated picture Corbalán found and removed from Gallego's lodgings. Given the physical and cultural resemblances between the two men, and the fact that the adulterous older beauty in the two men's lives is the same woman, their erotic liaisons also mirror each other.

Specularity extends beyond this point, for, when Gallego discovered the theft of his novel, he published a book denouncing Corbalán's plagiarism and offering detailed textual analysis of stylistic similarities (the *mise en abyme* does not require an exact reflection or "concordance," as Dallenbach explains, but may involve "discordance" [33]). The results, however, mirror (with slight distortion) the outcome of Gallego's attempt to displace his pseudonym "Ramírez" as author of the prizewinning translation: he fails, success eludes him again, and he is once more stigmatized and ridiculed. Shortly after publication of Gallego's translation of *Poetry and Truth,* Corbalán (then Itálican ambassador to Paris) published a volume of essays called *Lights and Shadows* (119–40) constituting yet another parallel between the work of the two. Thus, each man's work "mirrors" or coincides with the other's, as do their respective lives.

Over time, Gallego—originally more radically leftist than Corbalán, despite coming from a wealthier background—responded to family pressure by becoming less militant, more of a bourgeois liberal, while Corbalán found himself the target of the next rightist regime as a result of Gallego's militancy in the novel Corbalán had appropriated. Jailed, in an ironic twist of fate, unable now to disclaim authorship, Corbalán suffered torture, dying from lack of adequate medical attention (here, the mirroring refracts and distorts Gallego's first imprisonment). Again arrested following somewhat unwitting involvement in the politics of workers on his plantation, Gallego faces further torture (reflecting his own prior incarceration as well as that of his rival) and probable death. A secret offer from the government complicates the intrigue: to deflect international reaction to the death of Corbalán and conceal other human rights violations, Gallego must *become* Corbalán and complete the novel the late plagiarist began in jail. Gallego's physical resemblance to Corbalán (sufficient to qualify him as a double) had been noted by his landlady following his first imprisonment, when Señora Acosta described the man who had picked up the prisoner's belongings:

> alt com vostè, amb el mateix color de cabells. . . . El nas un poc més llarg. . . . Un tipus "guapo," amb tots els respectes, quasi diria que s'assemblen.
>
> [tall, more or less like you, the same color hair. . . . His nose was a little longer than yours. . . . A very nice looking man, if I may say so. There was a certain resemblance.] (86)

Following plastic surgery to enhance the similarity, Gallego "Es sotmès a un entrenament duríssim. Es xopa dels costums de Corbalán, dels seus gestos, de les lectures que li interessxen, del que li agrada menjar. Coneix perfectament la seva obra" [undergoes rigorous training. He absorbs Corbalán's habits, his gestures, his favorite books and meals. He has practically memorized his oeuvre] (181). Coached by experts, he studies Corbalán's biography, attitudes, and mannerisms while subordinating his own behavior patterns: he must successfully impersonate the internationally visible writer at a worldwide peace conference in exchange for his return to freedom.[14]

> Avancen els anys. Avancen I s'emporten un rostre: el bisturí manejat pel cirurgià canvia un rictus, transforma uns llavis, s'acobla a la imatge que vetlla en un retrat.
>
> [The years pass . . . and take with them a face. A face transformed by scalpels that copy a certain turn of the lips, another face's features, always in search of the image in the photograph.] (178)

The photograph here (like the one of Gallego in the newspaper, which resembles Corbalán) is another of the forms mirroring may take: Dallenbach notes that the *mise en abyme* sometimes uses allegorical pictures which summarize a story, a work of art that "mutely speaks" (73). And, while it is said that the camera does not lie, it can be fooled: makeup, disguise, angles, lighting, distances, retouching, and trick photography can produce deceptive photographs, resulting in images which, like the mirage or trompe l'oeil, do not reflect reality.

Aware that he and Corbalán are once more involuntary collaborators (as their joint writings will again appear as a single novel), Gallego reflects that "Tal volta és una mena de força estranya que els acosta I alhora els separa com si en una altra vida haguessin viscut plegats, como si haguessin estat una mateixa persona" [Perhaps there is a strange force that keeps on bringing them together just as it pushes them apart, as if they had been but one person in another life] (180)—another instance of internal duplication or *mise en abyme.* When the transformation is complete and the novel is finished, the government stages an amnesty, "releasing" Corbalán with much fanfare and publicity. Specularity reaches its extreme, with Gallego reduced to a "mirror image" of his rival,

> pendent d'un joc de miralls, sentint-se el seu doble com l'actor fracassat que s'arrisca, fent-se pasar per l'estrella en les seqüències perilloses, assumint la personalitat aliena.
>
> [depending on a mirror game, believing himself to be his double like the failed actor who takes the risks, passing himself off as the star in the dangerous sequences, assuming the other's personality.] (179)

—nothing but a skillfully prepared mirage. He assumes not only Corbalán's physical appearance but his legal identity, and Gallego's work appears once more with his rival's signature (thus "mirroring" the prior incident). The stand-in whom Teresa interviews in Barcelona, like the stunt man, eventually is robbed of his own identity, even in death. Having successfuly exploited the release of "Corbalán" for international public relations, the regime in Itálica orders the bothersome dissident assassinated under the guise of an overdose of medication. Gallego's body is buried in Barcelona under the name of his nemesis, the ultimate "mirage."

The novel abounds in metafictional elements, specifically mentioned and occasionally discussed at some length. Whereas specularity does not figure among them, Riera's Catalan title suggests her probable familiarity with the concept. It can be no accident that the archetypal situation of the famed, aging writer and his adoring youthful fan appears "mirrored" at least three times (Goethe/Bettina is echoed by Galdós and his nameless young admirer, Teresa/Corbalán and Teresa/Gallego). Furthermore, several passages in the novel suggest relevant poetics. First, Teresa speculates that her obsession with "Corbalán" results from an insatiable desire to know,

> "Força de la curiositat que engendra el coneixement. . . . Parences. Mascares. Focs d'artifici. Maquillatges. Ortopèdies. Exorcismes. Rius. Seducció del que és aparent I efímer, en funció de l'obscur reclam de les ombres."
>
> [Curiosity which engenders knowledge. But perhaps it is only masks. Appearances, trompe l'oeil, makeup, prostheses. Exorcisms, rites. The irresistible allure of that ephemeral apparition which camouflages the dark call of the shadows.] (19)

These words apply equally to Riera's text, describing both the novel as a whole as well as what Teresa encounters later in her search for Corbalán's history, which becomes the quest for restoring Gallego's identity wherein she must strip away "appearances, trompe l'oeil, makeup, prostheses."

Corbalán's description of his work could be read as a self-reflective commentary by Riera, a "mirror" of *Joc:*

> Mitjançant l'aparença de la meva escriptura, mitjançant els signes, les ambigüitats i connotacions que li ofereix el meu discurs (M'interessa seduir el lector).
>
> [The play with appearances, the ambiguous signs, the varied connotations that characterize my work are all aimed at . . . seducing (the reader.)] (23)

The significance of appearance, in its most superficial sense—and many specular images only *appear* to be what they reflect—surfaces again when "Corbalán" discusses his idea of art:

> Hom sedueix els déus a través de les mistificacions, que són la base dels ritus. . . . Allò que sedueix és sobretot la coberta, l'embocall, el signe, més no el sentit. [The gods are seduced by mystification, which is the basis of ritual. . . . What primarily attracts us is the wrapping, the cover, the symbol, much more than any deep meaning.] (24)

These words by Gallego/Corbalán convey an ironic charge, inasmuch as makeup has suppressed Gallego's own individual appearance to present the "wrapping, the cover" identified as Corbalán. Referring to his writing, Corbalán/Gallego affirms that "En *El relevo* . . . el joc és un dels principals elements. I un dels jocs és justament el de les disfresses, les màscares" [Play and games are key features of (my novel) *Relay,* which is precisely why costumes and masks are so prominent] (27), again insinuating deception. Although the ludic aspect is more visible in Part I, disguise is crucial throughout, making this self-reflective commentary fully applicable to Riera's text. Yet another statement with both political and literary double resonances appears near the end of the interview:

> els inquisidors, els tirans, els dictadors es creuen en possessió de la veritat, i la veritat no existeix . . . l'única possibilitat d'amagar la seva inexistència és mitjançant les aparences, les imatges.
>
> [inquisitors, tyrants, and dictators believe themselves in possession of the tuth, but the truth does not exist, there are only appearances, mirages to soften its non-existence.] (29)

In their next interview, Teresa and Corbalán/Gallego discuss

> "el punt de vista d'*El relevo,* sempre canviant, la utilització dels miralls, una constant al llarg de la novel.la que ens amplia les possibilitats dels angles de visió, però que alhora ens ofereix tots els paranys dels reflexos."
>
> [the ever-changing point of view in *Relay,* the constant use of mirrors which multiply the angles of vision and trap us in a tangle of false reflections.] (32–33)

These words leave no doubt that Riera's manipulation of specular structures is conscious and deliberate. Nevertheless, mirrors per se (as object or artifact) seldom appear in *Joc,* although they assume greater prominence in some of Riera's other works, where their functions are both literal and symbolic or metaphorical. One prior work in which Riera's use of the mirror as artifact or symbol and of mirroring techniques appears fairly complex is *Qüestió de amor propi* (1987). Narcissism is a major theme, and the major characters mirror each other's weaknesses and self-love (the narrator becomes a mirror of masculine desire in this essentially feminist text). The complex network of specular devices in *Joc de miralls* constitutes a logical extension of earlier experimentation with mirror tropes.

Riera does not allude specifically to Bakhtin or the concept of the carnivalesque, but disguise and pseudo-identities assume sufficient prominence to show that masks and disguise figure as significant motifs in the writer's mind. Disguise can be carnivalesque and ludic or sinister, or it can assume both faces simultaneously; to some degree, Riera's probe of the consequences of disguise for the identity of the disguised touches on all these. One relevant passage refers to Gallego's translation of Goethe's memoirs, *Poetry and Truth.* Gallego

> meravelava el seu enginy per trobar per a cada situació la disfressa més adient. Els dés sempre havien davallat a la terra disfressats, recordava Goethe a les *Memòries,* quan escrivia que amb vestits grollers, quasi esdernegats, d'estudiant pobre acompanyà el seu amic . . . i com després tornà a canviar aquelles per les de diumenge d'un pagès. 'Una màscara en porta una altra', es justifica a *Poesia I veritat*perquè desitja agradar a Frederic fent-se passar per algú que a ella li pot caure bé.
>
> [was awed by the way Goethe ingeniously came up with the most appropriate disguise for each unique situation. . . . Goethe recalls in his memoirs that the gods always wore costumes when visiting the earth. Later, perhaps because one mask often leads to another, Goethe changed those clothes for the garb of a country rustic in his Sunday best. He liked to woo Friederike pretending to be somebody else. . . .] (114)

Goethe's disguises and apocryphal identities or role-playing—yet another specular device—call attention to the key role of these motifs in the Corbalán/Gallego narrative, but the ludic aspect present in Goethe's disguise disappears when Gallego assumes the identity of Corbalán. As he works on the translation of Goethe's memoirs, various instances of dramatic anticipation permit the past—via his comments on Goethe's life—to "mirror" Gallego's future, for example, "es sap portador d'una maledicció. Tal vegada per això, perquè desitja que aquesta no s'acompleixi, vol fer-se passar per un altre" [knowing he had been cursed by fate, and perhaps hoping to fool fate, he tried to be taken for another man] (115). Dallenbach specifically mentions anticipation as a special instance of internal duplication (28–29). Similarly, certain passages relevant to annotating Goethe's memoirs could be lifted verbatim as *autocrítica* or description of *Joc,* for example, Goethe's delight in costumes, masks, doubles, evident in *Poetry and Truth,* which Gallego considered a motif of great importance (ibid.). These and similar concepts, repeatedly pointing to important motifs in *Joc de miralls,* suggest that Riera has consciously incorporated disguise, masks, and doubling within this novel's poetics. Another passage, synthesizing part of Goethe's memoirs, describes an encounter

> per un senderol i de sobte, no amb els ulls de la carn, sinó amb els de l'esperit, contempla un cavall igual que el seu i que ell mateix munta. En creuar-se amb la seva pròpia figura s'adona que és més vell i estrena un vestit gris, galonejat d'or.

> [suddenly along a path, with eyes not of the flesh but the spirit, he saw a horse identical to his own which he himself was riding. Upon comparing, he realized that he was older, but wearing the same coat with gold buttons, and recognized his own, if slightly aged, face.] (113)

The incident provides a ghostly anticipation of another journey Goethe would make eight years later (mentioned elsewhere in the text). Further discussion of the double constitutes yet another instance of specularity in *Joc,* inasmuch as Gallego is/becomes the double of Corbalán. Gallego's "shadow double" or pseudonymous identity as Ramírez offers another case in point.

Some instances of mirroring are true miniatures by virtue of their brevity (what Dallenbach calls "reduplication simple" or fragments similar to the larger work), as, for example, the grotesque mirroring of past infancy and domestic felicity when the now mature Gallego's aged mother, apparently a victim of advanced Alzheimer's disease or senile dementia, undergoes maternal regression; she

> Volia que Lucía donés de mamar, en presència seva, a Antonio per tal d'examinar si la llet de la qual es nodria era suficient. I com que tothom intentava treure-li del cap aquella obsessió, reaccionava amb uns plors desconsolats assegurant que tots volien la mort del seu fill.

> [demanded that Lucía breastfeed Antonio in her presence in order to check if he was getting enough milk. When people attempted to distract her from this obsession, she reacted with disconsolate sobbing, insisting that they were seeking to starve her baby to death.] (109)

Dallenbach points out that the "reflection" may be reversible, antithetical or complementary (49); it need not be identical, and may also "oscillate." The hallucinations of Gallego's mother offer such an oscillating or antithetical reflection. Another episode which mirrors a comparable, earlier moment in Gallego's life (but does so faithfully, exactly) involves his defense mechanism for escape from the reality of imprisonment and torture by conjuring up the loving image of his mistress, first Blanca, then Gabriela:

> Blanca era un punt de claror, una llumenera que deixava anar la petita flama blavosa, suficient per espantar la tenebra de la cel.la.
>
> [Blanca was a point of light, the luminosity of a little flame that sufficed to overcome the darkness of his cell.] (70)
>
> La paraula ressonant aquí a la cel.la, més que un nom, el nom de Blanca que el salvà en aquella altra cel.la . . . el nom-amulet o el de Gabriela, pedra foguera en les seves nits.
>
> [The resounding word here in the cell, more than a name, Blanca's name that saved him in that other cell, the amulet-name of Gabriela, firestone glowing in his darkest nights.] (174)

Gallego's fantasizing about his post-prison reunion with Blanca is grotesquely mirrored by the reality of his landlady's crude attempt at seduction after Blanca has abandoned him (99–101). He views Señora Acosta's sexual innuendos as a "parody" (imitation, degraded reflection) of his feelings for Blanca, especially as he ironically reflects on the governmental proclamation of women's equality (101).

On the level of rhetoric, also, Riera subliminally emphasizes doubles and doubling. For instance, even before his arrest and second imprisonment, long before the "official" supplantation, Gallego is haunted by the image of Corbalán:

> A estones són uns ulls del mateix color que els seus, molt més acerats, però que el persegueixen sense pertànyer a cap rostre; d'altres el que veu és un immens ocell, una mena de paó amb les plomes estufades I una garlanda de llorer envoltant-li el coll, que intenta envestirlo . . . el rostre del qual es concreta en la fesomia de Pablo Corbalán.
>
> [At times eyes the same color as his, but more steely, pursue him from a faceless void. At others he is chased by an enormous peacock

with fanned-out tail and wearing a laurel wreath that tries to attack him . . . a peacock whose face takes on the specific features of Pablo Corbalán's.] (118)

These comparisons and reminders of similarity/identity implicitly strengthen perceptions of Gallego as a mirror image of Corbalán. After Gallego's failed attempt to have himself recognized as the bona fide translator of the prizewinning edition of Goethe, the *Diario de Venusia,* "el més important de la ciutat, aconseguí que sortís la seva fotografia, una fotografia que l'afavoria malgrat accentuar la seva semblanç amb Corbalán" [the city's most influential paper publishes a flattering picture of him which accentuates his physical resemblance to Corbalán] (134). Similarly, Gallego's thoughts, conveyed by free indirect discourse, reinforce the notion of doubling before the fact: "En el fons no sabia si el seu odi anava dirigit contra Corbalán o era ell mateix" [Deep down, he was unsure whether his hatred of Corbalán was real or if it was self-hatred] (119). Although he knows his nemesis to be a plagiarist and a snob, Gallego envies Corbalán's success and self-confidence. Riera presents this sentiment via rhetoric which ironically anticipates (even though it negates) the future doubling or supplantation: Gallego "envejava el fet que Corbalán no hagués volgut deixar d'esser Corbalán. Ben al contrari, havia volgut ésser part d'Antonio Gallego, la millor part, robant-li . . ." [he envied Corbalán because he had never ceased to be himself. Instead, he had appropriated parts of Gallego, always the best part, robbing him] (112).

One key incident is *not* doubled: Gallego, fleeing after the awards ceremony for the translation prize, encounters Corbalán and silently acquiesces when invited to dinner. By the end of the evening, however, revolted by his rival's smugness, he forces a showdown and hits Corbalán in the face, knocking him down and breaking two front teeth (129–30), subsequently repaired by a renowned dentist in Paris. This dental work later enables Celia Bestard (recipient of Teresa's six letters from Itálica, as well as of Gallego's notebooks) to confirm Teresa's discovery that the man buried as Corbalán in Barcelona is *not* Corbalán, thereby exposing the hoax and ultimately bringing about the fall of the regime some eight years later, as detailed in the Epilogue (187–88). Gallego's unpremeditated (and perhaps, therefore, more genuine, authentic) act thus results in posthumous recuperation of his true identity.

History repeats itself, and such repetition constitutes further reflections or mirror episodes, as with the three coups that occur over the course of Gallego's narrative: "Altra vegada, la vegada vint-i-sisena des que Itàlica aconseguí la independència, una fracció de l'exèrcit s'alçava" [for the twenty-sixth time since Itálica became an independent nation, a faction of the Army revolted] (141). Following his mother's death, Gallego begins to write a fictionalized autobiography, another mirror:

> Intentava bastir un món de ficció perquè volia explicar-se el real i el probable d'uns personatges que s'assemblaven tant als que havia conegut que forçosament, si algun dia aquell escrit sortia a la llum pública no li quedaria més remei que disfressar-los.
>
> [He tried to create a fictional world because he wanted to explain the real one and the probable motivations of characters who so resembled those he had known that, if the book ever saw the light, he would have no choice but to disguise them.] (142)

The characters provide a means of self-analysis, mirroring his obsessions: "li serviren d'excusa per trobar-se com en un mirall amb el restre de les seves obsessions que era, tanmateix, bien igual que el seu" [they allowed him to find himself, as in a mirror, facing those obsessions whose visages were exactly the same as his own] (142). So successful is Riera's game of mirrors that the most careful reader will be baffled upon attempting to ascertain exactly what was "real" or genuine in Corbalán's life and works and what belonged to his "reflection." Gallego, though reduced to a mirage, the appearance of Corbalán, paradoxically appears to have more substance than the image he reflects.

Tempting as it may be to conclude that Riera's dazzling tour de force in exploiting specular structures is an end in itself ("the medium is the message"), certain things remain unexplained by such a conclusion. One is Riera's unprecedented use of a Latin American setting, albeit fictitious, which does not necessarily imply intended critique of a given Spanish American regime. Equally plausible is the oblique allusion to totalitarian regimes generally or to Spain's late rightist dictatorship, as certain early stories suggest, for example, "D'un temps, d'uns ulls" [About a Time, About Some Eyes] in *Je pos per testimoni,* whose dedication includes the words *en homenatge i memòria als assassinats per la dictadura feixista:* [In homage and memory of those assassinated by the fascist dictatorship] (21). Riera's sally into a new subgenre, the political thriller or novel of international intrigue, might simply be further experimentation with "paraliterary" forms, an extension of her ventures into the detectivesque. Harder to explain are certain aspects of *Joc de miralls,* which are not mirrored and thus lack aesthetic justification, specifically the theme of governmental manipulation of public opinion and political use of disinformation on a global scale. Once the specular images have been exposed, the latter remains as the most "real," perhaps the only, reality.

Notes

1. *Por persona interpuesta* (literally, Via an Intermediary [Person]—or "By Proxy") accurately denotes the process of transmission of the narrative "facts" as well as of the novel-within-the novel, but loses the ironic charge of the Catalan title (as well as the significant specular image). It does introduce a different ironic dimension, which may have appealed to Riera, who usually does her own versions in Castilian. Although I initially had access to the very competent English rendering, *Mirror Images,* translated by Cristina de la Torre (New York: Peter Lang, 1993), in the Catalan Studies Series, I have chosen not to use that title because it, too, loses the ironic charge of the Catalan original—the notion of "game" is part of an essential double entendre.

Also, translations into English of the Catalan citations in the text are largely my own, because de la Torre rendered meaning on a macro-level, sometimes far removed from literal translation of specific words or sentences. I have tried to adhere more closely to the wording of the passages cited.

2. There is no exact Castilian counterpart to these two collections, although *Palabra de mujer* (1980) contains, in a single volume, twenty-four of the thirty stories from *Te deix, amor . . .* and *Je pos per testimoni les gavines.*

3. Johnson provides one of the most sensitive readings, "Voice and Intersubjectivity in Carme Riera's Narratives," in *Critical Essays on the Literature of Spain and Spanish America,* ed. Luis González del Valle and Julio Baena (Boulder: Society for Spanish and Spanish American Studies, 1991), 153–59. Riera herself is forthcoming, as seen in the especially useful interview with Neus Aguado, "Epístolas de mar y de sol: Entrevista con Carme Riera," *Quimera* 57 (1991):32–37.

4. For fuller treatment of the search-for-self theme by a leading feminist critic, see Elizabeth Ordónez, *Voices of Their Own: Contemporary Spanish Narrative by Women* (Lewisburg: Bucknell University Press, 1991).

5. In her "The Paradox of Narrative Seduction in Carme Riera's *Cuestión de amor propio,*" *Hispania* 75 (1992):281–86, Tsuchiya proposes a reading that accords with Riera's numerous erotic texts.

6. Dallenbach's use of the term—not his invention but taken from Gide, who adopted the device from heraldry (whose artisan surely did not invent the crest, etc.)—illustrates another aspect of the concept of regression. See *Le reçit speculaire* (Paris: Editions du Seuil, 1977).

7. Found in Jacques Lacan, *Ecrits* (Paris: Editions du Seuil, 1966).

8. The principle of "infinite regression" exemplified by a series of opposing mirrors reflecting each other, as employed by Jacques Derrida, appears in *De la Grammatologie* (Paris: Editions du Minuit, 1967). In *Dissemination,* Derrida

refers to "écriture en abîme" and equates it with "l'écriture au carré" (297), writing raised by self-reflectivity to the second power (cf. Dallenbach, 216).

9. See Tvetzan Todorov, *Littérature et signification* (Paris: Larousse, 1967).

10. Found in Todorov's *Poétique de la Prose* (Paris: Editions du Seuil, 1971).

11. See Brian McHale, *Postmodernist Fiction* (New York and London: Methuen, 1987). Riera's readers do not ask "Which world is this?" for she does not completely destabilize her literary world or present paradoxes and inconsistencies without any identifiable center of consciousness, or treat space so as to disorient readers (further characteristics attributed by McHale [18–21] to postmodern fiction).

12. Another relevant intertextual mirror relationship—not mentioned by Riera, as is that of Goethe and Bettina—involves the couple in Unamuno's *Tulio Montalbán y Julio Maceda*. This "mirror" reflects a slightly different angle; but, again, a younger woman becomes enamored of the aura of glory surrounding a man she has never seen, a Latin American revolutionary political hero, and again, readers witness a "game" of changing identities, reflected or refracted from the angle of one man with two identities rather than that of two men sharing a single identity, as in *Joc*.

13. André Gide, *Journal, 1899–1939*. Paris: Gallimard, 1948, 229–30, 241.

14. The most illustrious antecedent wherein a Spanish novelist has studied governmental disinformation, censorship, and manipulation of public opinion appears in Francisco Ayala's *Muertes de perro* (1958) and its sequel, *El fondo del vaso* (1962), novels which—despite numerous differences vis-à-vis *Joc*—also involve political dissent or revolution, writers (or would-be writers), imprisonment, and questions of identity.

Textual Desire, Seduction, and Epistolarity in Carme Riera's "Letra de ángel" and "La seducción del genio"

MARY S. VÁSQUEZ

> La carta no es más que un diálogo aplazado . . .
>
> [A letter is only a deferred dialogue. . . .]
> Carme Riera, interview with Neus Aguado, 1991

AMONG THE NINETEEN METAFICTIONAL TALES COMPRISING CARME Riera's 1991 short story collection *Contra el amor en compañía y otros relatos* (Against Love with a Partner And Other Tales), two are epistolary narratives reflecting the Majorcan author's ongoing cultivation of this literary form little favored in Spanish letters. Both stories revolve around the generation and expression of textual desire and the process of textual seduction. I propose to examine here the discourse of textual desire and seduction, and the dialogic interchange between the two, in the stories "Letra de ángel" [An Angel's Handwriting] and "La seducción del genio" [The Seduction of Genius]. My discussion will further address the creation by a female author of both male- and female-gendered voice. In both cases, I will employ the Castilian Spanish version of the story rather than the Catalan original, because of the substantial alteration of the stories in their Castilian reworking, a topic addressed by Kathleen Glenn in her interview with Riera which appears in the opening section of this volume, "In Her Own Voice." The question of profound differences between Riera's Catalan and Castilian short story texts was broached as well by Geraldine Nichols in an earlier substantive interview, included in her 1989 book, *Escribir, espacio propio* [Writing, One's Own Space].[1] A side-by-side analysis of Riera stories in the Catalan original and in their Castilian version would be another critical undertaking, one especially needed in the field of Riera studies, due to the author's apparent reticence with regard to this topic.

In European literature, as well as in that of the Americas, the epistolary form is normally associated with women's literature and has been an important mode of expression within it. In patriarchal societies, correspondence was traditionally one of the few literary avenues open to women, whose writing was most properly confined to the personal and intimate instead of ranging into the public arena. Epistolary literature does, in fact, duplicate fictively the intimacy of actual correspondence. It has, implicitly, a dialogic base. It is in the communicative exchange between sender and addressee that narrative interest lies. To the implied reader of epistolary literature is assigned the role of voyeur who witnesses and judges this game for two. The reader's role, then, is one of transgression of a fictively private narrative space. In the two Riera stories considered here, there is also authorial transgression of a certain epistolary convention: the female-authored letter of spurned or betrayed love. Yet here, Riera inverts that pattern in the first story to be considered, offering the reader, in "Letra de ángel," a female-authored text with an embedded, internal male author who complains of female abandonment or betrayal. The second story, "La seducción del genio," features a re-gendered author of an epistolary text who is newly female following sex-change surgery, an author whose ambiguity of gender identity creates a dialogic space in which male and female, appeal and rejection, tactic and countertactic cross and re-cross, calling into question reader assumptions about gender.

"Letra de ángel," a tale of a thwarted desire and an all-too-successful seduction, presents a series of what I call "narrative" or "textual transgressions": unwitting violations by the story's protagonist of the conventions of a particular epistolary form. The driving narrative force of the tale is the tension and the distance between two discourses and two Spains. Don Ramón Vendrell Macià, a seventy-eight-year-old blacksmith from the Catalonian town of Tortosa, receives a promotional letter from a Barcelona company. Believing this form letter to be directed to him personally, Vendrell replies to its signator, one Olga Macià, supposing her interested in his person. Don Ramón's correspondence with "Olga Macià," consisting of subsequent commercial offers to don Ramón and his responses to them, culminates in his visit to corporate headquarters in search of the signator of the promotional mailings.

The three letters of offer and the four letters written by don Ramón belong to two mutually exclusive discourses. The communicative process is initiated with a typical advertising letter made up of stock phrases and flattering references and sprinkled with appeals to a regional pride in Catalonia, which the company knows to be salable.

> Estimado amigo: Me dirijo a vd. porque me consta que es una persona a quien le interesa la Cultura Catalana y que en más de una ocasión ha demostrado su patriotismo.
> Sé también que es una persona generosa dispuesta a colaborar en la tarea de normalización lingüística, asunto importantísimo para Cataluña, que nos afecta a todos, no sólo a las Instituciones.
> Es por esto por lo que quiero ofrecerle la posibilidad de adquirir con un estupendo descuento *La Gran Historia de la Sardana* en tres volúmenes.
> Una obra escrita, precisamente pensando en personas como vd., por importantes especialistas.
>
> [Dear Friend: I am writing to you because I know you to be a person interested in Catalan Culture who has demonstrated his patriotism on more than one occasion.
> I know, too, that you are a generous person disposed to cooperate in the task of linguistic normalization, a highly important matter which affects us all, not only our Institutions.
> It is for this reason that I wish to offer you the opportunity to acquire, at a wonderful discount, The Great History of the Sardana Dance in three volumes.
> This is a work written by important specialists, precisely with persons like you in mind.][2]

Don Ramón receives this text but reads another, superimposing on the commercial discourse of the offer a discourse very much his own. In his reinvention of the letter, in receiving it as a text and discourse which it distinctly is not, Vendrell commits his first narrative transgression. The distance between the discourse of the offer and the one he believes he is reading measures the marginalization of this protagonist. It is a distance of generation and period, of socioeconomic class, and of ideology.

Upon reading the salutation "Dear Friend" and the final sentence of the company's initial letter, "Reciba mis saludos amistosos" [With friendly greetings] (24), Vendrell is not equipped to see in them the formula of courtesy, the mechanical phrase neutralized by repetition and context. Since he has not moved in the business world and, in all likelihood, has never received such a letter in the past—his social circumstances would not make him the predictable recipient of one—he interprets the expressions literally. Coming from a context in which such words did mean what they seemed to say, he personalizes the discourse of the advertising letter. A friend is precisely that; the term connotes intimacy, confidence. The allusion to his proven patriotism to his region confirms his supposition that the sender knows him and may indeed be a relative. Seeing himself addressed in terms of familiarity, don Ramón is incapable of seeing the machinations behind the letter. He cannot know that these sentences are not generated by sentiment, personal by its very nature, but, rather, by techniques of mass marketing, the maximum depersonalization. The cold calculation of any publicity campaign is made greater here, for this one has as its object the fixed-income retiree, who is ably manipulated to nurture in him a belief that he belongs to the new Spain, so different from the one he knew. As a capstone, the ad letter broaches the topic of "linguistic normalization," a term widely employed in Catalonia today to refer to the use, cultivation, and promotion of the Catalan language. Ironically, the promotion also pretends to incorporate the recipient into this process on an individual basis. It is significant that access to the New Spain is here to be gained through a sale; it carries, then, a monetary value. The objects offered in the series of advertising letters received by Vendrell—The Great History of the Sardana Dance, in three volumes, a luxury alarm clock, a gold rose—are beyond the means of the retiree of modest means, not to mention the utter uselessness for a retired worker of the second and third items. The offers, then, are markers of distance and, hence, of marginalization. They evoke, and appeal to, a free-spending, consumer Spain enamored of the plastic credit card. (When don Ramón receives his prize, a small figure of the Virgin of Montserrat, he alludes in his next letter to the "reproducción en plástico—materia que no me gusta mucho" [reproduction in plastic—a material I don't much like]) (29). To the "easy money" mentality of today's Western world is counterposed Vendrell's concept of finance; he has the by now totally antiquated notion that one does not spend what one does not have. When he does decide to buy the alarm clock, he makes the purchase with savings he had kept in a piggy bank. Moreover, he buys as a gesture of compliance; he wishes to please the Olga Macià who has signed the advertising letters but who has not answered his personal replies. More than a manipulation in turn, the acquisition of the alarm clock is a bridge purchase between his Spain—that of the modest, elderly manual laborer—and the new Spain: young, modern, cosmopolitan. Don Ramón admits the possibility that access to this New Spain may carry a price, one he is willing to pay this once and hence for all, since his means do not permit more. This supposition of his possible access is, indeed, the protagonist's second textual transgression.

In addition to the distance generated by economic circumstance and age, the discourse employed by don Ramón contains an implicit ideology, while that of the offers lacks one—or, better said, its ideology is the profit motive. Responding to what he supposes to be a personalized allusion to his patriotism, he remembers: "Yo me exilié por defender mis ideas y a pie, con los zapatos rotos, no en coche como otros, pasé la frontera el 26, de madrugada" [I passed into exile to defend my ideas and on foot, in wornout shoes, not by car like some others, I crossed the border (into France) on the 26th, at dawn] (25). The protagonist's recall of the deeply moving crossing of the Pyrenees by hundreds of Spanish Republicans, in bitter cold, into French exile at the end of 1938, in the final months of the Spanish Civil War, suggests to him his possible blood link to "Olga Macià":

> ¿No resultará que usted es hija de mi primo Pere? Herrero como yo, el pobre. Se quedó en Francia, pero le recuerdo mucho, porque estuvimos juntos en Argelers.
>
> [Isn't it possible that you are the daughter of my cousin Pere? He was a blacksmith like me, poor man. He stayed behind in France, but I remember him often, because we were together in Argelers.] (25)

This is one of two references in Vendrell's letters to the time spent in Argelers; there, too, don Ramón taught some comrades from Madrid to dance the Sardana. The memory evokes the sense of shared mission, of struggle for a cause, which in its best moments, if rarely at the level of official politics, joined the Republican companions, bridging their regional differences. The blacksmith belongs to the Spain defeated in the war, repressed and punished for the transgression of its democratic aspirations.

Don Ramón asks indulgence several times for his lack of skill in written communication, his few years of formal schooling. Nevertheless, his true incapacity lies not in writing but in reading. He does not know how to read Olga Macià's letters. He reads one discourse; the letter is written in another. His lack of knowledge is a metaphorical one. He has not mastered the discourse—

the multiple discourses—of the New Spain, which, in some senses, has no room for him. Ironically so, since the democracy would seem to be, in some measure, a re-vindication of his sacrifice, his struggle a half-century earlier, the silencing of Republican Spain throughout the long Franco years. Despite this very legitimate, possible expectation on the character's part, don Ramón is marginalized from all directions: as an elderly person, as a retiree of modest means, but also as a Civil War veteran in a Spain which believes that it did not initiate the tragic fratricide of generations past from which it would seek distance. One of the tactics of distancing from the Civil War on the part of young Spain has been, precisely, trivialization; don Ramón is an antique in a culture which, by 1979, displayed in toystore windows a new Civil War board game (You too can play at war.) Finally, don Ramón is marginalized as a Republican of conviction in a Spain which not only wishes to move beyond the war and the eternal dictatorship but which also represents for many a considerable distance from the ideals surrounding the Second Republic of the early 1930s.

When the protagonist, now a widower, goes to corporate headquarters in Barcelona to pay a visit to Olga Macià and request an accounting for her silence, he commits his ultimate narrative transgression, this time one in which textual space has become physical. Vendrell is told that there is no such person, that the name is an invented one. The sign which he had endowed with deeply personal meaning turns out to connote anonymity, an anonymity worsened by the attempts of a receptionist to calm the elderly man by inviting him to have a cold drink in the depersonalized name of "la empresa" [the company] (34). That his dreamed-of relative—and, later, dreamed-of love interest—should not only prove to be no such thing, but, more than that, nonexistent, infuriates don Ramón. He feels deceived, ridiculed. He is right, of course; the attempt to exploit a group of retired laborers—a company representative confirms the advertising campaign's intent—inciting them to buy luxury items is to take cruel advantage of their vulnerability and reduce the value of their lives to the contents of a piggy bank, or, lacking that, to nothingness. The object of don Ramón's anger, however, is not the company or, less still, the New Spain. His fury is directed at Olga Macià, whose play of texts and silences has finally been resolved in the nonexistence which serves as culmination of the protagonist's marginalization. His absolute aloneness was, in fact, prefigured in the first advertising letter: "Y si prefiere darse un pequeño gusto, regáleselo a usted mismo. Nadie se lo agradecerá tanto." [And if you wish to treat yourself, give yourself (the books) as a gift. No one will appreciate (them) more.] (24)

The invective the retired blacksmith hurls into the air is the only vengeance he knows. "Zorra, mala pécora, ¿por qué no has querido verme? Bruja, cara de sapo. Mentirosa." [Whore . . . , why have you refused to see me? Witch, toadface. Liar.] (34). The whore lies at the opposite pole from the angel evoked in the story's title in a reflection of the saint/whore paradigm—elucidated so compellingly with respect to nineteenth-century literature by Gilbert and Gubar in their *The Madwoman in the Attic*—, which is still another marker of the distance between generations despite the persistence in our times of the paradigm in at least residual form. Irony is present in the fact that for most of the new generation, terms of insult and invective have lost their earlier meaning (precisely as has the term *friend* for the company in "Letra de ángel") as part of the break from the puritanism of the Franco years and have been retextualized in jokes and greetings between friends.

The story opens and closes with the same negative words—"whore," "witch"—to enclose don Ramón, who lives on *la calle Esperanza*, Hope Street, in his town of Tortosa, in a cycle of marginalization and impotence. What has happened to don Ramón Vendrell Macià has to do with two counterposed and mutually incompatible discourses of desire. A distance of incommunication stretches between the two discourses, within each of which is created a tension between desire and the potential for its realization. The communicative process is essentially different for the corporation and for the humble blacksmith. For the company, the object of the communicative process is the generation of an acquisitive desire and its subsequent manifestation in the purchase of the article. The prospective client responds either with silence or with money. In either case, the communicative process is complete, and a client's option for purchase of one of three products offered constitutes an advertising success. This client's name will remain in the computer program, and he will continue to receive offers, as occurs here. Hence, in reaching closure, the communicative process achieves aperture as well.

The company's offers inspire in the blacksmith a distinct desire: for a love, a hope to brighten his last years of life. Because this desire is unfulfilled, with don Ramón's repeated initiatives meeting a wall of silence, for him, the communicative process is truncated, incomplete—a perception quite different from that held by the company's computers. Fulfillment of don Ramón's very human desire proves much more problematical than the simple acquisition of a product, and the discourse of desire—a desire for connection with which the protagonist responds to the texts he believes he has read—ends in abject failure. He has transgressed the boundaries of commercial textual anonymity. An incompetent reader of the texts generated by the company, don Ramón proves a highly adept fabulizer. Upon misreading the received text, he initiates an imaginative labor of precision and invention: precision in attempting to re-endow words with the meanings they once had and invention in creating an incompetent new text. In gifting the letters' signer, maximally anonymous in her nonexistence, with an identity particularized in relation to his own person, don Ramón creates literature. The implied reader watches the character reader read; the character reader, in turn, imagines another character—who turns out not to exist—reading. With the impossibility of fulfillment of his textual desire revealed, the blacksmith and his discourse of desire end in defeat and impotence, which, at last, constitute closure.

In her *Extravagant Narratives* (1990), Elizabeth J. MacArthur examines the genesis of epistolary fiction in seventeenth-century European manuals of instruction in the art of letter writing, finding that such manuals often included brief narrative sequences. The step from epistolarity to fictional narrative is a natural one, as MacArthur observes: "Any letter already involves some of the essential elements of narrative: at least two characters, the writer and the addressee, and some sort of relationship between them. In order for a group of letters to form a narrative, this relationship must be prolonged and transformed in time."[3] MacArthur adds that, although such manuals quite naturally include models of numerous epistolary forms, "virtually all of the miniature narratives that develop arise out of love letters."[4] In "Letra de ángel," such a narrative "relationship" does develop as a discourse of desire in which that desire itself gives voice to—invents—a responding desire to create a fictional reciprocity. Vendrell's transgression of the code of corporate advertising yields the inevitable de-voicing of the reciprocal desire he has invented and the re-voicing, in humiliation and fury, of his own. An ongoing narrative tension between aperture and closure is the vehicle for such voicing, de-voicing, and re-voicing.

In this sadly humorous tale, Riera creates, on the one hand, a nuanced play of multiple voices and voicings, and on the other, silences and silencings. The question of gender in the matter of character and narrative voice is a pivotal one, subtly and playfully employed by Riera to subvert both societal and epistolary conventions. As an epistolary exchange protagonized by a male character, product of the pen of a female author, "Letra de ángel" is an example of cross-gender epistolary narration, what James Carson terms "narrative cross-dressing," in which an author of one gender creates a letter-writer of the other.[5] Here, a female author has created a male voice which is directed at an invented female, as, indeed, the male world historically has invented the female to its need and liking. In making the female be the voice that minimalizes, that enunciates a formulaic response, Riera performs a neat reversal of the classic paradigm. And then, in "revealing" what the reader has suspected all along regarding Olga Macià's nonexistence, to the surprise only of Vendrell, Riera continues her play, reminding us that the male-invented female has always proven elusive precisely because she was the product of a pre-cast mold, directed to articulate a male-authored script.

And yet, exclusionary societal discourse, at whose margins Vendrell finds himself, in uncomprehending mystification that becomes rage, is employed in the promotional correspondence specifically because of his marginalization. Advertising finds its market in the marginalized, those who wish to belong, to gain access to a world at which they believe they gaze from without. Vendrell's response subtly subverts, even as it rewards and perpetuates, the discourse of product promotion; in personalizing discourse, he deflects attention from product acquisition to human warmth and companionship.

In this Riera story, a male character is cast in a frequent and familiar female societal role. Vendrell is excluded from broader societal discourse through his membership in all but one (the Catalan, to which I will return) of the groupings to which he might be considered to belong: the elderly, the humble, the Civil War veteran in an age that wants to forget the ideological struggle, the sacrifice, and the camaraderie still so immediate to him. His multiple marginalization identifies Vendrell with the dilemma of female voicing and silence. The character's concerns are minimalized; the response to his own discourse is formulaic. His is the personalized voice that shares confidences and seeks intimacy. In the story's epistolary exchange, Riera plays with concepts, traditions, and patterns of gender voicing. The male character, Vendrell, is both destinataire of a masculinized female voice (the corporate, generic self which bears no correspondence to reality extratextual to the letter; a simulacrum) and subject of male voicing of (an invented) female object. It is in the space between these mutally nonexistent realities that the story occurs.

Vendrell's Catalan identity—the articulation of which is the lone societal discourse that might include him—serves Riera for another playful consideration of marginalization. In appealing to the blacksmith's regional and cultural identity—a highly politicized discourse in Catalonia today—the promotional material evokes in Vendrell memories of his sacrifices for Catalonia in the Civil War and, significantly, of a context in which Catalan self-identification was less exclusivist, as in Vendrell's anecdote of the Catalan soldiers' teaching the regional Sardana dance to comrades from Madrid. They all danced together, a phenomenon which has about it a flavor of antiquity given not only the long Francoist suppression of Catalan language and other cultural expressions but also the exclusivist politico-linguistic context of today, whose extremes Riera has criticized in the interview with Kathleen Glenn, included in the present volume. Through the genuineness of Vendrell's response to the advertising appeal to his pride in Catalan identity, Riera seems to gently mock the Catalanist linguistic hegemony of the present moment, which would trade the imperialism of a Castilian Spanish for that of Catalan, one hegemony for another.

Finally, Riera's treatment of the promotional letters and deeply personal responses offers a commentary on the arbitrariness of language. Advertising language is arguably the most arbitrary of discourses, its formulas varying little, its codes fixed, its register placed at a particular setting. It is unidirectional, commodifying—as women have often felt themselves to be commodified. The discourse of advertising is, paradoxically, at once open and closed, its enunciation a complete linguistic act, not to be countered or nuanced by a response, yet open because there is no interlocutor and, hence, no completion or closure. Paradoxically, too, it is that most depersonalized of discourses, rendered often in the discourse of familiarity and even intimacy.

Throughout "Letra de ángel," there is a tension between a (personalized and personalizing) private writing self and a public written self, inviting to reception and response—a reception and response problematized, annulled at the base, since the destinataire is, quite literally, nonexistent. So, too, have women frequently found their speaking and spoken selves unheard, their writing and written selves unread. In her preface to the present volume, Riera tells of a day spent on Ramblas Boulevard in Barcelona, at a bookseller's table. She stood behind tall stacks of copies of her first book, the short story collection *Te deix, amor, la mar com a penyora* [I Leave You, My Love, the Sea as a Token] (1975). As other (male) writers saw the piles of their books diminish, Riera's supply remained at 100 percent. She finally lured a buyer by promising to dedicate the book to him if he purchased it. It was her first sale, and she expresses in the article her enduring gratitude to the purchaser.[6] Having bought the book, he would presumably read it, hence completing the writing act by performance of the reading one. Don Ramón Vendrell Macià, like the woman writer, seeks to be read; at the company headquarters, he then seeks to be heard. Neither expectation is granted him. Even his fury takes on a heavily ironic tone as he finds himself hurling poisonous invective at a nonexistent name. As woman has historically found the "angel" self of her social, male-authored text subject to rewriting as "whore" should she transgress male-created social boundaries, Vendrell buys into, and responds in terms of, precisely this paradigm. Yet, Riera ironizes his text and his response to the silence on which it falls, feminizing the role of her protagonist and hence creating a multiply dialogic tension in her tale.[7]

The second story to be treated, "La seducción del genio," bears a number of striking similarities to Riera's 1987 novella *Qüestió d'amor propi* [A Question of Self-Love or, as I prefer, A Matter of Pride]. Both works consist of a single letter; we do not have in either case the benefit of the narratee's reply. In both narratives, the letter in question is cast as a confession. And, as in the earlier work, the story presents a textual tension, even combat, between the confessional and epistolary modes, the former tending, or pretending, to privilege emotion over reflection, spontaneity over plan, while the epistolary mode is normally expressive of a strategy, hence appropriating power and attempting to exert control. Confession is an expression of desire—for intimacy, understanding, forgiveness, redemption—while epistolarity acts out a plan for seduction, however crossed, conflicted or self-subverted the epistolary text—that is, however much it is a literary text.[8] Elizabeth MacArthur posits an essential ambiguity, instability, open-endedness—in her term, an "extravagance"—in epistolary narrative, which, for the sensitive reader, retains a metonymic quality resistant to critical efforts to close or freeze it into metaphor.[9] The tension between confession and epistolarity is a force creative of such destabilization; yet it is hardly accidental that confession and epistolarity should often be joined in fiction. The confessional mode is disarming, predisposing to receptivity both narratee and implied reader. Here, confession is innately seductive, drawing the listener/reader into a circle of intimacy and privilege. The narratee—and, through her, the implied reader—are cast in the role of voyeur, the narratee an invited guest, the reader an intruder into a private world, with narratee and reader both sought and seeking, both object of narrative seduction and pre-seduced accomplices. In this seductive power of confession lies its point of confluence with the strategy inherent in epistolarity.

In an interview in 1991 by Neus Aguado, Riera sees the seductive function as essential to literary creation and links this concept with epistolarity:

> . . . [C]reo que el escritor debe ser un buen seductor y la escritora una buena seductora, y que para seducir al lector lo que hay que hacer es encontrar un tono confidente, cómplice, envolvente, y ese tono suele darse precisamente en la carta. La carta no es más que un diálogo aplazado en el que tú no te sometes a las preguntas, al interrogatorio del otro, como ocurre en un diálogo directo. Cuando se escribe una carta se intenta explicar el punto de vista personal e intentar convencer, de la mejor manera posible, al destinatario, que siempre es el lector.

> [. . . I believe that the writer should be a good seducer and the woman writer a good seductress, and that in order to seduce the reader one has to find a confessional, complicitous, involving tone, and that tone is normally found precisely in the letter. A letter is only a deferred dialogue in which you don't submit to the questions, the interrogation of the other person, as occurs in direct dialogue. When we write a letter we try to explain our personal point of view, we try as best we can to convince the destinataire, who is always the reader.][10]

"La seducción del genio" is a tale of multiple failed seductions; the single letter which comprises it is itself a plan of seduction, at once ingenuous and wily, singleminded and ambiguous. It is directed to Carmen Balcells of Barcelona, by Juanita Chamorro of Brazil, who had been known until recently as Juan Chamorro. (Like all the literary figures alluded to in Chamorro's correspondence, Balcells has an extratextual identity, in this case, as a

Barcelona literary agent. This flavor of the roman à clef adds, of course, to the story's playfulness for Hispanists and, perhaps more still, to members of the Barcelona literary and publishing world, hence inviting reflection on the question of aperture and closure in the textual correspondence which is Riera's tale.) Juan Chamorro had wanted to be a writer but was dissuaded from this aspiration by his friends, who convinced him that he had no talent. Nonetheless, longing to dwell near the muses, Juan decided to become husband to a writer. After rejection in Brazil, he tries his luck in Spain. Upon hearing of his project, Rosa Chacel (a noted Spanish writer, who died in 1994 at age 95), "por poco se muere atragantada de risa" [nearly died laughing].[11] The Spanish poet Carmen Conde has the flu and cannot be approached. Rejections follow by Esther Tusquets (Barcelona novelist and editor, former head of Editorial Lumen) and Ana María Matute (celebrated Spanish novelist and short story writer). After the sex-change surgery, Juanita Chamorro cherishes the same dream and seeks a writerly husband.

At the level of *histoire,* "La seducción del genio" is a repetitive dialogue between desiring subject and rejecting object, the homogeneity of the approaches equalled by that of the responses. In flipping through the pages of one of those tiny moving-image books in which we delighted as children, we achieved a sense of vertiginous movement replicating and hyperbolizing that of life lived at its fastest. Were we to concoct such a book of drawings from the story of "La seducción del genio," the resulting sense would be one of stasis, of movement in place, a kind of flailing paralysis; images would succeed one another in rapidly experienced sameness.

One also recalls the sensation felt in the early junior high classroom when the appointed projectionist of the day might take advantage of the teacher's momentary preoccupation with a task to speed up the history or current events film, producing the same frenetic movement of the images on the pages of the book of drawings flipped by a child's hand but also a kind of poignant innate comicity arising from the fact that human figures were involved, because of the simultaneous surpassing of the bounds of reality and reduction of the human figure, and the human enterprise, to an ineffectual burlesque of itself.

Chamorro's epistolary text, too, doubles back upon itself in the dialogic relationship between desire, the force that drives the text, and seduction, its point of failure, which stalls it, sending it back again to desire and its new enactment, always the same as the one before. There is something almost Chaplinesque in Chamorro's continuous action of knocking on a door which is then slammed in his face. After a while, it ceases to matter, if it ever did, which door is knocked upon. Action, reaction, and action again become an exercise in themselves, a self-perpetuating circular movement propelled by desire. The story's cyclic nature is clearly marked by the consonance between Chamorro's letter to Carmen Balcells and the embedded tale, the history, it contains. The letter is written from Brazil to a narratee living in Barcelona. In the history recapitulated in the letter, we learn that Chamorro's seductive endeavor, in fact, began in Brazil. After failure there, the setting was moved to Spain, with stop two being, precisely, Barcelona. The initial Brazilian project, marriage to the Brazilian writer Nélida Piñón, presumably now being impossible, given Chamorro's gender change, the project moves, once again, to Spain. The cycle reopens; that is, it closes, moves backward, prepares to reenact the same steps, substituting only new names. The chances of success, the reader probably gauges, are totally unaltered.

In the dialogic desire-seduction relationship that lies at the heart of the story's *discours,* the rejections are as essential to the cycle's completeness as the initiatives themselves. In closure there is aperture, due to the intensity of the desire propulsion, and in aperture there has come to be assurance, even guarantee, of closure. The ultimate rejection in the cycle, one serving only to reopen the cycle once more, is the letter writer's choice of a sex change, the conversion from Juan Chamorro to Juanita Chamorro. Gender does not function here as a sociocultural determinant, nor is the decision to change gender a product of an imperative of personal identity, sexual or otherwise. Chamorro's recounting of the genesis of the idea trivializes its import as a personal revolution and underscores its nature as a caprice of the moment. Chamorro was walking with a writer at the time the idea hit.

> Una tarde, casi a punto de regresar al Brasil, paseando por el barcelonés Moll de la Fusta con la dulce Ana María Moix y a propósito precisamente de María Kodama, una especie de fetiche para mí, de pronto me percaté de que sólo me quedaba una alternativa factible si de verdad quería que mi deseo se cumpliera por encima de cualquier otra cosa. . . . Se lo confesé a mi amiga y nos abrazamos llorando en pleno paseo.
>
> La operación, querida Carmen, ha sido un éxito.

> [One afternoon, when I was about to go back to Brazil and was strolling on Barcelona's Moll de la Fusta with sweet Ana María (Barcelona short story writer, poet, and novelist), and a propos María Kodama (widow of the late Jorge Luis Borges), who is a kind of fetish for me, I suddenly realized that only one viable alternative remained to me if indeed I wanted, above all else, to see my desire fulfilled. I confessed my idea to my companion, and we hugged, in tears, right there in the middle of the sidewalk.
>
> The operation, dear Carmen, was a success.] (142–43)

Clearly, Chamorro's decision is a career choice. The entire letter, in fact, is written as though to a job placement service, detailing the applicant's motivations, qualifications for the position, willingness to work, and job expectations:

> A cambio de asistir al espectáculo—Chamorro writes—ofrecí mi colaboración de secretario, corrector, amanuense, mecanógrafo y hasta negro—para las páginas de relleno, claro—, además, naturalmente, de marido.
>
> De esta manera aseguraba mi escasa parcela de futura supervivencia como compañero de la escritora, quizá en forma de brevísima mención en las páginas de las enciclopedias pero, por supuesto, con los honores de bastantes páginas en las biografías bien documentadas, además de sentirme partícipe de una labor fundamental.

> [In exchange for attending the show, I offered my services as secretary, proofreader, scribe, typist, and even slave—for the filler pages, of course—as well as husband.
>
> In this way I ensured my scant portion of future survival as companion to the artist, perhaps in the form of the briefest of mentions in the pages of the encyclopedias, but, of course, honored with quite a few pages in the well-documented biographies, in addition to feeling part of a fundamental enterprise.] (140–41)

The self-repudiation implicit in making a change of such magnitude, in an aspect so fundamental to identity and in response to an unsubstantiated hope of enhanced prospects in the marketplace, makes of Chamorro the ultimate flexible employee. The project of this pliable self, however, remains unchanged. "Por ello," writes Chamorro with regard to the success of the operation, "estoy segura de poder conseguir por fin mi propósito" [For this reason, I feel certain that I'll be able to reach my goal at last.] (143). The self has been detextualized but not retextualized, her place in the unemployment line of would-be spouses of writers unchanged and the desire-seduction cycle ready to resume its self-perpetuating, self-consuming motion.

Significantly, Riera's character seeks its own self-perpetuation through a literary text, or a text written in response to the existence of a literary production. This nonwriter who is the letter writer wishes to be written, hence validated, confirmed, perpetuated, immortalized. Such is the import of the literary text for the letter writer that it takes precedence even over an identity marker as basic as gender. Ironically, the perpetuation that is sought is that of an obliterated, annihilated self. Chamorro's desire is ultimately a narcissistic one, doubling back upon itself precisely as does her/his epistolary text. It is a desire for immortality of a self-made Other in the search for a self. The self seeks . . . *itself,* a self to be created precisely by the written word. Project and process meet in the text. Chamorro thus endows the literary text with the power to create character, the power to create him/her—which is, of course, precisely what Riera has done. The desire-driven, failed seductions narrated in the story which is embedded within the framing seduction attempt—that of Carmen Balcells in the letter which constitutes the entire text of the story, itself framed by the marker "short story by Carme Riera" under the rubric "La seducción del genio"—all attempt literary invention. Chamorro's tale is metafictional, Riera's doubly so.

The framing seduction, that of Carmen Balcells, is never clear in any stated purpose beyond the plea for "muchos y buenos consejos" [much good advice] (143). But certainly, Balcells is to be the midwife in the birth of a new Chamorro posterity, made "other" and eternalized by literature. The letter writer employs a number of clever strategies to enlist her aid.

First among these strategies is recourse to hyperbole. "Tuve el inmenso placer de conocerla hace unos años" [I had the enormous pleasure of meeting you a few years ago] (139), writes Juanita Chamorro, referring just after to Nélida Piñón as "mi admiradísima escritora" [my so greatly admired writer] (139), although, near the story's end, she undercuts this alleged allegiance by stating that when she leaves Brazil for Spain, as Juan Chamorro had done before her, she will not deign to inform Nélida Piñón, since, after all, Nélida rejected Juan as a prospective husband.

Juanita Chamorro also employs the technique of familiarity, moving from an "Usted pensará, señora Balcells" [You (formal) will think, Mrs. Balcells] (140) to a "tú pensarás, querida Carmen [You (familiar) will think, dear Carmen] (140) in the same sentence. Apparently, Juanita is not deterred in the flattery department by any fear of seeming too obvious; she not only expresses assurance of the "muchos y buenos consejos" to be received but takes care to praise Carmen Balcells' city, Barcelona, citing no less an authority than the creator of Don Quijote and Sancho. "[No] en vano Cervantes habla de su hospitalidad" [Not without cause does Cervantes speak of her hospitality] (142). The letter writer does not hesitate, in an evident attempt to elicit sympathy, to detail the succession of humiliating rejections, then to acknowledge total defeat: "Todas y cada una cercenaron sin pied ad mis mejores ilusiones" [Every single one of them demolished my most cherished hopes] (143). It is only one step more to the kind of de-selfing implicit in the otherwise common phrases "*me llamaban* Juan Chamorro" [*they called me* Juan Chamorro] (139)—the letter's opening phrase—and "lo guapa que *me han dejado*" [how pretty *they've made me*] (144) near its conclusion (emphasis mine), a de-selfing accentuated by the contextualization of the expressions in the story. Once de-selfing has been effected, the self can conform to the contours of the other. It is, of course, a highly ironized de-selfing, as Juan chooses to become Juanita, then selects a new name in a play on traditionally held male privileges. Kathleen Glenn reminds us that "the godlike power to name and thereby confer identity has long been a male prerogative."[12] Juanita can now speak to Carmen "de mujer a mujer" [woman to woman] ("Seducción," 143), and, in soliciting advice, state, "Obedezco mujeramente feliz" [I obey in womanly happiness] (143). (The adverb *mujeramente*, whose English equivalent would be roughly "in a womanly way," is coined by the character.) She also initiates gossip about male writers who could—and could not—form part of her list of husbandly candidates. Juanita insists on the completeness of the change wrought in her by the operation—"Me siento verdaderamente otra" [I truly feel different (literally, another [feminine] person)] (143), as though the writing of the word, of which she exacts so much, could make it so. However, Juanita goes on to offer Carmen "un fraternal abrazo" [a fraternal embrace] (144), a phrase ambiguous both etymologically and as a possible expression of unresolved gender ambivalence.

It is significant that the "fraternal abrazo" phrase should appear in the letter's—and the story's—last sentence. It may well contain a subversive commentary on the arbitrariness with which our societies approach gender categorization, by a writer who frequently has treated lesbian and gay themes and topics of identity fusion and separation, sometimes across genders. The phrase, together with the use of an adjective invented by the letter writer, suggesting that there is no adequate existing word, or that the writer cannot find one, also evokes a topic taken up by Carme Riera in her article, "Femenino singular: Literatura de mujer" [Feminine Singular: Woman's Literature], text of a lecture delivered at the Seminario de Estudios de la Mujer [Seminar on Women's Studies] at the University of Granada in May 1988. Riera takes up the matter of women writers' inevitable and ironic need to have recourse to a borrowed, male-created language when they write. She states that perhaps woman's time in the world is now at hand:

> . . . la hora de reivindicar para nuestra escritura todo lo que antes fue privativo o característico de la del hombre desde la aventura a los temas eróticos, desde el lenguaje preciso y riguroso, sin sentir que este lenguaje es un préstamo en el que nos movemos incómodas hasta el que se ha considerado privativo de nuestra condición. Aunque el lenguaje puede, en cierto modo, marginar a la mujer—basta asomarnos a cualquier diccionario—porque no es más que un reflejo de la relación que el hombre establece con la realidad, debemos cambiar ese lenguaje, acoplarlo a nuestra medida, a nuestros intereses y tal vez así las palabras algún día vuelvan a ser lo que nunca fueron, es decir verbo, es decir, amor.

> [. . . the time to revindicate for our writing all that was exclusive to or characteristic of male writing, from adventure to erotic themes, from precise and rigorous language, and without feeling that such a language is a borrowed one in which we move uncomfortably, to the language that has been considered exclusive to our (female) condition. Although language may, in some ways, marginalize women—we have only to look in any dictionary (to confirm this)—because language is only a reflection of the relationship that men have established with reality, we must change that language, fit it to our measure, to our interests, and perhaps in this way words will again be what they never have been, in other words, the Word, in other words, love.][13]

Juan/Juanita Chamorro wishes to be present in the creative process, to attain immortality in the collective memory, or at least in *someone's* memory, through the generation of a series of literary texts, each dependent on the one before. He and she seek their end through the creation of a text, the articulation of a discourse of desire, in order to seduce the word. The word seduced must, however, be in *castellano*. Juan Chamorro rejected the thought of Montserrat Roig as writerly wife even though he had moved his search precisely to Barcelona, and Juanita is careful to praise that city. (Roig, who died in 1991, was a Catalan novelist, essayist, and television journalist who always composed her texts first in Catalan—as, indeed, does Riera.) Riera conflates marginalities, joining gender issues to those of regional identity. In this aspect of identity, too, categories limit and divide us, silencing our possibilities. The text whose creation Juan/Juanita Chamorro ultimately requests is, of course, the self. Through the depiction in "La seducción del genio" of a character's extreme faith in, and expectation of, the writing of her erased self—a word of which so much is asked and to which little is permitted—Carme Riera subverts, even as she writes, our sense of that word's power.

In her playful conflation of gender and regional identity, Riera clearly privileges the gender topic in "La seducción del genio." The matter of gender and its voicing are expressed through a multilayered irony which moves in a circular fashion, doubling back upon itself and, in a sense, reproducing, as each irony engenders yet another. The result is a playful social and metafictional commentary that addresses the creation—the engendering—of both social and literary texts. (It is important to observe at this point how essential to the functioning of this multiple irony it is that the protagonist's sex change be neither a matter of the imperative of fundamental identity and sexual orientation nor a caprice. Its nature as a considered career change and a step toward planned literary immortality frees the concept for play in this story of a seductive attempt to establish female complicity.) In Riera's tale, a female creator writes a male voice which rewrites itself as female, seeking a female code and register. Chamorro literally changes gender, appropriating—and ironizing—female identity. In a reversal of the classic pattern whereby a woman, to succeed in the male world, is tacitly asked to become part of it (then is chastised for having become "unwomanly"), here, a male approaches the female world, reinventing the self both in order to do so and in so doing. Riera plays with the long-held male concept of female intrusion into male space, female assumption of male voice. She also adopts a playful, authorial stance with respect to the theme of a search for self which is often associated with female-authored literature. It is in the present story a highly problematized theme, not a look within but a look out—to a desired role in the world, not a search for self but a fundamental alteration of the self in response to a perceived market advantage. The result is a movable self, mutable at the very core. In depicting a fictional and metafictional process of attempted re-gendering and re-engendering of language, Riera implicitly asks how a woman writer is to deal with a borrowed language, how she is to go beyond the writing of the body of Annie LeClerc and Hélène Cixous. Epistolarity fits the question well, in that a protagonist/letter writer pretends to seduction of both destinataire and reader—that is, of the reader both within and outside the text—into cooperation in the application of a corrective to failure—precisely, a masculine failure. Riera's (always playful) admonition seems to be that the woman writer write herself as self, as an individual, perceiving, writing being.

Several steps of ironic removal, then, mark the process by which a male narrator, product of a female pen, chooses to become female, then, re-engendered, seeks complicity with newly "fellow" women. The literary evocation of a (former) man, a man *rewritten* as woman, now seeking to write a female self, using a classically female literary form, may well be an ironic commentary by Riera on the condition of those women throughout history who have had recourse to the assumption of male literary identity—Aurore Dupin as George Sand, Caterina Albert i Paradís as Victor Català, Mary Ann Evans as George Eliot, Cecilia Böhl de Faber as Fernán Caballero—in order to publish their works. Riera plays, too, with the concept of male and female language, masculine and feminine writing. In her article "Femenino singular," she discusses the examples of Marguerite Yourcenar, thought by some to write "like a man," and Proust, whose writing has been said to be "feminine."[14] Riera pokes fun at those who historically have seen the woman writer as, inevitably, a cross-dresser, having to cloak her identity in linguistic masculinity, in male nomenclature. She inquires,

> ¿El desvío de la norma, configurador del estilo del autor, es doble si se trata de una escritora puesto que debe desviarse dos veces?: como escritora que rechaza el lenguaje de uso—es decir, los aspectos denotativos de éste—y como mujer que rechaza el lenguaje eminentemente masculino?
>
> [Is the departure from the norm, which is what configures an author's style, a double one if the writer is a woman: as a woman writer who rejects language as commonly used—in other words, its denotative aspects—and as a woman who rejects an eminently masculine language?][15]

"La seducción del genio" presents a reversal of this paradigm; Riera's protagonist is a former man who would seek to write as a woman, "mujeramente," as it has been supposed that a woman who would speak in public forum was aspiring to manhood. Riera's use of an ironized "female" language—the coined word *mujeramente,* the play with others in the sentence "Me siento verdaderamente otra" [I feel truly "other"], the "fraternal" embrace with which a letter closes—may express the author's doubt, and that of many others, as to just what female language is. In the Granada talk which became the article "Femenino singular," Riera finds female identity written into, and read in, tone and topic, and relayed through the sense of complicity that draws female readers to female-authored texts,[16] even as the protagonist and letter writer of "La seducción del genio" seeks to awaken a disposition to "female" complicity in the reception of "her" texts: the letter and future texts from "her" pen, that of her still-sought writerly husband, and, behind them, of the author herself, as well as through acceptance of the newly engendered social text of female identity.

The crossed gazes of male and female identity in "La seducción del genio" bring to mind a curious observation: that the dust jackets of both Goldsmith's 1989 *Writing the Female Voice* and MacArthur's 1990 *Extravagant Narratives,* each cited in the pages of this essay, carry the same reproduced image of a painting, although the books emanate from two distinct academic presses. The painting is Elisabeth Vigée-Lebrun's "Lady Folding a Letter" (1784). It portrays a woman folding a letter, her gaze turned toward the viewer. Her plume pen has been put down, and her text is complete, now being prepared for actual transmission. The woman, in sending the letter she presumably has authored, is completing her own text; she is not written by others but, rather, writing. In closing, she is opening: dialogue, perhaps understanding. The text of the painting, too, is open. We have interrupted her in the very act of folding her letter. Her intelligent, slightly mischievous gaze registers mild surprise, though absolute calm in face of it. Her look is complicitous and somewhat self-satisfied. Its aperture-closure tension suggests that of the dialogic process within each of the stories examined here, a cross-fertilization and, in the case of the second story, a cross-gendering. The very title, "La seducción del genio," suggests, in its ambiguity, this multiplication of meaning and duplicity of its engendering. Is the title to suggest a seduction *of* genius or *by* genius, or perhaps the seduction of or by a particular, individual genius? The space in reader receptivity opened by this unresolved ambiguity is akin to those spaces of suggestion created by the image in the painting.

The image of a crossed gaze between the respective covers of these two critical books, the Goldsmith and MacArthur texts, in turn, causes, reflection on a possible parallel with the Ana María Moix story “Las virtudes peligrosas,” much admired by Carme Riera.[17] In Moix's tale, two women maintain for years an exclusively female mutual contemplation, perfect in its absoluteness and utterly closed nature, open in its many ambiguities. It is seemingly a complete communication which occurs, however, without benefit at any moment of the spoken word.

These two book covers, of two women, the same yet appearing in different contexts, each folding a letter in unwitting replication of one another and suggesting the replicated gaze of “Las virtudes peligrosas,” are apt metaphors for the Riera texts considered in these pages. Both “Letra de ángel” and “La seducción del genio” are complicitous tales in which aperture and closure, male and female, success and failure, acceptance and rejection, self and other, are all placed in a dialogic position, crossing, conflating, separating again. The members of each pair engage in a gaze in which they become at once the same and different, even as Riera's stories speak to us of a Spain, and a human condition, of multiple texts within one. In a recent article, L. Teresa Valdivieso discusses feminism as a path to a new humanism of mutual tolerance and respect.[18] Riera's tales, indeed, point in this direction in their reflection of, and upon, the Other which is the self, the self which is the Other.

Notes

1. Nichols, “Carme Riera,” in *Escribir, espacio propio: Laforet, Matute, Moix, Tusquets, Riera y Roig por sí mismas* [Writing, One's Own Space: Laforet, Matute, Moix, Tusquets, Riera, and Roig Speaking for Themselves] (Minneapolis: Institute for the Study of Ideologies and Literature, 1989), 187–227.

2. Carme Riera, “Letra de ángel,” in *Contra el amor en compañía y otros relatos* (Barcelona: Destino, 1991), 21–34. Subsequent citations from this work will be indicated parenthetically within the text.

3. MacArthur, *Extravagant Narratives: Closure and Dynamics in the Epistolary Form* (Princeton, N.J.: Princeton University Press, 1990), 61.

4. Ibid., 61.

5. Carson, “Narrative Cross-Dressing and the Critique of Authorship in the Novels of Richardson,” in *Writing the Female Voice: Essays on Epistolary Literature* (Boston: Northeastern University Press, 1989), 95.

6. Riera, "Una ambición sin límites"/"An Ambition Without Limits" in the section of this volume entitled "In Her Own Words."

7. An earlier version, here recast and reworked, of portions of this section of my essay appeared in Spanish as "Epistolaridad, marginación y deseo en un cuento de Carme Riera," in *Cuadernos de ALDEEU* 10:2 (October 1994): 75–82. I thank the journal's editor, Dr. Juan Fernández-Jiménez of Pennsylvania State University–Erie, for permission to incorporate this material here in expanded and altered form and in English.

8. The 1992 article "Dialogic Discourse, Gender and Power in Carme Riera's *Cuestión de amor propio*," in *Misogyny in Literature: An Essay Collection*, ed. Kathleen A. Ackley (New York and London: Garland, 1992), 349–62, treats dialogic discourse in Riera's novella, published in Catalan in 1987 and in Castilian Spanish in 1988. That novella consists of a lengthy letter written by the protagonist, a Spanish writer named Angela Caminals, to her longtime Scandinavian friend, Ingrid, concerning Angela's brief love affair with her fellow writer, Miquel Orbajosa. Her narration to Ingrid encloses two sets of double-voiced discourse, one contained within the other. In the framing story—the act of composing the letter—we are able to speak of dialogic discourse, although there is at no moment an interruption, nor a reaction or reply from Ingrid. The dialogic quality arises from two factors: a narratorial appropriation of presumed narratee reaction, on the one hand, and, on the other, the narrator's deeply ambivalent feelings toward her narratee, the couching of her letter as confession in order to attain retribution, to employ the artifice of intimacy in order to achieve a more public gain, revenge. We may speak, then, of a *double* double-voiced discourse in the novella's framing story. In the embedded story of the love affair, a dialogic element is also present in the simultaneous narration and analysis of Angela's own motives and those of her lover as well.

9. Macarthur, *Extravagant Narratives*, passim.

10. Neus Aguado, "Epístolas de mar y de sol: Entrevista con Carme Riera." *Quimera* 105 (1991), 35.

11. Riera, "La seducción del genio," in *Contra el amor en compañía y otros relatos* (Barcelona: Destino, 1991), 139–44. Subsequent citations from this work are indicated parenthetically within the text.

12. Glenn, "Authority and Marginality in Three Contemporary Spanish Narratives," *Romance Languages Annual* 2 (1990): 428.

13. Riera, "Femenino singular: Literatura de mujer," in *Crítica y ficción literaria: Mujeres españolas contemporáneas* (Granada: Universidad de Granada, 1989), 37–38. Riera also addresses this topic in her "Literatura femenina: ¿un lenguaje prestado?" in *Quimera* 18 (1982): 9–12.

14. Riera, "Femenino singular," 26.

15. Ibid., 32.

16. Ibid., 32–33.

17. Riera speaks of her admiration for this story in the Neus Aguado interview, "Epístolas de mar y de sol: Entrevista con Carme Riera," 35–36. The story "Las virtudes peligrosas" was published in Moix's short story collection *Las virtudes peligrosas* (Barcelona: Plaza y Janés, 1985), 7–43.

18. Valdivieso, "Mujeres en busca de un nuevo humanismo," *Inti: Revista de Literatura Hispánica* 40–41 (1994–95): 289–98.

"Tras su hache mayúscula": Carme Riera and the Exploration of History in *Dins el darrer blau*

GERALDINE CLEARY NICHOLS

DINS EL DARRER BLAU [IN THE FURTHEST BLUE], PUBLISHED IN 1994 by the Majorcan author Carme Riera, is a momentous and ambitious work.[1] In pre-postmodern times, it would have been called a historical novel, but today we can say more precisely that it displays qualities of historiographic metafiction. It should be noted that the novel has made history of its own. In December 1995, it was awarded the Premio Nacional de Narrativa [Spanish National Prize for Fiction], becoming the first novel written in a Spanish language other than Castilian to win this prize. *Dins el darrer blau* re-chronicles the failed attempt of a group of *xuetes,* Majorcan New Christians of Jewish descent, to flee Majorca in 1688.[2] Those who tried to escape were crypto-Jews, or Judaizers, hoping to settle where they could practice their Judaism openly and properly, believing that to be their only hope for salvation. But this flight was organized hastily, in response to information that a *malsí,* or *converso* informer, had recently denounced their continuing observance of the Law of Moses to the Inquisition. This placed many of them at risk of being prosecuted as relapsed Judaizers, for which the punishment was death by fire. A ship was found and its captain bribed to transport the most endangered to the Continent. But a violent storm prevented the ship from departing, and all the *xuetes* on board, as well as many who stayed behind, were seized by the Inquisition; none escaped punishment. The novel ends in 1691 with the public burning of the community's leader, the rabbi Valls.

Dins el darrer blau is an arresting blend of so many diametrical elements that its title—literally, in the furthest blue; figuratively, there, where blue of sky melds into blue of sea—describes the novel as well as alluding to one of its principal messages, the hope that in some as yet undiscerned place or time, just at the horizon, the factitious divisions between peoples will disappear and only their common humanity will remain. Two elements cogently blended in *Dins* are history—for the events rechronicled have been exhaustively researched—and fiction, with its capacity to present enduring if not factual truths about human behavior. In an afterword, Riera explains that she took some liberties with history to intensify the novel's drama: she amalgamated four *autos de fe* into one and condensed the time elapsed between the frustrated embarkation and the *auto* in which Valls perished. Undoubtedly, however, her principal fiction and and greatest achievement lies in characterization. Some figures in the novel are drawn from composites of historical personages, while others are invented; but the novelist endows characters from both categories with dreams, beliefs, and fears, transforming them from one-dimensional markers into complex, desiring, and sometimes self-contradictory subjects.

More unusual than the novel's "scumbling," or combining, of history and fiction is its mixing of both subject matter and tone.[3] It begins with a tale as fanciful or fantastic as any in the *Arabian Nights,* but this frame soon merges into a more conventional narration that interweaves scenes of everyday life in disparate venues of seventeenth-century Palma—from palaces to bordellos to the cramped quarters of the ghetto—with the small but increasingly charged actions that will lead to the *auto de fe.* The final chapter closes the frame that opened the novel; its fictional protagonist, João Peres, returns to Majorca just in time to witness Valls' last moments.

The novel's tone is immensely varied, ranging from lyrical, to objective, to sardonic, to solemn, to humorous, to chilling. There is a strong admixture of eroticism in *Dins el darrer blau;* in the context of a work about 37 people immolated for practicing their religion, it is a startling presence. Such surprises merit analysis, but the particular focus of this essay on Riera's novel as a retextualization of history precludes more than a cursory consideration of the function of the erotic. Those familiar with Riera's fiction know that she frequently employs the erotic as an effective delivery system for other messages; in pharmaceutical terms, she has it serve as a tasty excipient for unpalatable medicine. In *Dins el darrer blau,* eroticism is used as the primary means to embody characters, even those who might have seemed too spiritual to have bodies like ours: Inquisitors, priests, rabbis, pious queen mothers.

At the same time, showing Eros to be as powerful a motivator as ambition, piety, or greed allows Riera to open a space for the reader to imagine women's protagonism in history. When desire is identified as a defining human trait, women can be portrayed on an equal footing with men. Blanca Maria Pires, a wholly invented but historically plausible character, makes the first contacts with a ship's captain to initiate the plan of escape from Majorca. Once she herself has left the island, she underwrites and helps arrange the flight of the most threatened of her correligionists. An object of desire as well as a woman of intellect and convictions, Blanca centers the gaze and fires the dreams of many of the most important male characters of the novel. A prostitute named Beatriu Mas, "La Coixa," also intersects with history as it is narrated in Riera's novel. Like Blanca, she leaves her trace on several lives but is invisible in official chronicles.[4]

In a novel as accomplished as *Dins el darrer blau,* it is not surprising to find that structure replicates content, blending unlike elements. Disparate narrative forms are combined; as was the case in Riera's first novel, *Una primavera per a Domenico Guarini,* the circularity of a frame tale is welded to the linearity of the chronicle. Although narrated in the third person, shifting focalizations make *Dins* a choral or heteroglossic work, allowing the reader the illusion of entering the thoughts of characters presented by history as impenetrable. The past tense predominates, but approximately six of the twenty-five chapters are related in the present. The novel also offers a paradoxical reading experience. It is utterly lacking in suspense, since readers—even those ignorant of history—will know the story's end before they start the first page, either from the information on the book jacket or from the description of the dramatis personae. Nonetheless, one reads its 426 pages with urgency, drawn in by the rhythm of the narration, several canny enigmas (or hermeneutisms, in Roland Barthes' term), and the sentiments—positive and negative—that one is led to feel for the characters.

Dins el darrer blau is sufficiently complex to respond to many critical approaches. This essay focuses on the novel as a retextualization of history, but it will also consider, albeit briefly, the work's status as a historical document in itself. *Dins* conforms in certain ways to what Linda Hutcheon calls historiographical metafiction, that is, fiction in which "theoretical self-awareness of history and fiction as human constructs . . . is made the grounds for its rethinking and reworking of the forms and contents of the past."[5] At the same time, *Dins* is intensely imbricated in the present, written from a specific site at a particular moment by a writer with an acute awareness of the weight of historical tradition. Following the paradoxical model of the novel, I conclude this essay with two opening gestures. The first places *Dins el darrer blau* in the religious, literary, historical and political context of the call to remembrance—*Zakhor* in the Jewish context, "ni olvido ni perdón" [no forgetting or forgiving] in the Latin American. The second assesses *Dins* as an instance of what feminists and postcolonialists call "speaking for the other."

The "tras su hache mayúscula" [behind the capital h] of my title is from a letter written by nineteen-year-old Ana María Moix to the exiled writer Rosa Chacel, whom she had adopted as mentor-by-correspondence. In the course of her letter, Moix explains the type of stories she would one day like to write: the "other" (hi)stories, the (hi)story of "others," precisely those tales that capital-h History ignores.

> Pienso que la Historia oculta infinidades de historias tras su hache mayúscula, y en esto está la razón de que se escriba con hache grande y no pequeña. La HISTORIA es la más pequeña, la más inverosímil, por eso hay que estudiarla y aprenderla. La otra es patrimonio de la imaginación en el tiempo, de nosotros en la otra cara de los otros que nos cuentan e intentan explicar.
>
> [I think that History hides an infinite number of histories behind its capital h, which is why it is written with a big and not a little h. HISTORY deals with the smallest things, the most implausible, and that is the reason it must be studied and learned. The other (hi)story belongs to imagination anchored in time, and to those of us who are on the other side of the coin from those who tell about us and try to explain us.] [6]

What Riera does in *Dins el darrer blau,* is to tell—to invent, literally to embody and en-gender—some of the "infinidades de historias" behind the capital-h Historical accounts of the last *autos de fe* resulting in loss of life in Majorca. In so doing, she compels a rethinking of this episode, told monologically and seemingly once-for-all in two sources; the copious *legajos* [files] of the Inquisition, and the vitriolic eyewitness account of the Jesuit Francisco Garau, titled *La fe triunfante.* Garau's history was published in the year of the last *auto,* but continuous reprints over the centuries have both fixed its status as the standard history of these events and ensured that its intemperate message about the perfidiousness of the *xuetes* never be forgotten in Majorca.

Dins el darrer blau does not question the historical facts related in contemporaneous sources; instead, it disputes the way the events and actors have been described and semioticized with a single meaning. In the most general sense, the novel critiques history by rewriting it, differently; by copying it "otherhow," to use Rachel DuPlessis's apt neologism.[7] For example, *Dins* imitates history's methodology—its archival research—and aspects of its written style; appropriates many of its bona fide characters; re-relates—albeit along a different axis—a story already consecrated as true. The novel's language, self-consciously archaic and realistically varied, adds to its air of authenticity while simultaneously underlining historiography's often unacknowledged dependence on language, itself historical insofar as it changes through time. In the afterword, Riera explains that she strove to ensure the novel's comprehensibility to the modern reader while reproducing as faithfully as possible the diverse registers, dialects, and sociolects that characterized written and spoken discourse in seventeenth-century Palma. Despite these carefully cultivated similarities to capital-h History, *Dins el darrer blau* is clearly marked and marketed as fiction. This purposeful crossing of the boundaries between history and fiction serves to make readers doubt the absolute veracity of historical discourse, especially with regard to the *Cremadissa* (the Catalan word for mass burning, used to refer to this episode in Majorca). When concrete certainty is breached, other versions may flower in the cracks.

Dins presents another challenge to historiography by constantly underscoring its textuality, its written-ness and resulting eventuality. This reminds readers of an unsettling fact about history's transmission of the "real" past, summarized by the new historicist, Louis Montrose: "we can have no access to a full and authentic past, a lived material existence, unmediated by the surviving textual traces of the society in question."[8] *Dins* draws attention to a particular bias that colors Garau's textual traces of the events, obstructing our access to the past. This is the pervasive teleology and triumphalism of his account, most evident in repeated assurances that Divine Providence had arranged every detail leading to the crypto-Jews' downfall, since "Los acasos son para los hombres y ninguno lo es para la Providencia Divina" [Contingencies exist for men, but never for Divine Providence] (20). Garau declares it unambiguously providential that the crypto-Jews were prevented from escaping Majorca, since their seizure allowed them to die as Catholics.

> Bien pudiera Dios rigurosamente piadoso dejarles apartar de estos mares y, sepultarles después en golfos de agua para eternizar su muerte en las llamas que merecían. Mas los adorables juicios de la Providencia Divina, aunque siempre inescrutables a la mayor perspicacia, también a veces se nos dan a venerar dejándose traslucir en la benignidad de sus efectos. Y a la verdad del devoto y católico modo de morir de casi todos, . . . juzgo se puede piadosamente creer que el embarazarles la fuga fué efecto de la predestinación eterna, que quiso librarles de perderse en el agua para que pereciendo en las llamas se lograran para siempre.
>
> [God in strict piety might very well have allowed them to escape from these seas only to bury them later in oceans of water, thus prolonging eternally their agony in the hellfire they deserved. But the adorable judgments of Divine Providence, even though always inscrutable even to the most perspicacious, at times move us to veneration by revealing themselves through the benignity of their effects. In light of the devout and Catholic death that almost all of them had, . . . I judge that one may in all piety believe that the frustration of their flight was the effect of eternal predestination, which desired to free them from being lost in the water so that by perishing in flames they should be won forever.] (21)

Dins el darrer blau vitiates this pervasive certitude by subtle but continuous mention of the randomness and abundance of factors, personal to sociological to meteorological, which, indeed, led to the *Cremadissa* but which might just as plausibly have led to the Judaizers' escape.

Riera's novel alters only in minor ways the shape and chronology of the events related in *La fe triunfante* or in Inquisitorial records; yet it changes the (hi)story completely. This is accomplished principally through characterization, both of concrete historical figures (or composites thereof) and of purely fictive personages. Using Kaja Silverman's distinction between the speaking subject (or agent of discourse), the subject of speech (the first person speaker), and the spoken subject ("the subject produced *through* discourse," in Hutcheon's words, p. 169), one can more easily appreciate the double operation carried out in *Dins el darrer blau.*[9] On the one hand, the novel embodies the "speaking subjects" of the historical documents, heretofore effaced behind their titles and free to discourse without interrogation. On the other, it transforms into subjects of speech those who were the "spoken subjects" of this grisly episode, the *xuetes*.

The most notable of the historical "speaking subjects" fleshed out in *Dins el darrer blau* are a Grand Inquisitor and a Jesuit hagiographer and religious historian, *el pare* Amengual, modeled on Francisco Garau. Amengual is first depicted as a man consumed by ambition and blinded by conceit, a writer amenable to stretching the truth to please his patrons or to turn an especially clever phrase. Once the reader has identified him as unreliable, his similarities to Garau begin to be emphasized. He decides, for example, to write a chronicle of the *autos de fe,* to be titled "El triunfo de la Fe en tres cantos" [The triumph of the Faith in three cantos] (p. 372). By creating a fictional Garau and using the otherwise unremarkable technique of constructing him as an unreliable narrator, *Dins* places in question Garau's trustworthiness as an historian. At the same time, Amengual's characterization as a *lletraferit* [literary dilettante] and a vain, third-rate stylist is another way of underlining the textuality and contingency of historiography.

Characterization is also the means by which the spoken subjects of this (hi)story are transformed into speakers. *Dins* reincarnates the "others" of this episode-turned-exemplum, the *xuetes,* whose bodies were burned but whose names, painted on penitential sanbenitos, hung in one of the central churches in Palma until the mid-nineteenth century. The Judaizers were quite literally expunged as subjects in the *autos de fe,* but Garau's book and the expedient of displaying their names—fifteen surnames in all, the infamous "quince linajes" [fifteen lineages]—ensured that their ignominy would be perpetuated, and that their descendants would continue to suffer discrimination in Majorca.[10] *Dins el darrer blau* restores the power of speech to those whose silence or silencing guaranteed the social and religious order in Majorca for three centuries; in so doing, it challenges the very bases of Majorcan identity. Rachel DuPlessis writes of the great changes that can be wrought when the silent are given tongues:

> An intense play between subject and object(ified) is created in the invention of stories for the semi-silenced, or unheard female, or other marginal characters in traditional tales (myths) . . . . [S]uch a story of the unreckoned is more than just one *more* tale; reckoned in, it wrecks the "in." Intellectual and political assumptions are ruptured, narrative sequence, causality, resolution and possibly the

meanings of words or apt language themselves are all brought into question. (146)

None of the heretofore mute crypto-Jews is given fuller voice in *Dins el darrer blau* than the rabbi, Gabriel Valls, whose fictional name is respectfully close to that of Rafel Valls, his historical model. Valls is afforded more past and more present—more subjectivity—than any other character in the novel. It is through his memories that we take the measure of this man, and through him, of his community, since the experiences he recalls are a composite of many recorded in the Majorcan Inquisition's files. Valls delves into his memory—"el garbuix sutjós de la memòria" [memory's dark tangle] (152, 392)—to counter the despair and boredom he experiences in prison. He conjures, for example, the moment in adolescence when he first learned that he was a Jew; his feelings of material and spiritual superiority to the peasants and parvenu nobles of Majorca; his arranged betrothal to a girl from another family in the ghetto; the farce of their Catholic wedding followed by a secret ceremony as faithful to the Jewish rite as anyone's memory permitted; the magnificent garden where he and his correligionists met to discuss matters close to their hearts; an earlier imprisonment by the Inquisition, with hundreds of his *xueta* brethren, from which all had emerged shaken and impoverished, but ostensibly "reconciled" to Catholicism. Interspersed with these purposefully evoked images come unbidden memories and unwelcome desire for the widow Blanca Maria Pires, whom Valls had counseled as rabbi.

Because they are contrary to all his religious beliefs, such feelings torment him, revealing self-contradictions that grow more acute during his final months of life. The novel portrays Valls as having lost his faith by the time he is executed.[11] He believes, instead, that "La vida és el do més preciós" [life is the most precious gift] (421), and that his humanity defines him more fully than his religion. It is loyalty to his people that keeps him from apostatizing, or committing suicide; he cannot abandon them by betraying the religion for which so many of them were also condemned to die (422–23).

Dins el darrer blau forcefully reminds readers that history is indeed written by the winners. In point of fact, the winners were the only survivors of this confrontation; the losers were compelled to renounce their history or religion—consubstantial in Judaism—and then die, or not abjure and die horrifically. Having the last word, as Garau did in *La fe triunfante,* means being able to fix any interpretation one wishes on the events narrated. Riera's novel works on many levels to unsettle this monological presentation of the Judaizers' last years, to wrest the last word away from Garau and Company, restoring some vestige of speech to the silenced. The contrast between Garau's history and Riera's is nowhere more evident than in the parallel passages describing Valls' death, which I present in counterpoint.

The Jesuit's account is appropriately filled with clichés; he wants readers to see Valls' end as part of an already known signifying chain whose meaning is as simple as the day is long: good vanquishes evil, the true faith vanquishes. The clichés also reproduce Garau's earlier depiction of Valls as contumacious; as duplicitous rather than brave; as impervious through stubbornness to reasoned arguments about the true religion. If Valls seemed firm in his religious convictions, intelligent in his responses to the Inquisitor, and calm in the face of torture, Garau had a ready explanation which no one was in any position to contradict: it was a performance. His description sentences the rabbi to die without a shred of dignity: "Estoy para decir, que aunque murió judío, no fue por serlo del todo de entendimiento, ni aún por quererlo de veras ser, sino por quererlo parecer" [I am prepared to say that although he died a Jew, it was not because he fully understood what that meant, or because he truly wanted to be a Jew, but because he wanted to seem one] (47). Garau writes:

> Ni le bastó al Valls la estoica insensibilidad afectada (que va mucho de hablar a obrar y donde llega fácil la lengua no acompaña siempre el corazón). Mientras llegó solo el humo era una estatua, en llegando la llama, se defendió, se cubrió y forcejeó como pudo y hasta que no pudo más. Estaba gordo como un lechonazo de cría y encendióse en lo interior, de manera, que aún cuando no llegaban las llamas, ardían sus carnes como un tizón; y rebentando por medio se le cayeron las entrañas como a Judas. *Crepuit medius; et diffusa sunt omnia viscera eius. Actuun. 1.18.*

> [Nor was Valls' fake stoicism enough (for there's a many a slip 'twixt cup and lip, and talk is cheap). He was as still as a statue while there was only smoke, but when the flames reached him he defended himself, covering himself and struggling however he could and until he could no more. He was as fat as a suckling pig and his insides caught fire, so that even before the flames reached him, his flesh burned like a torch; he split down the middle and his intestines fell

out, as befell Judas. *He burst open in the middle and all his bowels gushed out. Acts 1.18.*] (51)

Garau's drive to fix a single demeaning interpretation on Valls' death stands in contrast to Riera's desire to recuperate the rabbi's subjectivity, with its fissures and silences. She presents Valls' death as the last, quintessentially unknowable moment of a complex being whose words and thoughts have been forever lost to history. In contraposition to Garau's gruesome detail, her description is more distanced and respectful:

> Però Valls no veu ningú. Amb el cap una mica girat pareix que esguarda la mar. . . . El moment és arribat i es fa un silenci espès. El Virrei encén amb la tea el foc purificador. Valls es contorç. Al seu rostre hi cap de sobte tot el sofriment del món. Obre la boca, però no demana misericòrdia, gemega. Uns instants i aquestes flames que li fan rebentar el ventre ja seran calius. Cendres. Després res. No res. El seu cos es vincla cap al cantó esquerre, esclata i cau com un tió consumit.
>
> [But Valls sees no one. With his head slightly turned he seems to be gazing at the sea. . . . The moment has arrived and the silence grows heavy. The Viceroy lights the purifying fire with a torch. Valls writhes. His face suddenly reflects all the anguish of the world. He opens his mouth, but does not ask for mercy; he moans. Within seconds the flames that cause his bowels to burst will be coals. Ashes. Then nothing. Nothing at all. His body twists to the left, explodes, and falls like a burnt log.] (426)

To read *Dins el darrer blau* is to believe that a particularly monstrous injustice was carried out in the *autos de fe* of 1691; it is also to marvel at the strength of the Majorcan crypto-Jewish community, which had continued to practice Judaism—as much of it as they could remember, as much as they could hide from their servants and neighbors—for 250 years after all religions but the Catholic were proscribed in Spain.[12] Garau calls this persistence "la reconcentrada abominación de la obstinación depravada" [the consummate abomination of depraved obstinacy] (19), but Riera's novel presents it less monolithically; both Jews and Christians are shown to have complex, unstable, sometimes internally divided beliefs. Later historical accounts of this period in Majorca—principally those of Baruch Braunstein and Angela Selke—show that the ultimate, fatal difference between the two groups was not the quality of their religious beliefs but their varying access to several kinds of power: financial, governmental, and ecclesiastical.[13] The novel gives a remarkably complex account of the multiple interests that came into conflict and resulted in the crypto-Jews' extinction. None of the significant interest groups in Majorca is without representation in the novel's dramatis personae, from the Viceroy and his noble wife, to the Grand Inquisitor, to Palma's aging queen of the night, Beatriu Mas, "la Coixa." Just as Valls' remembered experiences serve to recapitulate those of the historical *xuetes,* so does the "thickly described" ambiance of Palma incorporate all the important historical elements that led up to the *Cremadissa.*[14] In the end, it is not a flattering picture of the Church or of the Majorcan nobility that emerges.

If *Dins el darrer blau* is a rewriting of the historiography and the events of 1688–1691, it is also itself an historical text, socially produced and socially productive, in Montrose's terminology (23). That is to say, *Dins* is as much a product of its moment, place, and speaker as are Garau's treatise and the Inquisition's records; that it aspires, as they did, to shape discourse about the actors and the meaning of the *Cremadissa.* To quote Montrose: "writing and reading are always historically and socially determinate events, performed *in* the world and *upon* the world by gendered individual and collective human agents" (23). *Dins el darrer blau* is Riera's first historical novel, but it is not difficult to see its relationship to her other works, which deconstruct totalizing visions—such as that of the capital-w Woman—by presenting the layered and self-contradictory subjectivities of little-w women or of others, notably the poor, arguably the homosexual, who have been left out of history and objectified in discourse.[15]

Looked at thus, *Dins*' contestation of the monological historiography of the *Cremadissa* represents a continuing rejection, on Riera's part, of the unity Franco imposed on Spain: "Una, grande, y libre" [One, great, and free]. Like many who lived in regions with their own history and who spoke a Spanish language other than Castilian, Riera grew up abominating the regime's brutal repression of pluralism. But that's a dead letter in Spain in the mid-1990s. Or is it? She has written this novel about the disasters born of intolerance at a significant point in Spanish history: when most Spaniards under thirty have difficulty identifying what Franco did or represented, and when violent racist incidents are not uncommon items in the Spanish news. A similar historical amnesia obtains in Majorca, where massive immigration since the 1950s has so changed the society that few would seem to remember the historical reasons for the *xuetes*' marginalization (see Moore, 202–203). Discrimination against the group persists, however, and one of Riera's aims in writing the novel was to stimulate a public discussion of its wellspring. Many of her fellow Majorcans, including descendants of the *xuetes,* would prefer that the black episode be forgotten rather than revisited, but Riera has stated her belief that an airing of the problem may, in time, lead to healing.[16] The novel's denunciation of ideological and religious/racist fanaticism is also a purposeful comment on the situation in the former Yugoslavia. Poignantly, some of the first Yugoslavs displaced by the war and resettled elsewhere in Europe were Sephardim, invited to live—three hundred years after the Spanish diaspora—in Toledo.

The artful complexity and seriousness of purpose that characterize *Dins el darrer blau* make it one of the most important Spanish novels of the past twenty years. Yet one cannot fully appreciate its significance without relating it to the politics or literature of memory. The novel is, in many ways, the re-creation of a memory: that of the long-vanished *xuetes,* contained within the remembrance of the frame tale's protagonist, João Peres. Indeed, Peres functions as Mnemosyne in *Dins el darrer blau;* he is witness to the *Cremadissa* and bearer of its history. Peres the rememberer is also Peres the desirer, and his appearance on the opening page of the novel signals the importance that will be given to the intertwined impulses of memory and desire in the structure, form, and meaning of this novel. Both center on lack, on that which one does not have and can only possess imaginatively; in this, they are not unlike literature, history, or religion. In metafictional terms, it could be posited that the desire to embody memory impelled the writing of *Dins el darrer blau.*

Memory, desire, and narration brought João Peres to Palma, where the novel commences. Carrying certain details "ben impreses en el full primer de la memòria" [firmly printed on the first page of his memory] (17), Peres arrives in search of a woman described by a boastful ship's captain. He has never met this woman, but he desires her passionately because he "remembers" her from his dreams. For numerous other characters in the novel, men and women, remembered desires are the narrative traces of their subjectivity. For Valls, and the community he hypostasizes, memory has an even more important function: it constitutes them as Jews. Not simply because they have had to rely almost exclusively on memory to fulfill the precepts of their religion, but also because remembrance and history are essential to Judaism. As Yosef Yerushalmi observes in his book on Jewish history and memory, *Zakhor,* "Only in Israel and nowhere else is the injunction to remember felt as a religious imperative to an entire people."[17] The Jewish mandate to keep memory alive, no matter the cost, is associated in our century with the Holocaust and its survivors, including the writers Primo Levi and Elie Wiesel, whose literary works bear doleful witness to the atrocity they survived.

The politics of memory, the plea to remember so as to prevent recurrence, is also an essential part of the human rights movement in Latin America, reflected in such mottoes as "nunca más" and "ni olvido ni perdón." In an evocative article, Elizabeth Jelin writes that in Argentina, "one of the most important aspects of the human rights movement's cause is its struggle 'against forgetfulness' and for the construction of memory."[18] Riera's long-standing interest in the political and human situation of Latin America, evidenced in her novel *Joc de miralls* [Game of Mirrors; translated into Castilian as *Por persona interpuesta,* (By Proxy)], allows us to postulate her familiarity with this more recent, if more geographically distant, call to remembrance.

Dins el darrer blau clearly aims to construct a memory. But it can be objected—I myself have heard it objected, by a *xueta*—that it is not Riera's memory to construct, since she is not a *xueta*. But she is a Majorcan, and the novel re-creates an episode in Majorcan history that involved Old Christians as well as *conversos*.[19] Her entitlement to speak about this case depends on how narrowly one draws the categories of belonging, to use a point from an extensive article by Linda Alcoff, in which she debates whether "the discursive practice of speaking for others [is] ever a valid practice."[20] Alcoff believes that the speaker should "strive to create wherever possible the conditions for dialogue and the practice of speaking with and to rather than speaking for others" (29). As mentioned, Riera has stressed her hope that this novel will stimulate dialogue in Majorca. Alcoff concludes warily that there cannot be "an absolute disauthorization of all practices of speaking for others," since in some cases it may "enable the empowerment of oppressed peoples" (29).

Elizabeth Jelin writes that it is dangerous to charge remembrance to a few trustees, for the efficacy of memory may be lost.

> Those who have suffered directly or through their immediate relatives define themselves as the bearers of pain and memory. By this very fact, they unwillingly claim a type of symbolic authority and power based on their "monopoly" of meanings of truth and memory. Such power may, in turn, obliterate the mechanism of intergenerational transmission of memory, preventing the new generations from reinterpreting the transmitted experiences in terms of their own historical circumstances. And this is dangerous, since only when the incorporation of historical events becomes an active and dynamic process can it feed into the construction of a democratic culture and collective identity. (53)

Jelin's words, read in the context of *Dins el darrer blau,* provide ample justification for Riera's exploration of a dark tangle in Majorca's memory, one involving both *xuetes* and Christians. Incorporating this event into the collective memory of Majorcans is a step toward preventing the recurrence of similar tragedies with different victims.

Dins el darrer blau goes behind the capital h of History to imagine lives and tell stories that speak about human dignity and pettiness, about fanaticism and obduracy, about faith, longing and fear. It does so in terms that resonate in Majorca, in Spain, in Bosnia, in Germany, in Argentina: in every corner of the torn world. *Dins el darrer blau* gathers up the metaphorical ashes of the *xuetes* and lays them to rest, enjoining its readers not to forget the promise that beckons at the horizon, in the furthest blue.

Notes

1. Riera, *Dins el darrer blau* (Barcelona: Destino, 1994). Subsequent references to this novel appear in the text.

2. The term *xueta* has been used in Majorca since the end of the eighteenth century, to refer to a *converso,* or New Christian, of Jewish descent. The word continues to be used as an insult, but anthropologists and other social scientists use it nonjudgmentally to refer to the bounded community it denominates; I adopt their usage. It should perhaps be made clear that *xueta* is not a synonym for Judaizer, since not all members of the Majorcan *converso* community continued to observe Mosaic law. Folk etymologies abound for the word, but it seems most clearly derived from the (disparaging) diminutive of the Catalan and Majorcan word for Jew [*jueu*]: *juetó,* once written *xuetó.* See

Angela Selke, *The Conversos of Majorca: Life and Death in a Crypto-Jewish Community in XVII Century Spain* (Jerusalem: Magnes Press, 1986), 10–11; Eva Laub and Juan Laub, *El mito triunfante: Estudio antropológico de los chuetas mallorquines* [The Triumphant Myth: an Anthropological Study of the Majorcan Chuetas] (Palma de Mallorca: Miquel Font, 1987), 29. Subsequent quotations from these works are cited parenthetically in the text.

3. I borrow the word "scumbling" from David Herzberger, who uses it to describe the purposeful confusion of previously distinct entities or categories: "I mean by scumbling both a creative device and a critical perspective: it overextends the folds of one thing (fiction) into those of another (history) without eliminating entirely the discreteness of each. As a way of approximating history and fiction, scumbling deliberately opens truth and meaning to the contingencies of configuration. . ."; *Narrating the Past: Fiction and Historiography in Postwar Spain* (Durham: Duke University Press, 1994).

4. Women have not had salient roles in standard versions of this episode, which has always been narrated as a struggle between men in thrall to competing patriarchal religions: "la ley vieja y caduca de Moisés" [the old, superseded law of Moses] as it was referred to constantly in the documents, vs. its historical successor, *la fe triunfante* [the triumphant faith]. In this light, it is curious to note that more women than men (46 vs. 38) were "relaxed" in the four *autos de fe* of 1691, suggesting that women were more steadfast than men in their religious beliefs. But Francisco Garau, eyewitness and principal chronicler of this episode, advanced a different interpretation for the gender disproportion: women were more easily duped than men. Referring to the large number of women who did not abjure their Judaism, he wrote: "De ésto se infiere con evidencia que el seguirse tan obstinadamente esta Secta, ni es por razón, ni por estudio, ni por saber, pues no puede sospecharse en ellas, que se entienden solo de aliñarse, hilar, coser y vender, sino puramente por engaño, error, tema, y pasión ciega y torpe, que todo es tan connatural en el sexo. Engañábanlas sus maridos o parientes, a unas con especie de piedad, a otras de codicia" [From this it can evidently be inferred that if women hew so obstinately to this Sect it is not the result of reason, or study, or knowledge, since none of these can be expected in them, who only know how to array themselves, to spin, sew or sell; but rather is the result of deception, error, manias, and blind, stupid passion, all so innate to their sex. Their husbands or relatives deceived them, appealing to their piety or to their greed]. I cite from the 1984 edition of Garau's work, which uses a simplified title, *La fe triunfante* (Palma de Mallorca: Miquel Font), 58. The full title of the 1691 edition is *La fee trivnfante en qvatro avtos celebrados en Mallorca por el santo oficio de la Inquisicion en que an salido ochenta, i ocho reos, i de treinta, i siete relaiados solo vvo tres pertinaces* [The Triumphant Faith in Four Acts Celebrated in Majorca by the Holy Office of the Inquisition in which Eighty-Eight Were Judged, and of the Thirty-Eight Relaxed There Were Only Three Recalcitrants]. Subsequent quotations from Garau are cited parenthetically in the text, and respect his orthography.

5. Hutcheon, *A Poetics of Postmodernism: History, Theory, and Fiction* (New York: Routledge, 1988), 5. Subsequent quotations from this work are cited parenthetically in the text.

6. Ana Rodríguez-Fischer, ed., *Cartas a Rosa Chacel* (Madrid: Versal, 1992), 172.

7. DuPlessis, *The Pink Guitar: Writing as Feminist Practice* (New York: Routledge, 1990), 151. Subsequent quotations from this work are cited parenthetically in the text.

8. Montrose, "Professing the Renaissance: The Poetics and Politics of Culture," in *The New Historicism,* ed. H. Aram Veeser (New York: Routledge, 1989), 20. Subsequent quotations from this work are cited parenthetically in the text.

9. Silverman, *The Subject of Semiotics* (New York: Oxford University Press, 1983), 47–50, discussed in Hutcheon, 168–69. Silverman's categories expand Benveniste's distinction between the speaking subject and the subject of speech.

10. So strong is the opprobrium still attached to the surnames of the "quince linajes" that Riera debated inventing last names for her fictional characters, rather than risk reopening old wounds (personal communication). About the term *quince linajes* and related debate, see Selke, 13–15; Eva Laub and Juan Laub, pp. 29–33; and Kenneth Moore, *Those of the Street: The Catholic Jews of Mallorca* (Notre Dame: University of Notre Dame Press, 1976), 13. Subsequent quotations from Moore are cited parenthetically in the text.

11. It cannot be known if the historical rabbi remained faithful to his faith or not, but some may feel that Riera's imputation of loss of faith to Gabriel Valls diminishes Rafel Valls' memory. Selke maintains that the failed escape led many *xuetes* to lose faith. "What finally broke down that tenacious adherence to the ancestral Law was not only the fact that the God of Israel, false to his word, did not save them on the night of their greatest tribulation and anguish; it was, above all, the conviction that their God, in permitting on that night that His people be delivered into the hands of their enemies because of a mere storm, had been *vanquished* by the Greater God of the Christians. His omnipotence, therefore, *was not true*" (190). A different opinion is expressed by Nissan ben-Avraham, a *xueta* who left Mallorca to settle in Israel in 1977, became a rabbi, and wrote a book on rabbinical law and the *xuetes: Els anussim: el problema dels xuetons segons la legislació rabínica* [The Coerced: The Problem of the Xuetes According to Rabbinical Law] (Palma de Mallorca: Miquel Font, 1992). His book is dedicated to those who died in 1691: "aquells Sants Màrtirs que moriren amb la fidelitat a llur Poble dins del cor i amb el nom de D-éu als llavis" [those Holy Saints who died with hearts faithful to their People and with the name of God on their lips] (10). In an endnote to this dedication, however, he recognizes that his affirmation of their faith may be contested: "Malgrat que, en un moment donat, per causa de turment o coacció, l'esperit de molts d'ells defallí, i es deixaren seduir per la possibilitat d'alleujar un poc l'amargor de la mort, són considerats com a màrtirs del Judaisme, ja que patiren i moriren just pel fet d'esser jueus" [In spite of the fact that at a given moment, from the effects of torture or coercion, many of them lost their spirit and allowed themselves to be seduced by the possibility of alleviating the bitterness of their death, they are considered martyrs of Judaism, since they suffered and died solely because they were Jews] (12). I am indebted to Pere Bonnín for bringing Ben-Avraham's book to my attention.

12. According to Ben-Avraham, many of the rites carried out by the *xuetes* would not have been valid in rabbinical law. Over the decades, many of the members of the *converso* community would have been too lax in observing Mosaic law to preserve their right to serve as witnesses. See Ben-Avraham, 50.

13. Braunstein, *The Chuetas of Majorca: Conversos and the Inquisition of Majorca* (New York: Ktav Publishing House, 1972). Subsequent quotations from this work are cited parenthetically in the text. Riera's familiarity with the original version of Selke's book (published in Spanish) is made clear at the beginning of "Horror," the chapter of *Escenarios para la felicidad* [Settings for Happiness] (Palma de Mallorca: R. y J.J. de Olañeta, 1994), which briefly relates the story of the *Cremadissa:* "Angela Selke en su interesantísimo libro *Los chuetas y la Inquisición* da cuenta pormenorizada de los últimos autos de fe con víctimas que tuvieron lugar en Mallorca a finales del siglo XVII" [Angela Selke, in her very interesting book *Los chuetas y la Inquisición,* gives a detailed account of the last *autos de fe* with live victims that took place in Majorca at the end of the seventeenth century] (46).

14. I will review briefly the most salient, drawing principally from Braunstein, 64–76, and Selke, 101–105. Many Majorcan Judaizers were prosperous merchants, often with extensive trade relations in the Mediterranean. Old Christian nobles entered into silent partnerships with these men in an attempt to shore up sagging family fortunes. At the same time, Inquisitorial activity on the island had languished, due in part to assiduous bribery of its officials by the Judaizers, in part to continuous feuding between the Viceroy of Majorca, who represented the Crown's interests, and the local Tribunal of the Inquisition. Finally, in 1678, the bare coffers of the Majorcan Tribunal, combined with financially and religiously motivated pressure from the Supreme Council of the Inquisition in Madrid, led the Majorcan body to move against the *xuetes.* With the help of *don dinero* [Sir Money], still the most *poderoso caballero* [powerful gentleman] in Majorca, every one of the 237 crypto-Jews imprisoned by the Inquisition in what was called *la Complicidad del año 1678* [Conspiracy of 1678] was eventually reconciled and released. Musing about those pardons, one *xueta* was reported—in later Inquisition records—to have said: "Our reconciliation was indeed very odd. Three taps with the rod, leave your money, and goodbye!" (quoted in Selke, 60). The trials had shaken the *xueta* community, and many were impoverished by the confiscations, but they continued to Judaize, albeit far more surreptitiously. They began to remake their fortunes and to plan in earnest for their escape. Had money continued to be the supreme arbiter in Majorca, much of the community might have succeeded in fleeing. But the arrival in Palma of not one but two unbribable Inquisitors, the first in 1687, the second in 1688 (Braunstein, 82), meant that orthodoxy replaced money as the highest value on the island.

15. For a provocative argument about the lesbianism presented in Riera's well-known stories, "Te deix, amor, la mar com a penyora" [I Leave You, My love, the Sea as a Token], and "Jo pos per testimoni les gavines" [I Call on the Seagulls as Witness], see Brad Epps, "Virtual Sexuality: Lesbianism, Loss, and Deliverance in Carme Riera's 'Te deix, amor, la mar com a penyora," in *¿Entiendes? Queer Readings, Hispanic Writings,* ed. Emilie L. Bergmann and Paul Julian Smith (Durham: Duke University Press, 1995), 317–45.

16. Riera's statements about the continuing discrimination against descendants of the *xuetes,* and her hopes that *Dins el darrer blau* could contribute to opening a therapeutic debate in Majorca, are found in two articles by C. G.: "Carme Riera: 'Voldria matar el monstre de la intolerància a Mallorca amb el meu llibre'" [Carme Riera: I would like to kill the beast of intolerance in Mallorca with my book] (*Avui,* 8 January 1995): 38; and "L'escriptora Carme Riera retrata la Mallorca jueva del segle XVII" [The writer Carme Riera portrays Jew-

ish Mallorca in the seventeenth century] (*Avui,* 25 February 1994): 44. In a brief note titled "Torna la polèmica xueta a Mallorca" [The *xueta* polemic returns to Mallorca] the newsmagazine *El Temps* (Valencia) reported recent opposition in Majorca to a planned monument memorializing the *xuetes* who fell victim to the Inquisition. "Va ser un grup de cinc persones, a través d'una carta a la premsa, totes elles descendants de xuetes, els qui mostraren la seva oposició a aquest monument, declarant que 'només servia per a ressuscitar vells menyspreus, odis i marginacions cap a tots nosaltres, quan ara ja tot estava pràcticament oblidat'" [It was a group of five, all descendents of *xuetes,* who expressed their opposition to this monument in a letter to the press, declaring that "it only served to revive the contempt, hatred, and relegation that used to be visited on all of us, just now when everything was practically forgotten"] (13).

17. Yerushalmi, *Zakhor: Jewish History and Jewish Memory* (Seattle: University of Washington Press, 1982), 9. I am indebted to Professor Harold Stahmer for suggesting that I consult Yerushalmi in this regard.

18. Jelin, "The Politics of Memory: The Human Rights Movement and the Construction of Democracy in Argentina," *Latin American Perspectives* 21 (1994): 49. Subsequent quotations from this work are cited parenthetically in the text.

19. In point of fact, more chapters of the novel are dedicated to Old Christians than to crypto-Jews: 14 versus 11.

20. Alcoff, "The Problem of Speaking for Others," *Cultural Critique* 20 (Winter 91–92): 7. Subsequent quotations from this work are cited parenthetically in the text.

The Ethics of Dissidence: Resistance and Relationality in Carme Riera's *Dins el darrer blau*

NEUS CARBONELL

CARME RIERA'S LATEST AND PRIZE-WINNING NOVEL *DINS EL DARRER blau* (In the Furthest Blue) is narrated from a position of historical and ethical dissidence; the past must be rewritten to change the present and to be carried over into the future.[1] When the Castilian translation was published, a news report stated that:

> Siglos después de los hechos que ella relata las heridas siguen abiertas. Riera todavía recuerda cómo en el colegio las niñas se reían de las compañeras que tenían apellidos judíos. La escritora guarda también un recorte de periódico, de hace dos años, donde se recogía la sentencia del Tribunal Supremo aprobando el cambio de apellido solicitado por una mallorquina que quería borrar esa huella de su linaje. "Ahora no hay hogueras físicas, pero hay mucha intransigencia y crispación"; dice la autora, quien se muestra partidaria de la palabra y el diálogo como único medio de posibilitar el cambio.
>
> [Centuries after the events that she describes there are wounds that remain unhealed. Riera still recalls how, as a child at school, the girls made fun of classmates with Jewish names. The writer still keeps a newspaper clipping from two years ago which summarizes the Supreme Court ruling approving a change of surname requested by a Majorcan woman who wanted to erase this vestige from her ancestral past. "Today there is no actual burning at the stake but there is a lot of intransigence and tension," says the author, who is in favor of the word and dialogue as the only means by which change can be brought about.][2]

Dins el darrer blau, however, also embodies all the pitfalls of contemporary discourses which confront the ethical issue of responsibility for the Other. Resistance to a particular representation is, in Riera's narrative, expressed by means of another representation. Paradoxically, the narrative does not take place outside mechanisms that ensure the reproduction of the very power that is otherwise being contested. As poststructuralist feminists have argued, it is difficult to denounce the repression of the Other without reenacting that repression, without lapsing once again into binary thinking in terms of purity and impurity and therefore reinforcing the outside/inside dichotomy situated at the core of the conflict in question. *Dins el darrer blau,* after all, is about the expulsion of those who resist assimilation. This has been a major concern for contemporary postmodern discourse after the loss of the traditional critical distance between knowledge and ideology. Robert Young has written about the issue:

> When science could set its knowledge against ideology, there was a noticeable lack of interest in the otherness of the other. Now that we are inextricably within the culture of postmodernism, the alterity of the other becomes the last trace of a ghostly knowledge.[3]

To avoid this impasse, I am going to consider how a discourse that endeavors to represent and defend the practices of heterogeneity is caught up in a web of heterogeneous contradictions. This is largely because the enunciative position is not a single, homogeneous one of forgiveness and correction but one of multiple sites. I would like to discuss in the next few pages the implications and scope of this plurality of writing positions, bearing in mind that *Dins* is written by a white European woman in a minority language about other minorities. It deals with the past in the context of contemporary ethnic violence, and here it is read framed within the critical literature of feminist and postcolonial practices.

Part II of *Dins* ends with the appalling, tragic story of Aixa and Laila, two young women enslaved by the Viceroy's orders. The representation of their submission to the powerful white man is informed by an orientalist ethos. The women are commodified as sexual slaves, portrayed as coming from a harem somewhere in the Orient, exotic, beautiful, and erotically playful. Aixa and Laila are first brutally mutilated by a drunk and impotent master and, later on, killed on his orders to avoid the scandal that would damage his social status. The young women *belong* to the Viceroy; they were brought to entertain him and his distinguished guests. Aixa and Laila are his property, and they emblematize the Oriental Other; they are objectified to enlarge the white man's sense of power and superiority. They are there, as the Orient is, to be gazed at and to be possessed:

> Fou una meditació vora el foc, vora d'aquesta mateixa foganya, davant unes flames paregudes—a estones, com ara, fins i tot blaves i quasi grogues—, meditació sobre el fugaç curs de la vida i l'efímera durada dels pocs plaers que ens atorga, que l'incitaren, feia tan sols quinze dies, a comprovar si aquelles moretes que li havien regalat i que només feia dansar de tant en tant per a ell o per a un grup d'amics selectes, serien capaces de fer-li reviscolar les flames del seu propi caliu.
>
> [It was a moment of meditation near the fire, near this very same fire, in front of some similar flames—sometimes, like now, even blue and almost yellow—a moment of meditation on the fleeting flow of life and on the ephemeral duration of the few pleasures granted to us, that had aroused him two weeks earlier to see if the Moorish girls given to him as a present (who he had dance for him or a group of select friends once in a while) would be able to revive the flames of his own desire.][4]

The story has its turning point when the Viceroy's impotence becomes visible to the slaves. Aixa and Laila cease to be the object looked at and become subjects of the gaze registering the Viceroy's inability to assert his superiority through the signifier of power and mastery. He is stripped of all phallic power when he proves to be incapable of responding to the sexual enticement of the women. The relationship between master and slave is revealed as unsustainable: the master cannot have what the Other represents. Power is exposed as a simulacrum:

> Les al.lotes dansaren com sempre ho havien fet, però aquesta vegada notaren sobre els seus cossos una mirada diferent. L'amo no intentava gaudir de la visió, pel pur plaer de contemplar aquells membres joves i elàstics lliurats al ritme, ballant en el seu honor. Ara cada esguard semblava amagar la menaça d'una torxa burxant a punt de penetrar-les. Fou Aixa la primera a observar que enmig de l'engonal del senyor Virrei els calçons no podien dissimular una creixent protuberància que mai no havia copsat. L'hem exitat, pensà l'al.lota, qualque dia havia de succeir. Veurem què ens manarà fer d'aquí a una estona. Però l'estona mai no arribà perquè tot succeí a partir d'aquell precís instant, com si també sa Excel.lència s'hagués adonat del pensament de la mora. D'una embranzida la féu agenollar al seu davant i . . . l'obligà a posar la boca sobre el seu sexe només a mitges erecte. . . . Però cap de les dues, malgrat els esforços disciplinats, no aconseguí convertir en tió encés aquell caliu minvat.

> [The girls danced as they had always danced, but this time they felt a different gaze upon their bodies. The master was not trying to enjoy the sight of them just for the pleasure of looking at those young elastic limbs surrendered to rhythm, dancing in his honor. Now every gaze seemed to hide the menace of a pointed torch ready to penetrate them. Aixa was the first one to notice that between the legs of the Viceroy his trousers couldn't hide a growing protuberance which they had never seen. We got him aroused, she thought, it had to happen one day. We'll see what he asks for in a moment. But that moment never came because everything happened from then on as if the master had realized what the Moorish girl was thinking. Impulsively, he made her kneel in front of him and put her mouth on his half-erect penis. . . . But neither of them, despite their disciplined efforts, succeeded in turning those embers into a burning log.][5]

The Viceroy attempts to regain his authority by turning his ridiculous position into an apparently playful situation he controls. He impersonates a dog and engages the young women in a game in which the roles of master and slave seem momentarily suspended, only to be brutally reestablished when he maims the clitoris of one woman and a nipple of the other. The cruelty of this scene can be interpreted as a metaphor for Western history as the history of intolerance of the Other and of its confinement to hierarchical relationships of power and subjugation, even when violence becomes the irretrievable sign of the master's own unbearable weakness.

The story of these enslaved women, "made to disappear" by the Viceroy's men so as to prevent them from talking to the Catholic Church's high-ranking officials and exposing the governor's morally dubious sexual behavior, illustrates the fall of a character despised also by his own class because of his transactions with people of other kinds whose impurity contaminates him—Jews, prostitutes, and Moors. The Viceroy's position is a contradictory one. On the one hand, his dealings with subaltern subjects secure the superiority of the privileged whites, and, through these acts he becomes an agent of colonization. On the other hand, his position engages him actively in exchanges with colonial subjects. The story of Aixa and Laila is strategically placed at the threshold of the events that narrate the repression of the Jewish community in seventeenth-century Majorca. It can be read as a display of the violence and contradictions ingrained in any narrative about race, class, and gender. Power and impotence, silence and speech, horror and pleasure mix and expose the paradoxes of an enunciative position regarding the repression of otherness.

The Viceroy's act of silencing the Orientalized women also narrates the story of their silence, for readers never hear their story. How could they? How could the subaltern speak to the reader? As repressed and objectified beings, Laila and Aixa occupy the place of the signifier and not the place of enunciation. They are spoken for, represented and representing somebody or something beyond themselves; they are not awarded the subjecthood necessary to assume an enunciative position.[6] But this becomes a paradigmatic question for the entire novel: how can otherness be narrated? If the Other is represented by the Self, the logic of silence that is being denounced is also being reproduced.

Cultural narratives of resistance are manifold, but they share a critique of power and a will to "change the subject" of textual practices, to use Nancy Miller's felicitous expression, to claim justice for the colonized. Criticism has expanded the boundaries in the notion of the colonized beyond its classical territorial reach "to include women, subjugated classes, national minorities, and even marginalized or incorporated academic subspecialties,"[7] that is, all those social groups or categories that are left outside the borders of hegemonic discourses. But, just as it has been recognized that the subaltern is not part of a homogeneous group, voices have recently been raised against the view of the dominant group as a monolithic discourse. Reina Lewis reminds the reader of Orientalist critique that

> power is never willed, owned (by individuals, groups or states), unitary or monolithic, but discursive: discourse, as an ordering of knowledge, produces positionalities (enunciative modalities) into which individuals are interpellated and from which they may speak or act (as policemen, lawyers, mothers) but which are never the truth of themselves.[8]

Resistance is not only produced against, but also as a result of, the dominant group. The place of enunciating identities, the place of belonging, is legitimized by what is forced not to belong—that is, by the Other. But, as this position is never a truthful one, there are fissures in the process of enunciating identities, and, through them, the Other permeates and subverts the self. When fissures are violently prevented, as has happened in Western history, the Other is aggressively constrained to a subaltern position. Hélène Cixous expresses it this way:

> What is the "Other"? If it is truly the "other," there is nothing to say; it cannot be theorized. The "other" escapes me. It is elsewhere, outside: absolutely other. It doesn't settle down. But in History, of course, what is called the "other" is an alterity that does settle down, that falls into the dialectical circle. It is the other in a hierarchically organized relationship in which the same is what rules, names, defines, and assigns "its" other. . . . The paradox of otherness is that, of course, at no moment in History is it tolerated or possible as such. The other is there only to be appropriated, recaptured and destroyed as other. Even the exclusion is not an exclusion. Algeria was not France but it was French.[9]

The paradox alluded to by Cixous is that History constructs its Other to ensure the dialectical circle of power and powerlessness, even though only the Other can effectively undermine this dialectic. Because violence and colonization are not random exercises, their subversion demands more than traditional practices of altruism and charity, because, in order to change the status of the subaltern, hegemonic practices must be radically contested. It is not a matter of sharing but of giving. This new ethical relationship with the Other is, for Cixous, a feminine practice of love and giving: "And there is a link between the economy of femininity—the open extravagant subjectivity, that relationship to the other in which the gift doesn't calculate its influence—and the possibility of love."[10] This may seem highly utopian, but, as Robert Young has also stated, it is significant as a new model of ethics being articulated from dissident voices in the West concerned with constructing paradigms of knowledge which can also contest imperialism on epistemological and moral grounds.[11]

Dins el darrer blau may be read as a narrative of resistance from the ethical perspective of the responsibility for the repressed. As stated at the outset, one of the main purposes of the novel is to pay homage to the last community of Jews burned by the Inquisition in Majorca in the seventeenth century, and to beg forgiveness of their descendants, cast out and humiliated by an intolerant Majorcan society during the centuries that followed the inquisitorial process. For Carme Riera, rewriting and revising the past is a present endeavor and a moral project for the future:

> Las hogueras del fanatismo y la ortodoxia son una constante del siglo XXI, en el que ya estamos. Seguimos proyectando nuestro peor

> yo sobre los débiles, los pobres y los emigrantes. Necesitaríamos matar el yo racista que llevamos dentro y eso sólo se puede conseguir colocándonos en el lugar del otro, sintiéndote agredida.

> [Execution at the stakes of fanaticism and orthodoxy is a constant of the twenty-first century, in which we are already living. We keep projecting our worst self onto the weak, the poor and the immigrants. We would need to kill the racist self that we all bear within us, and this can only be achieved by positioning ourselves in the place of the other, by making yourself feel assaulted.][12]

Here, Riera formulates the ethical and political issue of responsibility for the Other. She articulates a position that involves recognition of one's relationality with the Other, while trying to avoid its denial and its assimilation to the self. For this reason, "unlike a conventional ethics of altruism, such a relation remains one of alterity."[13] *Dins el darrer blau* represents Riera's effort to position herself *in relation to* the other; but it is also true that this cannot be done outside the cultural and historical discourses that create the position of alterity. Resistance and accommodation are tangled in discourse. The novel not only narrates, but also performs, the expulsion of the Other in order to safeguard the identity of the dominant self; in a certain sense, the scapegoat ritual is both denounced and carried out. Its denunciation is a political and ethical act which displays and evidences the violence exercised to preserve the privileges of the powerful. The plot focuses on the construction and repression of otherness, as the author's comments imply. The persecution of the Jewish community is represented as having been carried out for financial and political reasons, and the ideological and religious arguments brandished by the Inquisition are only a facade to ensure the impunity of their action. The categories of good and evil, and the compulsion to expel what is categorized as evil, are established by the powerful in order to preserve their privileges at all costs. Clearly, the conflict does not reside in the Other, but in the dominant self's intolerance and fears. Those Majorcans who are faithful to their ancestors' religion and traditions, despite their coerced conversion, are made to embody sin and evil by other Majorcans, the *pure-blooded* Catholics, and, as a result, they are exterminated. Everybody expects some gain from the inquisitorial processes: money, property, political or religious influence, distraction for the hungry peasants.

The narrative, however, opens up several questions: are the *gent del carrer* (*the people from the street,* the Jews are named after the street to which they are confined) the textual other?[14] And if so, in what way? Is the speaking position that of the Gentiles reconciling themselves with the persecuted? These questions bring us back to my previous concern that the novel, in its very act of denunciation, is a performance of the scapegoat ritual. If the intended audience is, in its vast majority, the white nominally Catholic but generally nonreligious Catalan-speaking community, then—and I borrow Lewis's words to formulate the question—is it possible "to bring Christian readers to a recognition of their debt to the Jews without collapsing the psychically essential distance between reader and textual other?"[15] Or, in other words, is it possible to recognize a historical and ethical debt from a position of exteriority to the subject to whom one wants to acknowledge such a debt? And, if distances are collapsed, how does this attitude differ from one of appropriation?

Either directly or in their representation, the Jews are unquestionably represented as being Majorcans. Their belonging to the island goes unquestioned: they speak the same language, share the same spaces, and participate in the same transactions as do non-Jews. Their difference amounts to no more than a few religious practices performed in hiding and some dietary customs. They, however, are obliged to maintain the secrecy of their attachment to their ancestors' practices and are confined to the island (they do not have access to permits to leave Majorca). But secrets and secrecy confer distinct identity. And their uncovering by the *malsí Costura* (the informer to the Inquisitor) leads the community to its fatal extermination. Secrecy and its exposure lie at the core of the conflict. The lives of the Jewish protagonists are represented as a struggle to maintain their identity in hiding; their fall is due to the discovery of their practices. The narrative revolves around clandestine activities such as their religious habits, meetings in the rabbi Gabriel Valls's garden, the concealed customs of Isabel Tarongí (the Jewish wife of a Catholic man, uncovered by her husband), and, finally, their furtive and failed flight to a land of freedom and tolerance. Secrecy, however, is also the burden of a community that strives to flee to a land where everyone will be free to abandon the constraint to live in secrecy: "Fugim per poder complir lliurement amb es preceptes que ens imposa sa nostra religió, per no haver d'amagar-nos, per poder dir amb veu ben alta que som jueus i morirem jueus" [We are fleeing so that we can freely comply with the obligations imposed by our religion, so that we don't have to hide, so that we can say aloud that we are Jews and will die Jews].[16] Secrecy is synonymous with repression and freedom with public disclosure. As a consequence, the story is articulated through a discourse that narrates and explains characters, situations, feelings, ideological positions. Contrary to many poststructuralist statements which praise secrets and secrecy on the grounds that Otherness cannot be known, in *Dins el darrer blau,* secrets and secrecy are the result of humiliation. The position of the Jew-as-Other becomes, as such, problematic in the novel. To what degree have they become yet again Otherness mastered? Have they become a projection of the self, of the White-as-privileged-position?

Riera's political project may, however, make other demands. The reader can identify with the Jews, with the victims, because they are not really alien, they are not really different, and therefore, a painful confrontation between the reader and the textual other does not take place. One could say that the text constructs a position that forces readers to identify with the victims of persecution, "positioning them in the expected place of the Other, making them feel assaulted," in Riera's own words quoted above.

The limits between good and evil are reconstructed in the form of the division drawn between the executioners, the Inquisitors, the agents of repression, and the intolerant, on one hand, and the victims, on the other. To the extent that good and evil are foregrounded, the novel risks reproducing what it criticizes. The demarcation between good and bad characters, clearly spelled out, threatens to reestablish what, on the other hand, has been undermined. And this statement is not made in the name of a radical relativism that leads to moral and ethical nihilism, but rather because the division between good and evil secures for the reader a position of certainty which identification with the Jews weakens. Certainty could be at odds with historical debt; it could comfortably wash away one's responsibility. The author's note at the end of the novel, however, opens up the conflict again to leave it unresolved and writes uncertainty back into the narrative and, more importantly, into history, not as past but as present and as future. By bringing the reader back into the present and into the need to recognize his or her own debt to the persecuted, the writer's note turns a narrative which recasts a historical past into a present contingency. It also creates the uncomfortable possibility of the self being situated both in the place of the executioner and of the victim. In this sense, it demands of the reader an ethical commitment. The first-person plural form of the verb in the last paragraph of the author's note forces the issue:

> *Dins el darrer blau* no té, encara que pugui semblar-ho, cap interès polèmic. No pretén burxar velles ferides ni tampoc obrir-ne de noves, fent referència a la intolerància de bona part de la societat mallorquina contra un altre grup de mallorquins de procedència jueva, ja que, per ventura, pitjor que els fets del 1691 foren les seves tràgiques conseqüències que marginaren i humiliaren durant segles els descendents dels màrtirs cremats en els *Autos de fe*. A tots ells, crec que els mallorquins de bona voluntat no podem fer altra cosa que demanar perdó. Aquesta és, també, una de les intencions de la novel.la.
>
> [*Dins el darrer blau* does not have, despite appearances, a polemical aim. It does not try to open up old wounds nor cause new ones when it refers to the intolerance of a large part of Majorcan society against another group of Majorcans of Jewish descent. Perhaps what was worse than the events of 1691 were the tragic consequences suffered by the descendants of those martyrs burned at the stake, who were outcast and humiliated for centuries after. To all of them, I think that Majorcans of good will owe an apology. This is, also, one of the novel's intentions.][17]

Dins el darrer blau presents a current issue as a result of the continuity of the past. Riera purports to have drawn on factual sources for raw material and articulates a distinction between fact and fiction in the Aristotelian tradition of truth and verisimilitude:

> He canviat noms, cognoms i malnoms a posta per remarcar que el meu llibre no és d'història, sinó de ficció. En els dominis de la història cap material no pot ser manipulable; en el de la novel.la, per molt històrica que sigui, mentre es mantingui la versemblança, la veritat de cohesió, tot és vàlid i es legitima en conseqüència.
>
> [I have changed names, family names and nicknames on purpose to stress the fact that my book is not historical but fictional. In the domain of history, nothing ought to be manipulated. In the domain of fiction, regardless of its historicity, as long as verisimilitude and truth of coherence are maintained, anything and everything is valid and, consequently, legitimate].[18]

According to this quotation, history has become the extra-discursive space of factuality, and fiction the supplementary realm constructed above the truth provided by the metalanguage of history. Statements such as this one have been contested by poststructuralism which, on the contrary, has argued the impossibility of any extra-discursive realm. For its practitioners, history—and, for that matter, any other form of knowledge—cannot be immune to the effects of the signifiers that produce its meanings. History cannot escape the effects of its own rhetoric; therefore, it cannot be a secure basis for any literary practices, neither as source nor as authority for interpretation. As such, the consequences go beyond the critique to the relationship between the two discourses that Western knowledge has traditionally categorized as related but nevertheless different—the discourse of facts (history) and the discourse of fiction (literature)—because, in their most radical approach, poststructuralist positions have denied the alterity of the past. Some critics, such as Patrick Wright, have claimed that the writing of history is not about past events but about present institutions of knowledge and truth.[19] To deny the force and influence of this critique would be shortsighted. There seems to be little opposition to the claim that history is a discourse enunciated from the present. On the other hand, to deny the alterity of the past poses serious problems for narratives which vindicate a rewriting of the interpretation of documents for political and ethical reasons. In the words of David Lowenthal:

> To doubt the historical past, however, raises additional problems. A world created during historical times would falsify not just some but *all* accounts of previous history, with dire implications for human credibility. . . . Would it make any difference had there been no past? Would we not behave just as we do anyway?. . . . But in fact nothing would be the same. Tradition would be farcical. Few would heed the consequences of their actions. No one would apprehend wrong-doers if there was no past when their crimes could have taken place.[20]

If the value of the past is denied because the past as such cannot exist, and all we are left with is a present discourse validated and legitimized only by the power of current institutions, there could be no recourse to the ethical revision of practices that have involved subalternity. In this sense, Riera's rewriting would make impossible the very alterity that the novel attempts to vindicate.

The force of the claim that history is an institution validated by forms of knowledge also institutionalized cannot be denied. However, to negate radically the existence of the past can become as absolutist a claim as the opposite assertion of its truthful nature. Because only when the past is constructed as a monolithic and ontological entity does it become irretrievable from the present. But if, following Lowenthal, a distinction is drawn between past as a multiform event, and history as a discourse that interprets, for the sake of the present, the relics and memories that leave traces of the past, then possibilities open up for new ways of understanding contemporary events.

To find new ways of thinking and writing about history has been a driving force behind discourses seeking to investigate the relation between the West and its others: the revision of what *History* entails, and which *histories* are left behind, has been undertaken from multiple sites. Young addresses the question:

> But how to write a new history? When, as Césaire observed, the only history is white? The critique of the structures of colonialism might seem a marginal activity in relation to the mainstream political issues of literary and cultural theory, catering only for minorities or for those with a special interest in history. But although it is concerned with the geographical peripheries of metropolitan European culture, its long-term strategy is to effect a radical restructuring of European thought and, particularly, historiography.[21]

Dins el darrer blau's revision of history can be read as a narrative that discusses the present need for tolerance even though it is also a rewriting of the past. Given its political and ethical nature, the novel questions the future of a community of nonmarked boundaries that, Riera seems to argue, ought to learn to live with multiplicity and dissidence. Writing about a minority which has long ceased to have any influence on dominant Catalan and Spanish social forms may seem a marginal exercise, one that does not threaten the identity of such hegemonic cultural forms.[22] But it may not be irrelevant to recall that Catalan nationalist discourse after the nineteenth century has drawn on historiography to represent a coherent self persecuted over the centuries, whose identity flows with an unquestioned continuity from the past into the present.[23] As a contrast, *Dins el darrer blau* represents the heterogeneity inherent in any form of human existence. As such, fantasies of unified identity are undermined through the ethics of relationality with the Other, with the subaltern subject, by unsettling positions of comfortable certainty in the addressees' identity.

Notes

1. *Dins el darrer blau* (Barcelona: Edicions Destino, 1994) was awarded the "Premio Nacional de Narrativa, 1995."

2. Amelia Castilla, "Carme Riera: 'Ya no hay hogueras pero persiste la intransigencia,'" *El País* (7 March 1996), 40. All translations are mine.

3. Young, *Torn Halves. Political Conflict in Literary and Cultural Theory* (Manchester: Manchester University Press, 1996), 20.

4. Riera, *Dins el darrer blau,* 275.

5. Riera, *Dins el darrer blau,* 277.

6. As an example of criticism on subalternity, I consider Spivak's article more than pertinent in this context: "Can the Subaltern Speak?" in *Colonial Discourse and Postcolonial Theory,* ed. Patrick Williams and Laura Chrisman (New York: Harvester Wheatsheaf, 1993), 66–111. It addresses the problem of the intellectual trying to work within a determinate frame of knowledge which is articulated by imperialism even when the intellectual tries to undo it.

7. Edward Said, "Representing the Colonized: Anthropology's Interlocutors," *Critical Inquiry* 15 (1989): 207.

8. Lewis, *Gendering Orientalism. Race, Femininity and Representation* (London and New York: Routledge, 1996), 18–19.

9. Cixous, "Sorties," in *The Newly Born Woman,* trans. Betsy Wing (Minneapolis: University of Minnesota Press, 1987), 71.

10. Cixous, "Sorties," 92.

11. Young, *White Mythologies* (London and New York: Routledge, 1990), 16–17.

12. José Martí Gómez, "Con los años ganas lucidez y sentido crítico," *La Vanguardia Magazine* (24 December 1995): 12.

13. Young, *White Mythologies,* 17. This quote is in reference to Cixous, Levinas, and Kristeva, but I have appropriated it for my new context.

14. For a study of how the crypto-Jews in the novel are reduced in terms of space by the Catholic community, see Luisa Cotoner, "Marco escénico e interpretación simbólica de los espacios en *Dins el darrer blau* de Carme Riera," in *Lectora. Revista de dones i textualitat* (Universitat Autònoma de Barcelona, forthcoming).

15. Lewis, *Gendering Orientalism,* 221.

16. Riera, *Dins el darrer blau,* 189.

17. Ibid., 432.

18. Ibid., 430–31.

19. Wright, *On Living in an Old Country: The National Past in Contemporary Britain* (London: Verso Editions, 1985).

20. Lowenthal, *The Past Is a Foreign Country* (Cambridge: Cambridge University Press, 1985), 189–90.

21. Young, *White Mythologies,* 119.

22. Catalan historiography includes the Balearic islands as well as Valencia, as they have formed part of the same political and linguistic entity since the Middle Ages.

23. Some historians have worked on the idea of Catalonia as a nation whose identity flows in a *continuum* from the past into the present, such as Ferran Soldevila, Pierre Vilar, and Albert Balcells. I do not mean to state that all that has been written about Catalan history has been nationalistic, but I would like to insinuate that *Dins el darrer blau* does question what kind of history should be written or, at least, as Young would put it, what histories are erased behind History.

Convergence and Disjunction: Doubling in the Fiction of Carme Riera

CATHERINE G. BELLVER

THE DOUBLE IS A SIGNIFICANT PHENOMENON THAT HAS SERVED AS the basis for many cosmologies over the ages, for major tenets of seminal philosophers such as Plato and Descartes, for concepts underlying modern psychology, and for the presentation of character development in literature. Doubleness, duplicity, and fragmentation have held special meaning for women, because they have been defined as the passive other "in whom the subject transcends himself without being limited" and cast in the role of mirror, of "looking-glasses possessing the magic and delicious power of reflecting the figure of man at twice its natural power."[1] Women's experience is also grounded in doubleness. Culturally, as Elaine Showalter has explained, women's existence is split between the muted group to which they belong and the dominant male group with which they partially overlap; therefore, when they write, they speak in a "double-voiced discourse" that embodies both groups.[2] Feminist theorists have also suggested that female psychology is based on a consciousness of the other or is manifested in a "binary unity."[3] Given the inextricable links between women and doubling, it is not surprising that the double frequently surfaces in their fiction. Annette Kolodny, for example, writes that "women writers repeatedly invest their female characters with 'reflexive perceptions,' a habit of mind that, itself, becomes a repeated stylistic device, as character after character is depicted as discovering herself or finding some part of herself in activities she has not planned or in situations she cannot fully comprehend."[4] The double also often appears in the fiction of contemporary women writers of Spain, as a number of Hispanists have already noted.[5] This, of course, is not to say that male writers of Spain have not resorted to the use of the double; but in current fiction, as women writers explore female experience and point their protagonists toward liberation from the constraints of otherness placed on them by patriarchal society, the use of the double becomes an indispensable tool in that enterprise.

One of the contemporary women writers of Spain who uses the double consistently in her fiction is Carme Riera. Duplication, duality, and reflection—all play a prominent role in her works. People, places, and objects often serve either as mirrors, in which the characters see themselves reflected, or as doubles that accentuate the feeling of loneliness, alienation, and vulnerability that many of her characters experience. In Riera's early short stories, the sea is an important agent of doubling. More than a stage setting for her narratives, the sea becomes a personified object of desire, the beloved other with whom her characters long to merge. In her novel *Una primavera per a Domenico Guarini* [A Primavera for Domenico Guarini], Riera creates a more complicated set of doubles that enable the protagonist not only to understand the motivations for the crime committed but also to resolve her own inner doubts. Images projected as if in a mirror form vehicles beneficial to self-realization and positive models for personal transformation. In Riera's recent narratives, doubles fail to prevent the dissolution of the self or the perpetuation of inner fragmentation. In *Contra l'amor en companyia i altres relats* [Against Love with a Partner And Other Tales], as the self-conscious quality of her fiction increases, doubling begins to lose its role as a means to unification of the self. Without the tragic and lyric elements of her earlier short stories, these later narratives exploit doubling to create ironic tales of disillusion, disappointment, and unheroic banality.

The first collection of stories considered here, *Palabra de mujer* [Woman's Word] (1980) is a Castilian translation of most of the narrations of Riera's first two books of short stories, written in Catalan: *Te deix, amor, la mar com a penyora* [I Leave You, My Love, the Sea as a Token] and *Jo pos per testimoni les gavines* [I Call the Seagulls as Witness]. In them the sea is only a partial double for the beloved in that it does not represent either an independent fictional character nor the source of counterbalancing required of the true second self as defined by C. F. Keppler.[6] Yet, from the subjective point of view of the narrator, the sea substitutes for the lost lover. The narrator of Riera's well-known epistolary story "Te entrego, amor, la mar, como una ofrenda" [I Leave You, My Love, the Sea as a Token] opens her evocation of her idyllic eight-month relationship some years prior with an allusion to the sea: "Desde aquí, desde esta ventana, no puedo ver la mar" [From here, from this window, I cannot see the sea] (*Palabra,* 9).[7] The sea was the literal stage for the illicit adventure between the adolescent narrator and the older woman (the love scene the narrator recalls in her letter took place in the cabin of a boat). The sea surpasses its function as spatial setting to become, as the narrator indicates, companion, accomplice, and spy and as Roberta Johnson has observed, a "silent witness" to their affair.[8] Beyond this associative value as metonym for the absent lover, the sea serves as a mimetic representation for that absent other, a poetic clone. References to the sea reconstruct the estranged woman, giving her a presence in the narrator's text that paternal authority had not allowed in real life. Through the metaphorical transposition of woman to sea, presence replaces absence and lyrical sublimation replaces profane reality. Like a mirror, the sea reflects back to the narrator images of her lost happiness.

The invisibility of the sea announced in the first sentence of the story duplicates the absence of the lover. The narrator begins the next two paragraphs with statements that could refer as easily to the sea as to her lost lover: "la amo" [I love her] and "Añoro la mar" [I miss the sea]. In her nostalgic evocations, the beauty of the sea and that of her beloved also overlap, colliding if not merging in her descriptions: "me fabriqué un calendario de uso personal, donde años, meses y días comenzaban en el preciso instante en que el azul era perfecto, tu cuerpo de seda, tibia, dulce, y suavísima la luz que se filtraba" [I've made a personal calendar in which the years, months and days begin at the very moment when the blue of the sea was perfect, your silky body warm, sweet, soft, the light filtering through] (*Palabra,* 10).[9] Although not a full-fledged fictional character, the sea acquires an equivalent nature through personification. The protagonist turns the sea into a dark feminine presence: "enlutada, grasienta, pestilente, mece, nodriza vieja . . . en cuyo regazo se acomodan cáscaras y plásticos, entre impúdicos coágulos de una menstruación aceitosa" [A mourning, greasy, almost stinking sea. Like a wet-nurse, the sea holds its debris in its lap among the clots of its oily menstruation] (Palabra, 9). The human qualities of the sea are amplified by the letter she writes to it in the hope of its becoming a courier to her estranged lover; and the mirroring of the beloved in the sea is enhanced when the narrator declares her desire to be buried at sea. Thus, the union with the real woman denied her on the empirical level is enacted on the sublimated level of poetic imagery and on the mythic level of desired cosmic unity.

According to Robert Rogers, to see mirror images indicates an internal, mental conflict that manifests itself in the replacement of logical thinking by "'thinking' archaically," as occurs in dreams, the fantasies of children, "primitive" superstitions, or myths.[10] The "archaic thinking" in operation within Riera's use of the sea as double for an absent love is that of the myth of the original androgyne. Keppler associates the second self as beloved with the archetypical concept of love as an irresistible search for the missing component of a mythical whole, "if necessary from the ends of the earth . . . as though they had inherited in its full strength the nostalgic yearning for each other experienced by the two halves of one of those once-whole humans long ago bisected by Zeus."[11] This same compulsion for unity is what motivates the protagonist in "Te entrego . . ." to want to be buried at sea. Riera accepts the idea of love as a desire for union of the self with the Other and has openly declared her special appreciation for the tale of the origin of the human race told by Aristophanes at Plato's banquet. Love rests, she says, on a relation with an Other, be it of the same or opposite sex, and therefore is implicitly a process of doubling: "la libertad de uno acaba donde empieza la libertad de otro . . . estamos siempre en función del otro, pero . . . si este otro acepta, cada uno sabe con las posibilidades que cuenta" [one's freedom ends where the freedom of another begins . . . we always function in relation with the other . . . if this other accepts, each one knows the possibilities with which he must contend].[12]

Among the possibilities on which one must count when entering into love is self-destruction. Attachment to the ghostly shadow of her drowned lover brings the narrator of "Y pongo por testigo a las gaviotas" confinement within a mental institution, alienation, and, presumably, madness. Her lover is reproduced in the tenuous, disembodied form of sensorial stimuli: the scent of sea mixed with that of roses, the feel of a few strands of algae, and the voice the protagonist purports to hear. Once again in its metonymic representation, the sea provides the mechanism for an imperfect copy of an absent lover, confirmed in their intertwined identification with palpable remembrances they left behind: "un trozo de alga enredado en un mechón de su pelo" [a piece of algae tangled in a lock of hair]. The metaphorical analogies between the sea and the beloved at play in "Te entrego . . ." become in this narrative a literal, physical fusion of the two.

Having committed suicide by drowning, the narrator's lover now dwells within the sea in one of its hidden grottoes. A physical union with the absent Other through drowning reappears in another story, in "Casi un cuento decimonónico, acompañamiento a cuatro voces" [Almost a Nineteenth Century Story, Accompaniment of Four Voices]. After suffering a bout of amnesia on stage, the diva Nora Giacometti shuts herself in a villa in Palma de Mallorca where she spends her days staring at the sea. She writes to the sea, transforming it into a personification of love; and, like the obsessive soul that incessantly seeks the missing component of some mythical whole, she surrenders to it in her act of suicide: "vado subito a rimettermi nelle tue braccia per sempre, mare, amore mio" [I will soon fall into your arms, sea, my love] (*Palabra,* 56). The sea in *Palabra de mujer* recalls and replicates love, allowing characters to relive a lost sense of idyllic unity.

Doubling also occurs in the stories of *Palabra de mujer* not involving the sea; but, instead of bringing about a simulated unity with love, it reflects the impossibility of resolving alienation from love. In "Sí, me llamo Helena" [Yes, My Name Is Helena], the male protagonist fails to duplicate an earlier lover, and in "Jaime-Juan" [James-John], the female protagonist succeeds in creating a double but without reconciling duality and her own existential dilemma.[13] Not unexpectedly, the doubling process is more extensive in Riera's novels than in her short stories, and it involves more thorough probing into the psychology of her characters. Riera herself recognizes that "desdoblamiento" fascinates her and comes into play in her novel *Joc de miralls* [Game of Mirrors] (1989), the story of a writer who passes himself off as someone else.[14] Here, however, the double can more accurately be called a mask than a second self, in the traditional sense. It is a consciously invented counterpart, an overt double, not a mysterious hallucination or an involuntary manifestation of anxiety. Similarly, Angela, in *Qüestió d'amor propi* [A Question of Self-Love] (1987) attempts to convert her friend, Ingrid, if not into a mask into a proxy for her conscious plan of revenge against Miguel for his seduction, ridicule, and desertion. For Akiko Tsuchiya, in this novel duplication stems from its "duplicitous discourse," from narrative seduction as a mirror of erotic seduction.[15] Although the element of replication figures prominently as the basis of the epistolary form, my concern lies not with the metafictive aspects of Riera's fiction, but with the double as an instrument of characterization.

In Riera's early short stories, doubling occurs outside the protagonist, usually between a past love and a new one. When the double is the sea, in its personified form it provides a mirror in which to behold the lost lover. The union these protagonists reexperience in this manner is a loving but tragic convergence, one built on delusion and leading to self-destruction. In Riera's novel, *Una primavera per a Domenico Guarini,* the doubling process centers primarily on the protagonist in the form of inner division and of reduplication in another character. The convergence ultimately achieved in this work unites the fragments of the self, conferring on her a sense of liberation and agency. Doubling, particularly in the form of inner psychic division, serves as an effective strategy for resolving the protagonist's personal dilemma and as the crucial step in her progress toward maturity. Isabel Clara Alabern, a journalist, travels to Florence to report on Domenico Guarini's act of vandalism against Botticelli's *Primavera.* What begins as a routine professional assignment, however, becomes the stimulus for a penetrating reevaluation of her own life. In parts I and II of the novel, the installments of her report on the bizarre Guarini case are interspersed with the narration of her personal life, and in part III, a lecture on Botticelli's famous painting evokes recollections of her past, especially those of her mother. The focus of the novel is divided between past and present, between private and public worlds, and between Clara and Guarini. Clara addresses much of her narration to herself, becoming both narrator and narratee, or, as Roberta Johnson affirms, she becomes her own interlocutor.[16] In the arduous process of self-reflection, Clara becomes her own double, addressing and observing herself as a discrete, albeit complementary, object.

Beyond the doubling of narrative structure, on the psychological level of characterization, Clara's fragmentation into "you" and "I," the observed and the observer, creates a mirror in which she sees herself as a detached image disposed to observation and analysis. This double does not enjoy autonomy as a separate fictional character or as "a recognizable, unified psychological entity," as Rogers would require; but the "you" she creates nonetheless confirms that the human mind in conflict is susceptible to inner division. Mental disassociation is a symptom of severe illness whose study falls within the jurisdiction of psychiatric analysis, but a consideration of this psychological phenomenon helps us understand the development of a fictional character like Clara. Rogers writes of the fragmentation of the mind that "the appearance of an alternating personality can be understood in terms of the drives which have been repressed and impulses which are defended against."[17] When Clara adopts the second-person point of view to distance herself from her life story, her reflections on her past compel her to confront the repressive gender-defined social agenda inculcated in her by her mother and manifested in her various relationships with men.

Her mother gave her lessons on silence, submission, and self-sacrifice. Clara recalls her mother's severe words:

> Un hombre te puede engañar, te quiere aunque lo haga. Una mujer no puede hacer lo mismo, a no ser que sea una perdida. Nosotras hemos venido al mundo para sufrir y aguantar. Es la voluntad de Dios: parirás con dolor, obedecerás a tu marido. . . . Nadie puede enmendarle la plana a Dios. Como Eva se dejó tentar, pecó y ahora hay que pagarlo. Por eso tenemos que perdonar siempre.
>
> [A man can deceive you, he loves you even if he does. A woman cannot do the same thing, unless she is a loose woman. We have come into the world to suffer and endure. It is the will of God: you will give birth in pain, you will obey your husband. . . . No one can criticize God. Since Eve let herself be tempted and sinned, we have to pay. That is why we always have to forgive.][18]

She remembers that she was forbidden to ride a swing or slide because her dress might get dirty or be blown up by the wind. Perhaps nothing epitomizes the dreariness of the social role her mother fulfilled and tried to teach her daughter better than the importance embroidery held in the lives of women.[19] Clara evokes the image of her mother seated with her embroidery frame on her lap, stitching dozens of tablecloths, towels, and aprons now yellowing in the closet. When she pictures herself telling her mother she will have a child out of wedlock, Clara rejects not only the traditional view of motherhood but the compulsory activity of embroidery that long defined the good housewife in Spain: "Siento no poder utilizar el 'ajuar' que se está pudriendo en los cajones, y que tantas horas de trabajo y tanto dinero te costó" [I am sorry I cannot use the 'trousseau' that is rotting in the drawers and on which you spent so much time and money.] (*Una primavera,* 141).

By reviewing her past, Clara can gather together the disparate pieces of her childhood and view with fresh eyes the forces that shaped her life. She sees a child restricted by rigid rules of conduct for women and a double standard that casts women in the role of victim. She also sees a self-sacrificing mother figure, who, nonetheless, was capable of a single public display of subversion. The mother's fleeting act of rebellion against the phallic order, as Elizabeth Ordóñez shows, indicates woman's own rewriting of her self through her body. This isolated lesson in subversion inspires Clara to rebel by accepting pregnancy as a source of transformation.[20] The doubling process also unlocks for Clara her early repressed picture of men as abusive and treacherous and of sex as repugnant or exploitative. She recalls the sexual abuse she suffered in a movie theater, the strong admonitions against masturbation she heard in childhood, and the blatant infidelity of her father. The reassessment of her past helps Clara put in perspective her adult relationships with men. When Carlos gave her an ultimatum to choose between marriage and a university degree, she chose education over marriage at that moment; but she now realizes that she still feels "para con él una extraña dependencia por el hecho de haber sido el primero para quien me desnudé" [a strange dependency on him because he was the first man for whom I undressed] (*Una primavera,* 167). In spite of her early instinct for self-realization, Clara repeats her dependence on men in her affair with Enrique, having become over their two years together his editor, babysitter, housekeeper, and, ultimately, his mother. An innate tendency toward autonomy impels her to stop living with him, but she does not overcome her dependency on him until after her experience in Italy.

The double Clara creates in the child allows her to enter her "dark side," the realm of fears, anxiety and social taboo, and to contemplate the social forces at work in the formation of her personality.[21] What initially signals inner conflict and psychic fragmentation facilitates her break from her oppressive upbringing. The confrontation between the two selves causes pain, but ultimately confers benefits by awakening the first self from complacency, stripping away the mask of self-deception, and forcing self-awareness. Clara is besieged by doubt and contradictory sentiments: "Y, ahora, esta sensación te resulta absolutamente necesaria para sedimentar toda esta ciénaga de sentimientos contradictorios" [And now, this sensation turns out absolutely necessary to having contradictory feelings settle down in this bog] (*Una primavera,* 13); she overcomes inner division, however, reconciling the opposition between the self and the world. Therefore, despite its pathological implications of psychological decomposition, doubling can be a sign of a healthy struggle rather than a symptom of mental collapse, a mechanism of self-exploration and self-realization rather than an instrument of self-destruction.

In addition to the child, Clara must contend with another double who ultimately helps her free herself from the myths, charades, and illusions controlling her thinking. That double is Domenico Guarini, the subject of her investigation. Like the child Clara, Guarini becomes a mirror in which to see her imperfections clearly and a double to confront. Unlike her younger addressee, Guarini becomes a model to emulate. Under the spell of conventional conceptions of womanhood and love, Guarini has created an ideal, inaccessible woman just as Clara—conditioned by traditional notions of love, marriage, and motherhood—has accepted established paradigms of gendered behavior. Both, in their own way, are trapped within the destructive web of patriarchal archetypes; but he has buried his copy of Petrarch's *Il Canzoniere,* thereby symbolically interring the myth of love. Clara must duplicate the actions of her double in order to dispose of the anachronistic myths that govern her actions. She succeeds when she finally discards Enrique and accepts her pregnancy as her own personal, demythified story.

Alberto, her former lover now working as a journalist in Florence and involved in a homosexual relationship with Piero, could be considered an "opposing self" to Clara. As Ordóñez argues, in their discussion of the Guarini case, Clara identifies "with the phallic imagination," while Alberto engages in a more objective, more "feminist" reading of the situation (287). But Alberto also forms a part of a more important double—the one between him and Enrique. The pair brings into view for Clara a polarity of masculine personalities. They seem to be the male equivalent of the fair maid/femme fatale archetype that Rogers studies.[22] As contemporary women writers have begun to assume the position of subjects, they strive not only to see themselves from a female perspective, but also to subvert the image of men perpetuated in literature. Within the context of this tendency to refocus patriarchal profiles, the contrast established between Enrique and Alberto can be seen as representing the male duality that confronts a female protagonist and the writer's attempt to outline masculine prototypes.

Enrique is the successful but inattentive politician; Alberto is the sensitive but unknown writer. Unlike the male-generated dichotomy of woman as saint or sinner, neither one of the polarized components of this double constitutes the ideal complement to the protagonist's inner desires. Enrique is self-centered, cold, and exploitative. He never understood that his public position did not satisfy Clara's emotional needs; as she confesses, "nunca conseguí que comprendiera que para mí carecía de interés ser la amante de un miembro de la ejecutiva, de un diputado que salía un día sí y otro también en los periódicos, que prefería ser la compañera de un ciudadano corriente" [I never managed to make him understand that it was of no interest to me to be the lover of a member of the executive board, of a delegate who came out in the newspaper every other day, that I preferred to be the companion of an ordinary citizen] (*Una primavera,* 173). Alberto, Enrique's apparent opposite—affectionate, supportive, and communicative—has also disappointed her. As well as becoming a drug addict, he has chosen his homosexual lover over her. The Enrique–Alberto double fails as an instrument for self-renewal; Clara realizes that true transformation must come, as it came for Guarini, through suffering and the destruction of love. She interprets the butterfly-shaped cut Guarini made at the bottom of the Flora figure as a symbol of the transformation to which she must aspire: "símbolo de cualquier renacimiento, metáfora del alma según los griegos, por su naturaleza metafórica: de oruga a crisálida, de crisálida a mariposa" [a symbol of any rebirth, a metaphor for the soul according to the Greeks, because of its metaphorical nature: from caterpillar to chrysalis, from chrysalis to butterfly] (*Una primavera,* 187). Thus, through a threefold doubling process—with her younger self, with Guarini, and between Enrique and Alberto—Clara reassesses her life and succeeds in freeing herself from her past, from the unsatisfying men in her life, and from the myths that have been inculcated in her.

For Clara, self-exploration becomes the essential first phase of her inner renewal. Rather than remaining confined to her inner life, she exploits vacillation as the prerequisite for crucial decision-making and as the springboard for decisive action. After experiencing doubling, Clara accepts pregnancy and solitude as the difficult, but necessary avenues to the integration of the self. Just as Clara compares Guarini's dramatic exorcism of his obsessions to the actions of "los catecúmenos de los ritos iniciáticos" [the catechumens of initiation rites] (*Una primavera,* 187), her experience with division, doubling, and mirroring can be equated with the arduous ordeals of the second of the three steps that constitute ancient initiation rites transposed in literature to "the solitude and despair through which every human being must pass in order to attain to responsible, genuine and creative life."[23] As in initiation rites, Clara literally separates herself from her familiar environment in Barcelona as a prerequisite to the alteration of her perception of herself, the world, and her place in it. The story of her adventure parallels several elements of the archetypical rite of passage Joseph Campbell enumerates: its analogous call to a "zone unknown" (Florence), appearances of agents helpful in her development (Guarini and Alberto), the equivalence of the magic flight (her quick departure from Florence), and the crossing of the return threshold (her return to Barcelona by train).[24] The trajectory of Clara's route of psychological development, however, differs significantly from the traditional rite of passage, in that she attains knowledge of the normal world, not to reintegrate herself into it transformed into a suitable adult, but to gain the strength necessary, as an autonomous individual, to resist societal norms. The female quest myth cannot conform perfectly to the male paradigm, for, as Janet Pérez has shown, instead of the heroism through physical prowess characteristic of the classic quest cycle, female protagonists seek self-realization or self-sufficiency.[25] In Clara's case, doubling provides the mechanism for passage from unconscious subordination to societal myths to a state of selfhood, a state which, by virtue of its divergence from the norm, promises to alter society.

The struggle for self-definition and the implication of an altered role for women suggested at the conclusion of the novel make *Una primavera per a Domenico Guarini* a feminist statement. Riera herself recognizes that this novel could not have been written until she had read the works of feminist theorists.[26] In contrast to her early short stories, in this work, preservation of the self has become more important than love, and life has won over death. Although it is indisputable that a concern for the problems of women unites almost all of Riera's fiction, the specific form this theme takes changes over the span of her career as a writer of fiction.

In *Una primavera,* liberation from love is paramount, while, in her early short stories, the destructive power of love exacts its victim. By the time she published *Contra l'amor en companyia i altres relats,* Riera, by her own admission, had lost interest in feminism.[27] Men are the protagonists in nearly half the nineteen stories included in the collection, and most of the characters grapple not with interpersonal problems but with those relating to the writer's craft and the impact of writing. The stories of *Contra l'amor* still treat the emptiness, loneliness, and banality of everyday existence that surround Riera's earlier characters, but gone is the lyrical atmosphere of tragic love. Instead, these stories project the cynicism, the "game of irony" that Umberto Eco identifies with postmodernism, and "the playful discontinuity" that Hassan associates with the era.[28] The novelist's own words confirm the ludic underpinnings of her stance in this 1991 collection: "Esta obra es un divertimiento donde el nexo común lo encontramos en el hecho literario, la escritura es simplemente el papel impreso" [This work is a diversion in which the common bond is found in the literary act, writing is simply the printed page].[29]

Riera still incorporates doubles or doubling in *Contra l'amor*, but the way she uses these devices reflects her shift in aesthetic orientation. The self-consciousness and ironic deconstruction that typify postmodern texts prevent the realization of unity, either of the type Clara Alabern achieved within herself or of the kind Riera's early protagonists acquired with the sea. In "Esto no es un cuento" [This Is Not a Story], the double does not appear in function of characterization as a well-integrated narrative device, but as a deliberately chosen strategy openly recognized and commented on by Andrea Hurtado, the author/narrator of the story-within-the-story of this selection. In a public display of her creative prowess, she explains that she surpassed the "tópico tan viejo como manido" [the old and trite cliché] of the double by replacing *desdoblamiento* [doubling] by what she terms *destriplamiento* [tripling]. In two other stories, the elaboration of spontaneous doubles is thwarted by ambiguity that stems not from the ambivalent relationship between a first and second self but on the level of reading from indeterminate endings.

"Un placebo llamado María López" [A Placebo Called María López] appears, at first glance, to reconfirm the playful tendencies of postmodernism in its suggestion of parody of Riera's earlier story "Sí, me llamo Helena"; but it also attests to the impossibility of definitive interpretation, either on the part of readers or of characters. A writer repeating a trip he made forty years earlier would like to believe that the young woman riding in his compartment is related to the unforgettable María López of that earlier ride. Conscious of the coincidences between his present trip and the one he took in 1948 (he is to lecture in the same city and the same cultural center as before), the protagonist purposefully attempts to make his second trip a repetition of the first: "Esa coincidencia le obligaba a poner de su parte todos los elementos posibles para facilitar al azar la tarea de la repetición copiando, al menos, las circunstancias que rodearon los hechos" [This coincidence forced him to put together all of the possible elements that would spontaneously facilitate the task of repetition, copying, at least, the circumstances that surrounded the facts].[30] He again chooses first class and evokes the details of his chance meeting with María López, the woman who became his muse and a symbol of his nostalgia for unattainable happiness. A potential for duplication of a past love, as occurred in *Palabra de mujer,* exists, but the common links between María and her double are dubious. A certain physical resemblance recalls the image of María López, but their radical difference in age, varying tastes in literature, and divergent attitudes make authentic doubling impossible. Any match in identities appears to respond more to an aging man's pathetic attempt to repeat the past than to the irresistible drive toward the beloved that motivates a convergence with the sea in Riera's early fiction. Yet the text leaves unresolved the faint possibility of a connection between the two women. When the writer gets off the train, he has an inexplicable lipstick mark on his cheek just like the one María left on him forty years before. It is unclear whether history has repeated itself or whether taking pity on the man, the young girl has indulged his illusions.

In "De Eva a María: relatos de mujer" [From Eva to María: Women's Stories], an expectation of doubling is established by the title in its reference to contrasting types of women—Eve and Mary. This initial hint of doubling is expanded by the story's central focus. The narrator, María, concerns herself with the publication of an anthology that has the same title as Riera's short story and that begins with a work by the young writer, Eva Guarini, and ends with one of her own compositions. The doubling process is further enhanced by Eva Guarini's duplication of María's unpublished story from 1950 and by the fact that the present situation of the young writer and the narrator's situation at the beginning of her own career are parallel.[31] However, any interpretation on the part of the protagonist and the reader of spontaneous repetition and mysterious kinship are undermined when María discovers that Eva is her own daughter, Amalia.

The element of fraud suggested at the end of this story reappears in "*Mon semblable, mon frère*" [My Double, My Brother], as does the ingredient of self-consciousness evident in the creation of a double in other stories in *Contra l'amor.* The irrepressible attraction between two selves in this narrative is reminiscent of the earliest works of Riera already discussed and the potential for inner growth as the result of contact between doubled characters recalls *Una primavera;* but the irony underlying "*Mon semblable, non frère*" undermines the grandeur of the destruction in a story such as "Y pongo por testigo a las gaviotas" and the healing effects of doubling in the novel.

The story tells of two university friends who become writers. Infected by Rafael's enthusiasm for literature, José Joaquín starts writing poetry and offers to translate his friend's work from French into Catalan. Rafael fails to acknowledge José Joaquín's role as translator and in addition passes off some of his friend's work as his own. A strange force, "un extraño pudor" [a strange modesty], prevents José Joaquín from accusing his friend of plagiarism. Meanwhile, Rafael ingratiates himself to his friend by calling him "mon semblable, mon frère." There seems to exist between the two the element of irresistible, almost fatal attraction and the "certain strange and special affinity" necessary as a basis for a second self.[32] The psychology of the two characters is not sufficiently developed to establish a full range of differences and identities between them, but the story contains evidence pointing to a mysterious bond between separate, yet steadfastly linked components of a double. At the precise moment Rafael commits suicide with barbiturates, José Joaquín is operated on in another city for a perforated stomach. Before his death, Rafael had left his friend a letter in which he states that he felt the two of them together formed one being in the manner explained by Aristophanes in Plato's work, and José Joaquín concludes his narration with a statement that confirms the lingering interdependence of the two of them:

> Dudé si la carta era una certera maniobra de Rafael para seguir viviendo en mí con mayor intensidad que cuando vivíamos los dos por cada lado. Porque desde entonces, desde su muerte, noto un terrible vacío que no se atenúa con el tiempo, que, al contrario, se acentúa.
>
> [I wondered if the letter was an intentional maneuver by Rafael to keep living in me with greater intensity than when we lived side by side. Because from then on, since his death, I have noticed a terrible emptiness that does not lessen with time but to the contrary, increases.] (58–59)

In the case of the second self as twin brother (whether literal or equivalent brother), each character exists as a component of a duality inexplicably dependent on his other-half for a sense of wholeness. As commonly occurs in this type of double, the second self tends to be the uncanny one, or at least the potentially disturbing one, but whether enemy or friend, the "twin" initiates action between them and the first self registers the effect of the action.[33] Thus, even after Rafael's death, José Joaquín will remain inextricably linked to Rafael and feel deprived of an independent identity.

The simple metaphorical doubling between the lover and the sea in Riera's early fiction has been complicated in this later story by a multiplication of the levels of doubling. In "*Mon semblable, mon frère,*" doubling exists on the level of story, reading, and writing. From the very beginning, the title alerts the reader to expect fraternal resemblance between the main characters. On the level of the narration, the characters themselves are conspicuously aware of the probability of doubling in their psychology. Before José Joaquín's final realization of his mysterious dependence on Rafael, there are signs of awareness on the part of the characters of their existence as doubles. José Joaquín begins his account with an implicit intention of disengaging himself from Rafael, in his own work as an artist and as a possible literary model for a story by Juan José Millás. An open declaration on the part of Rafael of his existence as a double for Joaquín and the fraudulent act of publishing José Joaquín's work as his own introduce a possibility of deliberate deception into the doubling process in the story. After his death, Rafael continues to manipulate his double psychologically through the letter of confession he left.

In keeping with the self-referentiality characteristic of the postmodern bent that surfaces in *Contra l'amor,* the self consciousness of the characters is replicated on the level of creative process. The echoes of previous texts resounding through "*Mon semblable, mon frère*" suggest that writing is but a process of doubling, of duplication of other authors. The title of the story is an intertextual reference to Baudelaire, and the narrative begins with a discussion of its relationship to texts by the Spanish author, Juan José Millás, and the Argentine, Angel Bonomini. Despite the similarities between his relationship with Rafael and Millás's story, "El pequeño cadáver" [The Small Cadaver], José Joaquín refutes the coincidences and argues that the Spaniard was inspired by Bonomini's versions of the dynamic between the two friends, thus suggesting that writing is the act of copying copies. The narrator's preamble on the authenticity of the literary textualizations of his friendship inscribes his own account within a fictional frame that produces a climate conducive to Rafael's prefabrication of José Joaquín's works and his usurpation of his friend's identity. The author herself recasts and appropriates narrative ingredients from both Millás and Bonomini to write her publication.[34] An author subsumes her predecessors in the amalgamation of existing texts in a new, personal elaboration just as the second self overshadows the first one. Thus, both life and literature are equated with the doubling process, with a replication that, although entailing copying, nonetheless creates a symbiotic whole totally different from its constitutive components. Only together could Rafael and José Joaquín produce publishable works.

The possibilities of polarity, duality, and duplication in the phenomenon of the double connote psychological fragmentation as well as the reproduction of the interplay of sameness and difference, of absence and presence, and of self and other inherent in interpersonal relations. The process of doubling generates frustration or fluidity, destruction or peaceful coexistence. Thus it can accentuate disjunction or serve as a therapeutic step toward convergence. The person repeated can be either the subject of focus in a narrative or a person separate from, but intimately related to, the primary self. Carme Riera is consistent in her preference for the use of the double, but she modifies its specific nature to match the changing contours of her fiction. What begins as lyrical doubling with tragic overtones passes through beneficial mirroring and ends with layered doubling with ironic implications. In the first short stories Riera wrote, the double appears as a substitute for a lost beloved with whom the protagonist wishes to unite. The autonomous self seeks in the other a fusion that remains unrealized and that, in its illusiveness, confronts the self with the distance from the object of desire. In this way, the stories capture the severity of the emotional turmoil provoked by love. In *Una primavera per a Domenico Guarini* the double becomes primarily a mirror in which the protagonist sees herself in the form of her childhood self or of Guarini. Self-contemplation leads to maturation; the doubling process functions as a route through which she passes to disengage herself from love and social myths in order to transform herself from a victim of socialization into an autonomous individual capable of articulating her own destiny. After this keen probing into the profound impact of doubling, Riera's subsequent short stories become excursions into irony and self-reflection. The double in *Contra l'amor en companyia i altres relats* becomes a malevolent, fraudulent, or artificial force that makes convergence problematic and the question of self-creation relevant. The varying manifestations of the double evident in Riera's works, as well as confirming the rich potential of this literary phenomenon, also attest to the breadth of her narrative artistry.

Notes

1. Simone de Beauvoir, *The Second Sex,* trans. H. M. Parshley (New York: Bantam Books, 1961), 174; Virginia Woolf, *A Room of One's Own* (New York: Harcourt Brace Jovanovich, 1957), 35.

2. Showalter, "Feminist Criticism in the Wilderness," in *Writing and Sexual Difference,* ed. Elizabeth Abel (Chicago: University of Chicago Press, 1982), 9–35.

3. Nancy Chodorow, *The Reproduction of Mothering: Psychoanalysis and the Sociology of Gender* (Berkeley: University of California Press, 1978); and Kathryn Allen Rabuzzi, *Motherself: A Mythic Analysis of Motherhood* (Bloomington: Indiana University Press, 1988).

4. Kolodny, "Some Notes on Defining a Feminist Literary Criticism," *Critical Inquiry* 2:1 (1975): 79.

5. Some examples of studies on the use of the double by contemporary women writers of Spain are the following: Catherine G. Bellver, "Division, Duplication, and Doubling in the Novels of Ana María Moix," in *Nuevos y novísimos,* ed. Ricardo Landeira and Luis T. González-del-Valle (Boulder: Society of Spanish and Spanish-American Studies, 1987), 29–41; Biruté Ciplijauskaité, "El 'espejo de las generaciones' en la narrativa femenina contemporánea," *Actas del IX Congreso de la Asociación Internacional de Hispanistas* (Frankfurt: Vervuert Verlag, 1989), 201–10; and Kathleen M. Glenn, "Gothic Indecipherability and Doubling in the Fiction of Cristina Fernández Cubas," *Monographic Review/Revista Monográfica* 8 (1992): 125–41.

6. C. F. Keppler, *The Literature of the Second Self* (Tucson: University of Arizona Press, 1972).

7. The original version of this story, written in Catalan under the title "Te deix, amor, la mar com a penyora," received the "Recull" prize in 1974 and was the first selection in the collection with its same title (Barcelona: Laia, 1975). This story is the lead selection in *Palabra de mujer* (Barcelona: Laia, 1980). Citations are taken from the Castilian collection.

8. Roberta Johnson, "Voice and Intersubjectivity in Carme Riera's Narratives," in *Critical Essays on the Literatures of Spain and Spanish America,* ed. Luis T. González-del-Valle and Julio Baena (Boulder: Society of Spanish and Spanish-American Studies, 1991), 154. The role of the sea is also outlined in Roxana Recio, "La lírica medieval y dos cuentos de Carmen Riera," *Torre de Papel* (Iowa City), 2 (1992): 28–38.

9. The translations from this story are by Alberto Moreiras and are found in *On Our Own Behalf: Women's Tales from Catalonia,* ed. Kathleen McNerney (Lincoln: University of Nebraska Press, 1988), 31, 32. The other translations are my own.

10. Rogers, *The Double in Literature* (Detroit: Wayne State University Press, 1970), ch. 2.

11. Keppler, *Literature of the Second Self,* 132.

12. Neus Aguado, "Epístolas de mar y de sol: Entrevista con Carme Riera," *Quimera* 105 (1991): 34–35.

13. In both narratives, doubling is a manifestation of ambivalent, unresolved feelings toward love. In the first story, the protagonist senses that in the young writer, Helena, he has found a replica of the woman with whom he lived after his exile from Spain. She shares the same name, smile, and curiosity. He feels toward her the same desperate and absolute passion, but the second Helena cannot duplicate the first one because he has changed. This partial doubling is the sad confirmation of the transience of happiness that most of the characters in Riera's early fiction must confront. Doubling is announced in the hyphenated title of the brief story, "Jaime-Juan." Alternately addressing her husband, Juan, and her lover, Jaime, the protagonist fails to reconcile the polarity between presence and absence, youth and old age, legal and illicit love. The anxiety of conflicting desires devours her, keeping her awake at night and exhausted during the day.

14. Geraldine C. Nichols, *Escribir, espacio propio: Laforet, Matute, Moix, Tusquets, Riera y Roig por sí mismas* (Minneapolis: Institute for the Study of Ideologies and Literature, 1989), 219.

15. Tsuchiya, "The Paradox of Narrative Seduction in Carme Riera's *Cuestión de amor propio,*" *Hispania* 75 (1992): 281–86.

16. Johnson, "Voice and Intersubjectivity," 157.

17. Rogers, *Double in Literature,* 92.

18. Carme Riera, *Una primavera para Domenico Guarini* (Barcelona: Montesinos, 1981), 139. In subsequent citations from this book, I refer to this edition.

19. Embroidery was always central to the education and socialization of girls in Spain. When girls began attending grade school in the nineteenth century, their limited curriculum included primarily music, French, and embroidery. Even when superficial notions of history, geography, art, and mathematics were added to girls' program of study, their education was still aimed at the creation of religious, socially gracious, and manually dexterous women. For a discussion of women and education in Spain, see studies such as Rosa Capel Martínez, *El trabajo y la educación de la mujer en España (1900–1930)* (Madrid: Ministerio de Cultura, 1986) and Pilar Folguera, *Vida cotidiana en Madrid. El primer tercio del siglo a través de las fuentes orales* (Madrid: Comunidad de Madrid, 1987). Although these authors examine women in Spanish society of the first third of the twentieth century, Riera's novel confirms that an ultra-conservative ideology still drove social attitudes and practices in Spain well into the Franco years.

20. Ordóñez, "Beginning to Speak: Carme Riera's *Una primavera para Domenico Guarini,*" in *La Chispa '85. Selected Proceedings,* ed. Gilbert Paolini (New Orleans: Tulane University Press, 1985), 292.

21. Keppler refers to the theory of the "darker side" as the figure that embodies the author's own shortcomings, "the self which he really is . . . as against the self that he would like to be"; *Literature of the Second Self,* 189. The purpose of this study is not to speculate on the psychological connections between the fictional characters of *Una primavera para Domenico Guarini*

and Riera, but to suggest that Clara's confrontation with the troublesome sectors of her personality has a therapeutic effect on her.

22. Rogers, *Double in Literature,* ch. 7.

23. Mircea Eliade, *Rites and Symbols of Initiation: The Mysteries of Birth and Rebirth* (New York: Harper & Row, 1958), 128.

24. Joseph Campbell, *The Hero with a Thousand Faces* (Princeton: Princeton University Press, 1968).

25. Pérez, "Presence of the Picaresque and the Quest-Romance in Mercè Rodoreda's *Quanta, quanta guerra,*" *Hispania* 76 (1993): 433.

26. Nichols, *Escribir,* 192.

27. The Spanish public saw her early works as feminist or at least as "women's" literature. Female readers received her stories enthusiastically as mirrors of their own lives, but male readers avoided them because they were uninterested in "literatura de mujeres." Riera comments on this discrepant response to her fiction in her conversation with Geraldine Nichols, but concludes that "mi 'contribución' al feminismo—entre comillas siempre—ya está hecha. A partir de ahora, creo que no me va a interesar demasiado" [My "contribution" to feminism—in quotation marks, always—is done. From now on, I think it is not going to interest me very much.] (*Escribir,* 193). Thus she recognizes both the feminist implications of her fiction and her eventual disengagement from this perspective.

28. Aguado, "Epístolas de mar," 26.

29. Eco, *Postscript to the* Name of the Rose (San Diego: Harcourt Brace Jovanovich, 1984), 68; and Ihab Habib Hassan, *Paracriticisms: Seven Speculations of the Times* (Urbana: University of Illinois Press, 1975), 24.

30. Carme Riera, *Contra el amor en compañía y otros relatos* (Barcelona: Destino, 1991), 75. References are to this edition.

31. It is unclear to me why Riera chose Guarini, the surname of the important double in *Una primavera,* for the double in this later short story. There is a hint of self-doubling in *Contra l'amor* on the part of the author herself in this repetition of the names of one of her earlier creations, just as there is an element of parody of an earlier story of hers in "Un placebo llamado María."

32. Keppler, *Literature of the Second Self,* 11.

33. Ibid., ch. 2.

34. An analysis of the details of the intertextual incorporations that Riera makes in this story was done in a paper by Horst Hina, presented at the 1995 conference of Asociación Internacional de Hispanistas, in Birmingham, England. I am grateful to Kathleen Glenn for calling my attention to this study.

Disappearing Acts: Configurations of Textual Elimination in the Fiction of Carme Riera

SUSAN LUCAS DOBRIAN

> If you cannot be my bride, then you shall be my tree.
> —Apollo to Daphne

> Estoy donde no estoy [I am where I am not].
> —Gabriela Mistral

> Let the priests tremble, we are going to show them our sexts.
> —Hélène Cixous

ONE OF THE MOST FAMOUS DISAPPEARING ACTS IN PATRIARCHAL LITerature is that of Daphne, a virgin nymph who, like so many others, faces sexual violence at the hands of the powerful, ruling Greek gods.[1] The young sun god, Apollo, pursues the resisting nymph, whose act of salvation occurs when, aided by her father, the river god Peneus, she is magically transformed into a laurel tree. Although Daphne thwarts the theft of her virtue and self-will, success comes at the price of her immobilization and removal from society. Her safety is guaranteed, but salvation of the self signifies the disappearance of her sexuality, body, and voice. Converted into a vegetative state, the young nymph now stands rooted firmly in place, representing one more woman who embodies the common connection drawn between female and nature.

Catalonian women writers often take on the task of disassembling imprisoning myths that attempt to convert all women into vegetative states within patriarchy. In many Catalonian feminist works, disappearance, both enforced and as an act of choice, swirls around issues of voice, body, and desire. These authors configure textual elimination in varied ways, transforming and altering Daphne's nullifying escape into a powerful act of subversion. In so doing, a critical mythopoesis takes shape in which each writer steps beyond the frame and engages in what Rachel Blau DuPlessis calls "writing beyond the ending," to give voice to previously muted experiences.[2]

The notion of disappearing acts, brought to mind by a story such as Daphne's, suggests several points relevant to this study. First, the phrase "disappearing acts" evokes magic and portrays an event that, in its true nonfraudulent form, overturns or subverts the norms and laws of the visible, rational world in which patriarchy is heavily steeped. Second, to make another person disappear invokes great empowerment. Although in the Daphne-Apollo tale, it is the young nymph who escapes through transformation, Catalonian women writers frequently turn the act of disappearance back onto patriarchal figures. In the process, these authors create a space unhampered by patriarchal regulation, in which to explore issues of female identity and to heal the self in crisis. Finally, the reference to both feminism and textual elimination in the title suggests the potential eradication of those acts or structures of violence that nullify and marginalize women. For it is only with the constant tugging at the deep roots of traditional gender structures that women transform female invisibility and paralysis into female presence and empowerment.

The fiction of Carme Riera offers a progressive series of disappearing acts, in the form of textual elimination, as is also displayed in the literary works of other Catalonian women. The means, functions, and motives of this narrative tactic are varied, extending from self-elimination to the excision of males from the text. Although the most obvious type of self-exile from the offending social fabric is represented through suicide, self-elected elimination of characters also appears as a positive ploy. In the process, a metamorphosis of the act of female elimination occurs, in which an Escher-like fading of the dominant into the recessive takes place, first through the wearing down of male phallic awe and, finally, through the total eradication of the male body from the female text of desire.

The Catalonian writer Maria Aurèlia Capmany evocatively recalls: "El 1939 va ser per a nosaltres, les dones catalanes, les dones que vivim i treballem a Catalunya, l'any de la derrota" [1939 was for us, Catalonian women, women living and working in Catalonia, the year of defeat]. Referring to the first day of Nationalist rule, she continues: "El meu subconscient va elaborar l'enveja de penis el dia 1 d'abril de 1939" [My subconscious created penis envy on April 1, 1939].[3] Capmany's words suggest the complex web of invisibility, disempowerment, repression, and desire that the Nationalist victory created in defeated Republican Catalonia. In particular, the linking of political defeat and gender-based repression portrays the double disappearance experienced by Catalonian women, first through linguistic and cultural repression, then through gender, both by the Nationalist government's laws and by the tenets of a male-oriented society. Swiftly and surely, the patriarchal Nationalist government excised women from the public sphere of Spain, legally and morally "liberating" them from salaried employment, financial autonomy, sexual freedom, and gender equality.

Although legal modifications took place during Franco's tenure and even more substantive changes occurred after his death, writers of Riera's generation, born after the Civil War, in many cases grew up in somewhat oppressive environments. Anne Charlon notes the theme of prohibition, resulting from an oppressive morality imposed on women, that runs through the narrative of female Catalonian writers born after the war.[4] Riera herself refers to the transgression of certain prohibitions that led her to write. She links her initial writing to her childhood church confessions, suggesting a connection between speaking transgressions and the act of writing. Furthermore, she describes her first narratives as "historias de amor que se me ocurrían para paliar mi imposible contacto con chicos, en casa no me dejaban" [love stories that occurred to me as a palliative for my impossible contact with boys, at home I wasn't allowed].[5] Frequently, the works of contemporary Catalonian women writers not only portray this oppressive environment, they also manifest the need to relive the traumas and to embody the defeat experienced by Catalonia. In fact, a sense of double oppression, experienced by being both Catalonian and female, remains evident in the narratives of many of these writers. As the histories of Catalonian nationalism and feminism run parallel courses in contemporary Catalonian fiction by women, so too does the threat of disappearance continually haunt their texts.

A Death of Her Own

Simone de Beauvoir observes that "[t]here is a way out that is open to the woman who has reached the end of her resistance—it is suicide."[6] Indeed, perhaps the most obvious display of female textual elimination concerns the act, implied or real, of self-destruction. Yet, male signifying processes frequently appropriate the scene of female suicide, contextualizing, interpreting, and projecting meaning and motives on the experience. For example, Sigmund Freud contends that "[t]o poison oneself = to become pregnant; to drown = to bear a child; to throw oneself from a height = to be delivered of a child."[7] Freud's words seem particularly remarkable for the way that they link female self-destruction and reproductive destiny, as if giving birth necessarily entails destruction of self. In her study on female suicide, Margaret Higonnet demonstrates other ways in which the suicidal act has been seized by men, who have typically interpreted self-destruction as giving in to one's femaleness, either in the form of illness or biological destiny. Indeed, female suicide has often been perceived to be motivated by a *mal de amor,* which causes a crisis in identity; that is, a woman who loses her man, loses her self. Suicide, however, may reveal an oddly empowering facet, in that, as Higonnet notes, taking one's own life forces others to read one's death.[8] Therefore, although suicide ultimately negates the self and may be "misread" as merely this, ironically, often it also represents for the protagonist a last signifying act of autonomy.

Carme Riera's "Es nus, es buit" [The Knot, the Void][9] represents a modern version of the violation of self-will and the silencing of voice experienced by Daphne, a situation that leaves no other alternative than to opt out of the male-driven social narrative. Riera's short story portrays a widow who sits passively in a rest home, having been placed there against her will by her family members, who remain convinced she has lost her reasoning faculties after she burns her wedding picture and the postcards her husband sent on his only trip to Barcelona. Elimination from the public world is made all the more poignant by the ripping away of the first true happiness and fulfillment experienced by the protagonist after her husband's death, during which time she discovers that her domestic skills, honed in marriage, can be applied equally well to eliminating all reminders of life with her husband. Her words reveal that her marriage was empty, her husband insensitive and unkind, and that his trip to Barcelona was to find prostitutes. Although society expects the protagonist to lose her sense of self through the loss of the defining presence of her husband, she instead gains a sense of identity and fulfillment not known to her within matrimony.

As often portrayed in feminist works, the storybook ending "and they lived happily ever after" is but a fiction. The real story begins when it becomes clear that society's promises of personal fulfillment will not be met in marriage. Instead, the marriage contract, as revealed by the protagonist of "Es nus, es buit," represents nullification of true affection, respect, and communication between the participants, as she becomes little more than a domestic servant for her husband, a fact alluded to in the Castilian title, "El detergente definitivo" [The Ultimate Detergent].[10] Traded from one institution (marriage) to another (the rest home), the tedium of her confinement and the anguish of her stolen autonomy lead her to the conclusion that her only option is to swallow lye, the ultimate detergent, to produce the definitive cleansing of her distress in order to dissolve the knot in her throat that threatens to suffocate her. Such a solution points to the murderous nature of domesticity, when it excludes self-development.

Like the laurel tree, the narrator sits immobile, with no hope of escape back into the world she so briefly enjoyed after her husband's death. Still, just as Daphne, now enclosed within bark and rooted in place, continues to shrink from Apollo's embraces, the narrator of "Es nus, es buit" refuses to submit to this violation of her selfhood, carried out under the pretext of familial caring. In monologue form, the female narrator's voice, silenced within marriage, in this very short narrative fills the space that was denied her within the public world. Her voice, and hers alone, fills and shapes the narrative, as she speaks her desire to escape the patriarchal embrace that threatens to suffocate her.

In *The Madwoman in the Attic,* Sandra Gilbert and Susan Gubar state that "masochistic or even suicidal behavior expresses the furious power hunger of the powerless."[11] "Es nus, es buit" portrays a woman who attempts to escape from the suffocating enclosure of powerlessness, now that she "has reached the end of her resistance." Having delighted momentarily in her autonomy and individuality, in the brief space of freedom between her husband's death and her institutionalization, she now feels the walls of demanding social conformity close in upon her. The only moment of power left becomes self-destruction, a last act of autonomy.

"I am where I am not"

Riera's story, "Variacions sobre el tema de Dafne" [Variations on the Theme of Daphne], appears in the collection *Dones soles*

[*Women Alone*],[12] a series of narratives dedicated to the theme of solitude, all written by contemporary female Catalonian authors. Like "Es nus, es buit," this narrative also configures escape as an elimination from the social structures that have offered an aging woman little more than prohibitive suffocation her entire life. However, instead of offering self-annihilation as a potential remedy, "Variacions" suggests elimination as a positive ploy, a freedom from the constraints of an oppressive society that seeks to deny woman access to her own sensuality.

Riera's story begins with the narrator, Caterina, wondering what her neighbor Rosa will think when she returns home to find that Caterina has disappeared. In an effort to comprehend what has occurred, Caterina muses on the events leading up to her current state. Recent and distant memories alternate as the narrator desperately attempts to hold onto the thread of the tale, to untangle the knotted skein of past and present events, that will reveal what has happened to her. Although she has experienced some happy moments, as a child playing in the cool grass under the warm sun, Caterina has since lived an arduous life, from an early age working long hours enclosed in a workshop in order to support herself and her ill father until his death. Later she hauls around a cart of toys and candies but remains unsuccessful in her attempts to sell to children, who, she imagines, are afraid of her withered face. Her only two friends are her neighbor, Rosa, and mestre Miquel, a gardener who tends the municipal flowerbeds. In fact, it is soon after mestre Miquel gives Caterina a sprig of mimosa and makes an overture that might be interpreted as an invitation to greater intimacy between him and Caterina, that a strange metamorphosis overtakes her. However, true to Riera's common narrative technique of seducing the reader by revealing and concealing at the same time, a technique Geraldine Cleary Nichols aptly refers to as a dance of the seven veils,[13] it is not until the last paragraphs that Caterina reveals uncategorically that she is indeed a tree. Nevertheless, the transformation is not only corporal, for Caterina now displays a full-bodied voice, that spreads across the text, rooting itself firmly into the pages. Typical of Catalonian texts that portray middle-aged or older females, who rarely have a voice within patriarchy's social structures, Caterina seems bereft of words in her earlier life at the margins of society as a human being. Her life in human form accords her an existence that appears phantomlike, isolated, unnoticed, almost disembodied as a member of a society that grants her so little value.

But here, in her new botanical form, the text absorbs her every word, filling the narrative space with her desire and her progressive move towards self-awareness.

That the story directly relates to the myth of Daphne is obvious from the title, although Riera herself creates a metamorphosis from Ovid's tale, transforming the original narrative into one that emphasizes a feminine textual erotics. Although Riera's tale remains a narrative regarding sexuality and the female body, the author redirects the original myth to establish a female point of view, transforming as well Ovid's narrative of attempted rape by the male Apollo into an embracing of fertile, sensual sexuality by the female protagonist within a nonviolent context. Whereas the need to escape the violence of Apollo causes Daphne to change into a tree, Caterina's tale implies the necessity of elimination from society in order to experience fully the erotic nature of female sexuality.

Janet Pérez observes that plant imagery often serves as a metaphor for feminine dependency and society's restrictive limits on women. For instance, Pérez notes that vines may suggest the necessity of support structures for dependent women, or they may serve to suggest the dehumanizing effect of total dependency, as in the case of Maria-Antònia Oliver's *Vegetal,* where a woman undergoes transformation into a potted plant.[14] Instead of using plant imagery as symbolic of female dependency, Riera presents Caterina's transformation into nature as a powerful recovery of the voice and body that have been denied her all her life. For Caterina, becoming a tree represents the embodiment of her sensuality, a newly acquired access to a corporal existence in which her voice becomes fleshed out as well. Further, the addition of Rosa and mestre Miquel to Riera's narrative adds nuances to the original tale which suggest that Caterina's unusual sensitivity to plants does not represent the traditional connection of female and nature that has so frequently been used to diminish women's power and active presence within culture. Instead, Riera breaks the gender boundaries of woman-nature and man-civilization by portraying mestre Miquel as possessing a comprehension of plant life to which Caterina's female neighbor, the ironically named Rosa, remains completely immune and hardened. Unlike the sensitivity to the plant world demonstrated by mestre Miquel, the narrator muses that Rosa will look for her neighbor but will not see her, nor will she notice anything different in the patio: "Si al manco no fossis tan burot i estimassis un poc ses plantes!" [If at least you weren't such a dolt and you loved plants a little bit!] (143). "Tot et pareixerá igual . . . perquè a tu un arbre florit no et diu res" [Everything will seem the same to you . . . because to you a flowering tree says nothing] (144). Later, imagining her future needs, the narrator notes: "Hauré d'aprofitar-me bé de ses pluges perquè el que és de tu, Roseta, no puc esperar un mal rec i creixeré i tornaré a florir tota groga" [I'll have to really take advantage of the rains because left up to you, Rosie, I can't expect even a bad watering and I'll grow and I'll blossom all yellow] (144).

In "Variacions," Ovid's aggressive young sun god, Apollo, takes the form of the sensual, nonanthropomorphic sun. Unlike Daphne's father, who urges the nymph to marry and make him a grandfather, Caterina's father warns his young daughter against exposing herself to the dangers of this sensual entity, when she rolls up her sleeves, takes off her shoes, and unbuttons her shirt: "'*Caterina, per l'amor de Déu, et veuran ets veïnats*[. . . .] *Caterina, per l'amor de Déu, et cremaràs ets pits*" ["*Caterina, for the love of God, the neighbors will see you* (. . . .) *Caterina, for the love of God, you'll burn your breasts*"] (136). Although she follows the dictates of this patriarchal figure, and later similar admonitions of the parish priest who urges her to pray against such desires, she never forgets, from her early experiences, the promises offered by this erotic presence which infuses a sweet warmth and sensation of fertility into her belly. It is this sensuality, known to her in her youth through the sweet stickiness of fruit juices dripping down her face, the feel of the sun on her arms and the upper part of her breasts, and the cool grass under her bare feet, that remains a fertile seed within her, even when repressed by societal constraints. The well-being Caterina experiences within a sensual, natural setting contrasts sharply with the oppressive nature of the workshop where she must spend long hours laboring to support herself and her ill father. Cut off from the warm light of the sun and the sweet aroma of flowers, Caterina grows toward death, enclosed within the dark, imprisoning walls of the workshop, illuminated by lightbulbs that emit a phlegmatic yellow light that casts a deadly pallor on the workers there, as they breathe into their lungs the noxious odor of benzene.

It is then that the recovery of a voice for Caterina remains intimately linked to knowing herself as a corporal, sensual being, something that is denied to her through the impositions of society. Ultimately, self-expression must blossom from the material body, a fact Caterina does not at first comprehend as she worries over how she will communicate with Rosa, now that she no longer has a voice audible to society. Like the first broken flowers mestre Miquel gives the protagonist after she leaves the workshop to begin selling toys from her cart, Caterina in her human form represents a wounded plant, a stem broken purposely by another human being or by the overbearing winds of an oppressive society. The catalyst for Caterina's metamorphosis, the sweetly scented and healthy mimosa sprig that mestre Miquel gives to her, suggests his recognition of Caterina's sensual connection to nature and perhaps issues a call to assume a life of the senses in a world where she is the most comfortable: "'*Són foravileres, madó Caterina. Als jardins de Ciutat mai s'hi fan tan bones ni crien tanta olor. Tot d'una vaig pensar en vós ...* '" ["They're from the country, Miss Caterina. They never grow so well or produce such an aroma in the City gardens. All of a sudden I thought of you . . ."] (138). Indeed, mestre Miquel's sensitivity to plants, and the fact that Caterina remains certain that, if he were to see her in her new form, he would recognize some feature belonging to her, contrasts vividly with Caterina's neighbor. Caterina notes that Rosa, looking for an explanation for Caterina's disappearance, will surely imagine that she is dead or that she has been taken away to jail. However, the transformation that has overcome Caterina is not imprisoning but, rather, liberating; for in the first sentence of the story, Caterina indicates that the door to her house has been left open, an image especially poignant, given the many years of dark enclosure she experienced in the workshop.

The freedom Caterina enjoys to express herself through a new corporal existence contrasts firmly with the prohibitions that have surrounded her life. As noted, it is mestre Miquel's gift of a healthy mimosa sprig, picked purposely for her with the intimation of erotic intentions, that catalyzes the metamorphosis. As Caterina sits in her patio the next day, the warmth of the sun throbs upon her lap and penetrates her, the sweet scent of the mimosa brings on a drowsiness, a voice without words calls to her, inviting her to embrace the sensuality that exists all about her. Unlike the Daphne myth, where the young nymph escapes sexual assault through her metamorphosis, Caterina welcomes the sensual encounter that brings out the latent erotic nature within her that she has not been given the opportunity to nurture. The warmth of the sun and the seductive scent of the mimosa sprig bewitch her, infusing Caterina with an awareness of her body and the desire to be fertile. She rubs the mimosa across her nose, lips, cheeks, and ears, and unbuttons her shirt until the sun fully caresses her breasts:

> Es sol untava de mel tot el que tocava i s'herba tendra tornà de vellut. Vaig ajonollar-me en terra, com quan era nina, sense deixar es ram, amb es ram ben estret sobre ets pits i ets ulls lentament se'm clogueren. Endevinava al voltant meu lluïssors i papallones, molses com de seda que davallaven del cel.
>
> [The sun anointed with honey everything it touched and the tender grass became velvet. I kneeled on the ground as I did when I was a girl, without letting go of the branch, with the branch pressed tight across my breasts and my eyes slowly closing. I sensed around me brightness and butterflies, mosses like silk that descended from the sky] (142).

Caterina defoliates the mimosa sprig, pulling the buds off into her mouth, dissolving them with the juices of her tongue. The loss of consciousness of her former world turns into an awareness of her new one, as the metamorphosis takes place:

> vaig estirar-me, això sí, tan llarga com som, damunt s'herba i sentia ses mans que s'obrien i ets dits dets peus que començaven a endinsar-se dins sa terra humida com si cercassin arrels i ets cabells, amb s'oratge, com a branquetes d'un desmai voleiant-se i després es buit i altre pic, de bell nou, humitats noves, altres correnties a ses entranyes i ganes de tornar a despertar. . . .
>
> [I stretched out, indeed I did, my full length, over the grass and felt my hands open and my toes begin to enter the moist earth as if searching for roots and my hair, with the wind, like soaring limbs of a weeping willow, and then there was emptiness and again, once more, new moistness, other currents inside and the desire to wake up again. . . .] (142–43)

Where words once might have issued from her mouth, now she feels "sa boca cosida plena de brancons a punt d'esclatar en flor . . ." [her mouth completely full of twigs on the point of bursting into flower . . .] (143). The natural world about her seeks to communicate with her, and she answers by moving her leaves and branches.

Only after the metamorphosis, as Caterina begins to analyze her transformation through recent and distant memories that have shaped it, does she find a voice. Like the monologue of "Es nus, es buit," Caterina's voice fills the text, and a new self-awareness blossoms from the communication of branches swaying, leaves brushed by the wind, the sound of the breeze rustling through the grass. The story after the transformation, the attempt to comprehend, to adjust, and to impose a narrative shape upon the transformation, manifests the need for this female voice to speak, to explain matters from her point of view. Ironically, it is now, when she forms part of the natural world where people like Rosa will perceive only silence, that Caterina speaks forth most forcefully. Denied a voice within society, it is through her body, outside those inhibiting societal structures, that she speaks.

Although through much of the narrative Caterina shows herself to be somewhat bewildered, dazed, and resistant to leaving behind her old world, her words speak her growing sense of self, of confidence, and of subjecthood as the narration progresses. Although there remains some sorrow in leaving behind the two people with whom she has established a relationship, she accepts the transformation as a happy one: "em quedarà es conhort de tenir sa visita des sol i poder-me'l beure amb llepolia quan m'arribi a ses fulles" [I'll have the consolation of being visited by the sun and being able to drink it in greedily when it reaches my leaves] (144). Toward the end, Caterina proudly accepts her new corporal identity and manifests a firm sense of subjecthood and self-value: "Perquè d'una cosa sí que n'estic segura: si som un arbre, som una mimosa y de bona casta, com sa que em regalà mestre Miquel. . . . Qui sap! A lo millor creixaré ben alta i passaré ses parets des corral de na Rosa" [Because one thing I am sure of: if I am a tree, I'm a mimosa and of good stock, like that the one that mestre Miquel gave me. . . . Who knows! Maybe I'll grow really tall and pass over the walls of Rosa's patio"] (144). Still, Caterina manifests a need to define this new world with the only terms that she has known and feels a drive to comprehend this event in a context that is familiar to her. Thus, she transfers into her new world some of the very same social categories that structured her former existence. The sun, then, will be her husband:

> I si em crema massa en cobrir-me i m'asseca ses entranyes serà com si m'hi hagués casat i hagués de compartir amb s'homo ets bons moments i ets dolents . . . Com una viuda l'enyoraré quan ses boires siguien baixes i es geli sa soada damunt ses branques.
>
> [And if the sun burns me too much as it covers me, and my insides dry out, it will be as if I were married and had to share with my husband good moments as well as bad ones . . . Like a widow I'll

miss him when the fog hangs low and the moisture freezes under my branches.] (144)

The last lines from "Variacions" recall the laurel branch snatched by Apollo from Daphne, to be granted to worthy men as a symbol of victory. Instead, Riera transposes the significance of the fragmented body of Daphne into a symbol of sensuality and power that can affect any woman who opens herself to the senses. Musing that maybe the neighbors will see her as she grows tall and will ask Rosa for a sprig, Caterina notes: "I llavors, tal vegada qualqú el regali a una dona perquè l'ensumi ben fort, ben endins i mentre ensuma vagi sentit una caloreta tèbia a ses entranyes i un pes a ses cames molt dolç i una son . . ." [And then, maybe someone will give it to a woman for her to drink in its aroma, deeply, and as she inhales its perfume she will feel a tepid warmth inside and a sweet heaviness in her legs and a drowsiness . . .] (144). Caterina's branches will flourish, she will rise above the patio walls that cannot contain her, as she reaches for the yellow warmth of her lover. Having been seduced by the heady aromas of the flowers and warmed by the sun's rays, she herself now evolves into the seducing body; the bewitched becomes bewitcher. Daphne's fragments, once destined for men, now function as erotic enticers for other women, leading them into the embodiment of their own sensual power.

Deflating Phallic Awe

What if Daphne's escape from violation rested not on her own elimination from social structure but, instead, occurred at the expense of Apollo's disappearance? Although Daphne herself disappears from society and becomes rooted in place, Catalonian women authors often turn the act of elimination back onto the offending male. As this occurs, a space for female development issues forth, somewhat beyond the autocratic imperatives of a masculine-oriented world. Obviously, to be completely free from the only world one knows may in itself be negating; but it may also offer a liberated imaginary space that surfaces to create new possibilities.

Montserrat Roig states that "[e]ls homes han explicat el món de les dones a través de la seva pròpia visió. Jo el que intento és explicar com veig els homes a través de la meva visió" [(m)en have explained the world of women through their own view.

What I seek to do is explain how I see men through my view].[15] Anne Charlon notes that two ways in which feminist Catalonian authors rebel is by creating a wholly female space exclusive of males, or by transforming male figures, rejecting the official male traditionally portrayed as dominant and controlling.[16] Although, at times, this latter strategy surfaces as a feminization of a male character or the creation of one without aggressive features, I would note that the traditional male figure is also transformed in another way. For, not only is it necessary for the male presence to be excised from these texts, but symbols of masculinity that denote patriarchal authority must disappear as well. The most obvious object-turned-symbol of all, that on which phallic power has not so surreptitiously hung its hat, is, of course, the penis. Many have noted the great Lacanian contradiction of denying that the concept of the phallus is based on the penis, while at the same time defining phallic power in terms of the visually tangible.[17] A number of stories by Catalonian women touch upon the issue of the awe that surrounds the male sexual organ and work to excise that awe and the power invested by society in the penis-turned-phallus.

For example, Maria-Antònia Oliver casts aspersions on the revered male organ in "La primera vegada" [The First Time].[18] A schoolgirl, curious about the "llapis sense punta" [pencil without a point] (85) that she and her friends have heard boys possess, eventually receives her first view of a penis. Instead of admiration, awe, and increased desire, she is filled with disappointment at what appears to her group of friends as a "llapis curt i tou" [short and soft pencil] (89) or, worse yet, a "pirulí" [lollipop] (89). The pencil image reveals the important underpinnings that give support to phallic awe and power. A "pencil without a point," however, excises the inscriptive power relegated to men as those who create civilization and project order onto the world by inscribing masculine signification on chaos or blankness. Equally negating, and much more frivolous, a lollipop, while gastronomically seductive to children, will quickly be consumed.

Riera continues this deconstructive trend in "As you like, darling," from her collection of erotic fiction, *Epitelis tendríssims* [*Most Tender Epithelia*].[19] However, instead of presenting the male sex organ as humorously frivolous or incomplete, Riera eliminates the penis as the erotic center of attention. In "As you like, darling," the male body appears bereft of importance when a woman carries on an erotic relationship with a fetishized male voice, eliminating his body as a necessary component to her own pleasure. The man in question, Helmut, is situated in the position of sexual object, not subject. Although the love relationship does become carnal, the motor of female desire rests with his disembodied voice, and it is the intangible, nonvisual voice that keeps her desire in play, thus explaining her frequent exhortations to "continua, amor, continua" [continue, love, continue] (27). Alas, Helmut's voice, trained quite well, given that he works as an announcer for a Dutch radio station, cannot withstand the insatiable demands of the narrator's powerful desire. Repeatedly asked to perform on command over a two-day period, the weakness of this objectified voice intensifies, and soon Helmut finds himself unable to raise his voice for her pleasure. Completely diminished, Helmut leaves his sleeping lover; he must end the aurally erotic relationship in order to go off to recuperate and gargle, thereby easing the stress on his over-used voice. Daphne no longer shrinks from Apollo's once aggressive overtures; instead, the sun god slips away under the cover of night, unable to stand his ground.

Two Lips that Touch

Apollo's crime against Daphne concerns female sexuality and the attempt to convert it into a male enterprise dominated, controlled, and utilized by males. One female strategy regarding the recovery of female sexual autonomy concerns the elimination or diminished role of the male as center of the eroticized female text. Instead, women carve new spaces of identity and desire, exclusive of a male presence. In short, Daphne's salvation through metamorphosis into a tree is cast back on the offending male; it is he who is eliminated from the weave of the female narrative.

Carme Riera revises the traditional paradigm of eroticism in several ways. In her well-known short story "Te deix, amor, la mar com a penyora" [I Leave You, My Love, the Sea as a Token],[20] the reader falls easily into the heterosexual trap laid by the author in which an older math teacher who has an affair with a young adolescent girl is revealed to be a woman. Males fall to a secondary position in the love paradigm, unable to upset and replace the intimate bond forged between the two women. Borders that would separate are washed away by the powerful force of the feminine imagery of the immense sea that links the two women.

The male body is further excised in Riera's two short stories, "Una mica de fred per a Wanda" [A Cool Breeze for Wanda] from *Epitelis tendríssims* and "Contra l'amor en companyia" [Against Love With a Partner],[21] from the collection of the same name, when female masturbation replaces male figures completely in the attainment of female erotic pleasure. In the first story, a father and his son find themselves in conflict when each desires and seeks the sexual attention of Wanda. But, eventually, the father-son suitors fall ill, the father dies, and Wanda discovers the inordinate pleasures that can be achieved when sitting before an air conditioning system, which refreshes her and pleases her in the most intimate of fashions, much more so than does any man. The second story, "Contra l'amor en companyia," presents a female poet-protagonist courted by a secret admirer who soon reveals himself to be a much older family friend. Although her verses have been stimulated by the awe expressed by the secret admirer, who then becomes her husband, soon he no longer is able to inspire poetic heights in his young wife. Sexual drive and narrative impulse intertwine as the writer's block experienced by the protagonist dissipates when she discovers the ability to pleasure her own body in a way superior to intimacy with a man.

These narratives portray female desire as self-contained and exclusive of male contact. Although Daphne herself disappears from the social structure inhabited by Apollo, nevertheless, from the other side of the coin, the myth might be seen to represent an excision of Apollo from her world, allowing her to choose, instead, a self-contained existence and self-possession, where her branches and leaves brush sensually against her trunk, recalling Luce Irigaray's writings in *This Sex Which Is Not One*. As Irigaray notes in her description of female sexuality, woman "enters into a ceaseless exchange of herself with the other without any possibility of identifying either." That is, female genitalia supplant the oneness of the male sexual organ, and instead create a continuous "contact of *at least two* (lips) which keeps woman in touch with herself, but without any possibility of distinguishing what is touching from what is touched."[22]

Caressing the Word

Finally, male corporal presence disappears completely behind the materiality of language wielded by female narrators to create a textual body. If true power lies in the word, in the ability to invest the world with symbols and meaning of one's own making, it is here that the greatest potential subversion for women lies.

Riera's "Octubre, octubre" [October, October], her contribution to *El primer amor* [*First Love*],[23] an anthology of contemporary Catalonian stories dedicated to the concept of first love, tells the story of a young woman at the cusp of sexual discovery who meets with her lover despite her family's discouragement and their attempts to intervene in the relationship. Eventually, it becomes clear to the reader that the lover is a diary, and that writing acquires an erotic nature, a caressing of "la llisa superfície blanquíssima" [a smooth, very white surface] by "un bolígraf de tinta vermella, com si una vena em ragés del palpís amb incontinència apassionada" [a vermilion-inked pen, as if a vein gushed from my flesh with uncontrollable passion] (96). The text becomes corporalized and the young writer attempts to fix moments of passion onto this "lover," despite the limits of language. Through this textualized lover, the protagonist learns that "només la passió és carn de poema [. . .] acabada sobre el teu cos de cel-lulosa premsada, presoner d'un esquelet de filferro en forma d'espiral . . ." [only passion is the flesh of the poem (. . .) completed upon the pressed fiber of your body, prisoner of a wire skeleton in the shape of a spiral . . .] (96).

The protagonist's writing displays the subversive nature of the text against the social unit, represented in this case by her family, who hide her notebook among clothes to be ironed or mended, suggesting that this budding female desire is a wrinkle or tear in the fabric of social conformity. "Octubre, octubre" reveals the elimination of the male as the center of the erotic text, and the narrator, now fifteen years older and facing death, desires to experience the pleasures of this text once more before dying. Although the protagonist's text appears masculinized to project the image of a lover, still it represents a nonaggressive, "feminized" lover, given that it is the female who traditionally has occupied the role of the tabula rasa inscribed by the male lover. Language swallows up the lover in an erotic capturing of his body, as the pen caresses the page, inverting the traditional image of the female page and the male pen. The traditional image of textuality draped in sexuality portrays the male semen-word that impregnates the female page with meaning, ordering the blank chaos of the text into visible signs authored by a father-creator. Here, the "vermilion-inked pen" represents blood splashed onto the white nothingness, an infusing of life into the lifeless white page. Riera, however, does not simply invert the gender roles within this image; rather, she changes the active-passive delineation of the male author-female page, turning it into an erotic relationship of reciprocal pleasure, in which neither page nor author assumes the dominant role. The essential autonomy of the text remains evident as the narrator realizes that she cannot fully possess or know the text, and thus questions what this textual lover has felt, whether it has shared the pleasure that she so wished. She wonders: "si les meves paraules, les meves mans lliscant pel teu cos joveníssim, pogueren contagiar-te eternitats" [whether my words, my hands sliding over your very young body, could communicate to you eternities] (94). Although her first writing was stimulated by a flesh-and-blood lover fifteen years earlier, this first carnal love takes second place in importance to the pleasure of the first writing, which surges as the narrator seeks to translate her emotion to the text, to make the page share what she feels, to pleasure the text just as the text pleasures her.

In "'The Blank Page' and the Issues of Female Creativity," Susan Gubar discusses the traditional association of female sexuality and textuality, noting the significance of blood in female creativity as well as its varied meaning within a woman's life. Blood—of sexual initiation, menses, childbirth—represents one of the principal metaphors of the female body, and since the body serves as the primary or only medium available to women for self-expression, the female artist may "experience herself as bleeding into print," and perceive the flowing of blood from the interior recesses of the body out onto the blank medium as "telling" or narration.[24] Rather than an ejaculation of pleasure, as might be described for male authorship, Gubar notes that female artistic creation may instead represent a reaction to rending, a painful wounding, a penetration that violates the boundaries of the self.[25] Although female creativity has for so long produced a "cal·ligrafia vacil·lant" [hesitant calligraphy] (96), the words used by Riera's narrator to describe her own writing, the vermilion-inked pen used by the protagonist of "Octubre, octubre" suggests the controlled use of the interior currents of female corporality to move beyond the homespun hieroglyphics of a bloodstained page. The corporality experienced by Caterina in "Variacions sobre el tema de Dafne" becomes in "Octubre, octubre" the subversive strategy of writing with the body.

Although Gubar notes that twentieth-century women often suggest that their talent emerges from a male master rather than from a female muse,[26] Riera pointedly moves away from such a patriarchal origin and instead establishes her protagonist's relationship with the text as a product of a female inheritance. The narrator senses a feminine genealogy of writers within her family, perhaps women with textual lovers: "Vaig adonar-me, gràcies a tu, que jo també podia escriure, com l'àvia Joana, amb la qual, segons tothom, guardava de nina una estranya semblança" [I realized, thanks to you, that I too could write like grandmother Joana, to whom, according to everyone, I had a strange likeness as a child] (96). This female genealogy that gives a sense of continuity and connection contrasts with the air of prohibition within the narrator's immediate family regarding this relationship she has taken up: "'ets massa jove', 'val més que estudiïs i no perdis el temps amb beneitures'" ["you're too young," "it's better that you study and not waste your time with nonsense"] (94). Indeed, the protagonist learns early on that her text represents an imbrication of writing, eroticism, and subversion. As a girl, she writes while sitting on her bed—the first sign of the erotic nature that will fill the text, and keeps the pages hidden under her bed, away from the prying eyes of those who might intercede. To pour herself into the text can only happen by "transgredint totes les prohibicions" [transgressing all prohibitions] (94).

"Octubre, octubre" begins on much the same note as Riera's *Qüestió d'amor propi* [*A Question of Self Love*],[27] creating a geographical space of sensual literary excess that the narrator culls and uses in her own writing. Yet, the use of sensual elements of nature functions to underscore the materiality of the text. As she returns to her "first love," the protagonist notes that the material residue of her creation remains lodged under her fingernails, and that she retains the memory of her ecstatic fingers caressing the textual body. Furthermore, the importance of nature, with its sensual sounds, aromas, and textures, offers "material" for the budding young writer of fifteen years earlier, as well as a liberating atmosphere in which to give free rein to her erotic imagination. In the city, where society maintains consistently ordered constraints, laid out like streets on a map, the transgressive nature of the erotic text would never have taken the same course: "A la ciutat les coses haurien succeït de manera diferent fins i tot durant la tardor" [In the city things would have happened differently, even in autumn] (93).

Invoking the myth of Ariadne, who gives Theseus a ball of twine with which to leave a path of return after confronting the minotaur in the labyrinth, the narrator delivers the thread of her story to this textual lover, not yet realizing the extent of the reciprocity that exists between them: "però no sabia que, regalant-te'l, seria jo la que cauria presonera del meu propi llaç" [but I didn't know that, by giving it to you, I would be the one caught in my own trap] (94). The thread of Ariadne represents the erotic desire initiated with the text, carnally satisfied with en Jordi, the narrator's cousin, and brought back to the textual lover to relive through his body, tailored to his measure. In fact, the narrator implies that en Jordi represents a surrogate lover with whom she reaches "les portes del laberint" [the doors of the labyrinth] (95). In other words, en Jordi provides the progatonist with an erotic experience that serves as a pretext, a preliminary foreplay for shaping the intimacy of the textual erotics that later come into play between the narrator and her textual lover: "intuïa que la nostra relació es beneficiaria molt de la seva visita" [I intuited that our relationship would benefit much from his visit] (95).

There is no lover like the first, even when bound in a cheap cardboard cover: "Cap quadern no m'ha seduït com tu saberes fer-ho" [No notebook has seduced me as you were able to do] (96). The narrator has experienced other textual pleasures, with notebooks from varied places, using those that bear prestigious brandnames, notebooks crafted with delicate textures, or scented with perfume, all of which "m'han ofert al llarg d'aquests temps el dret i el revés del seu cos per omplir-los amb les meves dèries, però a cap no m'he lliurat com a tu aquella nit, la primera vegada" [have offered up to me during this time the front and the back of their body to fill them with my manias, but I have not given myself to any as to you that night, the first time] (96). Therefore, the first love is the last love, the last textual experience is a return to the first, both through memory and by caressing words upon the textual body once more. Like "Te deix, amor, la mar com a penyora," Eros and Thanatos embrace as both narratives end with a narrator, approaching death, who desires a return to her erotic origin. In "Te deix" the female narrator writes to her former female lover, her text representing not only a last declaration of her love, but also a will, leaving to her beloved the sea, and inscribing her lover's name in her soon-to-be-born daughter. "Octubre, octubre" also presents the same sense of last testament and the same notion of an aquatic substance (the inscriptive blood) that breaks boundaries separating the lover and the self. The last words of "Octubre, octubre" display the narrator's desire once more to pleasure the text/be pleasured by the text: "avui, amb infinita delectança, ompl la teva darrera pàgina, un bocinet de la teva pell que, durant quinze anys, aviat els farà, he volgut reservar-te per dedicar-te les meves darreres paraules" [today, with infinite pleasure, I fill your last page, a small part of your skin that, for what soon will be fifteen years, I have reserved to dedicate to you my last words] (97).

From the pulp of Daphne's fleshy interior, material is derived and fashioned into a smooth, ready surface for inscription. Written on by Daphne herself, "the blank page is transformed into living wood that sighs and sings like a tree in the wind."[28] No longer willing to have her story told for her, the nymph speaks her own tale. What surfaces through Riera's narratives, as well as one step beyond the myth of Daphne and Apollo, is the urgency for female desire to recover its voice. Although Daphne slips out of Apollo's sexual embrace, the god transforms his defeat into victory. For tradition has it that Apollo plucks Daphne's branches in his name to crown the heads of literary men, as an eternal symbol of the victory of the word. Although Mary E. Barnard emphasizes that "[t]he laurel of victory, becomes, paradoxically, a symbol of his amorous defeat,"[29] we might note that the myth leaves Apollo with the word, which he uses to colonize further his social space and to enforce female elimination. By that process, Daphne's very body, fragmented and torn, is converted into a symbol of his word. Nevertheless, Carme Riera reveals the possibility of recovering these very fragments, in order to allow the breeze to sing through Daphne's leaves, speaking her desire. For it is through the recovery of her voice that female disappearance is healed and feminine presence may be embodied.

Notes

The frequent ellipses in the quotations from Riera's works are part of the original texts. On the few occasions that I have deleted words from a citation, this is indicated by ellipsis points placed within brackets.

1. The myth of Daphne and Apollo appears in Ovid, *The Metamorphoses of Ovid,* trans. A. E. Watts (San Francisco: North Point Press, 1980).

2. DuPlessis, *Writing Beyond the Ending: Narrative Strategies of Twentieth-Century Women Writers* (Bloomington: Indiana University Press, 1985).

3. Capmany, "El feminisme ara," *Dona i societat a la Catalunya actual* (Barcelona: "Llibres a l'abast," 140, Edicions 62, 1978), 8, 9; quoted in Anne Charlon, 119, *La condició de la dona en la narrativa femenina catalana, 1900–1983,* trans. Pilar Canal (Barcelona: Edicions 62, 1990), 119. This and all subsequent translations from Catalan materials are my own.

4. Charlon, *La condició de la dona,* 124.

5. Racionero, "Entrevista con Carmen Riera: Cada vez tenemos menos imaginación," *Quimera* 9–10 (July-August 1981):15.

6. de Beauvoir, *The Second Sex,* trans. H. M. Parshley (New York: Vintage Books, 1974), 678.

7. Freud, "The Psychogenesis of a Case of Homosexuality in a Woman," trans. Barbara Low and R. Gabler, *Sigmund Freud: Collected Papers,* vol. 2, ed. Joan Riviere (New York: Basic Books, 1959), 220.

8. Higonnet, "Suicide: Representations of the Feminine in the Nineteenth Century," *Poetics Today* 6: 1–2 (1985):103.

9. Riera, "Es nus, es buit," *Jo pos per testimoni les gavines* (Barcelona: Laia, 1977), 79–82.

10. Riera, "El detergente definitivo," *Te dejo el mar,* trans. Luisa Cotoner (Madrid: Espasa Calpe, 1991), 192–95.

11. Gilbert and Gubar, *The Madwoman in the Attic: The Woman Writer and the Nineteenth-Century Literary Imagination* (New Haven and London: Yale University Press, 1979), 285.

12. Riera, "Variacions sobre el tema de Dafne," *Dones soles* (Barcelona: Planeta, 1995), 135–44. All quotations from "Variacions" are cited parenthetically in the text.

13. Nichols, "Stranger than Fiction: Fantasy in Short Stories by Matute, Rodoreda, Riera," *Monographic Review/Revista Monográfica* 4 (1988):41.

14. Pérez, "Plant Imagery, Subversion, and Feminine Dependency: Josefina Aldecoa, Carmen Martín Gaite, and Maria Antònia Oliver," *In the Feminine Mode: Essays on Hispanic Women Writers,* ed. Noël Valis and Carol Maier (Lewisburg: Bucknell University Press, 1990), 78–79, 98; Maria-Antònia Oliver, *Vegetal i Muller qui cerca espill* (Barcelona: La Llar del Llibre, 1984).

15. Roig, "L'Hora," (January 1981); quoted in Anne Charlon, *La condició de la dona,* 14.

16. Charlon, *La condició de la dona,* 180.

17. Lacan, "The signification of the phallus," *Ecrits: A Selection,* trans. Alan Sheridan (New York: W.W. Norton, 1977). In this essay, Lacan states that "this signifier [phallus] is chosen because it is the *most tangible element* in the *real of sexual copulation*. . . . It might also be said that by virtue of *its turgidity,* it is the image of the vital flow as it is transmitted in generation," 287 (my emphasis).

18. Oliver, "La primera vegada,"*El primer amor* (Barcelona: Columna, 1992), 83–89. All quotations from this work are cited parenthetically in the text.

19. Riera, "*As you like, darling,*" *Epitelis tendríssims* (Barcelona: Edicions 62, 1981), 19–28. References to this work are documented parenthetically in the text.

20. Riera, "Te deix, amor, la mar com a penyora," *Te deix, amor, la mar com a penyora* (Barcelona: Laia, 1975), 19–36.

21. Riera, "Una mica de fred per a Wanda," *Epitelis tendríssims,* 63–78. "Contra l'amor en companyia," *Contra l'amor en companyia* (Barcelona: Destino, 1991), 63–74.

22. Irigaray, *This Sex Which Is Not One,* trans. Catherine Porter (Ithaca, N.Y.: Cornell University Press, 1985), 31, 26.

23. Riera, "Octubre, octubre," *El primer amor* (Barcelona: Columna, 1992), 91–97. All quotations from this work are are cited parenthetically in the text.

24. Gubar, "'The Blank Page' and the Issues of Female Creativity," *The New Feminist Criticism: Essays on Women, Literature, and Theory,* ed. Elaine Showalter (New York: Pantheon Books, 1985), 296, 301.

25. Ibid., 302.

26. Ibid., 303.

27. Riera, *Qüestió d'amor propi* (Barcelona: Laia, 1988).

28. Gubar, "'Blank Page,'" 309.

29. Barnard, *The Myth of Apollo and Daphne from Ovid to Quevedo: Love, Agon, and the Grotesque* (Durham: Duke University Press, 1987), 42.

Politics and Desire: Rosa and Mercè as Social and Erotic Models in Carme Riera's One-Act Play, *Senyora, ha vist els meus fills?* from *Dones i Catalunya*

PATRICIA HART

> En Germinal . . . m'ensenyà que jo era molt més que un sexe badat per acollir-ne un altre, una bestia de càrrega . . . la revolució em faria, ens faria unes persones lliures . . . construïriem un món més just, sense rics ni pobres, un món de justicia i d'amor.
> —Rosa, *Senyora, ha vist els meus fills?, Dones i Catalunya,* Carme Riera[1]
>
> [Germinal . . . taught me that I was much more than legs and sex spread open, more than a beast of burden. The Revolution would make me, would make us free people. We would build a new, more just world, without rich or poor, a world of justice and love.][2]
>
> Para una mujer, escribir literatura es en cierto modo una rebeldía doble, primero porque está escribiendo; es mujer y por esto está marginada. Y segundo, es el hecho de que está escribiendo en una lengua que también la margina, la propia lengua margina a las mujeres . . . Para nosotras escribir es un poco lo mismo que en el caso de los judíos conversos y el castellano, una lengua en que se les oprimía.
> —Carme Riera[3]
>
> [For a woman, writing literature is in a way a double rebellion, first because she is writing; she is a woman, and because of that she is marginalized. And second is the fact that she is writing in a language that also marginalizes her, language itself marginalizes women . . . For us, writing is a little like the case of the Jewish Converts who wrote in Castilian, a language that oppressed them.]

THIS STUDY WILL EXAMINE THE APPARENT EROTIC AND POLITICAL polarity between the two main characters in Carme Riera's one-act play, *Senyora, ha vist els meus fills?* [*Madam, Have You Seen My Sons?*], one of six scenes that formed the collaborative play, *Dones i Catalunya* [*Women and Catalonia*]. At first glance, this play seems to have a very simple sociosexual structure, with the liberal Republican forces associated with free love, while the conservative Nationalist forces are connected sexually to repression, exploitation, and an unhappy, embittered abstinence. In this essay, however, I will scrutinize this schematic structure to discover some surprising conflicts beneath the surface in Riera's dramatic re-creation of history.

In *Senyora, ha vist els meus fills?* three women, Elissa, Mercè, and Rosa, reunite in a war-battered villa in the exclusive neighborhood of Bonanova in 1939 to try to salvage whatever scraps may remain of their lives. Elissa was once the mistress of the mansion, and Mercè, her young daughter, is now a prematurely soured twenty-year-old. Elissa's husband was shot by leftist militiamen at the start of the war, and her three sons were killed in the fighting; as a result, Elissa has gone insane. Her daughter Mercè struggles to care for her, while at the same time bitterly resenting her mother for mourning her dead sons to the exclusion of loving her living daughter.

Rosa was formerly a maid in the household and lost her virginity to one of the young "masters," Jordi. She then met the significantly named Germinal,[4] a militiaman who awakened her both sexually and politically to her individual rights and worth before he was killed in action. She also had a subsequent brief affair with a young soldier who died in her arms after one night of passion.

By tracing the sexual and political trajectory of the two younger women, I will demonstrate Rosa's politics of desire and Mercè's of repression. The polarity of their positions is emphasized and mediated by the presence of Elissa, whose madness is the result of her evasion of the hard realities Mercè and Rosa both face, each within her own moral, political, and erotic sphere. Wrenched from the context of her social and sexual role as wife to her "superior" husband and mother to her "superior" sons, Elissa cannot face the only role the conservative society leaves her to play—namely, that of grieving, virtuous widow—so she takes refuge in a return to the coquetry of her unmarried youth, a time when sexual abstinence was a game of delayed gratification that promised to heighten eventual encounters with increased satisfaction. In this way, ironically, the repressive restraints of bourgeois society actually function for Elissa as pleasurably fetishistic trappings of the sort Luis Buñuel pretended to loathe but which both obviously actually adored and needed in order to achieve filmic *jouissance*. Jaume Martí-Olivella has written that "two of the most problematic and urgent cultural and political debates in Spain today [are] the need to rethink the concepts of nationalism and feminism."[5] Here, I argue that the same is true for Catalonia, and that Riera reframes these debates with acute skill in this play.

It is precisely the fusion of sex and politics that most interests me in this play. On the one hand, it is hardly surprising that the defeated Republicans, as embodied by Rosa, should be associated with free love, given the liberal social agenda of the Second Republic, which included provisions for civil marriage and for divorce. By contrast, the conservative National forces had an expressly stated allegiance to both Rome and the monarchy; therefore the sexual conservatism expressed by Mercè is completely congruent with their views. However, the notion that all Republicans were lusty yet sensitive lovers while all Francoists were repressed louts is naive, and Riera avoids falling into this trap. As the drama unfolds, a number of details emerge that tug at the tattered threads of the sociosexual fabric of the postwar society.

Initially, the play presents us with a Mercè who is an extreme example of repression and a Rosa who is conspicuously lacking in sexual complexes or shame. The explanation for both stances is clearly connected to their politics. The very first stage direction describes Mercè's sour expression as paradigmatic of the Sección Femenina.[6] Later, Rosa's awakening from her repressive role as servant is double, as she emancipates herself from Jordi's sexual exploitation to enter into a political and erotic partnership with the militiaman, Germinal.

When the two young women first encounter each other at the beginning of the play, Rosa is the one who insistently brings the topic around to sex. She does this, as we begin to see, with a specifically self-interested motive in mind: that of creating a feeling of shared confidences and intimacy that she hopes will persuade Mercè to let her stay on in the house, where she will be safe from the reprisals of Francoist forces that would kill her as an enemy of the state. First, Rosa makes a winking reference to her sexual relationship with Jordi, as the stage directions tell us: "Intenta cercar una certa complicitat" [She tries to create a certain complicity] (7). This attempt backfires, and Mercè answers with a moralistic response, "El teu capteniment, Rosa, no fou d'alló més moral amb el senyoret Jordi, si és això el que vols donar a entendre" [Your behavior with Master Jordi, Rosa, wasn't exactly of the most moral sort, if that's what you're referring to] (7). At this moment in the conversation, the sexual polarity between the two women is great, and is demonstrated linguistically as they choose opposing registers (Rosa, using that of popular speech suited for telling a confidence or a joke, and Mercè, mouthing moralistic bourgeois clichés). Mercè speaks of "la moral" as if it were an absolute on which they both agreed without question, and the word introduces the basic issue that the play will debate.

Seeing that she has not succeeded in creating complicity, Rosa tries to use her superior sexual experience as a tool to manipulate Mercè. Harshly, she says to her, "Senyoreta Mercè, què sap vostè de la vida? Ha estimat algú de debó? Ha fet l'amor alguna vegada?" [Miss Mercè, what do you know of life? Have you ever really loved anyone? Have you ever made love even once?] (7). At first, Mercè continues to respond in the hollow rhetoric of the "good" bourgeois woman. "Jo sabia fer-me respectar, Rosa. Jo no sóc com tu . . ." [I knew how to make them respect me, Rosa. I'm not like you . . .] (7). Rosa still tries to insist that her sexual experience makes her superior, saying, "Això ja es veu. . . . Sap quin gust tenen els petons?" [I can see that. . . . Do you know what kisses taste like?] (7)

It is in response to this question that the text surprises us, and begins insidiously to deconstruct the apparently simple sociosexual paradigms suggested at the beginning. First, Mercè startles us by recognizing that part of the reason for her supposed "virtue" is that before the war no one ever encouraged her to sin. Referring to her fiancé, she says, "Manel també morí a la guerra, és clar que mai no em feu masa cas . . . Jo no soc maca . . . Volia els meus diners, ho sé" [Manel died in the war too. Of course he never really paid any attention to me. I'm not pretty. . . . He wanted my money, I know] (7). What Mercè says next further complicates the stark dichotomy of the sensual Republicans versus the repressed Falangists, as she tells a story of her own sickening exploitation at the hands of the very militia where Rosa found such tender affection and liberating care. "La nit que se'n dugueren el papa van intentar violar-me. . . . Sé com pot ser d'agre i fastigós un petó" [The night they took Papa away, they tried to rape me. . . . I know how bitter and disgusting a kiss can be] (7).

Rosa's response to this revelation is interesting, and serves to further support my contention that the initial, apparently Manichean sexual/political schema are gradually pulled into unsettling tension by the details of the play. It now falls to Rosa to defend her comrades, and with them, the structure and belief system that represents her reason for living. Although she expresses regret, "Ho sento moltíssim, senyoreta, no sap com" [I'm very sorry, Miss, you don't know how much] (7), she then finds a way to rationalize this behavior to some extent. "Alguns companys pensaven que les dones eram només femelles" [Some of the comrades thought women were just females] (7). Then she contrasts Mercè's experiences at the hands of the militiamen with her own exploitation by Jordi:

> Jo he tingut més sort . . . clar que només en aquest sentit, senyoreta. Vaig estimar Jordi, el seu germà, no em fa vergonya dir-ho. No erem iguals, ho sé, però la nit era més curta als seus braços.
>
> [I've been luckier . . . of course just in that sense, Miss. I loved Jordi, your brother, I'm not ashamed to say it. We weren't equals, I know, but the night was shorter in his arms.] (8)

It is then that the two women essentially re-fight the war, but on the basis of sexual mores, rather than with bombs. Janet Pérez has noted that women writers from all regions of Spain who have treated the Civil War generally treat "small, seemingly insignificant moments. . . . Their sphere is largely war's 'intra-history' as Unamuno would have termed it."[7] Rosa and Mercè's topics certainly include relationships and quotidian detail, as Pérez's observation would imply. Their disagreement, however, is essentially political, and could not be more serious. It has already cost the life of most of Mercè's family and two of Rosa's lovers, and could also end Rosa's life at any moment. In this regard, Riera's play differs from other works studied by Pérez.

Rosa begins by trying to explain the reality of her relationship with the young "Master," Jordi, to the moralistically supercilious Mercè. "Fou [Jordi] el que em buscava. . . . Jo la cambrera també servia per a aixó. . . . Em tingué d'estrena. . . . No, no s'esborroni, no" [It was (Jordi) who sought me out. . . . I, the chambermaid, was good for that too. . . . He was the first one to have me. . . . No, no, don't be shocked, no] (8). Mercè, representing traditional morality, insists on placing the blame for sexual peccadilloes on the woman, no matter who initiates them. Rosa inverts the situation to postulate that each person is responsible for the acts he or she commits. In this, we hear echoes of Don Quijote's insistence to Sancho that "cada uno es hijo de sus obras" [Every man is the child of his deeds], and the Quijotesque reference is not casual, as we will see later in the *loca-cuerda* figure of Elissa, who suffers from delusions, but nevertheless enunciates some of the play's basic truths. Mercè's reaction is one of distaste, but Rosa's insistence, "No, no s'esborroni, no," [No, no, don't be shocked, no] again attempts to restore any shame to the place it rightfully belongs, namely, with the person who has had power and has abused it within a sexual relationship (8).

Earlier, Mercè justified her attack on Rosa with the pitiful spectacle of her mother, driven to madness by her father's death at the hands of the very militiamen with whom Rosa ran away. Mercè tries to show that her suffering has been greater than Rosa's, and therefore that she is in the right, both morally and politically. When Mercè says that her mother is locked in madness because her sons have not returned, Rosa tries to comfort Elissa, saying that maybe the sons have gone into hiding in France. Seemingly blind to the emptiness of the victory, Mercè responds sharply that *her* side has won: "Cap dels nostres no és a França, Rosa. Per què havien de fugir, si hem guanyat?" [No one on our side is in France, Rosa. Why should they flee? We won the war!] (6).

Rosa's response is meant as an answer to the question of whether the sons may still be alive. "N'està ben segura? ¿En té proves?" [Are you sure? Do you have proof?] (6). The words pretend to be a statement of optimism about the possible survival of the young "Masters," but the audience, observing this struggle, questions the permanence of the "victory" to which Mercè refers.

Rosa's next move in this microcosmic re-fighting of the Civil War is to describe the way her political and sexual awakenings occurred simultaneously:

> Després vaig conèixer en Germinal, ell m'ensenyà que jo era molt més que un sexe badat per acollir-ne un altre, una bestia de càrrega . . . la revolució em faria, ens faria una persona lliure . . . construiriem un món més just, sense rics, ni pobres, un món de justicia i d'amor. . . .

> [After I met Germinal, he taught me that I was a lot more than legs and sex spread open, more than a beast of burden. The revolution would make me, would make us free people. We would build a

new, more just world, without rich or poor, a world of justice and love . . . .] (8)

Mercè's only available defense here is a linguistic one that stresses the artificial class distinction between them. When Rosa says in a confidential tone, "Vaig seguir a Germinal a Mallorca, Mercè," [I followed Germinal to Mallorca, Mercè] the latter jumps at the opportunity to create distance and declare herself a victor in this symbolic recreation of the war (8). "Senyoreta Mercè, per a mi segueixes èssent la cambrera de la casa, Rosa. . . . La guerra s'ha acabat i heu perdut. ¿Està clar?" [That's *Miss* Mercè to you. To me, you're still the maid in this house, Rosa. The war is over and you all lost. Is that clear?] (8). This would seem to be an irrefutable response in a conversation in which words are arms in a symbolic battle, but Rosa manages to go Mercè one better once more. "Hem perdut. D'acord. La guerra fou terrible, però la revolució bellìssima" [We lost. I'll grant you that. The war was terrible, but the Revolution was really beautiful] (8).

In his "The Sociology of Modern Drama," George Lukács points out that, in a contemporary society where there is no essential agreement as to the basic ethical structure (and it is hard to imagine a place that fits that description better than Barcelona in the postwar years, although contemporary Spain can certainly boast its own ideological rifts), a drama must work through problems to create consensus by demonstrating morality. "When ethics cease to be a given," he says, "the ethical knotting within the drama . . . has to be created; whereupon ethics, as the cornerstone of the artistic composition, move necessarily into the vital center of motivation."[8] How completely Riera understands this, and how deftly her characters argue their positions! As a victim of a sexual attack, as one who lost father, brothers, and future husband, Mercè embodies Francoist "righteous indignation." By revealing the serious wounds inflicted on Mercè by the war, Riera allows the public to see and experience the complexities of her position. That way, when the play ends with Rosa in the more precarious position, and therefore more immediately deserving of our sympathy, the playgoers can feel that they experienced dramatic conflict instead of witnessing a diatribe.

"M'alegro de que tinguis tan bons records de la guerra" [I'm happy you have such nice memories of the war], responds Mercé to Rosa's assertion that "La revolució fou bellìssima" [The Revolution was very beautiful] (both 8). Thus, there is a constant tension in the dialogue. Even though contemporary theatergoers know that this is not what Rosa meant, still Mercè's words remind us that, philosophical positions aside, any war exacts a terrible price in human terms.

Rosa next recounts her experiences during the war itself, clarifying what she meant by saying that the Revolution was beautiful, while at the same time answering Mercè's criticism implying that Rosa is a promiscuous, hopelessly deluded woman who has no idea of the war's real cost. In fact, Rosa reveals that nothing could be further from the truth. Soon after her rapturous lovemaking with Germinal, he was sent on a secret mission and never returned. The audience already knows he is dead. However, instead of melodramatically setting Rosa up as "virtuous" sufferer in opposition to the "bad" Francoists, Riera cleverly uses a stage prop to avoid such a reductive presentation. "Tot el que he pogut guardar d'ell és una fotografla," Rosa says [All I have left of him is a photograph] (9). But when she takes out the photograph to look at it, the artefact and the act of looking remind Elissa of her missing sons, and she mistakes it for a photo of them. This trick serves to make the public remember that for mothers and lovers on both sides of the war, the beloved was in far too many cases reduced to nothing more than a tattered photo. The presence of Elissa on stage has the effect of upsetting easy, Manichean thought patterns. When Peter Brook rails against "the deadly theater" in his book, *The Empty Space,* he points out the importance of keeping the ideas alive. "A doctor can tell at once between the trace of life and the useless bag of bones that life has left;" Brook tells us, "but we are less practised in observing how an idea, an attitude or a form can pass from the lively to the moribund."[9] Carme Riera clearly knows that one sure way of killing an idea on stage is to present characters who embody ideological positions that are unchallenged by opposing viewpoints.

After reminding the audience visually that the antagonistic sides of the conflict are connected in human terms, Riera is in a much stronger position to continue the process Lukács called creating ethics on stage. It is now that the two main characters directly address the subject of morality. Here, sexual desire is the catalyst for the discussion. Rosa begins to speak longingly of Germinal, while looking at the photograph. "Ara si, veu . . . ells llavis molsuts . . . Em feia uns petons!" . . . [Now, look at his full lips . . . he gave me some kisses!] (9). A three-way conversation ensues, in which Rosa argues in favor of free love, Mercè of conventional morality, and Elissa serves to destabilize both with the "madwoman's" license to say anything that comes into her head.

"Rosa, em fas llàstima," Mercè says as she begins her direct attack. "No tens principis ni moral" [Rosa, I pity you. You don't have principles or morals] (9). This opening provides Rosa with the opportunity to create and explore a sexual ethic along with the audience:

> ¿Principis? No l'entenc, senyoreta Mercè. ¿Moral . . . ? ¿Qué vol dir-me ara? He après moltes coses durant aquest temps, i més interessants que no planxar camises o enmidonar faldilles. He descobert tantes coses que em fa por no tenir el temps suficient per a viure-les.
>
> [Principles? I don't understand you, Miss Mercè. Morals? What do you mean by that? I learned a lot of things during those times, things that are more interesting than ironing and starching shirts, I can tell you. I've discovered so many things that I'm afraid I won't have time to enjoy them all.] (9)

Mercè's response depends on blind adherence to unexamined clichés about a woman's "place" in the world. "No crec que es pugui descobrir res de bo al front. No és lloc per a una dona ni que sigui una minyona, Rosa" [I don't think you can discover anything good at the Front. That's no place for a woman, even if she is a maid, Rosa] (9). With the last words, Mercè adds a humiliating class put-down to the clichéd morality, but now Rosa contradicts her directly. "S'equivoca, senyoreta Mercè, jo li aseguro" [You're wrong, Miss Mercè, I assure you] (9). What follows is most lively, living theater, in Brookian terms, as it tears preconceived opinions about war and women to shreds and reassembles them with the audience's complicity. Rosa explains that she was assigned to work in a hospital, but that she tried to escape one night, hoping to find Germinal, to see where he had fallen. She was captured by her own side, who wanted to shoot her as a potentially traitorous deserter. This gives rise to the following ironic dialogue between her and Mercè:

> Rosa: Fou difícil que aceptessin el que deia, hom podia creure que em passava a l'enemic . . .
> Mercè: (Irònica) Jo mai no m'ho hagués pensat . . .
>
> [Rosa: It was hard for them to believe what I said; they could've easily thought I was deserting to the enemy.
> Mercè: (Ironically) I would never have thought that!] (10)

In this exchange, Rosa shows us her awareness of the precariousness of ideological polarities within which fellow believers can turn on each other just because one is in the wrong place at the wrong time, or does not know the correct password. Because Rosa knows this, we believe her more. Her credibility grows. By contrast, Mercè's bitter clinging to easy, monolithic animosity makes her seem less objective and therefore causes her believability to decrease.

Rosa's reply, that perhaps it would have been better if she had been shot, comes close to moving Mercè, as her reaction shows. "No diguis bestieses, Rosa," she says [Don't say such awful things, Rosa] (9). "A mes, tinc feina, no estic per a monsergues" [Besides, I have work to do. I'm not in the mood for nonsense] (9). One common, last-ditch reaction in the face of an argument for which there is no good response is to pretend not to hear it. This is exactly what Mercè does now right before our eyes on the stage. She turns from Rosa (by physical action showing her philosophical rejection) and tries to go back to work. These actions (made explicit by the dialogue) show Rosa's theatrical position to be stronger within the ethical struggle emerging from the work.

As if she had not heard Mercè, Rosa now recounts her intense story of the one night of love she experienced with the young militiaman who died in her arms at dawn. The poetic language of her description contrasts dramatically with Rosa's present, precarious situation. This must surely be an example of what Luigi Pirandello meant when he talked of "spoken action," an "artistic miracle" that can occur only when "the playwright finds words that are spoken action, living words that move, immediate expressions inseparable from action, unique phrases that cannot be changed to any other and belong to a definite character in a definite situation."[10] Rosa's monologue first stresses the sensual pleasures, "una esgarrifança infinita, una frissança dolcíssima . . . ens estimàrem tota la nit . . ." [an endless shiver, the sweetest yearning . . . and we made love all night . . .] (9–10). Mercè's uncomfortable reaction to this revelation serves to petrify her in a position that refuses to come to any understanding, and resists the possibility of adaptation:

> Rosa, si et plau, prou! Em molesten les teves inconveniències! Marxes amistançada amb un perdut i acabes seduïnt una criatura. I a sobre, m'ho expliques sense vergonyir-te!

> [Rosa, please! Enough! You're really bothering me with these stories you don't have the sense to keep to yourself! You run off, hook up with an immoral loser, and then you end up seducing a child. And to top it all off, you tell me all this without shame!] (10)

Again, the notion of shame is introduced as a tool to try to keep Rosa under control, to prevent her from exercising her freedom of speech. Therefore, once more, the very act of continuing to say her piece is another spoken action, and the bravery implicit in speaking joins with ethical power when Rosa says, "Vergonya, senyoreta, no, no en tinc" [Shame, Miss? No, I don't have any] (10). However, the beauty of her description of the night of love concludes when her lover's calming words are cut grotesquely short. "No ens mourem, digué ell, no tinguis por. . . . Un troç de metralla li buidà el ventre, morí als meus braços" ['We won't die,' he said. 'Don't be afraid.' . . . But a piece of shrapnel emptied his belly. He died in my arms] (10). By adding this conclusion, Riera fuses a moral weight to Rosa's words. Her free love has been purchased both times at the price of life itself. The freedom to even speak of free love (let alone practice it), like the freedom to work and live as one chooses, was sought by people who thought it was worth dying for.

Contemplating whether or not tragedy is possible in the modern world of moral relativity and existential crises, Arthur Miller, in 1949, wrote, "A tragic feeling is evoked in us when we are in the presence of a character who is ready to lay down his life, if need be, to secure one thing—his sense of personal dignity."[11] Thus, Rosa is elevated to heroic stature as she tells of her role in the Civil War, even though, according to Mercè's hollow assertions, Rosa was the loser. This play demonstrates that, from the tragedy of the national conflict, Rosa and others like her emerged with a continued will to struggle unceasingly for freedom. Or, in Miller's words, "if this struggle must be total and without reservation, then it automatically demonstrates the indestructible will of man to achieve his humanity."[12] Rosa is a "failure" in Mercè's narrow definitions of winners and losers. The audience, however, is likely to see that although both have sustained great losses, Rosa, through the vitality of her ethical convictions and her spirit, will eventually "triumph," if not in person, then in those who continue her struggle after her.

This play would be a tragedy in Miller's sense of the word if, before the public's eyes, Mercè turned Rosa over to the Francoist police, and she were shot like many of her friends. Even so, for

Miller, the play would not be pessimistic. "The possibility of victory must be there in tragedy," he reminds us. "In [tragedy] lies the belief—optimistic if you will, in the perfectibility of man."[13] However, an actual denunciation of Rosa to the police does not take place within the confines of the theatrical space of the play. Mercè's last words to Rosa are a harsh order to leave, but we notice that at no time does Rosa appear to hear them or accept them. The play invites us to observe Rosa struggling for survival, fighting with all her might, refusing to admit defeat. The situation echoes a moment in one of the most famous Civil War novels in contemporary Catalan letters, *La plaça del Diamant* [*The Time of the Doves*], by Mercè Rodoreda. In the scene in question, Natàlia ("Colometa") vainly attempts to get back her job as maid in a wealthy Catalan family after the war, and the "master" of the household answers her pleas with a vulgar insult: "El senyor . . . va dir que qui volgués feina que pugés aquí dalt" [The Master . . . said that anyone who wanted work could just climb this.][14] Natàlia is desperate to save not just herself, but her two small children as well. However, the bourgeois couple is unmoved by her plight:

> I quan els vaig dir que en Quimet havia mort a la guerra, el senyor va dir que ho sentia molt, però que ell no l'hi havia pas fet anar. I va dir que jo era roja, i va dir, ¿comprèn?, una persona com vostè més aviat ens compromet, nosaltres no hi tenim cap culpa. . . .
>
> [And when I told them that Quimet had died in the war, the Master said that was too bad, but *he* hadn't made Quimet go. And he said I was a Red, and he said, "You understand? Really, a person like you puts us in a compromising position. We're not to blame for this mess. . . ."][15]

Natàlia's despair over her inability to find work to feed her children is so great that it takes her to the brink of murdering them and committing suicide, but she eventually survives, thanks to the kindness of Antoni, senyora Enriqueta, and others, although she is permanently damaged by her suffering.

Rosa's situation is no less desperate than Natàlia's, but she is of a different, more dynamic character; for, as long as we see her in the play, she never gives up on her goal of finding shelter through her own hard work. Although Mercè orders Rosa out, the next actions that occur do leave the ending ambiguous. Mercè tries to resume unpacking, but Elissa continues to introduce chaos into Mercè's plans by once more wandering out into the "street" (here the audience) to look for her lost sons. The audience sees Mercè unable to cope with her mother and unpack at the same time. The next stage direction is supremely important: "Mentre Mercè segueix endreçant, d'un paquet treu un uniforme de minyona, el rebregà, i el tira amb rabia" [While Mercè is unpacking a box, she comes on a maid's uniform, unfolds it, and throws it out, enraged] (12). The physical presence of the uniform on the stage at the play's close leaves open several possibilities. It just might be that Mercè will reluctantly relent and allow Rosa to help her cope with the difficult Elissa. If Mercè did this, Rosa's position would be tenuous and dangerous, and each day would be a fight for survival. But even if Mercè remains intransigent, and as a result Rosa is caught and executed (a very real possibility), someone else must inexorably come, in time, to wear the uniform Rosa left behind when she joined the militia. Even though Rosa may perish, her "sisters," whether Catalan or Andalusian, will take up the struggle, and eventually, by 1982 (the year of the play's premiere), new possibilities of freedom will open up to them.

There is a spark of hope in Rosa's ideological strength for her survival. However, there is less reason to be optimistic about Mercè's moral "survival" at the play's end. If Mercè persists in leaving Rosa out on the street, she will essentially be a murderess, and Rosa has made sure Mercè understands this. If Mercè allows Rosa to be taken away today, tomorrow, or next week, the burden of guilt she will incur will also be clear. The tragic possibilities of the reprisals and betrayals of the postwar are all implicit in this terrible, fragile moment of the ending of the play, and the story could lead in many directions that would spell disaster for Rosa. Whether Rosa or another like her ends up toiling with Mercè, any future cohabitation will be painful and marked by chafing ideological beliefs. The forty years of difficult coexistence by triumphant right and never-vanquished left in Spain is foreshadowed by the play's conclusion. The ending is unsettling in the sense that David Herzberger uses that word to allude to "the recurrent and unresolvable tensions embedded in all attempts to write the past into being."[16] As things now stand, an apparent dichotomy exists between the sexually liberated Rosa and the repressed Mercè, with only madness, represented by Elissa, standing between them.

Elissa's "folly" (and I use this word in an etymological, Erasmic sense of the word to imply that it contains a grain of wisdom) enables her to return to the romantically charged time of her youth, when the horizon was crowded with suitors and the future was a soon-to-be-fulfilled erotic promise. Elissa's delusions make her a sort of flirtatious Quijota, a *loca-cuerda* of coming-out parties instead of jousting matches. Her presence serves to tip the scales of debate in Rosa's favor. In *The Madwoman in the Attic,* Sandra M. Gilbert and Susan Gubar probe the possibility of female madness in literature as a metaphor for defiance and suppressed rage that disrupts many texts written by women within Victorian patriarchy.[17] Surely this applies to Elissa as well, for she is a victim of the war just as clearly as those who fell in battle. Moreover, her presence in the household will continue to serve as a disruptive element. Since she is mad, she has some privilege within the newly emerging fascist-style state to speak out on topics otherwise forbidden. As Nina Baym puts it, the madwoman exists "in a society that brackets but cannot obliterate the innate disruptive, revolutionary force of the female. Since society is bad, this force is good."[18] Elissa's constant "inappropriate" comments may keep topics in the open in front of Mercè that otherwise might disappear into the silence of the repressive political moment. And Rosa's domestic successors may bring their simple strength into the postwar society represented by this household.

This play catches Rosa , Elissa, and Mercè at the end of the war when their world is in shambles. Repressed desire and enforced passivity have led one character to madness, and another to the solitude of cruelty. By contrast, the attempt to fight for freedom may lead Rosa to her death, as it did so many of her comrades. However, the frank exchange of vantage points provoked here could enable the public of this play, if not the characters within it, to choose saner solutions for the future, as well as inspire them to continue the fight that Rosa carried on so valiantly. As Claude Lèvi-Strauss has observed, "history is . . . never history, but history for."[19] This dramatic re-creation of a painful moment of Catalan history is for anyone who will enter into the dialectic honestly and participate in the lessons of this brutal history.

Notes

1. Carme Riera, *Senyora, ha vist els meus fills?,* scene from *Dones i Catalunya.* From a typescript provided by the author. This play was part of a collaborative effort produced and directed by Ricard Salvat in 1982. Salvat asked six women writers—Lidia Falcón (lawyer and director of the Feminist party), author Riera, Isabel-Clara Simó (writer, teacher, and editor of the journal *Can-*

igó), Marta Pessarrodona (writer), Maria-Josep Ragué Arias (journalist and playwright), and Marisa Híjar (journalist)—to each write a scene involving two characters, a maid and her mistress. The idea was that the scenes would be a backward look at the century in Catalan history from the point of view of women. Pessarrodona and Riera eventually each added a third character to round out their scenes. After the premiere of the play in Barcelona, 10 August 1982, Mercè Ibarz wrote that these last two wrote the most successful scenes with the best dialogue (*Avui,* 11 August, 1982, "Cultura," 24). The play was later entered in a competition in Athens, and played there, 23–25 August 1982. Further references will be cited parenthetically within the text.

2. All translations are mine.

3. Geraldine Cleary Nichols, *Escribir, espacio propio: Laforet, Matute, Moix, Tusquets, Riera y Roig por sí mismas.* Minneapolis: Institute for the Study of Ideologies and Literature, 1989, 203.

4. The name, Germinal, is significant, both etymologically, because the militiaman motivates Rosa's erotic and political awakening, and also as a literary allusion to the 1885 novel of the same name, by Êmile Zola, in which the suffering of downtrodden workers is exposed in the protagonist, Étienne Lantier's attempt to get a labor movement to take seed among oppressed French miners (Paris: E. Fasquelle, 1911). "Germinal" was the name the French revolutionaries gave to the seventh month of the Republican calendar, from March 21 to April 19. The name, which inspired Zola's title, implied both the literal germination of springtime and the sprouting of the Revolution.

5. Martí-Olivella, "Towards a New Transcultural Dialogue in Spanish Film," *Spain Today: Essays on Literature, Culture, Society,* ed. José Colmeiro, Christina Dupláa, Patricia Greene, and Juana Sabadell, Hanover, NH: Dartmouth College Dept. of Spanish and Portuguese, 1995, 47.

6. The Spanish Falange, an anti-Communist party with fascist tendencies, was founded by José Antonio Primo de Rivera in 1933. With Franco the head of the new Spanish state following the Civil War, the Falange became the official party, and the Sección Femenina was created to instruct Spanish women in practical and moral matters. Church and state were fused, and the Sección Femenina came to be associated with arch-conservative views and the repression of women.

7. Pérez, "Behind The Lines: The Spanish Civil War and Women Writers." *The Spanish Civil War in Literature,* ed. Janet Pérez and Wendell Aycock, Lubbock, TX: Texas Tech University Press, 1990, 172.

8. Lukács, "The Sociology of Modern Drama." In *The Theory of the Modern Stage,* ed. Eric Bentley. London: Penguin, 1989, 405.

9. Brook. *The Empty Space.* New York: Atheneum, 1968, 11.

10. Pirandello, "Spoken Action." In *The Theory of the Modern Stage,* ed. Eric Bentley. London: Penguin, 1989, 154.

11. Miller, "Tragedy and the Common Man." In *Dramatic Theory and Criticism,* ed. Bernard F. Dukore. New York: Holt, Rinehart & Winston, 1974, 895.

12. Ibid., 896.

13. Ibid., 897.

14. Rodoreda, *La plaça del Diamant.* Barcelona: Club Editor, 1989, 160. Translations my own. This expression is usually accompanied with a vulgar hand gesture. I chose to use my own translation, rather than quoting from David Rosenthal's respected version, *The Time of the Doves,* because, in this case, he used a free translation that was much softer, "Let them sink or swim"

(143), in which the impact of the sexual insult is lost. David H. Rosenthal, trans. Mercè Rodoreda. *The Time of the Doves.* New York: Taplinger, 1980.

15. Ibid., 160.

16. Herzberger, *Narrating the Past: Fiction and Historiography in Postwar Spain.* Durham and London: Duke University Press, 1995, 1–2.

17. Gilbert and Gubar, *The Madwoman in the Attic: The Woman Writer and the Nineteenth-Century Literary Imagination.* New Haven: Yale University Press, 1979.

18. Baym, "The Madwoman and Her Languages: Why I Don't Do Feminist Theory." *Feminist Issues in Literary Scholarship,* ed. Shari Benstock. Bloomington: Indiana University Press, 1987, 49.

19. Lévi-Strauss, *The Savage Mind.* Trans. G. Weidenfield. Chicago: University of Chicago Press, 1966, 257.

Part III
An Original Work by Carme Riera

Senyora, ha vist els meus fills? from *Dones i Catalunya*

Carme Riera

Febrer de 1939. interior d'un saló d'una torra de la bonanova, requisada al temps de la guerra pels milicians i a on fa pocs dies han tornat els antics propietaris. El terra i les parets tenen encara marques de fogueres. Els pocs mobles, un parell de cadires decó, un sofà esfondrat, una tauleta, estan en mal estat. D'una de les parets penja un inmens mirall de lluna ennegrida. Hi ha balics per terra i un bagul ple de roba. Mercè, uns vint anys, desfà paquets intentant posar ordre. Es alta, prima, té cara de prunes agres versus secció femenina. Al seu costat, Elissa, enveillida, vestida de negre, menuda, amb aspecta de fuita, endola, treu i fica vestits al bagul malmanant-les, fent-ne un garbull o allisant-les amb cura segons li va. Per les tales es nota que són vestits de festes i soires. . . .

Mercè: Mamà, si et plau, ¿es pot saber què busques?
Elissa: El meu vestit de moiré groc. Haig d'anar al Liceu aquesta nit. Hi va el rei.
Mercè: Mamà, mamà, deixa't d'històries! No hi ha Liceu, ni rei . . .
Elissa: (Mirant-la com si no la conegués)
¿Vostè qui és? ¿Ha vingut de visita?
(No espera resposta).
¿Per què no m'ajuda a buscar el meu vestit de moiré groc? Jo diria que el vaig penjar a l'armari, però l'armari
(baixa la veu)
ha desaparegut i sap on hem trobat la roba? En aquest bagul . . .
(Torna a mirar-la).
Jo a vostè la conec . . .
(Torna a buscar).
Un vestit de moiré groc arrapat a la cintura . . . Vostè veu quina cintura . . .

(Es posa les mans a la cintura).

Mercè: (Interromp el monòleg)

Mamà, Déu meu! ¡Com és possible! Escolta mamà, sóc jo, Mercè, la teva filla.

(intenta que deixi de remenar roba i l'agafa pel braç amb intenció de fer-la seure al sofà)

Deixa de buscar el vestit mamà . . .

Elissa: (Refusant-la amb força i excitada).

Però ¿qui s'ha cregut que és vostè?

(La mira de fit a fit)

Mireu en quantes desgràcies m'haig de veure! No haver trobat altra cambrera que aquesta murria tossuda que no m'entén. Li dic que busco el meu vestit per anar al Liceu. . . . Afanyi's dona, ajudi'm. Es de moiré. . . . La faldilla fa fru-fru quan pujo les escales i les ones grogues baixen els esglaons. . . . Bona nit senyoreta Elissa diu el *botones* en obrir-me la porta de la llotja, si no és molestia, puc dir-li, quin goig que fa . . . !

Mercè: (Torna a tallar-la amb crispació)

Mamà, si et plau, prou. Escolta mamà: no hi ha Liceu, ni vestit de moiré, ni tens vint anys. . . .

Elissa: (Torna a interrompre)

Vint anys com vint sols. L'ajudant de camp del rei acaba de dir-m'ho: "Veinte años como veinte soles, y ¡qué guapa es usted!"

(Segueix com ha fet durant tota l'estona remenant)

"¡Bonito vestido!"

(Finalment sembla trobar el que busca, estira i surt un vestit groc final dels anys 10, molt mastegat, arnat, etc. Elissa està exultant)

Miri, miri, vostè que no ho creia . . .

(amb el vestit a les mans va cap al mirall, silenciosament comença a treure's la roba i la va llençant. Es posa el vestit, es mira, dona voltes, mira el vestit i no la seva cara, l'escena es del tot esperpèntica. . . . Fins i tot mira reptadora a Mercè i xiuxiueja l'ària de "Tosca, visi d'arte")

Molt bé, Juanita.

(Es dirigeix a Mercè que contempla l'escena bocabadada i que ha anat recollint les robes de la seva mare de terra)

Molt bé, digui a les operaries que les felicito. . . . Un model preciós . . . i això que ha seguit el consell de la mamà res d'escots pronunciats . . .

(De sobte, des del carrer se sent el sorroll d'un camió i una altra veu cada vegada més aprop: "Catalanes, Franco viene a liberaros de la opresión comunista. Vuestro invicto caudillo proclama la indisolubilidad de España. . . ." La veu puja ara amb tota la seva potència. "La guerra ha terminado pero aun quedan enemigos de España. Catalanes, denunciad a vuestros enemigos." La vella sembla transformar-se en sentir la veu. Va cap a la finestra, la veu s'ha allunyat. Fa senyes a algú.

Eh, eh, escolti, ¿ha vist als meus fills?

(La pregunta queda sense contestar . . .)

Jordi, Joan, Antoni . . .

(Crida des de la finestra. . . . s'asseu en una cadira . . .)

Els meus fills no han tornat encara del front. . . . El meu home mort . . .

¿Com puc ésser viva?

Mercè: (La mira espantada i trista tota l'estona, ara s'hi acosta)

Mamà, mamà, treu-te aquest vestit, si et plau, vina.

(Fa que es posi dreta.)

El groc no t'escau, dus dol, mamà.

Elissa: ¿Vostè ha vist als meus fills? ¿No, no n'ha vingut ningú? Haig d'anar a buscar-los, si, si. Ara mateix. Potser tindràn fred, o gana. Fills meus. Antoni, setze anys, Joan divuit anys, Jordi, vint anys . . . Tres fills . . .

(Amb les mans fa el gest de dur un infant i comença a cantar molt fluixet una cançó de bressol)

Mercè: (Com si s'hagués acostumat a aquest tipus d'estats de la seva mare i aprofités el seu interval catatònic, doblega i torna a guardar el vestit groc i desa tot el que la seva mare ha tret, intenta tancar el bagul.)

Elissa: (Acostant-se)

¿Vostè no ha vist els meus fills? Tres fills. . . . Jo tinc quatre fills . . . no tres fills i una filla. . . . Primer nasquè la nena, però jo volia nois. Les dones només venen al món pero patir. . . . Ells per contra. . . . Tres fills com tres sols. . . . Vint sols . . . vint anys. . . . Un vestit groc de moiré i el somriure més bell de la terra. . . . El Liceu . . . ¿Vostè no coneix el Liceu . . .?

Mercè: Per Déu, mamà, prou. Mira'm bé, sóc jo. Mercè, la teva filla.

Pensa una mica en mi, mamá, ells mai no tornaràn, no tornaràn, ni el pare, ni els meus germans, ni Manuel, són morts, mamà . . .

(El discurs crispat de Mercè és interromput per uns trucs a la campaneta de la porta del reixat del jardí)

Elissa: (Escoltant)

Són ells, han tornat. Són ells . . .

(Surt corrent)

Mercè: Espera't, mamà, ja hi vaig jo.

(Surt. Escena sola uns segons)

(Es sent una veu que arriba des de la porta i que crida des de fora)

Veu: Senyora, senyora.

Elissa: (Des de fora)

¿Ha vist als meus fills? . . . ¿Si? Passi, passi . . .

(Es sent encara fora d'escena la mateixa veu entrant cap a dintre cada vegada més propera)

Veu: Senyora, senyora, quina alegria. Jo pensava que no hi havia ningú, i em deia ¿on eren els senyors? Senyora ¿I els senyorets i el senyor estàn bons? Eh, senyoreta Mercè! ¿Com está tan prima?

(El monòleg es va acostant. Entren per la porta Mercè i Elissa seguides per una noia d'uns 30 anys, maca, més aviat grassoneta. Es una miliciana que fou cambrera de la casa abans de la guerra. Esta apaorida, té cara de patiment, pero es veu una persona vital amb resistencia, malgrat que ho ha perdut tot. Les dues dones es miren en silenci. La noia es diu Rosa)

¿De qui porten dol? Ah, senyora! deixi'm fer-li un petó.

(S'acosta a la vella per petonejar-la)

Mercè: (Tallant)

El senyor i els senyorets son morts. ¿Vols dir que no ho sabies?

Rosa: Què em diu ara! Les acompanyo en el sentiment.

(Els ulls li llagrimejen)

Però, ¿com és possible? Quina desgràcia tan grossa, senyora! Moriren a la guerra? ¿Els tres nois? Ho saben ben cert, senyoreta? No ho puc creure! Oh, quin disgust. ¿Què serà de . . .?

Elissa: Expliqui's dona, què diuen els meus fills, vostè els ha vistos, no és així?

Rosa: (Bocabadada)

Senyora, per Déu! Com no em reconeix, sóc jo la Rosa, la cambrera. . . . "Ningú no em posa els biguidís com tu, Roseta," ¿Que no s'en recorda? Ali, senyora, quines ganes tenia de tornar-les a veure. . . . No em miri així, senyora, que no sóc una aparicío . . .

Mercè: (Interromp)

La mamà ha enfollit . . . no coneix ningú, ni a mí.

Rosa: Pobrissona, pobreta, tan bona senyora. . . . ¿I es pensa que viuen els seus fills? Potser és veritat senyoreta, els buscarem . . .

(Dirigint-se a la senyora)
Jo l'ajudaré a buscar-los senyora, potser són per aquests camins del món. Molts soldats han passat a França.

Elissa: (Interrompent exultant)
Si, si, anem a França. Es clar, són a Françą. . . . Les maletes ràpit.
(Tot dirigint-se a Mercè)
Fes el favor de fer les maletes. . . . Vaig a canviar-me . . . Un vestit sastre pel viatge, amb el barret de plomes d'estrús.
(Torna a anar cap al bagul a remenar. Dirigint-se a Rosa)
Sap, en aquesta casa passen coses extranyes; no tenim armaris, la roba es desa aqui, en aquest mundo. . . .

Mercè: Sembla mentida, Rosa, sempre fores una eixelebrada. La mamà ha enfollit, és ben clar, i tu a sobre li dones corda. . . . Cal que s'adoni que mai no torbarà als seus fills, són morts. Cap dels no és a França, Rosa. Per què havien de fugir, si hem guanyat!

Rosa: N'està ben segura? ¿En té proves? Jo entenc la senyora . . .! Fins que no em diguin on és enterrat el Germinal, jo no m'ho creuré. . . .

Mercè: (Sardònica)
Ah, però no us veu trobar? ¿De què et va a servir fugir, doncs . . . com una perduda . . .

Rosa: Senyoreta, per Déu, quines coses de dir . . .

Mercè: Jo em pensava que les milicianes no anomenaven Déu . . . si no hi creuen . . .

Elissa: (Que ha seguit remenant la roba)
¿Que busco? ¿Un vestit sastre de fil? ¿Busco un vestit de moiré? . . . París, qui m'ha dit que marxem a París, i el Frederic? Frederic, la senyora Jornet se'n va a París . . . Dona, el seu vestit em plau . . .
(Tot això dit com si coquetejés amb un personatge absent)

Rosa: (Que ha esperat per a contestar a que acabés de parlar Elissa)
Per què no senyoreta? Potser el que anomanem amb aquesta paraula no és el mateix . . . Jo crec en la revolució, en la justicia. No surt el sol per a tothom?

Mercè: No pas pels morts, Rosa. El papà morí a la presó de la FAI pocs dies després que tu marxesis. El vingueren a buscar per a interrogar-lo. Mai més no va tornar. Era un home bo, recte . . . Havia fet diners, ¿és un delicte ser ric?

Rosa: ¿Ho és ser pobre? Potser si, és clar, si es tenen idees . . . No, no ho dic jo, ho deia en Germinal.

Mercè: Els meus tres germans moriren al front . . . L'Antoni pogué marxar a França i després a Burgos . . . El mataren a Terol . . . El senyoret Jordi (la mira marcant perfectament el distanciament) fou tirotejat per l'esquena; intentava passar-se als nacionals a l'Ebre; havia vist com una granada dels nacionals destrossava el cos de'n Joan . . . Quin absurd . . .! El pobre Joan morí en que no creia . . .

Rosa: Ho sento tant, senyoreta Mercè! Deu anys a casa . . . defensant allò (Intenta cercar una certa complicitat)

Mercè: El teu capteniment, Rosa, no fou d'allò més moral amb el senyoret Jordi, si és això el que vols donar a entendre . . . Per què deixaves la porta oberta a les nits? Si la pobre mamà ho arriba a saber . . .!

Rosa: (Dura)

Senyoreta Mercè, ¿què sap vostè de la vida? Ha estimat algú de debó? Ha fet l'amor alguna vegada?

Mercè: Jo sabia fer-me respectar, Rosa. Jo no sóm com tu . . .

Rosa: (Mirant-la trista)

Això ja es veu . . . Sap quin gust tenen els petons?

Mercè: (Am tó escardat)

Manel també morí a la guerra, és clar que mai no em feu massa cas . . . Jo no sóc maca . . . Volia els meus diners, ho sé.

(Duríssima)

La nit que s'endugueren el papà, van intentar violar-me . . . Sé com pot ser d'agre i fastigós un petó.

Rosa: Ho sento moltíssim, senyoreta, no sap com. Alguns companys pensaven que les dones erem només femelles . . .

(Elissa ha estat remenant el bagul tota l'estona sense reparar amb la conversa; ara ha trobat un vestit sastre que comença a provar-se, mentre riu)

Jo he tingut més sort . . . clar que només en aquest sentit, senyoreta. Vaig estimar Jordi, el seu germà, no em fa vergonya dir-ho. No erem iguals, ho sé, però la nit era més curta als seus braços . . . Fou ell el que em buscava . . . Jo la cambrera també servia per això . . . Em tingué d'estrena . . . No, no s'esborroni, no . . . Després vaig conèixer en Germinal, ell m'ensenyà que jo era molt més que un sexe badat per acollir-ne un altre, una bestia de càrrega . . . la revolució em faria, ens faria, unes persones lliures . . . construïriem un món més just, sense rics, ni pobres, un món de justicia i d'amor . . . Vaig seguir a Germinal a Mallorca, Mercè . . .

Mercè: Senyoreta Mercè, per a mi segueixes essent la cambrera de la casa, Rosa . . . La guerra s'ha acabat i heu perdut. ¿Està clar?

Elissa: Si, si, s'han perdut, per això els anem a buscar . . . quasi bé estic, esperi's una mica . . .

Rosa: Hem perdut. D'acord. La guerra fou terrible, però la revolució bellísima. Ningú no podrà arrabassar-me els records d'aquelles platges, ni les ones que feien xap, xap, sobre el meu cap nu . . . El sol era una taca de mercromina. Els nostres vaixells encararen davant Porto Cristo . . Un altre capfico i un altre, sense que ningú no em cridés: Rosa que ens està mirant la senyora . . . Rosa que no li agrada que ens banyem!!!

Mercè: (Irònica)

M'alegro de que tinguis tan bons records de la guerra . . . Es veu que per a tu, malgrat haver perdut, tot són guanys . . .

Rosa: No ho cregui. Germinal fou anomenat d'una missiò secreta. Havia, crec, d'arribar fins el campament enemic de Sant Servera. Mai no va tornar. Tot el que he pogut guardar d'ell és una fotografia.

(La busca a la butxaca i treu una petita fotografia arrugada. Li ensenya).

Tot sovint he de mirar-la. El seu rostre se m'esborra . . . No aconsegueixo composar-lo sense aquest ajut. Ara si, veu . . . Els llavis molsuts . . . Em feia uns petons! El nas llarg i els ulls, quins ulls! . . .

Elissa: (Que ha seguit remanant, s'ha acostat. El rostre l'il.lumina) Ah, senyora, vostè ha conegut el meu fill . . . si? . . . Anem de gresca a buscar-lo, anem a París ara mateix. Vaig a ordenar al xòfer que ens porti a l'estació . . .

(surt)

Mercè: Rosa, em fas llàstima. No tens principis, ni moral.

Rosa: ¿Principis? No l'entenc, senyoreta Mercè. ¿Moral . . .? ¿Què vol dir-me ara? He après moltes coses durant aquest temps i més interessants que no planxar camises o enmidonar faldilles. He descobert tantes coses que em fa por no tenir el temps suficient per a viure-les.

Mercè: No crec que es pugui descobrir res de bo al front. No és lloc per a una dona ni que sigui una minyona, Rosa.

Rosa: S'equivoca, senyoreta Mercè, jo li aseguro. La desaparicío de Germinal fou un cop molt dur. Però la guerra continuava. Bayo m'asignà al petit hospital, lluny de la primera línia. Una nit vaig intentar escapar-me; volia arribar a San Servera, volia veure a Germinal, saber si era mort, on havia caigut. Naturalment em descobriren . . . Fou difícil que aceptessin el que deia, hom podia creure que em passava a l'enemic . . .

Mercè: Jo mai no m'ho hagués pensat . . .

Rosa: Vaig tenir sort, no m'afusellaren, encara que potser hagués estat millor . . . Ara no em veuria com em veig . . . però tampoc hagués conegut Angel, ni els seus records omplirien el buit de les meves hores tristes. Estic d'acord amb la senyora: només viu per a recorder els seus fills. De no haver-los tingut, no patiria, és cert, però son ells els que l'ajuden a aguantar i no morir . . .

Mercè: No diguis bestieses, Rosa. A més, tinc feina, no estic per a monsergues . . .

(Torna a endreçar els paquets)

Rosa: (Com si no l'hagués sentit)

Ens haviem vist al *Ciutat de Tarragona.* Era eixerit, una barba com un formiguer . . . Em feu l'ullet . . . Jo com si tal cosa. Després anà a veure a Bayo per a que no m'afusselessin, m'ajudà. Tenia divuit anys, senyoreta, com el seu germà Jordi, i una certa semblança . . . Cantava tangos i ranxeres amb una veu que traspassava el cor. Jo dormia sobre un munt de palla a la cotxera d'una torre que haviem requisat . . . Per la porta entraven les estrelles. La seva veu a cau d'orella molt fluixeta, i una esgarrifança infinita, una frissança dolcìssima . . . Ens estimàrem tota la nit . . .

Mercè: Rosa, si et plau, prou! Em molesten les teves inconveniències! Marxes amistançada amb un perdut i acabes seduïnt una criatura. I a sobre, m'ho expliques sense ergonyir-te!

Rosa: Vergonya, senyoreta, no, no en tinc. L'olor dels lliris era estabornidor . . . Els avions italians ens havien bombardejat terriblement aquell dia. Seré viva demà, pensava? Era tan jove, i tenia una veu tan bonica! Jo no havia oblidat Germinal, no, ben al contrari, a la butxaca del meu "mono," que ens servia de coixí, hi havia la seva fotografia . . . A la matinada els avions . . . No ens mourem, digué ell, no tinguis por . . . Un troç de metralla li buidà el ventre, morí als meus braços.

Mercè: He dit prou. No m'interessen les teves històries brutes. Tinc feina, fes el favor de marxar.

Rosa: Oh, no, senyoreta, jo he vingut per quedar-me . . . Vostès necessiten una cambrera.

Mercè: Tu ens deixares per fer-te miliciana. A més tampoc no podriem pagar-te.

Rosa: Per això rai, senyoreta, no es preocupi, me'n faig càrrec, fins que no tornin els senyorets!

Mercè: Per Déu, Rosa, els senyorets són morts! He dit que no necessitàvem ningú.

Rosa: Apa, senyoreta, si la terra sembla un femer i, vostè dispensi, sempre que en requisàvem alguna me'n recordava de la nostra.

(Mercè la mira dura)

Perdó, de la seva, i li haig de dir clar, em feia una malicia! Ja veurà, si vostè m'ajuda una mica, en dos dies ho tindrem tot net.

Mercè: He dit no, gràcies.

(S'aixeca per a acompanyar-la a la porta)

Rosa: Senyoreta Mercè, si pogués deixar-me quedar només uns dies . . . Vostè és la meva darrera esperança. Em busquen, ahir afusellaven la Teresina i la Neus. No tinc on anar, si torno al poble em pelaran de seguida. Jo pensava que vostè em faria el favor . . . per caritat, senyoreta, aqui no em buscaran. A més, vostès són del Franco, vostès han guanyat . . .

Mercè: El papà fou afusellat per milicians, potser tu mateixa el denunciares. Desvergonyida, hipòcrita.

Rosa: No! Quines coses a dir! I ara. Mai no li hagués fet una cosa semblant, si jo me l'estimava al senyor a la meva manera, sempre em volia pessigar el cul!

Mercè: Fastigosa, bruta! Respecta la memòria dels morts, mentidera!

Elissa: (Entra en aquest moment. Porta una maleta petita i tronada a la mà)

No he trobat al xòfer, però ho tinc tot a punt. Podem marxar quan vulgui. Agafarem un taxi fins l'estació, després el tren . . . París . . .

(S'acosta a Rosa i l'agafa pel braç)

Rosa: Senyora, senyora, sóc jo la Rosa, he vingut per quedar-me, vostè si que ho vol? Oi que si, senyora?

Elissa: Es clar, filleta, ara anem a París, buscarem els meus fills, i després tornarem tots a casa.

(Va cap a la porta i surt)

Rosa: La senyora és qui mana, no vostè, senyoreta Mercè.

Mercè: La senyora està trastornada, Rosa, qui man sóc jo, i no et vull a casa. Pertanyo a la secciò femenina de la Falange Espanyola, com comprendras a teva presència em compromet, a més em resulta insoportable.

Rosa: Uns dies tan sols, senyoreta, puc dormir a les golfes, pel menjar no es preocupi, estic acostumada a patir gana . . .

Mercè: (Seca)

No. Marxa ara mateix i dóna gràcies si no et denuncio . . . com seria la meva obligació. ¿No has sentit els altaveus?

(Se vent el soroll de la porta del reixat i des del carrer la veu de la senyora que pregunta)

Elissa: (Des de fora)

¿Sap on podria trobar un taxi? . . . Anem a buscar els meus fills a París . . .

(Surt sense dir res cap al jardí, cridant)

Rosa: Senyora, senyora, esperis, vostè no pot sortir sola.

(Mentre Mercè segueix endreçant, d'un paquet treu un uniforme de minyona, el rebregà, i el tira amb rabia. Mentre per redera, Elissa ha passat al pati de butaques i va preguntant a la gent com si fossin vianants, pels seus fills:)

Elissa: Senyora, ha vist els meus fills. . . .? (Ad libitum)

(Rosa l'agafa pel braç.)

Rosa: Senyora, si us plau, torni a casa. Per Déu, senyora . . . La senyoreta Mercè l'espera . . . Senyora, vingui, senyora. Faci'm un favor: tingui, guardi'm aquesta fotografia.

(El rostre de la vella s'il.lumina.)

Elissa: Es l'Antoni? Ara no el veig bé . . .

(El mira intensament)

Rosa: A mí em queda poc temps per a mirar-la . . . Digui'm quin encàrrec vol pels seus fills. Jo me'n vaig cap a on són ells, senyora . . . No crec pas en el cel, però la mateixa terra que els acull, m'acullirà . . . Germinal deia que si ens estimàvem, ens trobariem més enllà i ell tampoc no creia . . . Digui'm, senyora, quin encàrrec els he de donar?

Ma'am, Have You Seen My Sons? Women and Catalonia
by Carme Riera

translated from the Original Catalan by Patricia Hart

February 1939. Interior of a living room on a property in Bonanova,[1] requisitioned during the war by militiamen and where a few days earlier the old owners have returned. The floor and the walls still show the marks of campfires. The new pieces of furniture, a pair of Art Deco chairs, a sagging sofa, a little table, are in poor condition. From one of the walls hangs an immense, blackened mirror. There are suitcases on the floor, and a trunk full of clothing. Mercè, about twenty years old, undoes packages, trying to put things in order. She's tall and thin, and has the sour expression of a woman in the Sección Femenina of the Falange.[2] At her side is Elissa, aged, dressed in black, small, with a fugitive air about her. She is haphazardly rummaging through dresses from the trunk, mishandling them, throwing them in a heap or smoothing them out carefully, as she pleases. We see they are party and evening dresses.

Mercè: Mama, what on earth are you looking for?
Elissa: My yellow moiré dress. I have to go to the Opera tonight. The King will be there.
Mercè: Mama, Mama, don't be ridiculous! There is no Opera, no king . . .
Elissa: (Looking at Mercè as though she doesn't recognize her)
Now who are you? Have you come to pay a call?
(She doesn't wait for a reply)
Why don't you help me find my yellow moiré dress? I could swear I put it in the closet, but the closet. . . .
(She lowers her voice.)
has disappeared, and you know where we found the clothing? In this trunk . . .
(She looks at her again.)
I know you. . . .
(She goes back to her search.)
A yellow moiré dress gathered at the waist . . . you see what a waist I have?
(She puts her hands to her waist.)
Mercè: (Interrupting the monologue)

Mama, my goodness! How is it possible! Listen, Mama, it's me, Mercè, your daughter.

(She tries to get Elissa to stop rummaging through the clothing, and grabs her by the arm with the intention of making her sit down on the sofa.)

Stop looking for the dress, Mama!

Elissa: (Resisting her energetically, upset)

Who do you think you are!

(She looks Mercè up and down.)

Look how many catastrophes I'm having to live through! Imagine not being able to find another maid besides this stubborn self-absorbed thing who doesn't understand me. I tell you I'm looking for my dress to go to the Opera. Hurry up, woman, help me. It's moiré . . . the skirt rustles when I climb the stairs, and the yellow ruffles float over the steps behind me when I come downstairs . . . "Good evening Miss Elissa," the usher says when he opens the door to my loge for me. "Excuse me for saying so, but you look lovely. . .!"

Mercè: (She cuts her off, annoyed)

Mama, please, enough! Listen Mama, there's no opera, no moiré dress, and you're not twenty years old. . . .

Elissa: (Interrupting her again)

Twenty years like twenty shiny coins. The King's aide-de-camp just said that to me, "Twenty years like twenty shining coins, and how beautiful you are!"

(She has continued rummaging as she speaks.)

"What a beautiful dress, Miss!"

(Finally it seems she finds what she is looking for, she yanks, and a yellow dress from the turn of the century emerges, very crumpled, moth-eaten. Elissa is exultant.)

Look, look, you didn't believe it. . . .

(With the dress in her hands she goes to the mirror silently and begins to take off her clothing and throw it here and there. She puts the dress on, admires herself, turns this way and that, looking at the dress and not her face. The scene is grotesque. At last she glances defiantly at Mercè and hums the aria from *Tosca,* "Visi d'arte.")

All right, Juanita.

(She turns to Mercè, who is contemplating the scene open-mouthed, and who has been picking up her mother's clothes from the floor as they are thrown there).

All right, tell the seamstresses that I congratulate them . . . it's a beautiful number . . ., despite the fact that they followed Mama's advice and didn't make it the least bit low-cut. . . .

(Suddenly from the street we hear the sound of a truck and a loudspeaker that comes closer and closer: "Catalan people, Franco has come to liberate you from the Communist Oppression. Your undefeated leader proclaims Spain one nation, indivisible. . . ." The voice climbs now to full volume. "The war is over, but there are still enemies of Spain. Catalans, report on your enemies!" The old woman seems to be transformed on hearing the voice. She goes to the window, but the voice has faded away now. She waves at someone.)

Hello there! Excuse me! Have you seen my sons?

(There is no answer.)

Jordi, Joan, Antoni. . . .

(She cries out from the window . . . she sits down in a chair. . . .)

My sons haven't come back yet from the Front. . . . My husband is dead. . . . How can I be alive?

Mercè: (She looks at her mother, frightened and sad at the same time, and now she draws closer to her.)

Mama, Mama, take that dress off, please. Come on.

(She helps her straighten up)

You can't wear yellow; you're in mourning, Mama.

Elissa: Have you seen my sons? No? Nobody's come today? I have to go out and look for them. Yes, yes. Right now. Maybe they're cold or hungry. My sons. Antoni, sixteen years old, Joan, eighteen, Jordi twenty years old . . . three sons. . . .

(She pretends to rock a baby and begins to sing a lullaby very softly.)

Mercè: (As if she were accustomed to her mother's states, and taking advantage of the quiet interlude, she folds up the yellow dress and returns it to the trunk, and puts back everything her mother has taken out, then tries to close the trunk.)

Elissa: (Drawing closer)

Haven't you seen my sons? Three sons. . . . I have four children . . . no, three sons and a daughter. . . First the girl was born, but I wanted boys. Women just come into the world to suffer. Men, on the other hand . . . three sons like shining suns, three coins . . . twenty shining coins. . . . A yellow moiré dress and the most beautiful smile on earth. The Opera. Have you ever been to the Opera?

Mercè: For God's sake, Mama, enough! Look at me, it's me, Mercè, your daughter. Think a little about me, Mama. They will never come back, they won't come back, not Father nor my brothers, nor Manuel. They're dead, Mama. . . .

(Mercè's tense speech is interrupted by the jangling of the little bell at the garden gate.)

Elissa: (Listening)

It's them! They're back! It's them!

(She runs out.)

Mercè: Wait, Mama, I'll go.

(She goes out. The stage is empty for a few seconds.)

Voice: (A voice is heard offstage coming from the door)

Ma'am! Ma'am!

Elissa: (From offstage as well)

Have you seen my sons? . . . Yes? . . . Come in, come in!

(We hear the same voice from offstage coming closer and closer.)

Voice: Ma'am! Ma'am! What a pleasure! I thought nobody would be here, and I said to myself, I wonder where the master and mistress are? Ma'am, and the young gentlemen, and the master, are they all right? Oh, Miss Mercè! How did you get so thin?

(The voice grows louder. Mercè and Elissa enter through the door, followed by a young woman of about 30 years of age, attractive, somewhat plump. She is a militiawoman who was a chambermaid in the house before the war. She is frightened, and her face reveals the internal suffering of one who has lost everything. Yet one can see she is a vital person with stamina. Mercè and the newcomer regard each other in silence. The newcomer's name is Rosa.)

Who are you in mourning for? Oh, Ma'am, let me give you a kiss.

(She draws closer to the older woman to kiss her.)

Mercè: (Cutting her off)

The Master and the young gentlemen are dead. Do you mean to tell me you didn't know?

Rosa: Oh no! I'm so sorry for your loss.

(Her eyes fill up with tears.)

But how is that possible? What a disaster, Ma'am! Did they die in the war? The three boys? Are they sure, Miss? I can't believe it! Oh, how terrible! What will become of . . .?

Elissa: So tell me, woman, what do my sons say? You've seen them, isn't that right?

Rosa: (Open-mouthed)

Ma'am, my goodness! How can you not recognize me? It's me, Rosa, the chambermaid. You used to say, "Nobody can roll my hair like you, Roseta." You mean you don't remember? Oh,

Ma'am, I wanted so much to see you all again. . . . Don't look at me like that, Ma'am, I'm not a ghost. . . .

Mercè: (Interrupting)

Mama has gone crazy. She doesn't recognize anybody, not even me.

Rosa: Poor thing! Poor dear, such a good lady. And she thinks her sons are still alive? Maybe it's true, Miss. We can look for them. . . .

(Turning to Elissa)

I'll help you look for them, Ma'am. Maybe they're somewhere out there on the highways of the world. A lot of soldiers crossed over into France.

Elissa: (Interrupting, exultant)

Yes, yes, let's go to France! Of course, they're in France! Quick, the suitcases.

(She turns to Mercè)

Please pack the bags. . . . I'm going to change . . . a tailored dress for the trip, with a little hat with ostrich feathers.

(She turns back to the trunk and begins to rummage around in it. Now she turns to Rosa.)

You know, in this house strange things happen. We don't have closets, the clothing was all stored like this in boxes. In this world. . . .

Mercè: I can't believe it, Rosa! You always were a scatterbrain! Mama is crazy, that's clear as can be, and you sit there egging her on. She needs to realize that she'll never find her sons, that they're dead. No one on our side went to France, Rosa. Why would they flee? We won the war!

Rosa: Are you sure? Do you have proof? I understand the Mistress! Until somebody tells me where Germinal is buried, I'm not going to believe it. . . .

Mercè: (Sardonically) Ah, so you two didn't find each other, then? So what good did it do you to run off . . . like a slut?

Rosa: Miss, my God, the things you say!

Mercè: I thought in the militia you didn't mention God . . . since you don't believe in him.

Elissa: (Who has been rummaging through the clothing)

What am I looking for? A tailored linen dress? Am I looking for a moiré number? . . . Paris, you said we're going to Paris. And Frederic? . . . Frederic, Mrs. Jornet is going to Paris . . . Darling, I love your dress!

(She says all this as though flirting with an absent character, [playing both parts])

Rosa: (who has been waiting until Elissa stopped speaking to answer.)
Why not, Miss? Maybe what you and I call God isn't the same thing. I believe in the Revolution, in Justice. Doesn't the sun come up in the morning for everyone?

Mercè: Not for the dead, Rosa. Papa died in the FAI[3] prison a few days after you left. They came looking for him to interrogate him. He never returned. He was a good man, upright. He had earned his money. Is it a crime to be rich?

Rosa: Is it a crime to be poor? Maybe it is, of course, if you have ideas . . . No, I'm not saying this. Germinal used to say it.

Mercè: My three brothers died at the Front. Antoni managed to cross into France, and then he went to Burgos . . . They killed him at Teruel[4] . . . Young Master Jordi
(she looks at Rosa superciliously, marking the class gulf that separates them)
was shot in the back; he was trying to join up with the National Army[5] at the Ebro;[6] he had already seen how a Nationalist grenade destroyed Joan's body . . . How absurd! Poor Joan died defending something he didn't believe in . . .

Rosa: I'm so sorry, Miss Mercè! Ten years in this house! I loved the Master very much, and the young Masters. You already know that, Miss Mercè . . .
(She attempts to create a certain complicity.)

Mercè: Your behavior, Rosa, wasn't exactly of the most moral kind with Master Jordi, if that's what you're alluding to. Why did you leave your door open at night? If poor Mama ever finds out . . .!

Rosa: (Harshly)
Miss Mercè, what do you know of life? Have you ever really loved anyone? Have you ever made love even once?

Mercè: I knew how to make men respect me, Rosa. I'm not like you. . . .

Rosa: (Looking at her sadly)
That's obvious . . . Do you know what kisses taste like?

Mercè: (In a scathing tone)
Manuel died in the war too. Of course he never really paid any attention to me. I'm not pretty . . . He wanted my money, I know.
(Very harshly)
The night that they took Papa away, they tried to rape me . . . I know how bitter and disgusting a kiss can be . . .

Rosa: I'm very sorry, Miss, you don't know how much. Some of the comrades thought that women were just females. . . .

(Elissa has been rummaging in the trunk all this time without paying any attention to the conversation. Now she has found a tailored dress, which she begins to put on, laughing)

I've been luckier . . . of course just in that sense, Miss. I loved Jordi, your brother, I'm not ashamed to say it. We weren't equals, I know, but the night was shorter in his arms . . . He came after *me;* I didn't chase him . . . I, the chambermaid, was good for that too . . . He was the first one to have me . . . No, no, don't be shocked, no . . . After I met Germinal, he taught me that I was much more than legs and sex spread open, more than a beast of burden. The revolution would make me, would make us free people. We would build a new, more just world, without rich or poor, a world of justice and love. I followed Germinal to Mallorca, Mercè.

Mercè: That's *Miss* Mercè to you. To me you're still the maid of the house, Rosa. The war is over and you all lost. Is that clear?

Elissa: Yes, yes, they've gotten lost, but we'll go find them. I'm almost ready. Wait just a little. . . .

Rosa: We lost. All right, I'll grant you that. The war was terrible, but the Revolution was really beautiful. Nobody can snatch away from me the memories of those beaches, nor the waves that broke gently over my bare head . . . The sun was a spot of mercurochrome. Our boats anchored off Porto Cristo . . . I dive into one wave and another, and no one shouts to me: "Rosa, the Mistress is watching us . . . Rosa, she doesn't like us to swim!"

Mercè: (Ironically)

I'm happy you have such nice memories of the war . . . I can see that for you, even though you lost, everything was a success . . .

Rosa: Don't believe that. Germinal was called on a secret mission. I think he was supposed to reach the enemy camp at San Servera. He never came back. All I have left of him is a photograph.

(She looks in a pocket and takes out a small, wrinkled photo and shows it to Mercè)

I have to look at this all the time or his face fades away for me. I can't manage to picture him without this help. But now I can see him, look, those full lips . . . He gave me some kisses! His nose was long, and his eyes, what eyes!

Elissa: (who has been rummaging, now comes to Rosa's side. Her face lights up.)
Oh, Madam, you knew my son . . . yes? Let's go look for him in Paris right now. I'll order the chauffeur to take us to the station.
(She leaves)

Mercè: Rosa, I pity you. You don't have principles or morals.

Rosa: Principles? I don't understand you, Miss Mercè. Morals? What do you mean by that? I learned a lot of things during those times, things that are more interesting than ironing and starching shirts, I can tell you. I've discovered so much that I'm afraid I won't have time to enjoy it all.

Mercè: I don't think you can discover anything good at the Front. That's no place for a woman, not even if she *is* a maid, Rosa.

Rosa: You're wrong, Miss Mercè, I can assure you. Germinal's disappearance was a heavy blow. But the war went on. Bayo assigned me to a little hospital, far from the front lines. One night I tried to escape; I wanted to go to San Servera, I wanted to see Germinal, know if he was dead, where he had fallen. Naturally, they caught me. It was hard for them to believe what I said; they could've easily thought I was deserting to the enemy.

Mercè: (Ironically)
I would never have thought that. . . .

Rosa: I was lucky. They didn't shoot me, although maybe that would have been better. I wouldn't be in the fix I'm in now. But I never would have met Angel either, and his memory wouldn't fill the emptiness of my sad hours. I agree with Madam; she lives just to remember her sons. If she'd never had them, she wouldn't suffer, it's true, but they are the ones who help her bear being alive, and not dying. . . .

Mercè: Don't say such awful things, Rosa. Besides, I have work to do. I'm not in the mood for nonsense.
(She goes back to straightening up the packages.)

Rosa: (As if she hadn't heard her)
We had first seen each other on board the ship City of Tarragona. He was tall, with a beard like an anthill. He winked at me, and I ignored him. Then he went to see Bayo to talk them out of shooting me. He helped me. He was eighteen years old, Miss, like your brother Jordi, and he looked a little like him. He sang *tangos* and *rancheras*[7] in a voice that pierced your heart. I was sleeping on a pile of straw in the carriage house of a villa that we had requisitioned. Through the door you

could see the stars. His voice was at my ear, very softly, and I felt an endless shiver, the sweetest yearning . . . and we made love all night. . . .

Mercè: Rosa, please! Enough! You're really bothering me with these stories you don't have the sense to keep to yourself! You run off, hook up with an immoral loser, and then you end up seducing a child. And to top it off, you tell me all this with no shame!

Rosa: Shame, Miss? No, I don't have any. The smell of lilies struck me like a blow . . . The Italian planes had been bombarding us terribly that day. Will I be alive tomorrow? I asked myself. He was so young, and he had such a pretty voice! I hadn't forgotten Germinal, no, on the contrary, his picture was in the pocket of my overalls that we were using as a pillow. At dawn the planes came . . . "We won't die," he said. "Don't be afraid". . . . A piece of shrapnel emptied his belly. He died in my arms.

Mercè: Enough, I said. I'm not interested in your dirty stories. I have work to do. Please leave.

Rosa: Oh, no, Miss. I've come to stay. You two need a maid.

Mercè: You left us to become a militiawoman. Besides, we can't pay you anyway.

Rosa: That's all right, Miss, don't worry, I'll take care of things until the young Masters come back.

Mercè: For God's sake, Rosa, the young Masters are dead! I said we don't need anybody.

Rosa: Come on, Miss, the place looks like a dungheap and besides, if you'll pardon me, every time we requisitioned a villa, I thought of our place here.

(Mercè looks harshly at her)

Excuse me, *your* place. And I have to confess it made me feel bad. You'll see, if you help me a little, in two days we'll have the place all cleaned up.

Mercè: I said no thank you.

(She gets up to usher Rosa to the door.)

Rosa: Miss Mercè, if you could just let me stay here a few days . . . You're my last hope. They're looking for me. Yesterday they shot Teresina and Neus. I don't have anywhere to go. If I go back to my village, they'll wipe me out right away. I thought you might do me the favor . . . have pity, Miss! They won't look for me here. Besides, you people were with Franco, you all won . . .

Mercè: Papa was shot by the militia. Maybe you yourself turned him in, you shameless hypocrite!

Rosa: No! What a thing to say! I should say not! I would never have done something like that; I loved the Master in my own way. He was always trying to pinch my bottom.

Mercè: You disgusting, dirty thing! Respect the memory of the dead, you liar!

Elissa: (Enters at this moment, carrying a little battered suitcase in her hand)

I couldn't find the chauffeur, but I have everything ready. We can go when you like. We'll take a taxi to the station, and then the train . . . Paris . . .

(She comes up to Rosa and takes her by the arm)

Rosa: Ma'am, Ma'am, I'm Rosa, I've come back to stay. You want me here, right, Ma'am?

Elissa: Of course, child. Now we'll go to Paris, we'll find my son, and then we'll all come back home.

(She goes to the door and exits)

Rosa: The Mistress is the one who gives the orders, not you, Miss Mercè.

Mercè: The Mistress is unbalanced, Rosa. I'm the one in charge, and I don't want you in the house. I belong to the Women's Section of the Spanish Falange. As you can understand, your presence in this house puts me in a compromising position. Besides, I can't stand it.

Rosa: Just a few days, Miss. I could sleep in the attic. Don't worry about food; I'm used to going hungry. . . .

Mercè: (Dryly)

No. Get out right now, and give thanks that I don't turn you in . . . as would be my duty. Didn't you hear the loudspeakers?

(We hear the noise of the gate and Elissa's voice)

Elissa: (From offstage)

Do you know where I could find a taxi? . . . We're going to look for my sons in Paris . . .

Rosa: Ma'am, Ma'am. Wait! You can't go out alone.

(While Mercè is unpacking a box she comes on a maid's uniform, unfolds it, and throws it out, enraged. Meanwhile, Elissa has gone out into the audience and is asking the spectators, as if they were people on the streets, if they've seen her sons)

Elissa: Ma'am, have you seen my sons . . .? (She ad libs from here)

(Rosa takes her by the arm)

Rosa: Ma'am, please, come back home. For God's sake, Ma'am. Miss Mercè is waiting for you. Ma'am, come on, Ma'am. Do me a favor: take this photo and keep it for me.

(The old woman's face lights up.)

Elissa: Is it Antoni? I can't see it too well. . . .

(She looks intensely at the photo.)

Rosa: I don't have time to look at it now . . . Tell me what message you have for your sons. I'm going where they are, Ma'am. I don't believe in heaven, but the same earth that welcomed them will welcome me. Germinal said that if we loved each other, we'd find each other in the Great Beyond, and he didn't believe either . . . Tell me, Ma'am, what message should I give them from you?

Notes

1. A posh Barcelona residential neighborhood.

2. The Falange Española, an anti-Communist party with fascist tendencies, was founded by José Antonio Primo de Rivera in 1933. After the war, the Falange became the official state party. The relentlessly denominational Francoist state reinforced adherence to conservative Catholic policies at every level. Says Víctor M. Pérez Díaz in *The Return of Civil Society: The Emergence of Democratic Spain*, "The speeches and the signs of identity of [the Francoist State's leaders], the public rituals, the affirmations of ecclesiastics, and their presence in state offices emphasized it. . . . Protestants, Freemasons, freethinkers, non-Catholics, Marxists, anarchists, and so on . . . were repressed, harassed, ostracized, excluded from teaching posts, or censored [by the state]" (Cambridge, MA: Harvard University Press, 1933, p. 132). The Sección Femenina of the Falange was an organization formed for the purpose of instructing women in both practical and moral matters, and was associated with fiercely conservative repression of women.

3. Federación Anarquista Ibérica, the most intransigent and widely-feared of the Anarchist organizations. Says Hugh Thomas:

> The organization of the FAI in 1927 meant the development of a whole army of shock troops in a more or less perpetual state of war against the rest of Spain. The FAI retained their fantastically high ideals. But they believed that it was with a pistol as well as with an encyclopedia that freedom could be achieved. They were inclined to believe every word that they read. When they came across a passage in Bakunin suggesting that the new world would be gained when the last King was strangled in the guts of the last priest, they would be likely to wish to test immediately whether this was so. Their passionate concern was to create through 'the propaganda of the deed' an atmosphere of panic among the middle class. They might do this through burning churches—as in May 1931. They might place their faith in the violent, sudden, political and perhaps general strike in one town after another. Or they might murder . . . Thomas, *The Spanish Civil War*, New York: Harper, 1961, p. 43.

4. Teruel was the site of one of the most vicious battles of the Civil War, which lasted over two months, from December 1937 through February 1938. With bitterly

cold temperatures, many soldiers suffered frostbite, and casualties from the fighting were atrocious.

5. The Francoist forces united the Falange and the Juntas de Ofensiva Nacional-Sindicalista under the heading of National Forces, with a provisional capital in Burgos until besieged Madrid fell.

6. The Battle at the River Ebro, begun on July 24, 1938, was a Republican attempt to cut off the Nationalists' opening to the sea. Initially, the battle, hard fought with air power and ground artillery, was a success for the Republicans—a turning point in the war, they believed, a moment of hope. Eventually it served as a rallying cry for Nationalists, and as a goad to Franco to seek further aid from Nazi Germany.

7. Popular musical forms from Hispanic America, the *tango* from Argentina and the *ranchera* from Mexico.

Bibliography

Aguado, Neus. "Carme Riera or the Suggestive Power of Words." *Catalan Writing.* Vol. 6. (Barcelona: Institució de les Lletres Catalanes, 1991): 53–56.

Aguado, Neus. "Epístolas de mar y de sol: Entrevista con Carme Riera." *Quimera* 105 (1991): 32–37.

Alas, Leopoldo. *La Regenta.* 2 vols. Ed. Juan Oleza. Madrid: Cátedra, 1984.

Alcoff, Linda. "The Problem of Speaking for Others." *Cultural Critique* 20 (Winter 1991–92): 5–32.

Altman, Janet Gurkin. *Epistolarity: Approaches to a Form.* Columbus: Ohio State University Press, 1982.

Baldini, Umberto. *Primavera: The Restoration of Botticelli's Masterpiece.* New York: Harry N. Abrams, 1986.

Barnard, Mary E. *The Myth of Apollo and Daphne from Ovid to Quevedo: Love, Agon, and the Grotesque.* Durham: Duke University Press, 1987.

Barthes, Roland. *Fragments d'un discours amoureux.* Paris: Seuil, 1977.

———. *The Pleasure of the Text.* Trans. Richard Miller. New York: Hill & Wang, 1975.

———. *S/Z.* Trans. Richard Miller. New York: Hill & Wang, 1974.

Baudrillard, Jean. *Seduction.* Trans. Brian Singer. New York: St. Martin's Press, 1990.

Baudrillard, Jean. *Selected Writings.* Ed. Mark Poster. Stanford: Stanford University Press, 1988.

Baym, Nina. "The Madwoman and Her Languages: Why I Don't Do Feminist Theory." *Feminist Issues in Literary Scholarship,* ed. Shari Benstock. Bloomington: Indiana University Press, 1987, 45–61.

Beauvoir, Simone de. *The Second Sex.* Trans. H. M. Parshley. New York: Vintage Books, 1974.

Braunstein, Baruch. *The Chuetas of Majorca: Conversos and the Inquisition of Mallorca.* 1936. New York: Ktav Publishing House, 1972.

Brook, Peter. *The Empty Space.* New York: Atheneum, 1968.

Campbell, Joseph. *The Hero with a Thousand Faces.* Princeton: Princeton University Press, 1968.

Capmany, Maria Aurèlia. "El feminisme ara," in *Dona i societat a la Catalunya actual.* Barcelona: "Llibres a l'abast," 140, Edicions 62, 1978. Quoted in Anne Charlon, *La condició de la dona en la narrativa femenina catalana, 1900–1983.* Trans. Pilar Canal. Barcelona: Edicions 62, 1990, 119.

Carson, James. "Narrative Cross-Dressing and the Critique of Authorship in the Novels of Richardson." In *Writing the Female Voice: Essays on Epistolary*

Literature, ed. Elizabeth C. Goldsmith. Boston: Northeastern University Press, 1989, 95–113.

Castle, Terry. *Clarissa's Ciphers: Meaning and Disruption in Richardson's Clarissa.* Ithaca: Cornell University Press, 1982.

Charlon, Anne. *La condició de la dona en la narrativa femenina catalana.* Trans. Pilar Canal. Barcelona: Edicions 62, 1990.

Chodorow, Nancy. "Family Structure and Feminine Personality." *Woman, Culture and Society.* Stanford: Stanford University Press, 1974, 43–66.

———. *The Reproduction of Mothering: Psychoanalysis and the Sociology of Gender.* Berkeley: University of California Press, 1978.

Cixous, Hélène. "The Laugh of the Medusa." Trans. Keith and Paula Cohen. *New French Feminisms.* Ed. Elaine Marks and Isabelle de Courtivron. Brighton: Harvester, 1980, 245–64.

———. "Sorties." *The Newly Born Woman.* Trans. Betsy Wing. Minneapolis: The University of Minnesota Press, 1987, 63–132.

———. "La Venue à l'écriture." *La Venue à l'écriture.* Ed. H. Cixous, M. Gagnon, A. Leclerc. Paris: Union Générale d'Editions, 1977, 9–62.

Cotoner, Luisa. "Marco escénico e interpretación simbólica de los espacios en *Dins el darrer blau* de Carme Riera." *Lectora. Revista de Dones i Textualitat.* (forthcoming)

———. "*Una primavera para Domenico Guarini.*" *Cuadernos Hispanoamericanos* 390 (1982): 712–14.

Dallenbach, Lucien. *Le Reçit Speculaire.* Paris: Editions du Seuil, 1977.

de Lauretis, Teresa. "Desire in Narrative." In *Alice Doesn't: Feminism, Semiotics, Cinema.* Bloomington: Indiana University Press, 1984, 103–57.

———. "The Female Body and Heterosexual Assumptions." *Semiotica* 67:3–4 (1987):259–79.

Derrida, Jacques. *De la Grammatologie.* Paris: Editions du Minuit, 1967.

DuPlessis, Rachel Blau. *The Pink Guitar: Writing as Feminist Practice.* New York: Routledge, 1990.

———. *Writing Beyond the Ending: Narrative Strategies of Twentieth-Century Women Writers.* Bloomington: Indiana University Press, 1985.

Eco, Umberto. *Postscript to* The Name of the Rose. San Diego: Harcourt Brace Jovanovich, 1984.

Eliade, Mircea. *Rites and Symbols of Initiation: The Mysteries of Birth and Rebirth.* New York: Harper & Row, 1958.

Epps, Brad. "Virtual Sexuality: Lesbianism, Loss, and Deliverance in Carme Riera's 'Te deix, amor, la mar com a penyora.'" *¿Entiendes?: Queer Readings, Hispanic Writings.* Ed. Emilie L. Bergmann and Paul Julian Smith. Durham: Duke University Press, 1995, 317–45.

Felman, Shoshana. *The Literary Speech Act.* Ithaca: Cornell University Press, 1983.

Freud, Sigmund. *Civilization and Its Discontents.* Trans. James Strachey. New York: W. W. Norton, 1961.

———. *Group Psychology and the Analysis of the Ego.* Trans. James Strachey. New York: W. W. Norton, 1959.

———. "On Narcissism: An Introduction." In *General Psychological Theory.* Trans. Cecil M. Baines. New York: Macmillan, 1963.

———. "The Psychogenesis of a Case of Homosexuality in a Woman." Trans. Barbara Low and R. Gabler. In *Sigmund Freud: Collected Papers.* Vol. 2. Ed. Joan Riviere. New York: Basic Books, 1959, 202–31.

———. "Remembering, Repeating and Working Through." *The Standard Edition of the Complete Psychological Works of Sigmund Freud.* Ed. and trans. James Strachey. London: Hogarth Press, 1953–74, Vol. 12, 145–56.

———. "The 'Uncanny'." In *Collected Papers.* Vol. 4. Trans. Joan Riviere. New York: Basic Books, 1959, 368–407.

Fuss, Diana. "Fashion and the Homospectatorial Look." *Critical Inquiry* 18:4 (1992):713–38.

———. *Inside/Out: Lesbian Theories, Gay Theories.* Ed. Diana Fuss. New York: Routledge, 1991.

G. C. "Carme Riera: 'Voldria matar el monstre de la intolerància a Mallorca amb el meu llibre.'" *Avui,* 8 January 1995:38.

———. "L'escriptora Carme Riera retrata la Mallorca jueva del segle XVII." *Avui,* 25 February 1994:44.

Gallop, Jane. *The Daughter's Seduction. Feminism and Psychoanalysis.* Ithaca: Cornell University Press, 1982.

———. *Thinking Through the Body.* New York: Columbia University Press, 1988.

Garau, Francisco. *La fe triunfante.* 1691. Palma de Mallorca: Miquel Font, 1984.

Gide, André. *Journal, 1899–1939.* Paris: Gallimard, 1948.

Gil de Biedma, Jaime. *Las personas del verbo.* Barcelona: Seix Barral, 1991.

Gilbert, Sandra M., and Susan Gubar. *The Madwoman in the Attic: The Woman Writer and the Nineteenth-Century Literary Imagination.* New Haven: Yale University Press, 1979.

Girard, René. *Deceit, Desire, and the Novel: Self and Other in Literary Structure.* Trans. Yvonne Freccero. Baltimore: Johns Hopkins University Press, 1965.

Glenn, Kathleen M. "Authority and Marginality in Three Contemporary Spanish Narratives." *Romance Languages Annual* 2 (1990): 426–30.

———. "Las cartas de amor de Carme Riera: El arte de seducir." In *Discurso femenino actual,* ed. Adelaida López de Martínez. San Juan: Editorial de la Universidad de Puerto Rico, 1995, 53–67.

———. "Conversation with Carme Riera." *Catalan Review* 8:1–2 (1994):203–09.

Goldsmith, Elizabeth C. *Writing the Female Voice: Essays on Epistolary Literature.* Boston: Northeastern University Press, 1989.

Gubar, Susan. "'The Blank Page' and the Issues of Female Creativity." In *The New Feminist Criticism: Essays on Women, Literature, and Theory.* Ed. Elaine Showalter. New York: Pantheon Books, 1985, 292–313.

Hassan, Ihab Habib. *Paracriticisms: Seven Speculations of the Times.* Urbana: University of Illinois Press, 1975.

Herzberger, David. *Narrating the Past: Fiction and Historiography in Postwar Spain.* Durham and London: Duke University Press, 1995.

Higonnet, Margaret. "Suicide: Representations of the Feminine in the Nineteenth Century." *Poetics Today* 6:1–2 (1985): 103–18.

Hutcheon, Linda. *Narcissistic Narrative.* Waterloo, Ontario: Wilfrid Laurier University Press, 1980.

———. *A Poetics of Postmodernism: History, Theory, Fiction.* New York: Routledge, 1988.

Ibarz, Mercè. "Sis escriptores escenifiquen la història del segle actual." *Avui* 11 August 1982, "Cultura": 24.

Irigaray, Luce. *Ce sexe qui n'en est pas un.* Trans. Claudia Reeder. *New French Feminisms.* Ed. Elaine Marks and Isabelle de Courtivron. Brighton: Harvester, 1980, 99–106.

———. "La 'Mécanique' des fluides." *L'Arc* 58 (1974):49–55.

———. *Spéculum de l'autre femme.* Paris: Minuit, 1974.

———. *This Sex Which Is Not One.* Trans. Catherine Porter. Ithaca: Cornell University Press, 1985.

Jakobson, Roman. "Linguistics and Poetics." *The Structuralists: From Marx to Lévi-Strauss.* Ed. Richard and Fernande De George. New York: Anchor Books, 1972, 85–123.

Jelin, Elizabeth. "The Politics of Memory: The Human Rights Movement and the Construction of Democracy in Argentina." *Latin American Perspectives* 21 (1994):38–58.

Jensen, Katharine Ann. *Writing Love: Letters, Women, and the Novel in France, 1605–1776.* Carbondale: Southern Illinois University Press, 1995.

Johnson, Barbara. "The Frame of Reference: Poe, Lacan, Derrida." In *The Critical Difference: Essays in the Contemporary Rhetoric of Reading.* Baltimore: Johns Hopkins University Press, 1980, 110–46.

Johnson, Roberta. "Voice and Intersubjectivity in Carme Riera's Narratives." In *Critical Essays on the Literatures of Spain and Spanish America,* Ed. Luis T. González-del-Valle and Julio Baena. Boulder: Society of Spanish and Spanish-American Studies, 1991, 153–59.

Kauffman, Linda S. *Discourses of Desire: Gender, Genre, and Epistolary Fictions.* Ithaca: Cornell University Press, 1986.

———. *Special Delivery: Epistolary Modes in Modern Fiction.* Chicago: University of Chicago Press, 1992.

Keppler, C. F. *The Literature of the Second Self.* Tucson: University of Arizona Press, 1972.

Kolodny, Annette. "Some Notes on Defining a Feminist Literary Criticism." *Critical Inquiry* 2 (1975): 75–92.

Kristeva, Julia. *Desire in Language: A Semiotic Approach to Literature and Art.* Trans. Thomas Gora, Alice Jardine, and Leon S. Roudiez, ed. Leon Roudiez. New York: Columbia University Press, 1980.

Lacan, Jacques. *Écrits.* Paris: Éditions du Seuil, 1966.

———. *Le Séminaire, livre VIII. Le Transfert.* Paris: Seuil, 1991.

———. *Le Séminaire, livre XX.* Encore. Paris: Seuil, 1975.

———. "Le séminaire sur 'La Lettre volée.'" In *Ecrits I.* Paris: Seuil, 1966, 19–75.

———. "La signification du phallus." In *Ecrits II.* Paris: Seuil, 1971, 103–115. "The Meaning of the Phallus." Trans. Jacqueline Rose. In *Feminine Sexuality.* New York: W. W. Norton and Pantheon, 1982, 74–85.

———. "The Signification of the Phallus." In *Ecrits: A Selection.* Trans. Alan Sheridan. New York: W. W. Norton, 1977, 281–91.

Laclos, Choderlos de. *Les Liaisons dangereuses.* Paris: Gallimard, 1972.

Laub, Eva y Juan Laub. *El mito triunfante: Estudio antropológico de los chuetas mallorquines.* Palma de Mallorca: Miquel Font, 1987.

Leclerc, Annie. "La Lettre d'amour." *La Venue à l'écriture.* Ed. H. Cixous, M. Gagnon, and A. Leclerc. Paris: Union Générale d'Editions, 1977, 117–49.

Lejeune, Philippe. *Moi aussi.* Paris: Seuil, 1986.

Lévi-Strauss, Claude. *The Savage Mind.* Trans. G. Weidenfield. Chicago: University of Chicago Press, 1966.

Lewis, Reina. *Gendering Orientalism. Race, Femininity and Representation.* London and New York: Routledge, 1996.

Lowenthal, David. *The Past Is a Foreign Country.* Cambridge: Cambridge University Press, 1985.

Lukács, George. "The Sociology of Modern Drama." In *The Theory of the Modern Stage,* ed. Eric Bentley. London: Penguin, 1989, 425–50.

MacArthur, Elizabeth J. *Extravagant Narratives: Closure and Dynamics in the Epistolary Form.* Princeton: Princeton University Press, 1990.

Mallarmé, Stèphane. "L'Action restreinte." *Oeuvres complètes.* Paris: Gallimard, 1945, 369–78.

Martí Gómez, José. "Con los años ganas lucidez y sentido crítico." *La Vanguardia Magazine,* 24 December 1995.

Martínez Romero, Carmen. "Relaciones textuales en la novela femenina de la subjetividad: Gaite, Rodoreda y Riera." In *Ensayos de literatura europea e hispanoamericana,* ed. Félix Menchacatorre. San Sebastián: Universidad del País Vasco, 1990, 293–97.

Martí-Olivella, Jaume. "Towards a New Transcultural Dialogue in Spanish Film." *Spain Today: Essays on Literature, Culture, Society,* ed. José Colmeiro, Christina Dupláa, Patricia Greene, and Juana Sabadell. Hanover, NH: Dartmouth College Department of Spanish and Portuguese, 1995, 47–66.

McHale, Brian. *Postmodernist Fiction.* New York and London: Methuen, 1987.

McNerney, Kathleen. *On Our Own Behalf: Women's Tales from Catalonia.* Lincoln: University of Nebraska Press, 1989.

Miller, Arthur. "Tragedy and the Common Man." In *Dramatic Theory and Criticism,* ed. Bernard F. Dukore. New York: Holt, Rinehart & Winston, 1974, 894–97.

Miller, J. Hillis. "The Problematic of Ending in Narrative." *Nineteenth-Century Fiction* 33 (1978):3–7.

Miller, Jean Baker. *Towards a New Psychology of Women.* Boston: Beacon Press, 1976.

Mistral, Gabriela. "Niño mexicano." In *Poesía y prosa.* Prol. Jaime Quezada. Caracas: Biblioteca Ayacucho, 67–68.

Moix, Ana María. "Las virtudes peligrosas." In *Las virtudes peligrosas.* Barcelona: Plaza y Janés, 1985, 9–43.

Montrose, Louis A. "Professing the Renaissance: The Poetics and Politics of Culture." In *The New Historicism,* ed. H. Aram Veeser. New York: Routledge, 1989, 15–36.

Moore, Kenneth. *Those of the Street: The Catholic-Jews of Mallorca.* Notre Dame, IN: University of Notre Dame Press, 1976.

Nichols, Geraldine C. "Carme Riera." In *Escribir, espacio propio: Laforet, Matute, Moix, Tusquets, Riera y Roig por sí mismas.* Minneapolis: Institute for the Study of Ideologies and Literature, 1989, 187–227.

———. "'Mitja poma, mitja taronja': génesis y destino literarios de la catalana contemporánea." *Anthropos* 60–61 (1986): 118–25.

———. "Stranger than Fiction: Fantasy in Short Stories by Matute, Rodoreda, Riera." *Monographic Review/Revista Monográfica* 4 (1988): 33–42.

Oliver, Maria-Antònia. "La primera vegada." In *El primer amor.* Barcelona: Columna, 1992, 83–89.

———. *Vegetal i Muller qui cerca espill.* Barcelona: La Llar del Llibre, 1984.

Oller, Narcís. *La febre d'or.* Vol I. Barcelona: Edicions 62, 1980.

Ordóñez, Elizabeth J. "Beginning to Speak: Carme Riera's *Una primavera para Domencio Guarini.*" *La Chispa '85. Selected Proceedings.* Ed. Gilbert Paolini. New Orleans: Tulane University Press, 1985, 285–93.

———. *Voices of Their Own: Contemporary Spanish Narrative by Women.* Lewisburg: Bucknell University Press, 1991.

Ovid. *The Metamorphoses of Ovid.* Trans. A. E. Watts. San Francisco: North Point Press, 1980.

Pérez Díaz, Víctor M. *The Return of Civil Society: The Emergence of Democratic Spain.* Cambridge, MA: Harvard University Press, 1993.

Pérez, Janet. "Behind the Lines: The Spanish Civil War and Women Writers." *The Spanish Civil War in Literature,* ed. Janet Pérez and Wendell Aycock. Lubbock: Texas Tech University Press, 1990, 161–74.

———. "Plant Imagery, Subversion, and Feminine Dependency: Josefina Aldecoa, Carmen Martín Gaite, and Maria Antònia Oliver." In *In the Feminine Mode: Essays on Hispanic Women Writers,* ed. Noël Valis and Carol Maier. Lewisburg: Bucknell University Press, 1990, 78–100.

———. "Presence of the Picaresque and the Quest-Romance in Mercè Rodoreda's *Quanta, quanta guerra.*" *Hispania* 76 (1993):428–49.

Pirandello, Luigi. "Spoken Action." In *The Theory of the Modern Stage,* ed. Eric Bentley. London: Penguin, 1989, 153–57.

Pratt, Annis. *Archetypal Patterns in Women's Fiction.* Bloomington: Indiana University Press, 1981.

Preminger, Alex, ed. *Princeton Encyclopedia of Poetry and Poetics.* Princeton: Princeton University Press, 1974.

Rabuzzi, Kathryn Allen. *Motherself: A Mythic Analysis of Motherhood.* Bloomington: Indiana University Press, 1988.

Racionero, Luis. "Entrevista con Carmen Riera: 'Cada vez tenemos menos imaginación.'" *Quimera* 9–10 (July–August 1981): 14–16.

Riera, Carme. *"As you like, darling."* In *Epitelis tendríssims.* Barcelona: Edicions 62, 1981, 19–28.

———. "Contra l'amor en companyia." In *Contra l'amor en companyia.* Barcelona: Destino, 1991, 63–74.

———. *Contra l'amor en companyia i altres relats.* Barcelona: Destino, 1991. Published in Castilian as *Contra el amor en compañía y otros relatos.* Barcelona: Destino, 1991.

———. "El detergente definitivo." In *Te dejo el mar.* Trans. Luisa Cotoner. Madrid: Espasa Calpe, 1991, 192–95.

———. *Dins el darrer blau.* Barcelona: Destino, 1994.

———. *Escenarios para la felicidad: Estampas de Mallorca.* Palma de Mallorca: R. y J.J. de Olañeta, 1994.

———. "Es nus, es buit." In *Jo pos per testimoni les gavines.* Barcelona: Laia, 1977, 79–82.

———. "Femenino singular: Literatura de mujer." In *Crítica y ficción literaria: Mujeres españolas contemporáneas,* ed. Aurora López and María Angeles Pastor. Granada: Universidad de Granada, 1989, 25–38.

———. "Grandeza y miseria de la epístola." In *El oficio de narrar,* ed. Marina Mayoral. Madrid: Cátedra, 1989, 147–58.

———. "I Leave You, My Love, the Sea as a Token." Trans. Alberto Moreiras. *On Our Own Behalf: Women's Tales from Catalonia.* Lincoln: University of Nebraska Press, 1988, 31–45.

———. *Joc de miralls.* Barcelona: Planeta, 1989. Trans. Cristina de la Torre as *Mirror Images.* New York: Peter Lang, 1993.

———. *Jo pos per testimoni les gavines.* Barcelona: Editorial Laia, 1977.

———. *Jo pos per testimoni les gavines.* Barcelona: Planeta, 1990.

———. "Letra de ángel." In *Contra el amor en compañía y otros relatos.* Barcelona: Destino, 1991, 21–34.

———. "Literatura fememina: ¿Un lenguaje prestado?" *Quimera* 18 (1982):9–12.

———. "Una mica de fred per a Wanda." In *Epitelis tendríssims.* Barcelona: Edicions 62, 1981, 63–78.

———. "Octubre, octubre." In *El primer amor.* Barcelona: Columna, 1992, 91–97.

———. *Palabra de mujer* (*Bajo el signo de una memoria impenitente*). Barcelona: Laia, 1980.

———. *Palabra de mujer.* Barcelona: Laia, 1995. Castilian translations of some of the stories of *Te deix, amor, la mar com a penyora.* Barcelona: Laia, 1975; and *Jo pos per testimoni les gavines.* Barcelona: Laia, 1977.

———. *Una primavera per a Domenico Guarini.* Barcelona: Edicions 62, 1980. Published in Castilian as *Una primavera para Domenico Guarini.* Barcelona: Montesinos, 1981.

———. *Una primavera per a Domenico Guarini.* Barcelona: Edicions 62, 1992.

———. *Qüestió d'amor propi.* Barcelona: Laia, 1987. Published in Castilian as *Cuestión de amor propio.* Barcelona: Tusquets, 1988.

———. "La seducción del genio." In *Contra el amor en compañía y otros relatos.* Barcelona: Destino, 1991, 139–44.

———. *Senyora, ha vist els meus fills? Dones i Catalunya.* Typescript provided by author. Barcelona, 1982. The play premiered in Barcelona on 10 August, 1982, and the same year was put on in Olite (Navarra) and Athens, Greece.

———. One-Act Play, *Senyora, ha vist els meus fills?* from *Dones i Catalunya,* trans. Patricia Hart. Purdue University.

———. "Te deix, amor, la mar com a penyora." In *Te deix, amor, la mar com a penyora.* Barcelona: Laia, 1975, 19–36.

———. *Te deix, amor, la mar com a penyora.* Barcelona: Laia, 1975.

———. *Te deix, amor, la mar com a penyora.* Barcelona: Planeta, 1992.

———. *Te dejo el mar.* Trans. Luisa Cotoner. Madrid: Espasa-Calpe, 1991.

———. "Variacions sobre el tema de Dafne." In *Dones soles.* Barcelona: Planeta, 1995, 135–44.

Rodoreda, Mercè. *La plaça del Diamant.* Barcelona: Club Editor, 1989.

———. *The Time of the Doves* (English translation of *La plaça del Diamant*). Trans. David H. Rosenthal. New York: Taplinger, 1980.

Rodríguez-Fischer, Ana, ed. *Cartas a Rosa Chacel.* Madrid: Versal (Cátedra), 1992.

Rogers, Robert. *A Psychoanalytic Study of the Double in Literature.* Detroit: Wayne State University Press, 1970.

Roig, Montserrat. "L'Hora" (January 1981). Quoted in Anne Charlon, *La condició de la dona en la narrativa femenina catalana.* Trans. Pilar Canal. Barcelona: Edicions 62, 1990, 14.

Rorty, Richard. *Philosophy and the Mirror of Nature.* Princeton: Princeton University Press, 1979.

Ross, Andrew. "Baudrillard's Bad Attitude." In *Seduction and Theory: Readings of Gender, Representation, and Rhetoric,* ed. Dianne Hunter. Urbana: University of Illinois Press, 1989, 214–25.

Said, Edward. "Representing the Colonized: Anthropology's Interlocutors." *Critical Inquiry* 15 (1989):205–25.

Salinas, Pedro. *El defensor.* Madrid: Alianza, 1983.

———. *La voz a ti debida / Razón de amor.* Madrid: Castalia, 1984.

Selke, Angela S. *The Conversos of Majorca: Life and Death in a Crypto-Jewish Community in XVII Century Spain.* Trans. Henry J. Maxwell. Jerusalem: Magnes Press, the Hebrew University, 1986. Trans. and rev. ed. of *Los Chuetas y la Inquisición. Vida y Muerte en el Ghetto de Mallorca.* Madrid: Taurus, 1972.

Servodidio, Mirella. "Surfing the Internet with Borges and Carme Riera." *Revista Hispánica Moderna* 49:2 (1996): 434–45.

Showalter, Elaine. "Feminist Criticism in the Wilderness." *Writing and Sexual Difference,* ed. Elizabeth Abel. Chicago: University of Chicago Press, 1982, 9–35.

Singer, Godfrey Frank. *The Epistolary Novel: Its Origin, Development, Decline, and Residuary Influence.* New York: Russell & Russell, 1963.

Snow-Smith, Joanne. *The Primavera of Sandro Botticelli: A Neoplatonic Interpretation.* New York: Peter Lang, 1993.

Spivak, Gayatri Chakravorty. "Can the Subaltern Speak?" *Colonial Discourse and Postcolonial Theory,* ed. Patrick Williams and Laura Chrisman. New York: Harvester Wheatsheaf, 1993, 66–111.

Thomas, Hugh. *The Spanish Civil War.* New York: Harper, 1961.

Todorov, Tzvetzan. *Littérature et signification.* Paris: Larousse, 1967.

———. *Poétique de la prose.* Paris: Editions du Seuil, 1971.

"Torna la polèmica xueta a Mallorca." *El Temps* (Valencia) 8 May 1995:13.

Tsuchiya, Akiko. "The Paradox of Narrative Seduction in Carme Riera's *Cuestión de amor propio.*" *Hispania* 75 (1992):281–86.

Valdivieso, L. Teresa. "Mujeres en busca de un nuevo humanismo." *Inti: Revista de Literatura Hispánica* 40–41 (1994–95):289–98.

Vásquez, Mary S. "Dialogic Discourse, Gender and Power in Carme Riera's *Cuestión de amor propio.*" In *Misogyny in Literature: An Essay Collection,* ed. Katherine Anne Ackley. New York: Garland, 1992, 349–62.

Wright, Patrick. *On Living in an Old Country.* London: Verso, 1985.

Wyatt, Jean. "Giving Body to the Word: The Maternal Symbolic in Toni Morrison's *Beloved.*" *PMLA* 108:3 (1993): 474–88.

Yerushalmi, Yosef Hayim. *Zakhor: Jewish History and Jewish Memory.* Seattle: University of Washington Press, 1982.

Young, Robert. *Torn Halves: Political Conflict in Literary and Cultural Theory.* Manchester and New York: Manchester University Press, 1996.

———. *White Mythologies.* London and New York: Routledge, 1990.

Zola, Emile. *Germinal.* Paris: E. Fasquelle, 1911.

List of Contributors

CATHERINE G. BELLVER is the author of two books on twentieth century Peninsular Spanish poetry: *Rafael Alberti en sus horas de destierro* (1984) and *El mundo poético de Juan José Domenchina* (1979). She has published over 25 refereed articles, many of them on women writers of Spain, and over 70 book reviews. Her most recent book, soon to be published, is *Presence and Absence: Spanish Women Poets of the Twenties and Thirties.*

NEUS CARBONELL holds a Ph.D. in comparative literature from Indiana University. Her research deals primarily with French feminism and Catalan women writers. She is a faculty member at the Universitat de Vic, Barcelona.

SUSAN LUCAS DOBRIAN is Associate Professor of Spanish at Coe College, Iowa. Her special interest within Hispanism is the confluence between classics and contemporary Spanish narrative by women. She was a contributor to the Spring 1995 monographic issue of *Letras Peninsulares, The Search for an Interlocutor and the Quest for Identity: Female Narrative in Democratic Spain.*

CHRISTINA DUPLÁA is Associate Professor of Spanish at Dartmouth College. She has published articles on the metaphorical and symbolic roles of the feminine figure in turn-of-the-century Catalan nationalist discourse as well as intellectual history and women writers. Co-editor of *Las nacionalidades del Estado español: una problemática cultural* (1986) and *Spain Today: Essays on Literature, Culture, Society* (1995), she is the author of *La voz testimonial en Montserrat Roig* (1996).

BRAD EPPS is John L. Loeb Associate Professor of the Humanities at Harvard University. He is the author of *Significant Violence: Oppression and Resistance in the Narratives of Juan Goytisolo* (1996) and of numerous articles on modern Spanish, Latin American, Catalan, and French culture. He is currently at work on two books, *The Limits of Sense: Representation and Reality in Modern Spanish Literature, Film, and Art* and *Daring to Write: Homosexuality in Hispanic Literature.*

KATHLEEN M. GLENN is Professor of Spanish at Wake Forest University. She is the author of two books on Azorín and has published articles on a number of contemporary Spanish novelists, including Cristina Fernández Cubas, Carmen Laforet, Ana María Matute, Carmen Martín Gaite, Carme Riera, Montserrat Roig, and Mercè Rodoreda. She is co-editor of *Anales de la Literatura Española Contemporánea.*

PATRICIA HART is Associate Professor of Spanish at Purdue University. She is the author of *The Spanish Sleuth* (1987), a history of detective fiction in Spain, and *Narrative Magic in the Fiction of Isabel Allende* (1989), as well as the novel *Little Sins* (1980).

GERALDINE CLEARY NICHOLS is Professor of Spanish and Chair of the Department of Romance Languages and Literatures at the University of Florida. She has written extensively on women's fiction in twentieth century Spain and Catalonia.

JANET PÉREZ, Associate Dean of the Graduate School at Texas Tech University, is an internationally recognized authority on post-Civil War Spanish fiction and women writers of the twentieth century. She has published books on Ortega y Gasset, Gonzalo Torrente Ballester, Ana María Matute, and Miguel Delibes and has co-edited a major collection of essays on women writers of narrative in contemporary Spain. She has edited or co-edited nearly 100 books in the Spanish section of the Twayne World Authors Series. *Contemporary Women Writers of Spain* (1988) and *Modern and Contemporary Spanish Women Poets* are her most recent books.

MIRELLA D'AMBROSIO SERVODIDIO is Professor of Spanish and department Chair at Barnard College. She is the author of books on Azorín and Eugenio Florit and has edited or co-edited five other books, including the much-consulted *From Fiction to Metafiction: Essays in Honor of Carmen Martín-Gaite* (1983). An active scholar of women writers in contemporary Spain, she has authored numerous articles in this area, in addition to her scholarly work in poetry and short fiction.

AKIKO TSUCHIYA, Associate Professor of Spanish at Washington University, St. Louis, is the author of *Images of the Sign: Semiotic Consciousness in the Novels of Benito Pérez Galdós* and of numerous refereed articles on feminist critical theory and the reading of female-authored literary texts. She is currently completing a book on Spanish women writers of the post-Franco period.

MARY S. VÁSQUEZ is Professor of Spanish and Chair of the Department of Spanish at Davidson College. Founding editor of the journal *Letras Peninsulares,* she researches the narrative of contemporary Spain, with an emphasis on exile narrative and on women writers, and Hispanic/Latino literature in the United States.

Index